Collective Bargaining Developments in Times of Crisis

Bulletin of Comparative Labour Relations

VOLUME 99

Founding Editor

The series started in 1970 under the dynamic editorship of Professor Roger Blanpain (Belgium), former President of the International Industrial Relations Association. Professor Blanpain, Professor Emeritus of Labour Law, Universities of Leuven and Tilburg, was also General Editor of the International Encyclopedia of Laws (with more than 1,600 collaborators worldwide) and President of the Association of Educative and Scientific Authors Authors. He passed away in October 2016.

General Editor

In 2015 Frank Hendrickx, Professor of labour law at the Faculty of Law of the University of Leuven (Belgium) joined as a co-Editor. Frank Hendrickx has published numerous articles and books and regularly advises governments, international institutions and private organisations in the area of labour law as well as in sports law. He is the Editor-in-Chief of the European Labour Law Journal and General Editor of the International Encyclopaedia of Laws.

Introduction

The Bulletins constitute a unique source of information and thought-provoking discussion, laying the groundwork for studies of employment relations in the 21st century, involving among much else the effects of globalization, new technologies, migration, and the greying of the population.

Contents/Subjects

Amongst other subjects the Bulletins frequently include the proceedings of international or regional conferences; reports from comparative projects devoted to salient issues in industrial relations, human resources management, and/or labour law; and specific issues underlying the multicultural aspects of our industrial societies.

Objective

The Bulletins offer a platform of expression and discussion on labour relations to scholars and practitioners worldwide, often featuring special guest editors.

The titles published in this series are listed at the end of this volume.

BULLETIN OF COMPARATIVE LABOUR RELATIONS – 99

Collective Bargaining Developments in Times of Crisis

Editor

Sylvaine Laulom

Contributors

Pierre-Emmanuel Berthier
Elisabeth Brameshuber
Judith Brockmann
Berrin Ceylan Ataman
Teresa Coelho Moreira
Florence Debord
Kübra Doğan Yenisey
Sonia Fernández Sánchez
Nicola Gundt
Tamás Gyulavári
Jenny Julén Votinius
Gábor Kártyás

Fabienne Kéfer
Barbara Kresal
Auriane Lamine
Olivier Leclerc
Piera Loi
Yolanda Maneiro Vázquez
José María Miranda Boto
Łukasz Pisarczyk
Jeremias Prassl
Felicia Rosioru
Christophe Vigneau

General Editor

Frank Hendrickx

Founding Editor

Roger Blanpain

Published by:
Kluwer Law International B.V.
PO Box 316
2400 AH Alphen aan den Rijn
The Netherlands
Website: www.wolterskluwerlr.com

Sold and distributed in North, Central and South America by:
Wolters Kluwer Legal & Regulatory U.S.
7201 McKinney Circle
Frederick, MD 21704
United States of America
Email: customer.service@wolterskluwer.com

Sold and distributed in all other countries by:
Quadrant
Rockwood House
Haywards Heath
West Sussex
RH16 3DH
United Kingdom
Email: international-customerservice@wolterskluwer.com

Printed on acid-free paper.

ISBN 978-90-411-8999-8

e-Book: ISBN 978-90-411-9027-7
web-PDF: ISBN 978-90-411-9028-4

© 2018 Kluwer Law International BV, The Netherlands

All rights reserved. No part of this publication may be reproduced, stored in a retrieval system, or transmitted in any form or by any means, electronic, mechanical, photocopying, recording, or otherwise, without written permission from the publisher.

Permission to use this content must be obtained from the copyright owner. Please apply to: Permissions Department, Wolters Kluwer Legal & Regulatory U.S., 76 Ninth Avenue, 7th Floor, New York, NY 10011-5201, USA. Website: www.wolterskluwerlr.com

Printed in the United Kingdom.

Notes on Contributors

Pierre-Emmanuel Berthier, University Lumière Lyon 2, Center for Critical Legal Research (CERCRID UMR 5137), France

Elisabeth Brameshuber, WU Vienna University of Economics and Business, Austria

Judith Brockmann, Faculty of Law, Universität Hamburg, Germany

Berrin Ceylan Ataman, Ankara University, Faculty of Political Science, Turkey

Teresa Coelho Moreira, University of Minho, School of Law, Portugal

Florence Debord, University Lumière Lyon 2, Center for Critical Legal Research (CERCRID UMR 5137), France

Kübra Doğan Yenisey, Istanbul Bilgi University, Faculty of Law, Turkey

Sonia Fernández Sánchez, University of Cagliari, Italy

Nicola Gundt, Department of Public Law, Maastricht Centre of European Law (M-CEL), Faculty of Law, Maastricht University, the Netherlands

Tamás Gyulavári, Pázmány Péter Catholic University, Labour Law Department, Budapest, Hungary

Gábor Kártyás, Pázmány Péter Catholic University, Labour Law Department, Budapest, Hungary

Fabienne Kéfer, University of Liège, Belgium

Barbara Kresal, University of Ljubljana, Slovenia

Jenny Julén Votinius, Faculty of Law, Lund University, Sweden

Notes on Contributors

Auriane Lamine, Centre de recherches Droit, Entreprise et Société (CRIDES), Université catholique de Louvain, Belgium

Sylvaine Laulom, University Lumière Lyon 2, Center for Critical Legal Research (CERCRID UMR 5137), France

Olivier Leclerc, CNRS, Center for Critical Legal Research (CERCRID UMR 5137), France

Piera Loi, Faculty of Law, University of Cagliari, Italy.

Yolanda Maneiro Vázquez, University of Santiago de Compostela, Spain

José María Miranda Boto, University of Santiago de Compostela, Spain

Łukasz Pisarczyk, Faculty of Law and Administration, University of Warsaw, Poland

Jeremias Prassl, Magdalen College and Faculty of Law, University of Oxford, United Kingdom

Felicia Rosioru, Faculty of Law, Babes-Bolyai University, Cluj-Napoca, Romania

Christophe Vigneau, University Paris 1 Panthéon Sorbonne, France.

Summary of Contents

Notes on Contributors — v

Introduction
Sylvaine Laulom — 1

PART I
The Changing Structures of Collective Bargaining — 13

CHAPTER 1
From Decentralisation of Collective Bargaining to De-collectivisation of Industrial Relations Systems?
Sylvaine Laulom — 15

CHAPTER 2
Chasing the Holy Grail? Stumbling Collective Bargaining in Eastern Europe and the Hungarian Experiment
Tamás Gyulavári — 29

CHAPTER 3
How Can Decentralisation of Collective Bargaining Be Achieved? A Typology of Legal Incentives
Pierre-Emmanuel Berthier & Olivier Leclerc — 47

CHAPTER 4
The Impact of the Economic Crisis on Collective Agreements in Poland
Łukasz Pisarczyk — 63

CHAPTER 5
Collective Bargaining in Romania: The Aftermath of an Earthquake
Felicia Rosioru — 73

Summary of Contents

CHAPTER 6
The Importance of Sectoral Collective Bargaining in Austria
Elisabeth Brameshuber 89

CHAPTER 7
The Revival of Sectoral Collective Bargaining: The Portuguese Experience
Teresa Coelho Moreira 105

CHAPTER 8
The Spanish Example
Yolanda Maneiro Vázquez & José María Miranda Boto 117

PART II
The Contents of Collective Agreements: Old and New Issues 129

A Wages 131

CHAPTER 9
Decentralisation of Wage Setting Mechanisms and Statutory Minimum Wage: Towards the End of Sectoral Collective Bargaining?
Piera Loi 133

CHAPTER 10
Measures of Wage Moderation in Times of Crisis: The Example of Belgium
Fabienne Kéfer 153

CHAPTER 11
Decentralized Collective Bargaining: A Solution to Economic Crisis? – The Case of Turkey
Kübra Doğan Yenisey & Berrin Ceylan Ataman 169

B Working Time 187

CHAPTER 12
Negotiating Working Time in Times of Crisis
Łukasz Pisarczyk 189

CHAPTER 13
Negotiating Working Time in Time of Crisis: The 'El Khomri Law'
Christophe Vigneau 203

Summary of Contents

C New Issues   211

CHAPTER 14
Work-Life Balance in Collective Agreements
Barbara Kresal   213

CHAPTER 15
Older Employees, Extended Working Lives, and Collective Bargaining
Jenny Julén Votinius   231

CHAPTER 16
Collective Bargaining with Regard to Young Employees: Importance and Challenges
Judith Brockmann   249

PART III
Expanding Spaces and New Boundaries of Collective Agreements   267

CHAPTER 17
Collective Autonomy for On-Demand Workers? Normative Arguments, Current Practices and Legal Ways Forward
Auriane Lamine & Jeremias Prassl   269

CHAPTER 18
Are Agency Workers Protected by Trade Unions?: A Case Study from the Netherlands
Nicola Gundt   293

CHAPTER 19
Multi-Employer Situations and Collective Bargaining: The Hungarian Cases
Gábor Kártyás   309

CHAPTER 20
A Study in Red and Blue: A Comparison of Collective Bargaining in Carrefour in Some EU Countries
José María Miranda Boto, Teresa Coelho Moreira, Florence Debord, Sonia Fernández Sánchez, Yolanda Maneiro Vázquez & Łukasz Pisarczyk   319

Table of Contents

Notes on Contributors   v

Introduction
Sylvaine Laulom   1

PART I
The Changing Structures of Collective Bargaining   13

CHAPTER 1
From Decentralisation of Collective Bargaining to De-collectivisation of Industrial Relations Systems?
Sylvaine Laulom   15
- §1.01 The European Context: The Aim of Decentralising Collective Bargaining   17
- §1.02 Towards Decentralisation of Collective Negotiations   19
  - [A] Absence of Decentralisation   20
  - [B] Maintaining a Centralised System of Collective Bargaining   23
  - [C] Legislative Intervention to Help Drive Decentralisation of Labour Relations Systems   24
- §1.03 Conclusion   27

CHAPTER 2
Chasing the Holy Grail? Stumbling Collective Bargaining in Eastern Europe and the Hungarian Experiment
Tamás Gyulavári   29
- §2.01 Why Is Collective Agreement Coverage Low in CEE Countries?   30
- §2.02 Development of Collective Bargaining in Hungary   35
- §2.03 Legal Reform to Increase Collective Agreement Coverage: 'Free Derogation'   40
  - [A] Farewell to 'In Favour Principle'   40

Table of Contents

	[B] Is Motivation Enough to Affirm Collective Bargaining?	42
§2.04	Conclusions: Reasons for Restrained Collective Bargaining in CEE Countries	46

CHAPTER 3
How Can Decentralisation of Collective Bargaining Be Achieved?
A Typology of Legal Incentives
Pierre-Emmanuel Berthier & Olivier Leclerc — 47

§3.01	Introduction	47
§3.02	Facilitation	51
§3.03	Reward	54
	[A] Financial Advantage	54
	[B] Relief from Legal Constraints	55
§3.04	Taxation	58
§3.05	Conclusion	59

CHAPTER 4
The Impact of the Economic Crisis on Collective Agreements in Poland
Łukasz Pisarczyk — 63

§4.01	Introductory Remarks	63
§4.02	The Structure of Collective Agreements in Poland	64
§4.03	The Current State of Collective Agreements	66
§4.04	Personal Scope of Collective Bargaining	67
§4.05	The Content of Collective Agreements	68
§4.06	Parties to the Collective Agreements and the Bargaining Procedure	70
§4.07	Conclusions	71

CHAPTER 5
Collective Bargaining in Romania: The Aftermath of an Earthquake
Felicia Rosioru — 73

§5.01	Once upon a Time…General Trends in the Evolution of the Collective Bargaining System in Romania	74
	[A] Collective Bargaining During the Communist Regime	75
	[B] Legislative Overview of the Industrial Relations in the Democratic, Post-communist Regime	76
§5.02	Social Dialogue Reform and the Reasons Behind It	77
	[A] The Reasons Behind the Legislative Reform	78
	[B] Collective Bargaining in the Public Sector	80
§5.03	The Impact of the Social Dialogue Reform: The Aftermath of the Earthquake	81
	[A] The Impact of Decentralization of Social Dialogue on Wage-Setting Mechanisms	83
	[B] Tripartite Institutions	85
§5.04	Conclusions	86

CHAPTER 6
The Importance of Sectoral Collective Bargaining in Austria
Elisabeth Brameshuber 89
§6.01 Introduction 89
§6.02 Sectoral Collective Bargaining as Stabiliser 90
    [A] Functions 91
        [1] Cartelising Function 91
        [2] Peace Function 93
        [3] Innovation Function 94
    [B] Stabiliser in Times of Crisis 95
§6.03 The System of Sectoral Collective Bargaining 95
    [A] Legal Background 96
        [1] Registration of Business 96
        [2] De-facto Bargaining Monopolies 97
        [3] Mandatory Applicability to All Members of the Concluding Party 98
        [4] Outsider Validity for Employees 98
        [5] Deviation from the Collective Bargaining Agreement Only to the Employee's Advantage 99
    [B] Critical Assessment 100
        [1] No Sectoral Bargaining: No Cartelising 100
        [2] Deviation to the Employee's Advantage: Another Threat to the Cartelising Function? 101
        [3] The Difficulty of Defining a Sector 102
§6.04 Sectoral Collective Bargaining: 'Best Practice Model'? 103
§6.05 Conclusion 103

CHAPTER 7
The Revival of Sectoral Collective Bargaining: The Portuguese Experience
Teresa Coelho Moreira 105
§7.01 Introduction 105
    [A] The Crisis in Portugal 105
    [B] The Right to Negotiate 106
    [C] The Traditional Tripartite Concertation 107
§7.02 Sectoral Collective Agreements in Portugal 108
§7.03 The New Political Cycle 114
§7.04 Conclusion 115

CHAPTER 8
The Spanish Example
Yolanda Maneiro Vázquez & José María Miranda Boto 117
§8.01 Collective Bargaining Regulation in Forty Years 117
§8.02 Sources and Outcomes of the Reforms 119
§8.03 The Public Sector: The Demise of Collective Bargaining 120
§8.04 The Agents of Collective Bargaining: The Double Channel 121

Table of Contents

§8.05	Structure of Collective Bargaining: From Branch to Company	122
§8.06	The Legal Effects of Collective Agreements: The Opting-Out and *Ultractividad*	124
§8.07	Content and Parameters of Collective Agreements	126

PART II
The Contents of Collective Agreements: Old and New Issues   129

A   Wages   131

CHAPTER 9
Decentralisation of Wage Setting Mechanisms and Statutory Minimum Wage: Towards the End of Sectoral Collective Bargaining?
Piera Loi   133

§9.01	Wage-Setting Mechanisms under the New Economic Governance	133
§9.02	Changes in Wage-Setting Mechanisms and European Economic Governance	136
§9.03	Soft and Hard Interventions of EU Institutions on National Wage Regulatory Sources	138
§9.04	Wage Setting Between Law and Collective Bargaining	142
§9.05	Wages Between Legal and Collective Sources and a Statutory Minimum Wage: Some Comparative Remarks	145
§9.06	Conclusion	150

CHAPTER 10
Measures of Wage Moderation in Times of Crisis: The Example of Belgium
Fabienne Kéfer   153

§10.01	Architecture of the Belgian Model of Social Dialogue		153
§10.02	Impact of the Crisis on the State's Role in Collective Bargaining		157
	[A]	Description of the Mechanism	159
		[1] Procedure	159
		[2] Content of the Cross-Sectoral Agreement	160
		[3] Impact of the Economic Crisis	162
	[B]	Legality of State Intervention	164
	[C]	Conclusion	166

CHAPTER 11
Decentralized Collective Bargaining: A Solution to Economic Crisis? – The Case of Turkey
Kübra Doğan Yenisey & Berrin Ceylan Ataman   169

§11.01	Introduction		169
§11.02	Legislative Overview of Turkish Collective Bargaining System		170
	[A]	Historical Evaluation	170
	[B]	Mandatory Decentralized Model	171

		[1]	Industry Level Unionism and Collective Agreements at the Workplace Level	171
		[2]	Bargaining Parties and Their Competency	172
§11.03	Wage Setting and Working Time Clauses in Enterprise and Group Collective Agreements			173
	[A]	Data and Methodology		173
	[B]	Wage Increase Rates		174
	[C]	Working Time Clauses		180
§11.04	Other Possible Factors			183
	[A]	Power Relations and the Size of Companies		183
	[B]	Union Rivalry		183
	[C]	Unions Approach to Flexibility		184
§11.05	Conclusion			184

B Working Time   187

CHAPTER 12
Negotiating Working Time in Times of Crisis
Łukasz Pisarczyk   189
§12.01 Introduction   189
§12.02 Working Time: The Social Dialogue and the Legislation   190
§12.03 Levels of Negotiations and Parties to Collective Agreements
       Regulating Working Time   194
§12.04 Content of Collective Agreements   196
§12.05 Conclusions   201

CHAPTER 13
Negotiating Working Time in Time of Crisis: The 'El Khomri Law'
Christophe Vigneau   203
§13.01 Retraction of the Law in Favour of Collective Agreements   204
§13.02 Primacy of Company Agreements over Branch Agreements   208

C New Issues   211

CHAPTER 14
Work-Life Balance in Collective Agreements
Barbara Kresal   213
§14.01 Introduction   213
§14.02 Framework Agreements on Work-Life Balance and Gender Equality   216
§14.03 Work-Life Balance Measures in Sectoral and Company Level
       Collective Agreements: Typical Issues   217
§14.04 Recent Developments During the Crisis   221
§14.05 New and Old Challenges   223
       [A]   Special Work-Family Balance Measures as a Response to the
             Ageing of Population   223

Table of Contents

	[B]	Special Measures in Collective Agreements That Promote Active Fatherhood	224
	[C]	Special Measures in Collective Agreements Supporting Women in Leadership Positions	225
§14.06	Other Issues		226
§14.07	Conclusion		227

CHAPTER 15
Older Employees, Extended Working Lives, and Collective Bargaining
Jenny Julén Votinius 231

§15.01	Introduction	231
§15.02	The Greying Work Force of Europe	232
§15.03	The EU Ban on Age Discrimination in Working Life	234
§15.04	The Active Ageing Agenda in EU Employment Policies	236
§15.05	Extended Working Lives and Collective Bargaining on a National Level	238
	[A] Regulatory Approaches and Strategies to Promote Extended Working Lives	238
	[B] Working Conditions, Work Organization and Part-Time Pension Schemes	239
	[C] Lifelong Learning and Mobility on the Labour Market	242
	[D] Age-Awareness and Attitudes Towards Older Employees	244
§15.06	Discussion and Final Remarks	245

CHAPTER 16
Collective Bargaining with Regard to Young Employees: Importance and Challenges
Judith Brockmann 249

§16.01	Introduction	249
§16.02	Who Are 'Young Employees'?	251
§16.03	Examples of Collective Bargaining with Regard to Young Employees	253
	[A] Youth Wages	253
	[B] Intake of Young Employees	254
	[C] Qualification of Young Employees and VET	254
	[D] Intergenerational Bargaining	255
	[E] Interim Conclusions	257
§16.04	The Institutional Framework: Challenges for Collective Bargaining with Regard to Young Employees' Matters	258
	[A] European Policies	258
	[B] Ban on Age Discrimination	261
	[C] Trade Unions and Young Employees	261
	[D] Labour Market Situation	264
§16.05	Other Options for Social Partners' Involvement	265
§16.06	Conclusions	266

PART III
Expanding Spaces and New Boundaries of Collective Agreements   267

CHAPTER 17
Collective Autonomy for On-Demand Workers? Normative Arguments,
Current Practices and Legal Ways Forward
Auriane Lamine & Jeremias Prassl   269
§17.01 Introduction   269
§17.02 Collective Autonomy for the On-Demand Worker? Exploring the
Practical Challenges   271
    [A] Practical Challenges   271
    [B] Legal Challenges   272
§17.03 Collective Autonomy for the On-Demand Worker? Building
Normative Arguments   273
    [A] Aim and Method   273
    [B] A Utilitarian Argument   274
    [C] A Libertarian Argument   277
    [D] A Marxist Argument   280
    [E] A Rawlsian Argument   285
§17.04 Conclusion: From Justice to Democracy – Finding Inspiration in
Habermas and Dewey   289

CHAPTER 18
Are Agency Workers Protected by Trade Unions?: A Case Study from the
Netherlands
Nicola Gundt   293
§18.01 Introduction   293
§18.02 The Definition of the Triangular Employment Relation   294
§18.03 Which Triangular Relations Are Covered by Article 7:690 and/or
Article 7:691 BW?   295
    [A] Parliamentary Debates   296
    [B] Doctrine   297
    [C] Supreme Court   298
    [D] Assessment   299
§18.04 The Collective Labour Agreement   300
    [A] Scope of Application   301
    [B] Flexibility   302
    [C] Wages   303
    [D] Other Provisions   304
§18.05 Assessment of the Collective Labour Agreement on Agency Work   304
§18.06 Why Is the Collective Labour Agreement as it Stands?   306
§18.07 Is the Trade Union the Most Appropriate Protector of Agency
Workers?   307

Table of Contents

CHAPTER 19
Multi-Employer Situations and Collective Bargaining: The Hungarian Cases
Gábor Kártyás — 309
§19.01 Introduction — 309
§19.02 A Case Study: Lost Between Four 'Employers' — 310
§19.03 General Remarks: Is This Just a Question of Power? — 311
§19.04 Public Funding Entities — 312
§19.05 Company Groups — 313
§19.06 Large Employing Entities — 314
§19.07 Micro-employing Entities — 315
§19.08 Employee Sharing — 316
§19.09 Conclusions and Questions — 317

CHAPTER 20
A Study in Red and Blue: A Comparison of Collective Bargaining in Carrefour in Some EU Countries
José María Miranda Boto, Teresa Coelho Moreira, Florence Debord, Sonia Fernández Sánchez, Yolanda Maneiro Vázquez & Łukasz Pisarczyk — 319
§20.01 Goals and Foundations of This Chapter — 319
    [A] Into the Heart of Collective Bargaining — 319
    [B] On the Methodology of the Study — 321
§20.02 The International Agreement — 323
§20.03 Formalities of the Agreements: Scope, Subjects, Duration — 325
    [A] Scope of the Agreement — 325
    [B] The Bargaining Agents — 328
    [C] Duration of the Agreement — 330
§20.04 Material Content of the Agreements — 331
    [A] Working Time — 331
    [B] Professional Classification — 333
    [C] Remuneration — 334
    [D] Work Contracts and Employment — 336
    [E] Health and Safety — 337
    [F] Trade Union Rights & Representation — 338
    [G] Discrimination and Diversity — 339
    [H] Other Provisions — 339
§20.05 Specific Issues Derived from Other Parts of the Research — 340
    [A] Work-Life Balance and Gender Equality — 340
    [B] Agency Work — 341
    [C] Age — 341

Introduction

Sylvaine Laulom

The articles published in this volume dedicated to collective bargaining developments in times of crisis are the results of research by INLACRIS (International Network for Labour Law Studies in times of Crisis), financed by the European Commission (INLACRIS VS/2014/0532) with the participation of ASTREES.[1] The emerging network INLACRIS was set up for two previous projects and the results of the research presented here follow on from them.[2] It gathers together experts on social issues – particularly social law – from different Member States of the European Union, as well as Turkey;[3] the aim is to analyse developments in progress in the different Member States of the European Union related to the crises affecting the European Union, in order to offer knowledge and expertise on these developments and as a way to propose innovative solutions. Another aim is to contribute to the continuous strengthening of relations between the academic world and social actors. The network is grounded in the asserted will of this collective of independent experts to contribute to the renewal of social policies in Europe in a way that respects peoples' rights and freedoms.

---

1. Association Travail, Emploi, Europe, Société and Christophe Teisser, Project Manager at ASTREES.
2. M.-C. Escande-Varniol, S. Laulom, E. Mazuyer & P. Vielle, (eds), *Quel droit social dans une Europe en crise?* (Brussels: Larcier, 2012); *Which Securities for Workers in Time of Crisis*, European Labour Law Journal (No 3-4, 2014), Project VS/2012/0223.
3. Austria: Franz Marhold et Elisabeth Brameshuber, WU Vienna University of Economics and Business; Belgium: Auriane Lamine, Université catholique de Louvain; France: Christophe Teissier (ASTREES), Sylvaine Laulom, Marie-Cécile Escande Varniol, Florence Debord, Cécile Nicod, Pierre-Emmanuel Berthier, Carole Giraudet, University Lumière Lyon 2, Olivier Leclerc, Emmanuelle Mazuyer, CNRS, Center for Critical Legal Research (CERCRID UMR 5137); Germany: Judith Brockmann, Universität Hamburg; Greece: Aristea Koukiadaki, University of Manchester; Hungary: Tamás Gyulavári & Gábor Kártyás, Pázmány Péter Catholic University in Budapest; Italy: Piera Loi, University of Cagliari; Netherlands: Nicola Gundt, University of Maastricht; Poland: Lukasz Pisarczyk, University of Warsaw; Portugal: Teresa Coelho Moreira, University of Minho; Romania: Felicia Rosiuru, Babes-Bolyai University, Cluj-Napoca; Slovenia: Barbara Kresal, University of Ljubljana; Spain: Yolanda Maneiro Vázquez, José María Miranda Boto, University of Santiago de Compostela; Sweden: Jenny Julén Votinius, University of Lund; Turkey: Kübra Doğan Yenisey, University of Bilgi; United Kingdom: Jeremias Prassl, University of Oxford.

The aim of the research was to conduct a comparative analysis of developments in systems of collective bargaining in fifteen mainly European Union countries (Austria, Belgium, France, Germany, Greece, Hungary, Italy, Netherlands, Poland, Portugal, Romania, Slovenia, Spain, Sweden, Turkey, United Kingdom). This is a broad range with countries with very different systems of industrial relations represented.

The term 'crisis', used in a very generic manner throughout this study, must be properly defined. Since 2008, the European Union has suffered a series of crises of unprecedented magnitude: the financial crisis, the euro crisis, the public debt crisis, the unemployment crisis (particularly amongst young people and older people), the migration crisis and the Brexit crisis. These different crises have not affected States in a uniform manner, with some of them already in 'crisis' prior to 2008 (e.g., unemployment crisis). This study does not intend to examine the reality of these crises and their effects on the countries studied, nor look into the intricate causalities between these crises and developments in industrial relations systems. One fact remains: these crises have been used systematically to legitimise reforms which, far from being cyclical, are intended to be structural.[4] J. Prassl concluded thus: *'what is perhaps the deepest crisis of employment law yet has been entirely overlooked: as labour markets continue to develop away from received paradigms; and worker-protective norms break down, the rhetoric of "financial crisis" and responses thereto have only served to increase moves into a deregulatory direction, instead of facing the key challenges at hand'*.[5]

The subject of this research is precisely these reforms and the links that will be established, notably through European and national legislative and institutional discourse, between these reforms and the crises.

Analysis of national developments in labour rights since 2008 shows an emerging trend apparently common throughout Europe: that of the decentralisation of industrial relations systems, specifically the transfer of collectively agreed regulations to the company level. Even if this trend towards decentralisation is not new and may have been observed over a long period in some countries, there is no doubt that it has been reinforced by the financial crisis, which allowed developments already underway on a national level to be legitimised, and even reinforced. This trend has been reinforced by a renewed European context. The new European economic governance, i.e., 'the European Semester', put in place during the 2011, is a great incentive for Member States to decentralise their collective bargaining systems.

The aim of this study is therefore to analyse these national developments, first of all in terms of the structure of the industrial relations systems, and then going beyond to look at this decentralisation and determine its real nature. It will also be concerned with the subjects of collective bargaining, and not just the traditional subjects (wages and working time) but also potential new themes: the work-life balance, young people, older people. It will also look at changes in productive organisations (e.g., the development of the digital economy) and the adaptation necessary for collective bargaining.

---

4. J. Prassl, *Contingent Crises, Permanent Reforms: Rationalising Labour Market Reforms in the European Union*, European Labour Law Journal, 211 (Nos 3-4, 2014).
5. *Ibid.*, p. 230.

Introduction

In order to conduct a comparison, questionnaires were created on these different aspects, as well as national reports, which were discussed and debated in two seminars that were also attended by the social partners. The preliminary results were also presented at a conference held in Lyon in September 2016. Comparison makes it possible to identify common trends and new, emerging issues in collective bargaining; it also means widely reported topics, such as those around the decentralisation of collective bargaining, can be discussed. The limits of comparison must however be taken into account, which are also set out by each of the authors of this work. Industrial relations systems are still in rare diversity: the rates of union membership, the rates of collective cover, union practices, the articulations of levels of collective bargaining and the role of the State are not the same and the conclusions we arrive at must take this context into account. This is also the reason why we made the choice, in tandem with comparative analyses, to show examples of national situations which make it possible to better understand the developments described within a specific system. A transversal approach was favoured, with the choice made to analyse a single question from different angles: thus the question of decentralisation is handled simultaneously through the structures of collective bargaining but also its subjects of negotiation (working time and remuneration).

The first part (*The Changing Structures of Collective Bargaining*) looks at the meaning of decentralisation of industrial relations systems. The different processes for decentralising collective bargaining are demonstrated by way of several national examples. The Austrian case (*E. Brameshuber, The Importance of Sectoral Collective Bargaining in Austria*) shows first of all that there is nothing inevitable about this decentralisation. Sectoral collective bargaining remains the essential level for regulating working conditions, and the Austrian system is characterised by its remarkable stability. Romania (*F. Rosioru, Collective Bargaining in Romania: The Aftermath of an Earthquake*), Portugal (*T. Coelho Moreira, The Revival of Sectoral Collective Bargaining: The Portuguese Experience*) and Spain (*Y. Maneiro Vázquez, J. M. Miranda Boto, The Spanish Example*) have, on the other hand, undergone extremely significant reforms since 2008. In these three countries, the legislator has intervened massively to restructure industrial relations systems in order to 'liberate' the company level from the restrictions of the sectoral level. The consequences have been dramatic, with a very significant reduction in the number of employees covered by sectoral agreements. In Spain, and particularly in Portugal, there is nevertheless some resistance at sector level, and in Portugal a change in public policies. A final national example is provided in this section. Unlike the four other countries, it is difficult to discuss Poland in terms of the decentralisation of collective bargaining, as it has never been centralised and is kept to a minimum in companies. In this regard, *L. Pisarczyk* shows that the polish system of industrial relations is experiencing a real crisis. The three opening chapters of this part offer a comparative analysis of these developments. *S. Laulom* (*From Decentralisation of Collective Bargaining to De-collectivisation of Industrial Relations Systems?*) shows in detail that with the exception of the countries maintaining a centralised system of collective bargaining, decentralisation that is not controlled by sector level agreements rather amounts to a de-collectivisation of industrial relations, where collective bargaining has very limited powers to regulate the field of labour relations. In Chapter 2, *T.*

Gyulavári (*Chasing the Holy Grail? Stumbling Collective Bargaining in Eastern Europe and the Hungarian Experiment*), explains the reasons why Central and Eastern European countries have not developed an articulated system of collective bargaining. He also shows how the most recent attempts by the Hungarian government to develop collective bargaining at company level by encouraging employers to engage in negotiations to conclude derogating agreements have not yet been successful.

The State has often been a central actor, intervening directly to remodel articulations of the levels of collective bargaining. The chapter by O. Leclerc et P.-E. Berthier (*How Can Decentralisation of Collective Bargaining Be Achieved? A Typology of Legal Incentives*) analyses precisely the different mechanisms that the States have been able to use as part of their social policy to encourage actors to negotiate. A typology distinguishing three types of measures is put forward (facilitation, reward and taxation). The authors conclude that:

> the core of the incentive-based mechanisms highlighted in our study aim to encourage collective bargaining; incentives are used to support an employment policy that is implemented directly at company-level. It is, however, still necessary to bear in mind the fact that the incentive-based mechanisms that we have identified are not particularly linked to the decentralisation of collective bargaining. These incentives (facilitation, reward, taxation) could also be used in support of policy aimed at the development of collective agreements at a branch level or indeed national, inter-professional agreements.

Incentives to decentralise have often consisted of authorising companies to derogate from the statutory norm, and the legislator has also sometimes strongly limited the framing powers of sector level collective agreements (this is the case in Greece, Portugal, Spain and France). Our conclusion is that it would certainly be preferable to consolidate the sector level and, through various measures, to encourage parties to organise at this level, even if it is not an easy path.

In the second part (*The Contents of Collective Agreements: Old and New Issues*), we look at the contents of collective agreements, whether this be the classic themes of collective bargaining (wages and working time) or less traditional themes. The objective here was to grasp the reality of the decentralisation of industrial relations, focussing however on the essential issues of wages and working time. Here it seems appropriate to cross-examine approaches, and we present a comparative analysis as well as particularly illuminating national examples of developments in collective bargaining. Beyond developments related to collective bargaining systems and to the traditional subjects of collective bargaining, our research also questioned the emergence or not of new issues for collective bargaining in Europe. Young people and older people are two categories particularly affected by the crisis and European institutions are encouraging social partners to address the employment issues affecting them. Work-life balance is also a societal issue at the heart of problems of real gender equality. The aim of the project was to measure the capacity of social partners to address potential or new subjects of collective bargaining.

P. Loi (*Decentralisation of Wage Setting Mechanisms and Statutory Minimum Wage: Towards the End of Sectoral Collective Bargaining?*) analyses the issue of decentralisation of collective bargaining and wages in more detail. The setting of wage

Introduction

levels has always been one of the primary functions of collective bargaining and it is precisely this function that has been called into question by European institutions, in the name of, according to *P. Loi*, an erroneous analysis of the causes of the crisis.

Determining wages is traditionally perceived as the core of collective bargaining. In every country where it has been developed, sector level negotiation has, in effect, aimed to compensate for a very unbalanced power relationship, to the detriment of employees, with regard to the determination of their wages, at the same time as making it possible to equalise competition conditions between companies in the same sector through labour costs.

The works and reflections our project sets out confirm that this situation is being called into question in the context of economic crisis. This is what is behind a destabilisation of collective bargaining systems which has until now conferred sector level collective bargaining a role of centralising the determination of wages. The development of company level negotiation, encouraged singularly by European institutions, through prescriptions by the Troika or the European Semester, is motivated by an objective of improving the competitiveness of companies by moderating or reducing wage costs. It is a question of opening up the options offered to negotiators in the company to achieve this objective, which leads to the increased significance of company level negotiating to the detriment of the sector level, through the option to derogate, through agreement at company level, from the provisions of the agreements made on the subject at a higher level. National examples are mixed but developments observed in Italy, Spain and Greece are very significant in this regard. There are thus clear examples of increased European and/or national state intervention in the determination of wages, leading to the structure of collective bargaining being changed in several countries. This increasing role for the State on this subject also extends to the implementation, or at least questions being raised around the implementation, of a statutory minimum wage in countries where this does not traditionally exist.[6] The fixing of minimum wages is/was usually left to actors in sector level collective bargaining. In this regard, the investigation carried out by *P. Loi* rests on the incidence of the introduction of such statutory minimums on pre-existing collective bargaining systems. The response to this question attempts to take into account specific characteristics of the different systems of collective bargaining in the EU. *P. Loi* nevertheless advances the idea that the very pertinence of introducing such minimum statutory standards, where they do not already exist, must be left to the judgment of the trade unions to avoid the risk of weakening or losing meaningful collective bargaining at sector level. The Italian example in this regard is revealing, where wages are the driving force behind sector level collective bargaining and, above all, the power of this sector level to produce effects well beyond just the determination of agreed minimums.

The role of collective bargaining in determining wages is then approached from the perspective of two countries: Belgium and Turkey, two completely opposing examples, which make it possible to question several predominant ideas around collective bargaining and fixing salaries. Belgium is one of the countries where the

---

6. See the recent introduction of a statutory minimum wage in Germany, and, in the opposite case, the absence of such legislation to date in Italy.

minimum wage is the responsibility of social partners and where no national minimum wage exists. F. *Kéfer* (*Measures of Wage Moderation in Tme of Crisis: The Example of Belgium*) shows how, even if the crisis disturbed the standard process for establishing wages (there is no legal minimum wage in Belgium), it does not lead to a decentralisation of the system. She concludes:

> In Belgium, the land of consensus and surrealism, social dialogue has flourished as almost nowhere else in Europe. Even the wage moderation system is backed by social dialogue. Social partners, who must submit biennially to a certain level State constraint by negotiating a margin for payroll cost increases for the next two years, are free to set this margin when they reach an agreement. State authorities may not oppose their agreement. The system's framework, bodies set up on an autonomous basis and encouraged by public authorities, was not undermined by the crisis in 2008. Nevertheless, social dialogue has proved difficult since then. The deadlock in negotiations at cross-sectoral level has led to increased interventionism by the government in the decision-making process for wage increases. However, one observes a twofold movement, that may appear paradoxical. On the one hand, wage negotiations are placed under governmental control. On the other, this interventionism makes it possible to revive social dialogue. Once the margin has been set by the government, social partners who failed to reach an agreement at multi-industry level, regain the power to negotiate new wage benefits at sector and company levels within the limits of the margin, based on their specific characteristics.

While decentralised systems are supposed to be more flexible and this is one of the main reasons that this kind of decentralisation has been favoured by the European Union as an internal labour costs adjustment variable, *K. Doğan Yenisey* and *B. Ceylan Ataman* (*Decentralized Collective Bargaining: A Solution to Economic Crisis? The Case of Turkey*) demonstrate that a decentralised system is not necessarily flexible. '*Decentralization is assumed to bring required flexibility to companies during times of crisis. However, our findings do not totally confirm this assumption. There are surely factors other than the bargaining level to induce such a result*'. According to the authors, '*a one-level decentralized model risks weakening the collective bargaining system and supporting growing earnings inequality. The Turkish experience confirms these observations. In the absence of extension practice, one-level small bargaining units are associated with narrow coverage and result in a reduction of the functions of collective agreements as an institution. The primary activity of Turkish unions has always been concluding collective agreements and wage settlements have always been the crucial item. However, we believe that the one-level bargaining model strengthens bread-and-butter unionism*'.

The crisis has also impacted regulation in terms of working time, even if once again, the crisis only accentuated the trends which were already underway (*L. Pisarczyk, Negotiating working time in time of crisis*). '*To summarise, the natural tendency for working time to shape its organisation at plant level has been strengthened by the economic crisis. Many aspects of working time (including the number of working hours) are regulated by the social partners within companies. The crisis also caused some changes in the structure of employee representation. The legislators had to confront the growing importance of collective negotiations with the crisis of the trade union movement. As a result, employees are more and more often represented by elected bodies (also created ad hoc). This applies to all aspects of collective bargaining, but is particularly visible in the area of working time (while some other aspects of the employment relationship may be devoted to trade unions only)'*. With regard to the subject of the collective bargaining, the collective agreements on working time are not unrelated to the issue of remuneration. In reducing working time, partial unemployment devices impact on remuneration, which has consequences that are often partially borne by the State. The flexibility sought can also lead to working more or differently with a level of remuneration that remains the same. If we analyse the different devices for flexibilising working time *'the provisions of collective agreements are intended to flexibilise working time, to organise work in a more efficient way, and to improve the situation of the employer. The extension of reference periods, or annualisation of working time, has proved very popular. More and more often, collective agreements introduce atypical organisation of working hours. The finest example is working hours accounts which over recent years have been developed or even introduced in some countries. When it comes to the length of the working day and week, collective agreements play an important role in various forms of balancing daily working time. A separate problem is systems of short-time work that have been developed in almost all European countries. They must be treated as a typical anti-crisis instrument usually introduced on the basis of collective agreements. Their application is, however, very controversial; their usefulness and effectiveness questioned'*.

The economic slowdown encouraged some tendencies that had been observed earlier (annualisation of working hours, flexible schedules of working time, short-time work). Flexible solutions are deployed in a more consequent way and to a broader extent. Some of them are becoming a normal element in the organisation of working time. Moreover, there are countries such as Poland and Portugal where the scope and nature of changes is more serious and significant. The scale of changes depends on a number of factors, including the economic situation of a country, the actual role of collective agreements (in some countries the economic crisis coexists with the breakdown of collective negotiations), the position of trade unions, and other political scenarios.

In light of these national variations, it seems necessary to dedicate a chapter to a national experience that is particularly enlightening in terms of the developments in progress. As *Ch. Vigneau* shows (*Negotiating Working Time in Time of Crisis: The 'El Khomri Law'*), in France:

> Working time is one of the areas in which legislative intervention has been most intense over the last twenty years, through an increasing number of reforms of varying scope. The method used was first that of derogation from branch agreements, allowing collective negotiations of a branch or company to derogate from legal provisions, including derogations that were not favourable to employees. Combined, in terms of discussion, by the active promotion of social dialogue as a means of regulation, these reforms have gradually made collective branch agreements, followed by collective company agreements, major sources of legal derogation as regards the length and planning of working time. As such, working time law has become a key lever in the flexibility and individualisation of working conditions. More recently, the legislative authority has turned to another method

of organising sources with respect to the length and planning of working time. Setting aside that of derogation, the legislative authority now favours a suppletive method. It was this rationale that was enshrined in the law of 20 August 2008 on revitalising social democracy and the reform of working time. Under this reform, the law plays, with regard to many aspects of regulating working time, no more than a suppletive role with respect to collective agreements. Furthermore, collective company agreements prevail over branch-wide agreements.

L. Pisarczyk and *Ch. Vigneau* note that collective bargaining on working time is today focussed on another issue, that of the work-life balance. Multiple actors, including the European Union, recognise it as a subject that is important to realising gender equality.[7] Does this mean that actors in collective bargaining are increasingly attracted by this problem?

The analysis conducted as part of our project shows a very variable degree of penetration of the subject through collective bargaining (*B. Kresal, Work-Life Balance in Collective Agreements*). This is true of the existence of framework agreements (notably those concluded at the interprofessional level) on the specific themes of work-life balance or gender equality, or the integration of specific clauses on these subjects in the general conventions and collective agreements. Furthermore, while even intuitively the crisis context and its implications (organisation of working time and level of wages for example) might appear conducive to new developments in collective bargaining in terms of these issues, the comparisons show that it is not.

A similar question can be posed with regard to the employment of young and older people. These are without any doubt the categories most severely affected by the crisis and the role that social partners and collective bargaining should play is regularly emphasised by European institutions (*J. Brockmann, Bargaining with regard to young employees – Importance and Challenges*; *J. Julén Votinius* (*Older Employees, Extended Working Lives and Collective Bargaining*). In this regard, we cannot neglect to mention the internal contradictions of the European Union: on the one hand, the European Semester encourages Member States to restructure their industrial relations systems, while on the other hand, the social partners are encouraged to address the problems of employment and/or labour equality and thus participate in the public policy of employment, while their capacity to act is attacked. *J. Brockmann* and *J. Julén Votinius* demonstrate the specificities of each of these categories, how they are addressed by law and the policies of the European Union, and the reasons why collective bargaining has struggled to date to address this subject. At a time when young people and older people represent serious societal issues, collective negotiation is struggling to address these subjects.

Finally, in the third part, we focus on the relationships between the figures of the employer and the capacity of social partners to address new complexities with productive organisations (*Expanding Spaces and New Boundaries of Collective Agreements*). The question of determining the boundaries of the company is a path well

---

7. See in particular *European Commission* (2015), New start to address the challenges of work-life balance faced by working families (http://ec.europa.eu/smart-regulation/roadmaps/docs/2015_just_012_new_initiative_replacing_maternity_leave_directive_en.pdf).

trodden in labour law and calls into question their ability to take into account the reality of productive organisations. To cite just one example from the field of collective labour relations, the invention of European works councils makes it possible to adapt to representing workers collectively in complex organisations. The problem of constant restructuring processes in companies and groups of companies that make it difficult for trade unions to identify the relevant interlocutor is however still real, as this is an important step in starting the negotiation process at the right level. This question is once again enhanced by a double trend: decentralisation of collective bargaining and digitalisation of the economy.

Among the new forms of work organisation, the development of the digital economy has, of course, already been the focus of attention of a growing body of scholarship which has begun to explore the practical implications of digitally mediated on-demand work, as well as potential legal responses. This attention has mainly concentrated on questions such as the scope of employment, and the issue of collective autonomy for on-demand workers has hardly been explored. However, the current legal and institutional environment might at first glance appear to be largely detrimental to the development of the collective autonomy of on-demand workers. The nature of their activities often isolates them from other workers, which hampers possible organisation, and legal obstacles stand in the way of collective action by (genuinely) independent contractors. This makes an analysis of potential opportunities to design new categories and measures conducive to collective autonomy all the more relevant and timely. This is the very purpose of the chapter of *Auriane Lamine and J. Prassl* (*Collective Autonomy for On-Demand Workers? Normative Arguments, Current Practices and Legal Ways Forward*) who analyse the consequences of the development of the digital economy and how on-demand workers' interests could be represented: should on-demand workers enjoy broader collective autonomy? And if so, how could this objective be achieved?

They examine the question of the desirability of introducing institutional or legal measures to support on-demand workers in their capacity to organise, to associate in order be better placed to voice their interests, and to have a broader say on the circumstances in which their activities are taking place. On the basis of the theories they used (Utilitarian, Libertarian, Marxist and Rawlsian arguments), they defend the notion that on-demand workers should benefit from broader collective autonomy. Finding inspiration in Habermas and Dewey, they conclude that 'We should favour institutional solutions which are directly inspired from on-demand workers' expressed aspirations and from their various creative attempts to realise them. This requires first to look closely at these initiatives. Then, we should as legal scholars, perpetuate and extend their experiment, proposing solutions aimed at being tried and tested in reality'.

In the three last chapters, the issue of the relationships between the figures of the employer and the capacity of social partners to address new complexities with productive organisations is addressed through three case studies.

N. Gundt (*Are Agency Workers Protected by Trade Unions? A Case Study from the Netherlands*) looks at the issue of temporary work in the Netherlands. Her contribution analyses the position of employees in triangular employment relations in the collective bargaining process at the example of the Netherlands. It aims to show that regulating the employment conditions of these employees is difficult for several reasons. In the first place, the category of persons employed in triangular employment relationships covers a wide range of – sometimes very different – situations. Therefore the question is whether the same legal rules should apply to the whole group. Here, questions concerning the reasonableness of derogations from protective labour law will be raised. In the second place, due to their short stay in an enterprise or sector combined with the usually fragmented employment history and frequent spells of unemployment, most persons working in triangular employment relations, specifically the classic agency workers, are hard to organise. Many will not remain in the enterprise or sector long enough to gain anything from (lengthy) collective bargaining processes, and therefore lack the motivation to join a trade union which could speak in their name. This means that trade unions as classic employee representation bodies may be legitimised to a lesser extent than usually. In addition and consequence, they may simply lack bargaining power to ensure a balanced mix of rights and duties, flexibility and protection. The central question is, whether the legislator should offer as much leeway to derogate in *peius* from protective employment law provisions in a sector where union density is low, the unions' bargaining position is correspondingly weak and the unions may be more interested in the fate of other employees.

Borrowing from several case studies related to various productive structures (franchise networks, employee sharing, etc.) observed in Hungary, G. Kártyás (*Multi-Employer Situations and Collective Bargaining, The Hungarian Cases*) points to the multiple difficulties for workers and their representatives with the development of networks of companies. In particular, it is clear that the freedom accorded to companies to freely structure their activities must not lead, in practice, to depriving employees from their rights to collective bargaining. This presumably presupposes further work to point out the different regulations or existing national practices in a wide range of situations that form the basis of a harmonised approach to the difficulties encountered.

The final chapter of this work summarises, in a case study, the different transversal approaches we adopted and the comparison in action that we tended to favour (J. M. Miranda Boto, T. Coelho Moreira, F. Debord, S. Fernández Sánchez, Y. Maneiro Vázquez, Ł. Pisarczyk, *A Study in Red and Blue: A Comparison of Collective Bargaining in Carrefour in Some EU Countries*). 'That is the main justification for this case study: a trip into the heart of collective bargaining, taking on the role of a collective Marlowe, trying to identify if the legal harmonisation has also meant an actual harmonisation of the structures, actors and contents of collective bargaining'. According to the authors, 'the case study could also mean a synthesis of very important parts of current INLACRIS research, incorporating a transversal approach. The most specific parts, concerning, e.g., work-life balance, older and younger workers, the role of agency work, or the impact of crisis on collective bargaining, could easily be incorporated into it'. Throughout this case study, the changes concerning the structuring of

Introduction

labour relations systems and the subjects of collective bargaining are illustrated and confirmed. The idea is to address the reality of collective bargaining through the study of collective agreements that have been concluded, to show 'whether the legislator's will has been implemented or if, on the other hand, social partners have their own points of view about the management of industrial relations.

PART I   The Changing Structures of
            Collective Bargaining

CHAPTER 1
From Decentralisation of Collective Bargaining to De-collectivisation of Industrial Relations Systems?

Sylvaine Laulom

Analysis of national developments in labour law since 2008 highlights a common trend: the decentralisation of industrial relations systems. This is a marked trend that is noted by observers of this period across the board:

> Once this rapid reaction stage was over, the situation in the various countries began to diverge, and developed very differently depending on the scale or perception of the crisis. Some practices or projects were nevertheless fairly widespread. There were frequent examples of civil service pay freezes or pay cuts, sometimes accompanied by job losses. Various methods were used to reduce the level or duration of certain social benefits, and VAT was sometimes increased. The crisis has sometimes had an accelerating effect, being used to justify reforms which had already been announced. Pension reform is the key example of this. In terms of labour law reform, three types of measure are very common and could have a major impact on national social rights (although not all countries are affected by these changes). The first of these are the sweeping reforms to the civil service, which call into question the specific nature of the rules applying to this type of employment. Secondly, at a time when it has become clear that the employment situation in EU countries is not dependent on job protection legislation, this very legislation is being challenged in various ways. Some measures have already been adopted, while others are in the pipeline. These include redundancy avoidance measures, avoiding recourse to the courts in the event of disputes, increasing the length of service required before redundancy rules apply, reducing the level of compensatory sanctions, calling into question the principle of reinstatement asa penalty for unfair dismissals, increasing the thresholds used to define specific obligations in the area of redundancy, etc. Finally, in some countries the crisis resulted in the adoption of new relationships between labour law rules, amounting to a decentralisation of collective bargaining. Company level collective bargaining

has gained ground and the normative function of branch level collective agreements has become less important.[1]

This finding has been made by several other authors. For example, I. Schömann and S. Clauwaert state that *'a clear policy and/or ambition can be identified in many countries to decentralize collective bargaining, shifting from national/sectoral level to company level. The professed aim is to give businesses more flexibility and help them adjust to labour market conditions'*.[2]

This trend towards decentralisation is not new and predated the 2008 crisis. After World War II, the professional sectoral level was confirmed in many European countries as the favoured level for regulating labour relations and a space structuring labour relations;[3] the first trends towards decentralisation of collective bargaining, in particular in terms of regulating working time, appeared in the 1980s and the movement has since intensified, from 2008 onwards in particular.

From this point of view, while widely disseminated rhetoric has highlighted the need for labour market reforms to tackle the crisis, in reality this is essentially a device permitting the legitimisation of processes already broadly underway prior to 2008. Another aspect of this decentralisation is apparent throughout this period: the emphasis placed hereafter on uncontrolled decentralisation of industrial relations systems at the expense of controlled decentralisation. New articulations of labour law standards have been implemented, granting precedence above all others to standards negotiated at company level.[4] The recent French law, known as El Khomri, is particularly revealing of this trend which is likely to be still further exacerbated in France by the reforms announced by the President of the Republic, E. Macron and his Prime Minister, E. Philippe.[5]

These national developments have been broadly encouraged by the European Union particularly in the context of the 'European Semester'. The next step, therefore, is to consider the reality behind this decentralisation of collective bargaining. Comparative study reveals very varied forms of decentralisation of collective bargaining systems with very different consequences. However, it can be observed that the term decentralisation often masks a situation which is more one of de-collectivisation of labour relationships, namely the absence or rarity of collective regulation of labour relationships at a company level.

---

1. S. Laulom, E. Mazuyer, Ch. Teissier, C.-E. Triomphe and P. Vielle, *How Has the Crisis Affected Social Legislation in Europe?*, ETUI Policy Brief, (2/2012).
2. S. Clauwaert and I. Schömann, *The Crisis and National Labour Law Reforms: A Mapping Exercise*, ETUI Working paper 04 (2012). See also N. Brunn, K. Lörcher and I. Schömann, *The Economic and Financial Crisis and Collective Labour Law in Europe*, (Oxford: Hart Publishing 2014).
3. A. Jacobs, *Collective Labour Relations*, in B. Hepple and B. Veneziani (eds), *The Transformation of Labour Law in Europe*, 201-231 (Oxford: Hart Publishing 2009).
4. A. Jacobs, *Decentralisation of Labour Law Standard Setting and Financial crisis*, in B. Hepple and B. Veneziani (eds), *supra*.
5. Law no. 2016-1088 of 8 August 2016 on work, the modernisation of labour relationships and securing of career paths. See Part II Chapter 13 by Ch. Vigneau (*Negotiating Working Time in Time of Crisis: The 'El Khomri Law'*) *infra*.

§1.01 THE EUROPEAN CONTEXT: THE AIM OF DECENTRALISING COLLECTIVE BARGAINING

National developments have been taking place within a European context that strongly supports this decentralisation of collective bargaining.[6] Traditionally, and particularly since the 1980s under the leadership of Jacques Delors, the European Union has supported action by social partners, in particular European social partners. Article 154 of the TFEU which institutionalises the participation of European management and labour in the European decision-making process particularly attests to this support. However, the economic means of governance[7] have been implemented on the whole without any consultation with European social partners, to the extent that in 2013 the European Commission published a communication calling in particular for the strengthening of social dialogue.[8] Above all, these very governance mechanisms have revealed themselves to be formidable instruments of convergence between national policies. One of the consequences of the new economic governance is a massive intrusion into collective bargaining systems, encouraging their decentralisation. To put it simply, national policies in the euro area have not been able to use traditional monetary mechanisms to support national economies and European institutions have put the emphasis on wage restraint or decreasing labour costs to ensure that companies are competitive. The aim of decentralisation of collective bargaining is precisely that: to impact on salary negotiations and decrease the cost of labour.

It is within the framework of the European semester, an annual cycle of coordination of economic policies and the main pillar of this new governance, that the

---

6. Also *see* in this volume, Part II Chapter 9 by P. Loi (*Decentralisation of Wage Setting Mechanisms and Statutory Minimum Wage: Towards the End of Sectoral Collective Bargaining?*), *infra*.
7. The terms of the new European economic governance refer to a set of rules and procedures that have been developed since 2008, but particularly since 2010, aimed at implementing more restrictive coordination of national economic policies. These new rules were adopted in the framework of the 'six pack', (Directive 2011/85/EU, of 8 November 2011, on the requirements for budgetary frameworks of the Member States, JOUE, L 306 of 23/11/2011, p. 41), the 'two pack' (Regulation (EU) no. 473/2013, of 21 May 2013, on common provisions for monitoring and assessing draft budgetary plans and ensuring the correction of excessive deficit of the Member States in the euro area, JOUE, L 140 of 27/05/2013, p. 11) and the Treaty on Stability, Coordination and Governance (the TSCG is an intergovernmental agreement, signed by twenty-five Member States excluding the United Kingdom, the Czech Republic and Croatia). The six-pack strengthened the Growth Pact and introduced a new macroeconomic surveillance tool: the procedure on structural imbalances. The two-pack requires Member States in the euro area to submit their draft budget plans in mid-October for the following year, so an examination of budgetary policies can take place at an early stage and the European Commission's guidance can be taken into account prior to the adoption of national budgets.
8. COM(2013) 690 final, *Strengthening the social dimension of the economic and monetary union*, Brussels 2.10.2013: '*the EU-level social dialogue plays an essential role in advancing our social market economy, producing benefits for employers, workers, and for the economy and society as a whole. When strengthening economic governance, it is critical to involve the social partners in policy debates and decision-making processes. This is not only to increase the ownership of policies and to ensure meaningful implementation, but also to enhance the effectiveness of policy coordination at euro area level. It is therefore vital that we invest in strengthening social dialogue at both European and national levels*'.

European Commission explicitly provides an incentive to Member States to contribute to the decentralisation of collective bargaining.

Each year, the European Commission analyses in detail the plans for Member States' macro-economic and structural budgetary reforms, providing them with recommendations for the following twelve to eighteen months. In this framework, euro area countries are subject to specific obligations and, in particular, a sanctions mechanism has been defined for States that do not respect the recommendations issued as part of the alert mechanism. There are even greater restrictions for countries where European financial aid is deemed to be indispensable. In exchange for financial loans, these countries have been obliged to bring in major reforms, set out either in 'Memoranda of Understanding', with the troika composed of the EU, the ECB and the IMF (this is the case for Greece, Ireland and Portugal) or 'Stand-by Arrangements' with the IMF (in the case of Hungary, Lithuania and Romania).[9] Spain, which likewise benefited from aid to support its financial sector, was obliged to commit itself to the implementation of specific national recommendations in the context of the European semester.

All the Member States have therefore been subject to injunctions from the European Union, and while the degree of restriction may vary, it is no longer a matter of entirely voluntary recommendations. Analysis of the subject of these recommendations[10] reveals a high number of them fall into the category of social policies. So while the TFEU Treaty explicitly places salaries outside the competence of the European Union,[11] salary policy is one of the ongoing concerns of the European semester as salaries are the main adjustment variable for tackling economic imbalances and boosting competitiveness.[12] Taking salary-related action is basically taking action on collective bargaining, and decentralisation of collective bargaining is a central component of the structural reforms to labour markets that Member States are called upon to perform. Company-level collective bargaining, which must be separated from that at a sectoral level, must be encouraged.

Using just a few examples of the pressure brought to bear by the European Union on the restructuring of collective bargaining, it is possible to cite the specific recommendations made to the Member States by the European Commission in the context of the European semester.[13] Thus for France in 2016, the Commission's diagnosis was that: '*the reforms carried out recently only gave employers a few options to derogate from*

---

9. D. Natali, B. Vanhercke, (eds.), Bilan social de l'Union européenne 2012, 14th annual report, 190 (Brussels: ETUI, 2013).
10. S. Clauwaert, *The Country-Specific Recommendations (CSRs) in the Social Field. An Overview and Comparison Update Including the CSRs 2014-2015* (Brussels: ETUI, 2014).
11. We should revisit here the terms of Article 153.5 TFEU under which, 'the provisions of this Article shall not apply to pay, the right of association, the right to strike or the right to impose lock-outs.' Introduced by the Social Protocol of the Maastricht Treaty, this article excludes salary policies from European policies, at the precise moment when the Economic and Monetary Union is being put into place.
12. D. Natali and B. Vanhercke (eds), Bilan social de l'Union européenne 2012, 14th annual report, 192 (Brussels: ETUI, 2013).
13. All these documents can be accessed on the European Commission Site, Europe 2020. https://ec.europa.eu/info/publications/2017-european-semester-country-specific-recommendations-commission-recommendations_en, accessed 5 June 2017.

sectoral agreements.[14] In Italy's case, the Commission found that *'second-level collective bargaining is not sufficiently widespread in Italy, which hinders the adoption, at a company level, of innovative solutions that could improve productivity and make salaries more reactive to labour market conditions'*.[15] As some countries have never had or no longer have collective bargaining at a sectoral level and some countries have already reformed their system, the Commission does not provide, or no longer provides, them with any incentive to carry out reforms in this area. Thus in 2014, the Commission found that the Spanish 2012 reform of the labour market had contributed to *'granting companies greater internal flexibility and limiting job losses, while giving priority to collective agreements at a company level and providing more opportunities for companies to derogate from a collective agreement'*.[16]

While it is difficult to establish direct causality between European recommendations, or more generally the objectives defined by the European Union in the context of the European semester, and national legislative policies, it should be noted that the majority of States will sign up for this European scheme and propose reforms that are intended to be structural in terms of labour relations systems, where the aim is their decentralisation.[17]

§1.02 TOWARDS DECENTRALISATION OF COLLECTIVE NEGOTIATIONS

Comparison of national experiences (some of which are in quasi permanent evolution) does not challenge the widely apparent trend towards decentralisation of collective bargaining. Indeed it highlights very varied forms of decentralisation of collective bargaining systems with very different consequences. In this regard, it is possible to distinguish three different groups of countries: those where it is not possible to talk of the decentralisation of a system because it is no longer or has never been centralised, systems where the sectoral level is still strong and finally systems where the State has been heavily involved in helping to drive the decentralisation of collective bargaining with varying results. The aspect that sometimes distinguishes the second group from the third is the State's role, because a country may maintain a strong role at sectoral

---

14. COM (2016) 330 final, Brussels, 15.05.2016, *Recommendation on the 2016 national reform programme of France and delivering a Council opinion on the 2016 stability programme of France.*
15. COM (2016) 332 final, Brussels, 18.05.2016.
16. COM (2014) 410 final, Brussels, 02.06.2014.
17. M.-C. Escande-Varniol, S. Laulom, E. Mazuyer and P. Vielle, (eds), *Quel droit social dans une Europe en crise?* (Brussels: Larcier, 2012). S. Clauwaert and I. Schömann, *supra*; A. Koukiadaki, I. Tavora and M. Martinez Lucio, *The Transformation of Joint Regulation and Labour Market Policy in Europe During the Crisis, Comparative Project Report* (University of Manchester, 2014). http://www.research.mbs.ac.uk/ewerc/Portals/0/Documents/Social%20Dialogue%20 and%20Collective%20Bargaining%202015%20Comparative%20report%20-%20final%20vers ion.pdf,accessed 20 July 2017.

See also, Conseil d'orientation pour l'emploi, *Les réformes des marchés du travail en Europe*, (5 November 2015), http://www.coe.gouv.fr/Detail-Nouveaute.html%3Fid_article=1 275.html, accessed 20 July 2017.

level, while at the same time the State may implement reforms aimed at decentralisation. This comparison highlights another trend which often masks the use of the term decentralisation: that of the de-collectivisation of industrial relations systems where in reality the absence of actors capable of negotiating at company level should be observed.

[A] Absence of Decentralisation

The term decentralisation, frequently used to describe national systems of labour relationships, may refer to two distinguishable situations. On one hand, the term evokes the idea of evolution of a system where collective negotiation is relocated to company level; on the other, the term likewise evokes a state where collective bargaining is to be situated mainly at a company level. Obviously this is a very simplistic depiction, the degree of evolution, the articulation of the levels and the definition of the negotiation unit may appear in a wide range of configurations from State to State. For various reasons Turkey, the United Kingdom, Hungary and Poland may not be used as examples of systems where collective bargaining is decentralised. First, collective bargaining at a branch or sectoral level is kept to a minimum and sometimes even non-existent nowadays; consequently there is no decentralisation of these systems. Second, collective regulation of labour conditions at a company level remains low.

Thus in the United Kingdom, the challenge to the more centralised system of collective bargaining which took place in the 1980s did not really lead to the development of collective bargaining in private-sector companies where the rate of unionisation was decreasing. Labour conditions there are, therefore, increasingly defined by the employer unilaterally, and it is even possible to ask whether collective laissez faire, the famous expression used by O. Kahn Freund to describe the British system of industrial relations,[18] has given way to laissez faire or to a law of the labour market.[19]

In Turkey, the collective bargaining system has been broadly structured and developed by the State, and since 1982, collective bargaining has only take place at company level (the establishment, company or group of establishments). The last reforms took place in 2012 and were basically justified by the need to integrate international labour standards, namely ILO Conventions Nos 87 and 98 and Articles 5 and 6 of the European Social Charter revised in 1996. Unlike the majority of Member States of the European Union, the economic situation was not invoked to justify the reforms: '*During the last 30 years, collective agreements have not been considered either among the reasons for, or the solutions to economic crisis. This result is also related to*

---

18. O. Kahn-Freund, *Labour Law* in M. Ginsberg (ed.), *Law and Opinion in England in the 20th Century* (Stevens 1959).
19. R. Dukes, *The Labour Constitution: The Enduring Idea of Labour Law (Chapter: From Collective Laissez-Faire to the Law of the Labour Market)* (OUP, 2014).

the narrow coverage of collective agreements.[20] With some rare exceptions, the collective agreement does not appear as a labour conditions flexibility instrument. It may also be governed fairly strictly as when, for example, legislation prohibits collective agreements from improving on legal provisions. As a result, since a 2003 law came into effect, the amount of unfair dismissal compensation, defined in legislation, may not be increased under a collective agreement. The implicit aim of the legislation here is to protect the public budget in public companies where union membership is still high. In a similar vein, a provision of Law no. 6356 of 2012 prohibits collective agreements from increasing the legal compensation set out for cases of trade union discrimination. The growing number of these provisions is such that they represent a major curb on the collective autonomy of social partners.

Poland and Hungary demonstrate many common features. In these two countries, as elsewhere in the ten Member States of Central and Eastern Europe,[21] industrial relations systems are characterised by the decentralisation of collective bargaining, low coverage of collective agreements and a low rate of unionisation. Can these systems really be described as decentralised collective bargaining systems? On one hand, they were never really centralised and collective sectoral bargaining is very rare and, on the other, collective bargaining at a company level remains low. Again, in these two countries, legislation has intervened with the aim of developing collective bargaining particularly with a view to introducing more flexibility, notably in matters of working time. However, these new collective bargaining spaces are struggling for implementation. At the same time, legislation has authorised negotiation of these agreements with non-trade union actors, a situation which offers fewer guarantees, and which is likely to weaken trade union representation. However, until now, collective bargaining has likewise failed to gain ground with these new staff representatives.

Thus in Poland, only a small proportion of employees is covered by the provisions of collective agreements. Consequently, the Polish system is characterised by the important role of the law and collective agreements hold a rather more marginal place in the regulation of labour conditions. Thus, as L. Pisarcszyk observes, the economic crisis which, for Poland, began in the early 2000s when unemployment reached 20%, exists alongside a profound crisis in collective bargaining.

The legislator was able to adopt certain provisions aimed at favouring the signature of 'anti-crisis' collective agreements. These might allow new flexibilities to be introduced in areas such as working time along with the temporary erosion of labour conditions or even the introduction of partial unemployment mechanisms. Thus, when so justified by the company's economic situation, social partners may sign collective agreements where labour and salary conditions are at stake. Under these agreements, it is possible to suspend the applicable provisions of collective agreements and take a new look at the labour conditions defined in employment contracts. Agreements may

---

20. See in this volume, Part II Chapter 11 by D. Yenisey and B. Ceylan Ataman, (*Decentralized Collective Bargaining: A Solution to Economic Crisis? The Case of Turkey*), *infra*.
21. See in this volume, Part I Chapter 2 by T. Gyulavári, (*Chasing the Holy Grail? Stumbling Collective Bargaining in Eastern Europe and the Hungarian Experiment*), and Part I Chapter 4 by L. Pisarczyk, (*The Impact of the Economic Crisis on Collective agreements in Poland*), *infra*.

not be for a duration of more than three years. No obligation to safeguard jobs has been acknowledged and the employer may undertake a collective redundancy procedure even when it has signed such an agreement. Thus, according to L. Pisarczyk, *'the agreement modifying individual employment standards refers directly to the conditions arising from employment contracts concluded with individual employees. It can therefore be criticized as a far-reaching interference in the autonomy of the will of the parties to the employment relationship'*.

The articulation of different levels of collective bargaining has also undergone changes. Development of derogatory negotiation has nevertheless remained limited: *'Polish law leaves very limited space for deviation from statutory standards. The list of legislative provisions that can be modified is closed and concerns only selected matters. During the economic crisis, the list was extended mainly when it came to working time regulations (e.g. longer reference periods). With regard to the structure of collective bargaining, the legislation allows the suspension of multi-establishment collective agreements concluded at a company level. This possibility does not play a particularly important role due to the very limited practical importance of sectoral negotiations'*.

These new fields of bargaining are open not only to trade union actors but atypical agreements can be adopted in the absence of trade unions. In such cases it is down to 'ad hoc' representatives to negotiate these agreements. Works councils themselves cannot enter into negotiations, even though legislation does not grant these 'ad hoc' representatives sufficient guarantees to allow for balanced negotiation.

The situation in Hungary is relatively similar. Labour law was the subject of major reform in 2012 with the adoption of a new Labour Code, the aim of which was to achieve the most flexible employment market in the world.[22] One of the mechanisms for rendering employment conditions more flexible has been promotion of the role of collective agreements in labour regulations and making it very broadly possible for company collective agreements to derogate from the law, even where this is unfavourable. Therefore, the aim has been to develop company collective bargaining in a country where, like Poland, the collective agreement norm is rare, even at a company level. The incentive consists of derogation authorised by law: *'The legislator expected that the wide possibility of in pejus derogations (...) would increase collective agreement coverage, because employers would be motivated to conclude such agreements'*.[23]

The new labour code also reforms the relations between collective agreements at different levels, relationships that were previously regulated by the favourability principle. Now, a company agreement may derogate from the sectoral agreement, if this sectoral agreement so authorises it. Nevertheless, sectoral agreements are rare so this mechanism should not be used.

According to Tamás Gyulavári, it is possible that the new labour code could eventually strengthen the role of unions if they are in a position to negotiate quid pro quo. Nevertheless, union organisations risk not reaching the level of 10% membership

---

22. T. Gyulavári & G. Kártyás, *The Hungarian Flexicurity Pathway? New Labour Code after Twenty Years in the Market Economy* (Budapest: Pázmány Press, 2015).
23. In this volume, Part I Chapter 2 by T. Gyulavári, (*Chasing the Holy Grail? Stumbling Collective Bargaining in Eastern Europe and the Hungarian Experiment*), infra.

which is now required in order to sign an agreement and at the same time, reforms might have contributed to weakening trade union organisations. Finally, the fact that works councils are given the possibility of signing such agreements represents a real danger because this can also lead to the weakening of trade union presence in companies.

[B] Maintaining a Centralised System of Collective Bargaining

Developments in national systems of labour relations and the major incentives that exist with regard to the decentralisation of collective bargaining must not mask the fact that some countries have not undergone such developments, or only to a very limited degree.

Within the range of countries studied, Austria, Germany, Belgium, Sweden and the Netherlands are in this situation, although their systems may be subject to a greater or lesser degree of pressure. These countries are all characterised by the fact that they have maintained a high level of unionisation (even if here once again, this rate might come down) and persistent abstentionism on the part of the State. Above all, the processes of decentralisation that exist remain controlled by high levels of collective bargaining and sectoral salary negotiations are still essential.

Austria is certainly the country where the labour relations system appears the most stable. Sectoral agreements still represent the main level of collective bargaining; it is at this level that minimum salaries are fixed and 95% of employees are covered by agreements at this level. Works councils agreements may only be entered into on matters defined under the law or if the sectoral agreement so authorises and they may not contravene the provisions of sectoral agreements. This is confirmed by Elisabeth Brameshuber:

> the Austrian system of sectoral collective bargaining has proved to be quite successful. It leads to a cartelisation of wages, with hardly any sector of industry currently offering a minimum wage of less than EUR 1,500/month for a full-time position. The regulatory function of the cartelised wages should not be underestimated either, leading to a de facto perishing of low-performing companies in the long run. By bargaining the wages and working conditions for one sector rather than just a single employer, the employer's position especially is reinforced, thus leading to relatively low strike rates. In this way, the Austrian system provides for a very distinct peace function. Another important feature is its innovation function, which was particularly visible during the crisis of the past few years where important decisions to stabilise the labour market were taken at the level of sectoral collective bargaining. Although current political developments are threatening the system's stability, it seems highly unlikely that it is going to change in the near future.[24]

Tensions may appear, but so far it has been possible to find solutions and they do not threaten the system's stability.

---

24. *See* in this volume, Part I Chapter 6 by E. Brameshuber, (*The Importance of Sectoral Collective Bargaining in Austria*), *infra*.

The Swedish system has also traditionally been depicted as a centralised system and this description is still valid, even though nowadays collective bargaining, particularly in relation to salaries, may take place at a decentralised level. *'In Sweden, collective bargaining has traditionally been described as highly decentralized. This description is still valid. Nevertheless, the collective bargaining structure also contains significantly decentralized elements – particularly regarding bargaining on wages. The decisive steps towards this partial decentralization of collective bargaining in Sweden was not taken during the crisis years, but mainly in the early 1990s. Furthermore, this partial transition of the collective bargaining system is not a product of political decisions that have been implemented through legislation. Instead the development has taken place in the area of industrial relations, and its outcome has been operationalized in collective agreements'.*[25]

Finally in Germany, the sectoral level is still important. However, the development of opt-out clauses and the decrease in extension procedures has led to the weakening of this level. Opt-out clauses set out in sectoral agreements related to establishments, namely employers and works councils, have progressively changed the structure of collective agreements by moving the centre of gravity closer to the company. In practice and under existing law, trade unions have accepted the need to sign opt-out clauses more frequently in sectoral agreements. These opt-out clauses appeared in the 1980s and authorised amendments made by agreements entered into between the employee and works councils on the subject of pay and working time. By the end of the 1990s, these opt-out clauses were spreading to companies experiencing major financial difficulties which could lead to redundancies. Such agreements were basically related to salaries and working time and were able to derogate unfavourably from the sectoral agreement standard. But while in the 1980s and 1990s these opt-out clauses on the whole concerned companies in difficulty, nowadays they can be found in companies who are not yet experiencing problems. Another development is that nowadays sectoral agreements may no longer contain clauses on salaries and working time which thus leads to a reduction in the scope of bargaining. The introduction of a minimum salary bears witness in part to this decline in the sectoral agreement.

[C] Legislative Intervention to Help Drive Decentralisation of Labour Relations Systems

The third group of countries (Italy, Spain, Portugal, Greece, Romania, Slovenia)[26] is characterised by legislative intervention, to a greater or lesser degree, aimed at decentralising industrial relations systems. The movement towards the decentralisation of collective bargaining, in itself, is not a recent phenomenon. What is new is the desire on the part of different regulators to prioritise the company level over the sectoral level.

---

25. J. Julén Votinius, internal report on Sweden, INLACRIS VS/2014/0532.
26. *See* A. Koukiadaki, I. Tavora & M. Martinez Lucio, *Continuity and Change in Joint Regulation in Europe: Structural Reforms and Collective Bargaining in Manufacturing*, 22 European Journal of Industrial Relations, 1 (2016).

The notable common thread among these companies is the intervention, in some case massive and in others repeated, by the State. Some reforms have been at the demand of the European institutions, in particular in the context of Memoranda of Understanding. For example, this is the case with Portugal and Greece. Social partners have sometimes been associated with reforms; however in the majority of countries studied the main trade union organisations have been opposed to them.

The measures adopted in order to develop company collective bargaining are varied and more often than not a set of measures is adopted and combined. Despite certain specific national characteristics, there are some common traits.

A country's legislation may revise the conditions for signing collective agreements at a sectoral level. This is the case for example in Portugal and Romania, where new conditions of representativeness have led to a reduction in the number of agreements entered into at this level. Procedures aimed at extending sectoral agreements may also be reviewed and the options of extension reduced. A limit on the term of the duration of agreements made at a higher level may also be allowed. The favourability principle may be called into question or see its field of application reduced and the regulator may review the articulation of bargaining levels by granting company level the possibility of derogating from higher level agreements in a way that is unfavourable to employees. The desire to develop collective bargaining at a company level also involves the acknowledgement of new actors in collective bargaining. In this way, elected or ad hoc representatives are sometimes granted the option of negotiating company agreements.

Thus the State has intervened in the regulations governing articulations between collective agreements and employment contracts to prioritise company agreements.

This State intervention is of a kind to call into question the very collective autonomy of social partners. This is the case particularly when the regulator seeks to impose a certain type of articulation between collective agreement standards themselves, granting precedence to company agreements over sectoral collective agreements. This type of intervention has sometimes even been acknowledged as being contrary notably to basic ILO standards. In 2012, when discussing the reforms made in Greece at the request of several Greek trade union organisations, the ILO Committee on Freedom of Association found *'numerous, significant interventions against the principle of the inviolability of freely concluded collective agreements'* and an extensive deficit of social dialogue. *'The elaboration of procedures systematically favouring decentralized bargaining of exclusionary provisions that are less favourable than the provisions at a higher level can lead to a global destabilization of the collective bargaining machinery and of workers' and employers' organizations and constitutes in this regard a weakening of freedom of association and collective bargaining contrary to the principles of Conventions Nos. 87 and 98'.*[27]

---

27. 365th report of the committee on freedom of association, GB316-INS_9-1_[2012-11-0030-01]-Web-Fr.docx http://www.ilo.org/wcmsp5/groups/public/---ed_norm/---relconf/documents/meetingdocument/wcms_193264.pdf, pp. 286 et seq., accessed 20 July 2017.

The effects of reforms on these collective bargaining systems are very diverse. Examination of the results of the research carried out by Aristea Koukiadaki brings to light three groups of countries: countries where the collective bargaining system has collapsed (Greece, Romania), countries where the system is being eroded (Portugal, Spain, Ireland, Slovenia) and countries where the system demonstrates continuity or resilience, such as Italy or up until now France.

One of the major consequences of these reforms has been the sometimes drastic reduction of a sectoral level due both to the contraction of the field of application of sectoral agreements and the contraction of the subjects of negotiation. Thus in Portugal, *'the number of employees covered by collective agreements fell from almost 1.9 million in 2008 to some 246,643 in 2014'*.[28] The conclusion for Portugal is *'the changes in the collective bargaining legal framework during the period of financial assistance did not promote organized decentralisation but a dramatic erosion of sector bargaining and coverage by collective agreements'*. The conclusion for Romania is still more pessimistic: *'The legislative intervention was brutal, without involving the social partners, and has ruined the social dialogue and the system the social partners had managed to build over the two decades, following the fall of communism. Decentralisation of collective bargaining to the lowest level has weakened the social acquis achieved so far by the trade unions at national and local level and affected sectoral collective bargaining. It has also lowered the standard of rights recognised so far, anchored in higher-level collective agreements'*.[29]

Another fairly general consequence and where there has not been parallel development of company-level collective bargaining. We might take Spain as an example. Post 2012, the law granted priority to company agreements. However, the option of negotiating at company level has not been exercised. One of the reasons for this is related to the specific characteristics of the Spanish industrial base, which is comprised basically of small- and medium-sized companies. The size of the companies means that it is difficult for negotiation to take place at this level. The disappearance or weakening of negotiation space at a sectoral level results in an extension of the employer's unilateral decision-making power.[30] This same observation has been made in Portugal.

It can also be seen that in countries where this erosion has taken place, recent developments have demonstrated that the sectoral level can stand its ground. In Portugal, since 2015 the government has been seeking to strengthen sectoral bargaining and the country has seen an increase in the number of agreements signed at this level, which has not been the case since 2012. In France, until the adoption of the Labour Law of 8 August 2016, the development of collective bargaining at a company level had basically not called into question the coordinated articulation of standards negotiated at company and sectoral level. This is the finding of the Combrexelle report:

---

28. In this volume, Part I Chapter 7 by T. Coelho Moreira, (*The Revival of Sectoral Collective Bargaining: The Portuguese Experience*), infra.
29. In this volume, Part 1 Chapter 5 by F. Rosioru, (*Collective Bargaining in Romania: The Aftermath of an Earthquake*), infra.
30. In this volume, Part I Chapter 8 by Y. Maneiro Vázquez & J. María Miranda Boto, (*The Spanish Example*), infra.

'the effects of the law of 4 May 2004 allowing derogation by company agreement from a higher level, including outside of the favourability principle, appear to have been limited. A review of the law made in 2008 demonstrated that social partners in fact had a tendency to "lock" the companies' power to derogate in sectoral agreements, as they were authorised to do by law. Over the following years, there was no monitoring, either by the social partners or the State, that would make it possible to provide an assessment of the importance of "derogatory" company agreements'.[31] The Labour Law of 8 August 2016 aims to go well beyond this and sets out a new labour law architecture where company agreements must prevail over sectoral agreements and the law. This law only targeted the field of working time, and the aim of the Macron rulings and the reform that should be implemented in summer 2017 is to go beyond this.[32]

§1.03 CONCLUSION

In many EU Member States, the crisis provided grounds for a rarely equalled level of state intervention in the regulation of labour relations with an explicit aim: the decentralisation of collective bargaining. This movement began long before the crisis, but without a doubt intensified from 2008 onwards. This evolution calls into question the role that the State can or must play in the field of labour relations.

Traditionally, the State has intervened by means of various measures to support collective autonomy and favour an environment conductive to the development of collective bargaining. State interventionism which, as we have seen, could be particularly intense, nowadays takes new forms. It is not so much a matter of supporting actors and helping to drive collective agreement-making activity, as allowing businesses to conclude a certain type of agreement and take action with regard to the structures and indeed content of collective bargaining. The majority of reforms are of little interest to actors in collective bargaining, other than, in the absence of union organisations within the business, in terms of allowing negotiation with other actors without really giving them the means to engage in balanced negotiations.

The consequences of these policies are not uniform. The decline in coverage by collective agreement can be dramatic, as has been the case in Greece, Portugal and Romania. The main lesson is that the decline in regulation of working conditions by professional sector has not been twinned with the development of collective bargaining at a company level and that decentralisation that is not sector-led generally leads to the absence of a collective agreement, namely a de-collectivisation of labour relations. Today this is the situation in which Poland and Hungary find themselves.

In this context, comparative analysis indicates that another path could be taken by national policies which would consist in engaging in reflection on how best to develop and support the sector level. Changes in productive organisations that are

---

31. J.-D. Combrexelle, *La négociation collective, le travail et l'emploi, Rapport au Premier ministre* (France Stratégie 2015) http://www.gouvernement.fr/sites/default/files/document/document/2015/09/rapport_combrexelle.pdf, accessed 20 July 2017.
32. See in this volume, Part II, Chapter 13 by Ch. Vigneau, (*Negotiating Working Time in Time of Crisis: The 'El Khomri Law'*), *infra*.

currently taking place, which see the development of small and very small businesses, networked businesses and work via digital platforms likewise suggest this is the right approach. Tamás Gyulavári and Lukasz Pisarczyk also conclude their analyses with the need to rebuild a collective bargaining system. There can be no doubt that this (re)construction would require complex measures and that it is anything but a certainty. As a result, the question is necessarily raised as to the evolution of labour rights in the absence of collective regulation of labour conditions. The process of decentralisation has more often than not led to an extension of the employer's unilateral power where salaries and labour conditions are ever more frequently determined by direct negotiations between employer and employees, with the State becoming the sole guarantor of employee protection. Paradoxically, there is no certainty that the flexibilities sought by companies are necessarily achieved, except in terms of extending the employer's unilateral powers still further.

CHAPTER 2
Chasing the Holy Grail? Stumbling Collective Bargaining in Eastern Europe and the Hungarian Experiment

*Tamás Gyulavári**

While industrial relations in central and eastern Europe exhibit certain differences across the ten EU Member States, this group of post-socialist countries have many important things in common, such as the predominance of decentralised wage bargaining,[1] a low density of social partners and sparse collective agreement coverage. Hungary has long been an excellent example of all these attributes, since trade union membership and collective bargaining is low and declining, and sectoral collective bargaining hardly exists.

The new Hungarian Labour Code of 2012 therefore sought to increase the role of collective agreements in regulating employment relationships. Free derogation from the Labour Code was designed as the central measure to motivate employers to conclude collective agreements. Nevertheless, the reform restricted certain trade union rights and shifted several roles from trade unions to works councils. Diminishing collective agreement coverage shows the failure of the Hungarian experiment to increase collective agreement coverage by means of a single legal incentive.

This paper analyses first the attributes of industrial relations in central and eastern Europe, second the Hungarian situation, and third the details of the 2012 reform of Hungarian collective labour law. The central issue of the paper is whether the present low level of collective bargaining coverage might be increased at all in central

---

* The author is grateful to Erzsébet Berki, Gábor Kártyás, Barbara Kresal, Sylvaine Laulom, László Neumann, Lukasz Pisarczyk, Imre Szabó and Felicia Rosioru for their comments on the draft.
1. L. Funk and H. Lesch, *Industrial Relations in Central and Eastern Europe – Organisational Charactistics, Codetermination and Labour Disputes*, Intereconomics, 264 (September/October 2004).

and eastern European (hereinafter CEE) countries[2] – and if so, what reform measures could work.

§2.01 WHY IS COLLECTIVE AGREEMENT COVERAGE LOW IN CEE COUNTRIES?

During the communist period, collective bargaining was not an essential mechanism for setting terms and conditions of employment. Generally, the state determined wages directly by wage scales, or indirectly by regulations. In countries such as Hungary and Poland (where there was a degree of decentralisation), limited collective bargaining at company level took place, but for instance in Romania there was no tradition of voluntary collective bargaining.[3] Moreover, sector level bargaining never played an important role in most of the CEE countries before 1990, as collective bargaining had always taken place mainly at company level.[4] For instance, in Poland before 1989 there was a system of sectoral collective agreements. They covered a large number of branches and employees. However, they were not a result of 'real' social dialogue (official trade unions were strictly connected with the political regime). After 1989, the whole structure collapsed and social partners were not encouraged to launch autonomous negotiations or to create a system of normal collective agreements.

Consequently, collective bargaining was a relatively new feature of the transitional model and was generally supported by a legal framework from shortly after the political changes.[5] However, the absence of real collective bargaining before 1990 has rendered the reform in CEE countries more difficult than expected. Since the beginning of the 1990s, there have been repeated attempts to advance towards free collective bargaining. Although legislation exists on paper, actual practice is quite different, as collective agreements are still limited in number and the process is also often far from a dialogue of autonomous and independent social partners, as is common in western Europe.[6]

One indicator of the importance of collective bargaining is the proportion of employees affected by it – namely its coverage. Across the EU as a whole, more than six out of ten employees (62%) are covered by collective bargaining, although there are important variations between countries.[7] Collective bargaining coverage is on average

---

2. The CEE countries are defined in this paper exclusively as those joining the EU in 2004 (Czech Republic, Estonia, Hungary, Latvia, Lithuania, Poland, Slovakia, Slovenia), in 2007 (Bulgaria and Romania) and in 2013 (Croatia).
3. A. Trif, *Collective Bargaining in Eastern Europe: Case Study Evidence from Romania*, 13 European Journal of Industrial Relations, 241 (2007/2).
4. *Industrial Relations in Europe 2010.* European Commission, 131 (2011).
5. J. Thirkell, R. Scase and S. Vickerstaff, *Changing Models of Industrial Relations in Eastern Europea and Russia*, in J. Thirkell, R. Scase, S. Vickerstaff (eds.), *Labour Relations and Political Change in Eastern Europe. A Comparative Perspective,* 20 (London: UCL Press 2005).
6. G. Casale (ed.), *Social Dialogue in Central and Eastern Europe,* 17-20 (Budapest: ILO 1999).
7. L. Fulton, *Worker Representation in Europe.* Labour Research Department and ETUI. 2013, http://www.worker-participation.eu/National-Industrial-Relations/Across-Europe/Collective-Bargaining2 (accessed 28 December 2016).

much lower in the EU-10 (CEE countries)[8] than in the EU-15.[9] Nevertheless, the coverage of collective agreements varies in CEE countries, from below 20% in Lithuania to around 100% in Slovenia, where collective agreements were mandatory before 2006.[10]

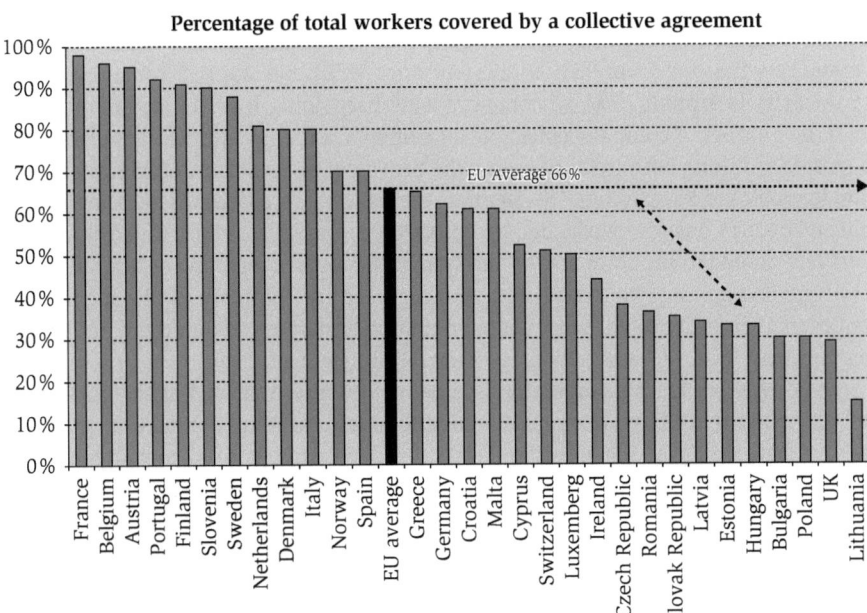

Figure 2.1 Percentage of Total Workers Covered by a Collective Agreement

Source: Fulton (2013) Worker representation in Europe, labour Research Department and ETUI (online publication).

The low(est) coverage in CEE countries is associated with several reasons, such as the decentralised (company-based) structure of collective bargaining and low level of organisation of employees and employers alike.[11] In the countries with low coverage, it is bargaining at company level that predominates. Almost by definition, company level bargaining depends on union activity at company level and is therefore more closely related to levels of union density.[12] Divisions between and within employers' organisations and the trade union movement are also at the root of the failure to build an efficient system of collective bargaining. Employers in particular are

---

8. Supplemented by the new CEE Member State, Croatia (EU-11 after 2013).
9. V. Glassner, *Central and Eastern European Industrial Relations in the Crisis: National Divergence and Path-Dependent Change*, 19(2) Transfer 161 (2013).
10. A. Trif, *Collective Bargaining in Eastern Europe: Case Study Evidence from Romania*, supra n. 3, p. 241.
11. L. Funk and H. Lesch, *Industrial Relations in Central and Eastern Europe – Organisational Charactistics, Codetermination and Labour Disputes*, supra n. 1, p. 267.
12. L. Fulton, *Worker Representation in Europe*, supra n. 7.

often reluctant to negotiate with trade unions in CEE countries.[13] Collective bargaining in the new Member States has actually declined with EU accession, at company as well as sector level. In Poland, for instance, the decline in registered company-level agreements has been constant: from 1,389 in 1996, to 405 in 2004, to 199 in 2008.[14]

As has already been mentioned above, the absolute lack or at least very weak presence of sector level bargaining has always been a basic feature of collective bargaining in the CEE countries,[15] except Slovenia and Romania.[16] However, in Romania collective bargaining was forcibly decentralised in 2011, resulting in a coverage rate that fell from 98% in 2011 to only 35% after 2011.[17] Romanian trade union density is around 20%, so company level bargaining leads to lower coverage, even if the number of company collective agreements is rising.[18] Romania is one of the two countries (along with Ireland) where the prevalent regime has shifted from multi- to single-employer bargaining. The fact that the national, cross-sector agreement was abolished in 2011 has also weakened coordination across sectors and wage bargaining has largely moved to the company rather than to the sector level. The decentralisation of collective bargaining was associated with the need for company level trade unions to re-organise in order to convince more company employees to join them and to get their company level representativeness recognised by courts.[19]

In general, collective bargaining is most commonly practised at the enterprise level. Although there have been legislative attempts in several countries to promote collective bargaining at the industry level, the development of such bargaining is impeded by the lack of well-structured organisations on both sides of industry and the lack of motivation on the employer side.[20] Industry-wide wage agreements tend to be most common in branches with monopolistic or oligopolistic structures, such as the energy sector and the railways.[21]

Evidently, trade union density is regarded as an important indicator of the ability of unions to negotiate collective agreements. Since 1990, trade union membership has decreased considerably in the post-socialist states, despite the reform of the previous communist employee associations and the founding of new ones. This development can largely be explained, firstly, by the revocation of the obligation to belong to a

---

13. G. Casale (ed.), *Social Dialogue in Central and Eastern Europe*, supra n. 6, p. 17.
14. G. Meardi, *Social Pacts: A Western Recipe for Central and Eastern Europe?*, 2:1(3) Warsaw Forum of Economic Sociology, 81 (Spring 2011).
15. *See* for example Poland (P. Grzebyk, *Legal Position of Trade Unions in Polish Collective Labour Law: Enterprise-Based Trade Union*, Hungarian Labour Law E-Journal, 73-86 (2014/1), http://www.hllj.hu.
16. G. Meardi, *Social Pacts: A Western Recipe for Central and Eastern Europe? supra* n. 14, p. 81.
17. Eurofound, *Collective Bargaining in Europe in the 21st Century*. Luxembourg, 2015, http://adapt.it/englishbulletin/wp/collective-bargaining-in-europe-in-the-21st-century, p. 42 (accessed 8 February 2017).
18. *Industrial relations in Romania – background summary* https://www.etui.org/Reforms-Watch/Romania/Industrial-relations-in-Romania-background-summary (accessed 1 February 2017).
19. F. Rosioru, *El salario in Rumanía – The Facts Behind the Myths*, III Doc. Labor, 131 (108/2016).
20. G. Casale (ed.), *Social Dialogue in Central and Eastern Europe*, supra n. 6, p. 18.
21. L. Funk and H. Lesch, *Industrial Relations in Central and Eastern Europe – Organisational Charactistics, Codetermination and Labour Disputes*, supra n. 1, 266.

union; second, by the increase in unemployment; and third, by the increasing number of small and medium-sized enterprises that resulted from privatisation.[22]

Recent economic changes have also greatly contributed to dismantling representation on both sides of industry. The world of business has generally been transformed in the direction of a multitude of small and medium-sized enterprises. Small business structures have replaced the previously dominant corporate entities. Trade union presence is not merely fragmented, but largely non-existent in these new structures, with the exception of formerly state-owned larger companies. Given the large number of non-union companies (up to 80%) and even non-union sectors (also lacking employers' associations), the essential conditions for collective bargaining are missing.[23]

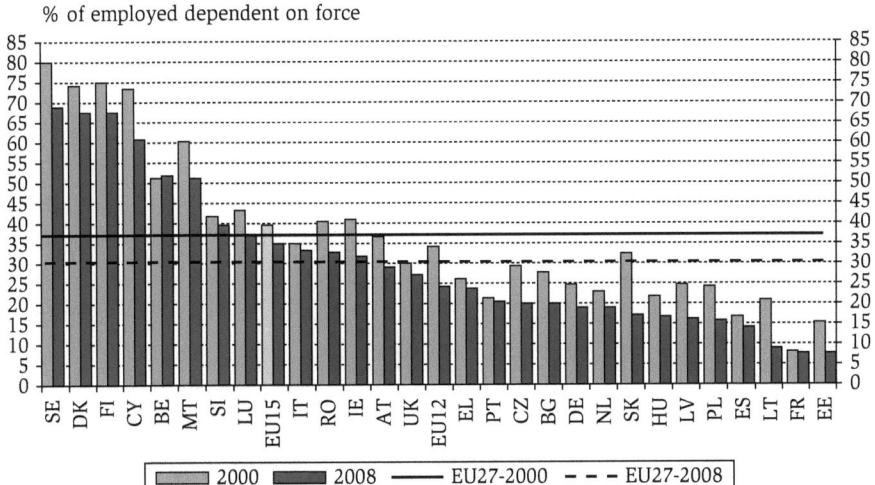

Figure 2.2 Union Density by Country, 2000-2008

Source: J. Visser, ICTWSS database 3.0, 2010 quoted in: Industrial Relations in Europe 2010 report. Brussels, 3 March 2011.

Since 2000, trade union density has declined throughout the EU (with the exception of Belgium). However, the trend towards dwindling employee unionisation has been more pronounced in the CEE countries, where average union density shrunk from around 30% to below 20% between 2000 and 2008, with the decline largest in Lithuania and Slovakia. The causes are manifold. In addition to the general trend towards de-industrialisation, growing unemployment and extensive migration to western Europe, legal obstacles to the recognition of trade unions, lack of institutional

---

22. Ibidem, pp. 264-265.
23. H. Kohl, *Where Do Trade Unions Stand in Eastern Europe Today? Stock-Taking after EU Enlargement*, Internationale Politik und Gesellschaft, 111 (2008), http://library.fes.de/pdf-files/ipg/ipg-2008-3/09_a_kohl_gb.pdf (accessed 20 July 2017).

support of unions in key policy fields such as collective bargaining, and the marginalization of unions in political decision-making all contribute to unions' waning organisational power.[24]

On the employers' side, a weakness in the industry associations can be observed. The main reasons for this are the short tradition of private employers in CEE, rivalries between different associations, and the structural changes in the economy.[25] Employers are more strongly organised in the EU-15 than in the EU-10. On average, almost two-thirds of all employees in western EU countries were working in companies affiliated to an employer organisation, while the respective figure was below 40% in the EU-10 in 2008. Organisational strength was most limited in Poland, Lithuania and Estonia at around 20% in 2008, while Romania, Bulgaria and Slovenia featured density rates of 55%-60%. Employer organisation density shrunk most in Slovenia, following abolition of obligatory membership in the Chamber of Industry and Commerce in 2006.[26] These trends have not been changed even after the economic crisis.

Figure 2.3 Organisation Rates of Employers by Country, 2000-2008

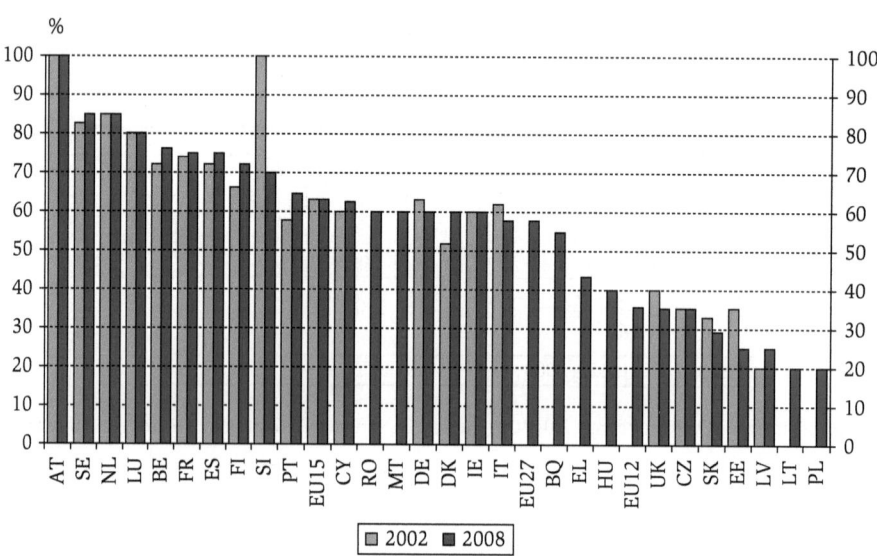

Source: J. Visser, ICTWSS database 3.0, 2010 quoted in: Industrial Relations in Europe 2010 report. Brussels, 3 March 2011.

---

24. V. Glassner, *Central and Eastern European Industrial Relations in the Crisis: National Divergence and Path-Dependent Change*, supra n. 9, pp. 160-161.
25. L. Funk and H. Lesch, *Industrial Relations in Central and Eastern Europe – Organisational Charactistics, Codetermination and Labour Disputes*, supra n. 1, pp. 264-265.
26. V. Glassner, *Central and Eastern European Industrial Relations in the Crisis: National Divergence and Path-Dependent Change*, supra n. 9, p. 161.

In consequence, industrial relations in the CEE countries (with the exception of Slovenia) are characterised by weak employers' organisations and trade unions, fragmented and decentralised bargaining, limited bargaining autonomy of both employer associations and trade unions.[27] Central and eastern European industrial relations contrast with the prevalent continental European, Scandinavian, and even Anglo-Saxon industrial relations models, although the latter is relatively close to the eastern European type in some respects. Kohl argues that a separate CEE transition model of industrial relations can thus be identified, distinct from other typologies dominant in the EU. While the initial situations may have been comparable, the results of social dialogue and union activities are clearly disparate.[28]

§2.02 DEVELOPMENT OF COLLECTIVE BARGAINING IN HUNGARY

In Hungary before 1990, the socialist Labour Code[29] and its many implementing decrees played the ultimate role in the regulation of both private and public employment relationships. Collective agreements could deviate from the Labour Code if the few provisions specifically allowed it. Employment law was therefore *ius cogens* (as the main rule) and collective bargaining was in fact neglected.

In marked contrast, the 1992 Labour Code[30] in the newly regulated market economy aimed at providing statutory minimum standards that could be substituted and supplemented by collective agreements. Thus, collective agreements were designed to play a more important or even a substantial role in employment regulation. However, it was acknowledged, that both workplace and higher-level collective agreements would be concluded only slowly and gradually over a longer time. Thus, the adoption of the 'in favour principle', allowing only *in melius* derogations, filled the potential gap and cogent rules remained an exception.[31] *In pejus* derogation also existed in principle, though only within a marginal range. Sectoral collective bargaining was not specifically regulated by the Labour Code, but a separate law[32] regulated sectoral dialogue committees in 2009, which could conclude sectoral level agreements.

Collective agreement coverage has been among the lowest in the EU at around 30%-40% in recent decades,[33] without huge changes. There used to be a fairly high coverage of company agreements in an eastern European comparison, but case studies reveal that only a small proportion functioned as in developed market economies. Many company agreements are still far from being genuine negotiated agreements, but

---

27. *Ibidem*, p. 158.
28. H. Kohl, *Where Do Trade Unions Stand in Eastern Europe Today? Stock-Taking after EU Enlargement*, *supra* n. 23, p. 112.
29. Act 2 of 1967.
30. Act 22 of 1992 on the Labour Code.
31. Gy. Berke, *A munkaviszonyra vonatkozó szabályok (Regulation of employment)*, in Gy. Kiss, Gy. Berke, Z. Bankó, E. Kajtár (eds), *Emlékkönyv Román László születésének 80. Évfordulójára*, 68-70 (Pécs: PTE 2008).
32. Act 74 of 2009 on Sectoral Dialogue Committees.
33. In 2000 it was even as high as 51%, including all leveles of collective agreements (L. Neumann, *Does Decentralised Collective Bargaining Have an Impact on the Labour Market in Hungary?*, 1 European Journal of Industrial Relations, 11-12 (2003).

are either defined unliterally by the employer or, following state socialist traditions, simply repeat the law (so-called parrot clauses).[34]

Since there is no reliable data on the number of collective agreements after 2013,[35] we must rely on Central Statistical Office data,[36] which reflects a shrinking coverage of around 20%-30%[37] in 2015.[38] The ILO also reported an almost 15% drop to around 25% between 2008 and 2013.[39] The new coverage level, revealing a decline in collective bargaining, is really one of the lowest in the EU, along with those of with Bulgaria, UK, Poland and Lithuania.[40] It must be emphasised that available data on Hungarian collective agreement coverage seems to be contradictory, making it hard to assess current figures and analyse trends.[41]

In spite of the establishment and detailed regulation of sectoral dialogue committees, sectoral collective bargaining has lacked vitality since 1990 and even after 2009 in Hungary. Just as in Poland,[42] if there is a collective agreement, it is typically concluded at workplace level. There have been only a few collective agreements with an extended scope over a sector. These agreements are concluded in sectors with a strong sectoral trade union and a smaller number of employers' organisations, such as construction, bakery, catering and electrical supply industries.[43] Such agreements do not regulate wages effectively, anyway, not only because their coverage is small, but also because their contents are weak and the guarantees of implementation are doubtful.[44] However, even these sectoral agreements are not presently in force.

---

34. *Ibidem*, p. 12.
35. All employers have to inform the authorities about the conclusion of a collective agreement. However, failing to meet this obligation does not bring any sanction; and the register does not contain hard figures or quality information on content issues. Not only is a reliable database missing, but research has been limited regarding collective agreements (Eurofound data shows 31% coverage in 2013 (http://www.eurofound.europa.eu/observatories/eurwork/comparative-information/national-contributions/hungary/hungary-working-life-country-profile, accessed 19 January 2017). Therefore, only the figures provided by the Central Statistival Office (KSH, www.ksh.hu) are available, which partly based on interviews (for instance: http://szabim.blog.hu/2016/05/17/_hianyopotlo_adatokat_kozolt_a_kozponti_statisztikai_hivatal).
36. KSH, Munkaerőfelmérés 2015. II. negyedévi kiegészítő felvétel, https://www.ksh.hu/docs/hun/modsz/modsz21_kieg.html (accessed 12 January 2017).
37. Eurofound 2017.
38. S. Hungler, *Public and Company Welfare in Hungary*, in W. Chiarmonte, M.L. Vallauri, (eds.), *Company Welfare* [working title], CNA Toscana, (2017) (forthcoming).
39. J. Visser, S. Hayter and R. Gammarano, *Trends in Collective Bargaining Coverage: Stability, Erosion or Decline? Labour Relations and Collective Bargaining*, Issue brief No. 1., ILO 9 (2015), http://www.ilo.org/wcmsp5/groups/public/---ed_protect/---protrav/---travail/documents/publication/wcms_409422.pdf (accessed 1 February 2017).
40. Eurofound comparative data: http://www.worker-participation.eu/National-Industrial-Relations/Across-Europe/Collective-Bargaining2 (accesse 25 January 2017).
41. There are two sources with different methods and both have methodology problems. The registry is probably biased upward, and the survey downward, the latter being mainly due to proxy answers.
42. P. Grzebyk, *Legal Position of Trade Unions in Polish Collective Labour Law: Enterprise-Based Trade Union*, supra n. 15.
43. Sz. Soósné Csikós, *A kollektív szerződés lefedettségi rátáját meghatározó tényezők*, Acta Juridica et Politica, PTE, Szeged 31 (2005).
44. L. Neumann, *Does Decentralised Collective Bargaining Have an Impact on the Labour Market in Hungary?*, supra n. 33, p. 12.

Table 2.1 Collective Agreement Coverage in Hungary (2008-2013)

	2008	2009	2010	2011	2012	2013
Coverage of single employer agreements, %	20.8	23.2	27.18	23.52	25.05	24.24
Coverage of multi-employer agreements, %	19.13	20.43	19.86	19.94	19.34	19.13

Based on selected data in: Borbély Sz. and Neumann L.: Similarities and diversity in the development of wages and collective bargaining in central and eastern European countries – a comparison of Hungary, Slovakia and the Czech Republic in: Van Gyes G. and Schulten T. (eds.): *Wage bargaining under the new European Economic Governance Alternative strategies for inclusive growth.* ETUI, Brussels, 2015, 202.

There are several related reasons explaining the weak regulatory function of collective agreements in Hungary. First, mass privatisation hampered the spread of collective agreements. The end of the socialist economic model based on large, state owned 'socialist firms' considerably weakened trade unions and their capacity to enforce collective bargaining in the new private companies.[45] As a result of privatisation and economic changes, micro, small and medium workplaces became the dominant employers, presently accounting for over 70% of employees,[46] and the enforcement of the Labour Code is generally problematic in these workplaces.[47] Furthermore, it has not been feasible to conclude a collective agreement in the small firms due to the lack of trade unions (and works councils) and the strict rules of the former Labour Code on trade union representation.[48]

Evidently, trade union activity and collective bargaining is confined to companies of over 1,000 (75% coverage) or 500 employees (67%), but it is almost non-existent for those under 50 (11%) and particularly below 20 workers (0.1%).[49] Trade unions have been gradually confined to large state-owned (e.g., National Railways, Budapest Transport Company) and large, mostly multinational companies (e.g., Audi, GE, MOL). The weakness and decline of the Hungarian trade union movement can be explained by a set of factors, such as inadequate financial, scientific and organisational background, dependence on state support, service-oriented activities and low organisational potential of the society.[50] Trade unions are now old and tired, without new

---

45. T. Laky, L. Neumann, D. Boda, *A privatizáció foglalkoztatási hatásai (Employment effects of privatization).* (Budapest, 2001).
46. Central Statistical Office (KSH): *A kis- és középvállalkozások helyzete hazánkban (Situation of small and medium entreprises).* Statisztikai Tükör, 2013/108, http://www.ksh.hu/docs/hun/xftp/stattukor/kkv12.pdf (accessed 17 January 2017), p. 2.
47. T. Laky, *Az atipikus foglakozásokról (Atypical employment).* http://docplayer.hu/932249-Laky-terez-az-atipikus-foglakozasokrol.html, p. 14.
48. Article 33 of the 1992 Labour Code.
49. Sz. Soósné Csikós, *A kollektív szerződés lefedettségi rátáját meghatározó tényezők,* supra n. 43, p. 48. Although this data is rather old, however, the problem is unchanged.
50. I. Krén, *A szakszervezetek helyzete Magyarországon (Situation of trade unions in Hungary)* (Budapest: Friedrich Ebert Stiftung 2012), http://www.fesbp.hu/common/pdf/Nachrichten_aus_Ungarn_07_2010_hun.pdf (accessed 14 January 2017), p. 5.

members even in their traditional fields, and struggle to reach the 10% density required to conclude a collective agreement at many employers.

Figure 2.4   Trade Union Membership in Hungary (2001-2015)

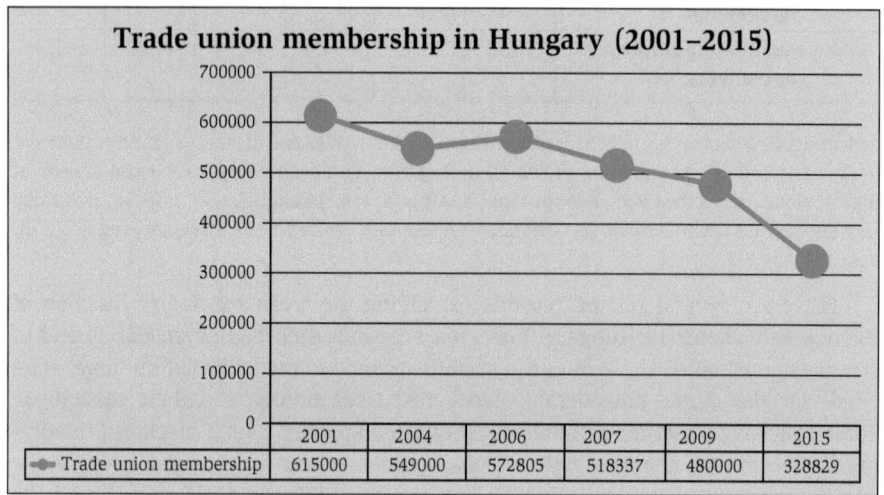

Source: http://szabim.blog.hu/2016/05/17/_hianypotlo_adatokat_kozolt_a_kozponti_statis ztikai_hivatal, based on data of the Central Statistical Office (www.ksh.hu).

On the other hand, the employers' side is also voluntary[51] and poorly organised (21% density in 2013).[52] Moreover, employers and their organisations have not been motivated by flexible employment regulation since 1990, which has even been 'further flexibilised' by the 2012 Labour Code (*see* table below). Before 2012, the old Labour Code allowed deviation via collective agreements to the benefit of employees (*see* details later). Therefore, employers were not interested in amending the statutory rules if it meant employment conditions less favourable to them. Since the new Labour Code provides an even more flexible legal environment and free deviation from statutory provisions, employers seem to be rather satisfied with statutory minimums and thereby neglect derogations by collective agreement(s).[53]

---

51. Since 1 January 2012 companies and entrepreneurs have had to register at the relevant chamber of commerce. This mandatory registration costs an annual registration fee, but does not provide the same rights and obligations as those of full members of chambers. Employer organisations were hostile to the mandatory registration, since it does not give companies any benefit and could simply be considered as a tax. It weakens companies' willingness to join employer organisations, which are based on the freedom of association (Eurofound 2017).
52. Eurofound: Hungary working life country profile – Actors and institutions http://www.eurofound.europa.eu/observatories/eurwork/comparative-information/national-contributions/hungary/hungary-working-life-country-profile (accessed 19 January 2017). This figure is much lower, than the 40% indicated in table above in the first chapter.
53. Employers may be a party to workplace and also higher (sectoral, subsectoral) level collective agreements.

Figure 2.5 Employment Protection Is Relatively High in the Euro Area Index Scale from 0 (Least Restrictive) to 6 (Most Restrictive)

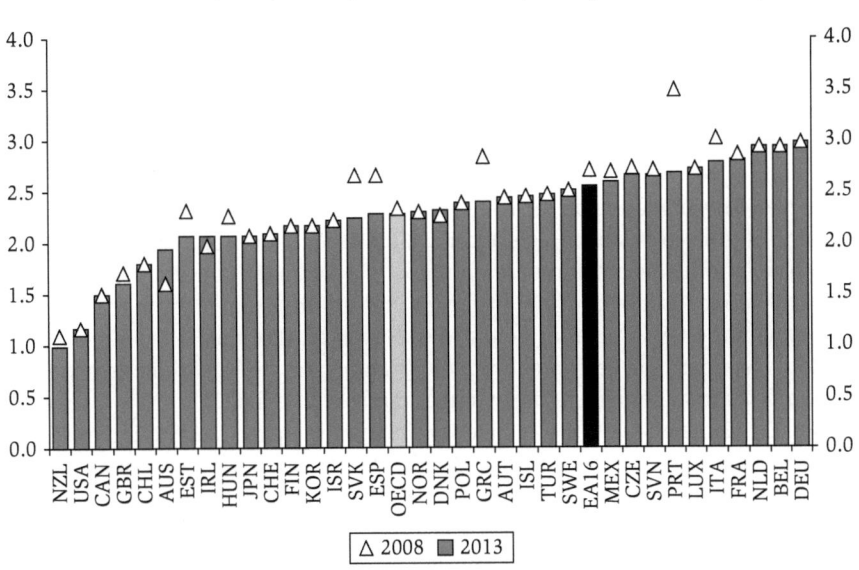

Source: OECD, Employment Protection Legislation Database.

As should be clear from the development of Hungarian collective bargaining, it is extremely difficult to reach tangible results without strong, prepared and motivated partners on both sides. On the employee side, we find weak, poor and declining trade unions that are more or less motivated to conclude collective agreements, yet seem unable to achieve them. As for employers, they are in fact also poorly organised and not motivated by flexible labour law. Consequently, existing collective bargaining is restricted to large state-owned and multinational companies. However, the quality and practical effect of these existing agreements is somewhat questionable.

Therefore, the constant support of legal, institutional and financial strength of trade unions and employers' organisations is a precondition for an efficient national collective bargaining system. As a whole, the Hungarian model is an excellent illustration of the weaknesses and failures of collective bargaining in central and eastern Europe. Despite some national peculiarities, Hungary has a declining trade union movement, an undeveloped employers' organisation, respectively low collective agreement coverage and a recently flexibilised employment protection framework.[54]

---

54. By contrast, in the Czech Republic there has been no significant attempt to reduce existing legal protection of employee or trade union rights, even under right-wing governments (Sz. Borbély, L. Neumann, *Similarities and Diversity in the Development of Wages and Collective Bargaining in Central and Eastern European Countries – a Comparison of Hungary, Slovakia and the Czech Republic*, in G. Van Gyes and Th. Schulten (eds), *Wage Bargaining under the New European Economic Governance*, 197-198 (Brussels: ETUI 2015).

§2.03 LEGAL REFORM TO INCREASE COLLECTIVE AGREEMENT COVERAGE: 'FREE DEROGATION'

[A] Farewell to 'In Favour Principle'

The 'in favour principle' (Günstigkeitsprinzip, inderogability)[55] governs, among other things, the relationship between law and collective agreements.[56] It means that legislation takes precedence over contractual regulation, as far as stipulations *in pejus* are concerned. This limitation on the freedom of contract of course is the very purpose and function of protective labour legislation. On the other hand, contracted provisions *in melius* have priority over statutory minimums.[57] Accordingly, collective agreements can in principle modify the law only *in melius* and not *in pejus* – i. e. they can only provide terms more favourable for employees. However, this general rule is usually subject to exceptions: the legislator frequently authorises collective agreements to derogate *in pejus* from certain statutory terms, rarely with a limit.[58]

In the EU Member States, the 'in favour principle' is applied to deviation from the law by a collective agreement. However, Member States are divided into two clusters regarding *in pejus* derogations. In one group of Member States, only *in melius* deviations are allowed (from dispositive rules) for collective agreements, but in the other group, *in pejus* derogations are also possible from some (limited number of) statutory provisions. Eastern European countries adopted the German 'in favour principle' after 1990,[59] but legislation later gradually relaxed this strict rule by allowing *in pejus* derogations from some rules[60] of the Labour Code in some CEE countries (e.g., Czech Republic, Hungary, Slovakia and Slovenia).[61] At the same time, free (*in melius* and also *in pejus*) derogation is a generally unknown hierarchy of labour law sources in the European Union.

In Hungary the in favour principle was first adopted by the 1992 Labour Code, which meant a fundamental change at that time (*see* above). There were three kinds of exception to the general rule of *in melius* derogation. First, several provisions stated

---

55. M. Freedland and N. Kountouris, *The Legal Construction of Personal Work Relations*, 151 (Oxford: Oxford University Press, 2011).
56. It may be assessed in relation to derogations by an emloyment contract as well, however, this context is not analysed here.
57. S. Evju, *The Relationship Between State Law, Collective Agreement and Individual Contract*, in Gy Kiss (ed.), *Recent Developments in Labour Law* 21 (Budapest: Akadémiai Kiadó, 2013).
58. Italy is a good example for this system: T. Treu, *Labour Law in Italy*, 203 (The Netherlands: Kluwer Law International 2011).
59. Sz. Borbély, L. Neumann, *Similarities and Diversity in the Development of Wages and Collective Bargaining in Central and Eastern European Countries – a Comparison of Hungary, Slovakia and the Czech Republic, supra* n. 54, p. 196.
60. For instance in Slovakia amendments to the Labour Code introduced in 2011 permitted collective agreements to worsen legal provisions in some areas, such as probation periods and overtime arrangements. However, the government elected in 2012 rejected these changes (*Ibidem*, p. 196.).
61. *Study on the characteristics and legal effects of agreements between companies and workers' representatives*. Final Report, DG Employment, Social Affairs & Inclusion, 2011, http://ec.europa.eu/social/main.jsp?catId=707&langId=en&intPageId=214, pp. 28-30 (accessed 20 July 2017).

that any alteration to it is null and void (*ius cogens*). Second, the Labour Code later exceptionally allowed collective agreements to deviate to the detriment of employees (*in pejus*) from a few provisions, and the amendments to the Labour Code slightly increased the number of these derogations after 2001 (e.g., on working time).[62] Third, there were statutory provisions which allowed for *in pejus* derogation only to a limited extent.

The new Labour Code came into effect on 1 July 2012, changing the previous law after twenty years.[63] Reorganisation of the hierarchy of labour law sources was the central element of the reform, since rigidity of labour law was partly explained by low collective agreement coverage. The main aim of this conceptual change was, therefore, to enhance the role of collective agreements by radically widening the possibility of *in pejus* deviations from the Labour Code.

Above all, the general rule was changed, since collective agreements may now derogate from most of the rules on both individual labour law[64] and collective labour law,[65] also to the detriment of employees.[66] There are over fifty provisions allowing both *in melius* and *in pejus* derogation. However, there are still three exceptions to this general rule (called 'absolute dispositivity'):

(a) Above all, there are over thirty cogent rules which do not allow any deviation (*ius cogens*). Only the second and third parts (on employment relationships and collective labour relations) of the Labour Code are dispositive; all the other parts (1, 4 and 5)[67] are *ius cogens*. Moreover, the general provisions concerning industrial relations and the rules on works councils are also *ius cogens*.[68]
(b) Only *in melius* derogation is allowed by certain provisions (called 'relative dispositivity') – for example, in the entire chapter covering employer liability for damages incurred by the employee.
(c) Finally, a few statutory provisions allow for *in melius* and *in pejus* derogation only to a limited extent (called 'limited absolute dispositivity') – for example, the number of extra hours may be 250 per year, which may be raised to maximum 300 in the collective agreement.[69]

---

62. *See* especially Act No. 16 of 2001 on the amendment of the 1992 Labour Code concerning transposition of nine Directives.
63. Act No. 22 of 1992 on the Labour Code came into effect on the 1st of July 1992.
64. Part 2, Articles 32-229.
65. Part 3, Articles 230-284.
66. Article 277 of the 2012 Labour Code.
67. Part I contains general provisions, part IV is on labour disputes and part V on closing provisions.
68. Section 277(3) The collective agreement: a) may not contain derogations from Chapters XIX and XX; and b) may not contain any restrictions concerning the provisions contained in sections 271-272.
69. Article 135(3) of the 2012 Labour Code.

The system described above of a general rule and three exceptions[70] is quite complicated, so the exceptions are listed at the end of each chapter within the second and the third part of the Labour Code.[71]

This novel hierarchy of the Labour Code and collective agreements represents a radical change in dogma. As has been stressed, legislation has traditionally concerned itself with contractual regulation in the hierarchy of labour law sources, and this limitation on the freedom of contract followed from the purpose of labour legislation. The drastic expansion of *in pejus* derogations curtails this set-up and may jeopardise the efficient functioning of protective labour law in an active collective bargaining system. As this measure was introduced in a moderate collective bargaining environment, in this case it does not seem to be a clear and present danger.

The legislator expected that the wide possibility of *in pejus* derogations outlined above would increase collective agreement coverage, because employers would be motivated to conclude such agreements. This strategy was thus confined to a single measure: motivating employers. I will question below, first, if this single measure is sufficient in itself to reach this ambitious goal, particularly in the reformed employment law framework; and second, if employers have really become motivated by free derogation. Since collective agreement coverage dropped as a result of the reform, the ultimate question is – why did the reform fail?

[B]   Is Motivation Enough to Affirm Collective Bargaining?

The first question here is whether the strategy was adequate in the light of its own goals and Hungarian labour market conditions. We cannot discard from our analysis the attributes of CEE countries described above, such as specifically a) declining trade unions, b) poorly organised employer organisations and c) lack of sectoral collective bargaining.

As for the altered position of trade unions, there is some good news and more bad news. The good news is that the conceptual change described above may strengthen the bargaining position of trade unions, for they can demand more favourable conditions in other areas (e.g., wages) in exchange for accepting detrimental changes (e.g., working time). Furthermore, the new representation criteria of trade unions was declared to foster collective bargaining: a trade union will be entitled to conclude a collective agreement if its membership reaches 10% of all employees of a given employer.[72] However, this threshold seems to be quite high and unreachable for declining trade unions at more and more employers. As a consequence of rapidly declining trade union density, this limit will slowly become a more and more important obstacle to collective bargaining.

---

70. For a detailed analysis: Gy. Berke, *The Collective Agreement in the New Labour Code*, in Gy. Kiss (ed.), *Trade Unions and Collective Agreements in the New Labour Code*, 122-127 (Budapest: Akadémiai Kiadó, 2015).
71. *See* also Article 277 on further exceptions.
72. Article 276 of the 2012 Labour Code.

However, it is questionable whether the players on the two sides of industry are prepared for active collective bargaining. On the employers' side, their organisations were not affected by the reform, so density remained at the former low level.

By contrast, the two-faced reform deliberately weakened trade unions. Further and even accelerated downfall of the trade union movement is clearly reflected by shrinking union membership, diminishing power and fewer collective agreements. Legislation substantially undermined unions' operating conditions (legal protection, time-off, financial support) and curbed trade union rights in the workplace.[73] For instance, the new law curtailed working time exemption and legal protection of union activists.[74]

The workplace status of trade unions is also undermined by the promotion of works councils, often to the disadvantage of unions.[75] Works councils have been elected at employers of over fifty employees since 1992; however, their powers have been rather weak.[76] Therefore, the shift of rights towards works councils reveals the new concept of strengthening duality of the Hungarian industrial system. This policy is symbolised by the novel possibility that works councils may conclude collective agreements.[77] The new Labour Code allows a works council agreement concluded between the works council and the employer to function as a collective agreement under certain conditions.[78] Works council agreements may contain rights and obligations regarding employment relationships, if the employer is not covered by a collective agreement[79] and there is no representative trade union.[80] The only restriction regarding its contents[81] is that it cannot regulate wages.[82]

Although the promotion of collective bargaining in medium sized companies is a positive aim, the legal nature and potential practical effect of normative works council

---

73. Sz. Borbély, L. Neumann, *Similarities and Diversity in the Development of Wages and Collective Bargaining in Central and Eastern European Countries – a Comparison of Hungary, Slovakia and the Czech Republic*, supra n. 54, pp. 197-198.
74. A. Tóth, *The New Hungarian Labour Code – Background, Conflicts, Compromises*, Friedrich Ebert Foundation Budapest, Working Paper, 2012, http://www.fesbp.hu/common/pdf/Nachrichten_aus_Ungarn_june_2012.pdf (accessed 17 January 2017), p. 9.
75. It must be mentioned here that trade unions have traditionally had a dominant presence in works councils, which was incentivised by the representation criteria of the 1992 Labour Code based on the number of votes at works council elections.
76. Article 236 of the 2012 Labour Code.
77. The possibility of works council agreements replacing collective agreements was already in place between 1999 and 2002 (Article 31 of the 1992 Labour Code).
78. Before the 2012 reform, works council agreements had a very different legal nature, since the law stipulated that only 'issues pertaining to the privileges of a works council and its relations with the employer' shall be set forth in such an agreement (Article 64/A of the 1992 Labour Code amended in 1995).
79. As a result, the employer may conclude a normative works council agreement, should it fall under the scope of a subsector or sector level collective agreement.
80. Article 268 of the 2012 Labour Code.
81. Chapter XII., Articles 136-165.
82. This exception is mistaken, since higher wages usually compensate flexible provisions on working time or resting periods. Since such a pecuniary compensation is not allowed by the law, the conclusion of a balanced agreement may be frustrated (T. Gyulavári, G. Kártyás, *The Hungarian Flexicurity Pathway? New Labour Code after Twenty Years in the Market Economy*, 30-31 (Budapest: Pázmány Press 2015).

agreements is problematic. Works councils were designed to foster cooperation between employers and workers, and to take part in the employers' decisions.[83] Participation seriously contradicts the attributes of collective bargaining, where employees' representatives confront the employer to better working conditions. Furthermore, works councils must not organise, support or obstruct strikes,[84] and the lack of collective action weakens their bargaining position.[85] In addition, only the chair of a works council enjoys protection against dismissal.[86] Unfortunately, we do not have any data on the number of such agreements, which is probably insignificant for the moment due to the same reasons as those given for collective agreements.

The reform also failed regarding sectoral collective bargaining, though this was not even a declared objective of the government. Collective bargaining remained at workplace level, and the conclusion of sector level collective agreements is not facilitated by the new legal and economic framework either, with the detailed rules still entirely missing from the Labour Code. As an exception to the lack of special provisions on sector level collective agreements, the Labour Code regulates the relationship between higher (e.g., sector) and lower (e.g., workplace) level collective agreements. Although the new Labour Code retained the 'in favour principle' regarding their relationship, it added an important exception, opening the door to decentralisation of collective bargaining.

Accordingly, higher level collective agreements may allow *in pejus* derogations in lower agreements by designating some rules for this purpose.[87] This new possibility may weaken the capability of higher-level collective agreements to standardise working conditions in an entire sector.[88] Thus, it may be considered a harmful legislative step, even if this opportunity is presently not exploited, due to the lack of sectoral agreements.

Since motivation of employers was the central element of the reform, we must finally raise the question of whether at least this measure succeeded in encouraging employers to conclude collective agreements. Certainly, employers can change many of the rules of the Labour Code also *in pejus*, but the protective nature of the legal basis is a key issue here. As we can see, Hungarian employment protection has been rather flexible since even long before 2012, but the new Labour Code is one of the most flexible in a European comparison, since the Orbán government has pursued a radical neoliberal reform including the flexibilisation of employment relations and the curtailing of union rights.[89]

Dropping collective agreement coverage after 2012 suggests that employers may be satisfied with the low level of employment protection and do not wish to give rights

---

83. Articles 235 and 262 of the 2012 Labour Code.
84. Article 266 of the 2012 Labour Code.
85. T. Gyulavári (ed.), *Munkajog (Labour law)*, 53 (Budapest: Eötvös Kiadó, 2012).
86. Article 260 (3)-(5) of the 2012 Labour Code.
87. Article 277 of the 2012 Labour Code.
88. G. Kártyás, *Kollektív szerződés (Collective Agreement)*, in T. Gyulavári (ed.), *Munkajog (Labour law)*, supra n. 85, p. 491.
89. I. Szabó, *Between Polarization and Statism – Effects of the Crisis on Collective Bargaining Processes and Outcomes in Hungary*, Transfer 213 (2013/2), http://journals.sagepub.com/doi/pdf/10.1177/1024258913480702 (accessed 18 January 2017).

(e.g., extra payments) for *in pejus* derogations. In practice, the management often uses derogations from the law that are favourable for the employer simply to apply pressure.[90]

Employers would be motivated, if *in pejus* derogations could somehow remarkably flexibilise employment conditions, such as working time and rest periods. Evidently, working time is the best example of this problem, as it has always been the main field of derogations to the benefit of employers since legal harmonisation of the Working Time Directive in 2001. Nevertheless, current provisions on working time and rest periods are extremely flexible. For example, the Labour Code widely allows work on six (sometimes even seven) days a week, twelve regular hours daily, only one rest day monthly on a Sunday, in a reference period of four or even six months.[91] The only benefits of *in pejus* derogations would be a fifty-two-week reference period or change in the work schedule within seven days of the start of scheduled working time.[92] In my opinion, setting higher statutory minimums on working time and rest periods would increase motivation of employers even in the present employment law framework. It would be a logical correction of the original strategy, if the government seriously wants to increase the role of collective agreements.

Motivation may be hindered by the Labour Code on the trade union side as well by setting detailed rights at a fair level for employees and union officials. Working time reduction is an important benefit for union officials and several extra payments or severance pay provide a solid statutory minimum for employees. Therefore, the employee side also automatically obtains some substantial advantages without collective bargaining. However, lowering this statutory protection would not increase in itself higher collective bargaining coverage.

It must be mentioned here that there is a special chapter in the Labour Code on so-called public companies in which the state (local government) has majority ownership. The evident purpose of these special provisions[93] was to prevent abuse by employment contracts or collective agreements, limiting deviations from statutory provisions, particularly on working time and termination of employment. It thus created a double employment regulation, one for public companies and the other for all other employers, a solution that raises the issue of unconstitutional difference in treatment. As a result, collective bargaining hardly exists in such public (service) companies.

The failed Hungarian reform has some crucial messages for reformers in the region. In CEE countries, the starting situation is characterised by low collective agreement coverage, sporadic density of trade unions and employers' organisations, and a corresponding lack of efficient sectoral dialogue. Above and beyond statutory regulation, social partners on both sides should be strengthened to ensure their financial, professional stability and motivation. Sectoral dialogue may be incentivised

---

90. L. Neumann, *The Practice of Collective Agreements: A Corporate Research Experience*, in Gy. Kiss (ed.), *Trade Unions and Collective Agreements in the New Labour Code*, 58-59 (Budapest: Akadémiai Kiadó, 2015).
91. Articles 99, 94, 105 of the 2012 Labour Code.
92. Articles 94(3) and 97(4)-(5) of the 2012 Labour Code.
93. Articles 204-207 of the 2012 Labour Code.

by organisational improvement at sectoral level and detailed regulation on sectoral collective bargaining. The Hungarian reform failed because it focused on only one problem regarding social partners – employer motivation – yet not even this goal was achieved. In addition, the weakening and general decline of trade unions contributed to the shrinking of collective bargaining.

§2.04　CONCLUSIONS: REASONS FOR RESTRAINED COLLECTIVE BARGAINING IN CEE COUNTRIES

CEE countries wished to copy the collective bargaining culture of Western European Member States as an attractive model after 1990, just as in many other fields of law and life. They wanted to reach a long-term high collective agreement coverage with substantial contents, also at sectoral level, with strong social partners. By contrast, twenty-five years later their social partners are the weakest, collective agreement coverage is still the lowest among EU Member States, and sectoral collective bargaining hardly exists. Certainly there are some exceptions, such as Slovenian social dialogue, but the overall picture is rather gloomy. The original aim of this legislation was good, as sectoral collective dialogue and strong social partners would help national economies and societies to work better and particularly to resist crisis situations. After this unsuccessful twenty-five years, the feasibility of this project is doubtful.

Investigation of the reasons for this premature social dialogue system leads us directly to weaknesses of social partners. Density, culture, experience and knowledge is missing on both sides. In addition, employer motivation is also hindered by low and decreasing levels of employment protection. It must be acknowledged that collective bargaining cannot improve in a flexibilised labour law with diminishing employee and trade union rights, or financially and professionally weak social partners.

Hungarian collective bargaining is a typical eastern European patient with all the above-mentioned symptoms. Therefore, the meritorious aim of the 2012 reform was to increase collective agreement coverage. At the same time, the neoliberal labour law concept of the government consisted of diminishing employment protection and trade union rights, plus motivation of employers by multiple options for *in pejus* derogation. The Hungarian lesson is that motivation as a single measure cannot work miracles, especially if employers have not become truly motivated in the end. The goal is attainable in the long term, but complex legal measures and partnership are essential.

CHAPTER 3
How Can Decentralisation of Collective Bargaining Be Achieved? A Typology of Legal Incentives

Pierre-Emmanuel Berthier & Olivier Leclerc

§3.01 INTRODUCTION

In numerous European countries, collective bargaining law is notable for its ever-greater tendency towards decentralised collective bargaining. Obviously, situations vary from one European country to another.[1] In some countries, branch level collective bargaining and national, inter-professional bargaining are still fairly common. However, on a European scale, these countries are the exception rather than the rule. The general trend is towards collective bargaining centred on the company and the establishment.[2] Decentralised collective bargaining is deemed to better respect the financial situation of the companies concerned and be more closely attuned to the wishes of employees and their representatives. The backdrop of the economic crisis experienced by Europe since the late 2000s has accentuated this trend, making collective bargaining a preferred tool for national legislations seeking to adapt to ongoing economic changes.[3]

---

1. For an overview, *see* the contribution of Sylvaine Laulom in this issue.
2. For more information on the roots of this movement, see Harry C. Katz, *The Decentralization of Collective Bargaining: A Literature Review and Comparative Analysis*, vol. 47, no. 1, ILR Review, 3-22 (1993); A. Lyon-Caen, A. Perulli (eds), *Trasformazioni dell'impresa e rapporti di lavoro*, (Padova: Cedam), 2004.
3. B. Hepple, B. Veneziani (eds), *The Transformation of Labour Law in Europe. A Comparative Study of 15 Countries 1945-2004*, (Oxford: Hart Publ., 2009); G. Loy (ed.), *Diritto del lavoro e crisi economica. Misure contro l'emergenza ed evoluzione legislativa in Italia, Spagna e Francia*, (Roma: Ediesse, 2011); M.-C. Escande-Varniol, S. Laulom, E. Mazuyer, P. Vielle, *Quel droit social*

The growing popularity of company-level collective bargaining has already been widely studied. Some praise the increased flexibility of labour law, while others underline the limited ability of employees to influence the outcome of collective bargaining. This article does not aim to revisit the diagnosis of this decentralisation. Our interest lies in tackling a question that has been largely neglected to date: how can public authorities obtain the signing of collective agreements by social partners at a decentralised level? Since the conclusion of company-level collective agreements is the goal of public authorities, how is it possible to ensure that social partners actually sign such agreements? In fact, there is nothing to guarantee that the labour law reform sought by the public authorities will lead to a change in behaviour on the part of the social actors targeted by these reforms. Clearly, the mere promulgation of regulations does not automatically lead to compliant behaviour on the part of the actors at whom they are aimed. In short, there is nothing *a priori* to guarantee that employers, employees or union organisations will agree to engage in decentralised collective bargaining. Consequently, how can political impetus towards more decentralised collective bargaining be effectively translated into a change in bargaining practices in companies and professional sectors? Until now, this question has received three different responses. The first response is favoured by labour lawyers and consists in making collective bargaining obligatory at a company-level. Of course, the obligation to negotiate is not an obligation to reach agreement. However, it is implicitly supposed that at least part of these negotiations will lead to collective agreements. This procedure can be found in place in several European countries. Under the French Labour Code, employers must engage in regular negotiation on an ever-increasing number of subjects within the company.[4] During the negotiation period, the employer loses the power to take unilateral action on the matters that are the subject of the negotiation.[5] Likewise, in Italy, employers are obliged to enter into negotiation in the event of collective redundancies or a transfer of undertaking. Similarly, under Romanian law, there is a general obligation to negotiate collective agreements, applicable to all professional sectors. This obligation also extends to companies which normally employ a staff of twenty or more. The common thread between these examples is that they suppose a very simple – indeed simplistic – relationship between the rule and the actions: the rule sets out obligatory action (negotiation) and it will be obeyed because anyone contravening it would be liable to a sanction (if they refuse to negotiate or negotiate in bad faith). Thus, it is hoped that, by making negotiation obligatory, collective agreements will finally be concluded. However, the decision of whether or not to sign agreements remains outside the scope of the law.

---

dans une Europe en crise?, (Bruxelles: Larcier, 2012); E. Peskine, *La célébration de l'accord collectif d'entreprise. Quelques enseignements de la loi relative à la sécurisation de l'emploi*, 5 Droit social, 438-445 (2014).

4. Negotiation must be undertaken every year with regard to pay, working hours, the sharing of added value created by the company, professional equality between men and women and quality of work. In companies with more than 300 employees, the employer must, every three years, open negotiations on the management of employment and career paths (Article L. 2242-1 of the French Labour Code).
5. Article L. 2242-3 of the French Labour Code.

The second response given by labour lawyers, built on this finding, focuses on the consideration that the very decision to enter into collective agreements falls outside the scope of the law and is based rather on sociological considerations that it is not their role to examine. It is more the job of labour sociologists and economists to endeavour to establish the reasons that lead trade unions and employers to sign collective agreements. Notions such as 'trade union cultures' (more or less reformist), the 'balance of power' (more or less favourable) and the 'economic interests' of the parties to the agreement, etc. are particularly highlighted. In short, labour law regulations allow collective bargaining and put the relevant organisational framework in place, but the decision whether they wish to sign any agreements is left to the social partners. From this perspective, legal analysis can only relate to the context of the actions but not to the actions themselves. This has been the classic distinction since Weber between the point of view of lawyers who are interested in the rules of law ('what normative meaning ought to be attributed in correct logic to a verbal pattern having the form of a legal proposition')[6] and the point of view of sociologists who consider what the social actors actually do with this ('What actually happens in a group due to the probability that persons engaged in social action, especially those exerting a socially relevant amount of power, subjectively consider certain norms as valid and practically act according to them, in other words, orient their own conduct towards these norms').[7]

Between these two paths – one concerned with the obligation to negotiate collective agreements, the other advocating that the signing of collective agreements is outside the field of legal analysis – some authors have highlighted the possibility of implementing reflexive regulations. Respect for the rules of law arises not only from fear of sanctions but also from the integration of these rules into the instruments created by social actors themselves, rooted in self-regulation. This is how Simon Deakin, Colm McLaughlin and Dominic Chai describe how the pay gap between men and women could be reduced in companies through the use of voluntary instruments, such as salary audits, good practice dissemination mechanisms and *benchmarking* of competitors' practices.[8] As these authors say:

> reflexive regulation offers a critique of voluntarist approaches on the one hand and 'command and control' forms of law on the other. Voluntarist approaches which assume that the interests of business will automatically align themselves with the wider public good are seen as ignoring a range of barriers to this occurring, including externalities and related forms of market failures. The 'command and control' approach, in contrast, is criticised as involving excessive reliance on prescriptive controls. (...) Regulation should aim instead to be reflexive in the sense of both responding in its form and content, to social contexts, and in triggering a range of responses from social actors which can form the basis for effective self-regulation.[9]

---

6. M. Weber, *Economy and Society*, ed. G. Roth and C. Wittich, 311 (Berkeley: University of California Press, [1922] 1978).
7. *Id.*, p. 311.
8. S. Deakin, C. McLaughlin, D. Chai, *Gender Inequality and Reflexive Law: The Potential of Different Regulatory Mechanisms*, in L. Dinkens (ed.), *Making Employment Rights Effective. Issues of Enforcement and Compliance*, 115-137 (Oxford: Hart Publ., 2012).
9. *Id.*, p. 119.

These reflexive regulations likewise have a place in the field of collective bargaining. There are many examples of companies adopting good conduct guides to negotiation or undertaking to hold periodic discussions on one subject or another.

These three ways of considering the relationship between collective bargaining law and the signing of collective agreements by social partners are present, to varying degrees, in the current legislation of European countries. However, in our opinion, the three mechanisms identified do not seem to take all the relationships between the rules and the actions sufficiently into account. We propose to identify a fourth, incentive-based method of bringing rules into operation. The notion of incentive is a familiar one in economic theory. The theory of incentive agreements has undergone significant development by focusing on establishing financial mechanisms that incite rational economic agents to adopt certain behaviour that is deemed desirable.[10] The theory behind incentive agreements thus constitutes a serious attempt to take account of the limited rationality of economic agents and asymmetries of information. Within the employment relationship, it seeks, above all, to establish a salary level capable of inciting workers not to lower their productivity to the detriment of the employer.[11] Outside of the flourishing field of law and economics, this research has had a limited impact on labour law for a long time. In this respect, we have also characterised[12] rules of law that we would classify as incentive-based. We have proposed identifying incentive rules as legal provisions that leave to actors the choice of adopting one or another course of action, but whose aim is to render the hoped-for course of action more attractive. Incentives do not impose; they allow for a particular form of behaviour and encourage its adoption on the basis of the supposed interests of the beneficiary of the rule. Beneficiaries will abide by the rule not because they are obliged to do so and would be sanctioned if they did not, but because it is in their interest to do so. As a consequence, legal analysis does not simply cover what the law imposes or prohibits, but also the legal techniques put into place to encourage certain actions.

In this study, we examine the rules of law that provide an incentive to social partners to enter into collective agreements. It is our contention that labour law is not limited to *imposing the bargaining* of collective company agreements: it also puts mechanisms into place that *provide incentives to enter into* collective agreements. These rules are too often ignored by labour lawyers even though they play a key role in the effectiveness of the decentralisation of collective bargaining.

In order to identify mechanisms that provide an incentive to enter into collective company agreements, we conducted a comparative survey of eleven European countries. This survey was performed over 2016 with insights from the research group

---

10. There is an extraordinarily number of published texts. For a classic introduction, see J.-J. Laffont and J. Tirole, *A Theory of Incentives in Procurement and Regulation* (MIT Press, 1993).
11. See Janet L. Yellen's seminal paper, *Efficiency Wage Models of Unemployment*, 74/2 American Economic Review, 200-205 (1984).
12. P.-E. Berthier, *Les incitations légales*, 1680 Semaine sociale Lamy, 36 (2015); O. Leclerc, T. Sachs, *Gouverner par les incitations. La diffusion d'une logique incitative dans le droit du travail*, 2 Revue française de socio-économie, 171 (2015). *See* also on this subject, in French law: S. Leroy, *Droit social et incitations: contribution à l'étude des transformations de la normativité juridique*, (thèse Université Paris Nanterre, 2014); in Italian law: V. Pietrogiovanni, *Le sanzioni positive nel diritto del lavoro*, (Universita degli studi di Bari Aldo Moro, 2013).

INLACRIS (*Independent Network for Labour Law and Crisis Studies*) in the context of a research project entitled *Collective bargaining developments in time of crisis* (project VP/2014/004, project coordinated by S. Laulom). We sent members of the INLACRIS network participating in the project a questionnaire aimed at identifying, in their country, the use of mechanisms aimed at providing an incentive to enter into collective agreements. This research enabled us to gather information on the following eleven countries: Austria, France, Italy, the Netherlands, Portugal, Slovenia, Romania, Spain, the United Kingdom, Hungary and Sweden.[13] This article is based on information drawn from this comparative survey. Responses to the questionnaire highlighted a variety of national situations. In some cases, several incentive mechanisms have been identified. By contrast, in other cases it seems that nothing of this kind exists in certain national laws. Consequently, our research enabled us to identify the diversity of incentive mechanisms present in national employment laws. Therefore, this article aims to set out a typology of incentives identified in collective bargaining law.

The comparative survey allowed us to characterise three principal incentive mechanisms in collective bargaining law. The first seeks to *facilitate* collective bargaining conditions for employers or unions. It entails removing material obstacles that could dissuade actors from entering into discussions and reaching agreement. Legislation can, for example, provide a subsidy aimed at covering negotiation costs. In this case, the incentive takes the form of facilitation. The second process consists in *compensating* actors who have actually signed a collective agreement. For example, a French employer can receive a 'bonus' for signing an agreement permitting the employment of young workers. The incentive is expressed here in a second form: reward. A third method of encouraging negotiation of a collective agreement consists in *taxing* companies who do not engage in the process. In this case, the incentive consists in making the undesirable situation more expensive (but without making it illegal). Taxation is, therefore, a third form that the incentive can assume.

In the light of French experience, and in view of the elements that we have been able to gather on other legal systems, it is our opinion that the following three procedures aimed at incentivising the signing of collective agreements can be identified: facilitation §3.02, reward §3.03 and taxation §3.04.

§3.02 FACILITATION

Facilitation is a rule of law aimed at making the conduct set out by law more simple: in this case, negotiation and signing of a collective agreement. Facilitation is aimed at simplifying the reputation of collective bargaining with a view to making it more attractive – a clear contrast to the unwieldiness and complexities sometimes attributed

---

13. We extend our sincere gratitude for the responses that were given to our questionnaire to: Pr Teresa Coelho Moreira (Universidade do Minho), Dr Nicola Gundt (Maastricht University), Prof Tamás Gyulavári (University of Budapest), Prof Barbara Kresal (University of Ljubljana), Prof Piera Loi (University of Cagliari), Prof Franz Marhold (Wirtschafts Universität Wien), Dr José María Miranda (University of Santiago de Compostela), Dr Yolanda Maneiro (University of Santiago de Compostela), Dr Felicia Rosioru (University of Babeş-Bolyai, Cluj-Napoca), Dr Jenny Julén Votinius (Lund University).

to it. Collective bargaining may well appear costly, difficult and risky, and this image may deter actors from embarking upon it. It is therefore important to help them to enter into negotiation and reach an agreement. To do so, the law must shed its reputation as a 'prescriber of action' and instead tackle the constraints of collective bargaining: its cost, lack of information, unavailability of negotiators or their mutual misapprehensions. Facilitation is aimed at removing these various obstacles. Although they are still very rare, such mechanisms aim to reduce the cost of negotiation for companies. In France, for example, the State may bear 70% of the costs incurred when implementing a 'generation contract'. This is a mechanism that favours the employment of young people and which is implemented, first and foremost, by the signing of a collective agreement.[14] Another form of facilitation consists of establishing, as they have in Sweden, a mediation body to which the parties to the negotiation can appeal when they are finding it difficult to reach agreement.[15]

However the forms of facilitation that are best represented at a European level are mainly aimed at removing two obstacles: the lack of information available to parties and a lack of availability on the part of trade union negotiators.

Lack of information can be a disincentive to negotiation and is the target of various types of facilitation. It might be, for example, that the union or employer is not aware of the different forms of collective bargaining or does not know the legal consequences of signing an agreement. Facilitation might, therefore, consist of establishing a commission responsible for informing employers and unions about collective bargaining 'good practice' and the rules applicable to it. This is the case in the United Kingdom, where ACAS ('Advisory, Conciliation and Arbitration Service') drafts 'Codes of Practice' covering various aspects of employment relationships. These guides are aimed at aiding comprehension and implementation of texts introduced by the legislator. Among these guides, the 'Code of Practice on settlement agreements'[16] deals specifically with collective bargaining. This text is not legally binding on the parties to the negotiation, although judges can refer to it when ruling on disputes in this field.[17] The code of practice has more of an educational purpose of explaining the law. It is aimed at enhancing 'understanding' on the part of negotiators, of the provisions of the *Employment Rights Act* of 1996[18] on collective bargaining. The aim is to make negotiation accessible to all actors, employers and unions. Likewise, in France, certain

---

14. Article D. 5121-6 of the French Labour Code.
15. Negotiators can call on the 'National Mediation Office' when they are finding it hard to make any headway in negotiations, even when there is no collective labour dispute. This body was established under The Co-Determination Act (1976:580), sections 46-53.
16. Code of practice 4, 'Settlement Agreements' (under section 111 A of the Employment Rights Act, 1996).
17. The following is specified in the preamble to the Code: 'The Code is issued under section 199 of the Trade Union and Labour Relations (Consolidation) Act 1992 and comes into effect by order of the Secretary of State on 29 July 2013. Failure to follow the Code does not, in itself, make a person or organisation liable to proceedings, nor will it lead to an adjustment in any compensation award made by an employment tribunal. However, employment tribunals will take the Code into account when considering relevant cases'.
18. This aim is set out in the introduction to this Code: 'This Code is designed to help employers, employees and their representatives understand the law relating to the negotiation of settlement agreements as set out in section 111A of the Employment Rights Act (ERA) 1996'.

facilitation methods have been proposed, aimed at making collective bargaining more accessible to a greater number of companies – particularly the smallest ones – as well as to trade unions. Thus the 'Combrexelle report' advocates the drafting of 'standard collective agreements' by professional sectors aimed at small companies.[19] The French law of 8 August 2016 likewise has an educational aspect, stating that 'employees, employers and their representatives may benefit from joint training aimed at improving social dialogue practices within companies'.[20]

However lack of information is not the only material obstacle to collective bargaining. The unavailability of actors, in particular the unions, is likewise an issue for facilitation. The time spent on collective bargaining within the company, if unsalaried, can be an obstacle to union negotiators, who have to interrupt their work in order to join in the negotiations. Several European countries grant union representatives the right to absent themselves from their work, without loss of pay, so they can fulfil their union role. This is specifically the case in Sweden,[21] Austria[22] and France.[23] Sometimes, for example in Hungary, such a right is specially organised in order to allow unions to hold discussion with their employer.[24] Even more specifically, under French law, union representatives are allocated additional 'credit hours', especially for the purposes of collective bargaining.[25] These supplementary hours allow a union representative, and employees called upon to take part in negotiations, to prepare the negotiation of an agreement without loss of salary, and without using up the monthly delegated hours to which the former is normally entitled. The employer is then bound to pay both for the time spent preparing the negotiation and their actual working hours.

There is, therefore, facilitation every time labour law establishes a mechanism that aids negotiation that underpins it. The aim is to put the actors in a position where they can fulfil the role that is expected of them: entering into negotiations and reaching agreement. Such facilitation must be distinguished from another form of incentive, which has often been found within the legislations analysed: reward.

---

19. J.-D. Combrexelle (dir.), *La négociation collective, le travail et l'emploi*, 89 (France stratégie, September 2015).
20. Article L. 2212-1 of the French Labour Code.
21. The Trade Union Representatives Act (1974:358) contains specific rules on employment protection for union representatives, and rules on paid leave for performing trade union activities.
22. When members of works councils are involved in their role as union representatives, they receive payment although they are generally not obliged to work as they would normally at their post (in enterprises with at least 150 employees §117 Arbeitsverfassungsgesetz) or because of the performance of their office as members of a works council (§116 Arbeitsverfassungsgesetz).
23. Articles L. 2143-13 et seq. of the French Labour Code.
24. Article 274(1) of the Labour Code: 'With a view to discharging their trade union functions of representation, employees shall be entitled to a reduction of working hours, and the employees designated according to Subsections (2)–(3) of Section 273 shall be exempted from work for the duration of consultation with the employer'.
25. Article L. 1243-16 of the French Labour Code.

§3.03 REWARD

Reward is a means of incentive that, according to Norberto Bobbio, should be carefully differentiated from facilitation. This distinction can be more easily understood by means of a simple example, inspired by the one given by the Italian author himself.[26] In order to encourage my daughter to do well in her English exam, I can do all that I can, in advance, to ensure that learning this language is a pleasure for her rather than an obligation. The incentive might consist in making learning English more fun so that my daughter is in a position to do well in her exam. This incentive is aimed at eliminating the obstacles that could cause her to do less well and constitutes facilitation.

Another way of encouraging my daughter – which is not exclusive of the first – consists in promising her a reward if she does well in her exam. I could offer her a gift or take her to the cinema, depending on her wishes. Unlike facilitation, a reward is not based on adverse factors that arise before or at the same time as the exam (the fact that the child does not like English for example). The reward is given after the performance that I expect of my daughter, and is a consequence of her success.

In terms of collective bargaining, the 'reward' is given once a collective agreement has been signed. It rewards the actors who have actually signed an agreement. To this end, the reward sometimes consists of providing a financial advantage [A] and, more often than not, reducing the legal constraints that may be a burden to the employer [B].

[A] Financial Advantage

Some reforms adopted since the start of the economic crisis have introduced financial advantages linked to the signing of a collective agreement. These incentives are aimed at achieving the objectives that public policies seek to achieve in terms of employment through collective bargaining. The agreements sought are designed to keep in employment or training the workers most affected by unemployment. In France, it is now possible, under a collective agreement, to reduce severance pay payable to an employee taken on under a fixed-term contract in exchange for 'preferential access' to vocational training.[27] Likewise, a 'bonus' may be paid to any employer who, via a collective agreement, undertakes to employ a young worker while keeping on an older worker in their job.[28] Such financial incentives are not only being developed in France. As Barbara Kresal points out, they were implemented on a temporary basis in Slovenia at the start of the economic crisis. In early 2009, two measures aimed at preserving existing jobs were introduced by two legislative acts: on the one hand, a partial subsidy for shorter working hours and, on the other hand, partial reimbursement of wage compensation allocated to workers during temporary lay-offs. These two legislative

---

26. N. Bobbio, *De la structure à la fonction. Nouveaux essais de théorie du droit*, trad. et présentation D. Soldini, 56 (Paris: Dalloz, 2012).
27. Article L. 1243-9 of the French Labour Code.
28. Articles L. 5121-6 et seq. of the French Labour Code.

acts linked entitlement to public subsidies either to the conclusion of a company agreement or consultation with trade-unions or other workers' representatives at a company level. These temporary measures have now expired.

Financial aid granted to companies in order to maintain employment can also take the form of more perennial mechanisms, such as in Austria, where a company with serious financial difficulties may request a grant from the Austrian Public Employment Service (AMS) to temporarily reduce working hours and pay for its workers by between 10% and 90% for a maximum period of six months. This requires the social partners to conclude a specific agreement. The employer receives a grant from the AMS based on the national unemployment benefit and compensates employees who suffer proportional pay cuts.

Reward, therefore, in the form of a financial advantage, is a means of encouraging employers to sign agreements on safeguarding employment or salary levels. Other rewards consist of relieving legal constraints to which employers are subject.

[B] Relief from Legal Constraints

In this scenario, the incentive consists in granting employers a more flexible legal system than if they had not signed an agreement. This may take two forms, with unequal representation across the countries analysed.

The first, which is found in Spanish and Portuguese law, consists in temporarily suspending application of a collective agreement. Thus in Portugal, social partners can agree to suspend application of other collective agreements on working hours or salaries at a branch or company level.[29] The Spanish provision also offers an incentive to negotiate, although it still leaves more room for a unilateral decision on the part of the employer.[30] It effectively allows the employer not to apply the provisions of a collective agreement at a branch or company level, in particular in relation to salaries and working hours, in the event of economic, technical, organisational or production difficulties. In this context, the employer does not need to obtain the consensus of the parties to the agreement or even that of the company's workers' representatives. He must, however, hold negotiations on the causes justifying recourse to the suspension of the collective agreement. This negotiation, which must not last more than fifteen days, ends with obligatory arbitration by the authorities in the event of disagreement. The prospect of an intervention by the authorities is meant to encourage the parties to reach agreement. While the Spanish and Portuguese mechanisms are different, they share the same aim: to relax application of an agreement to allow a company to tackle the difficulties it is facing, and, therefore, on the employer's side, to eliminate the constraints arising from this agreement.

The second technique used as an incentive to collective bargaining is in evidence in several European countries and involves derogation from the law or from a collective

---

29. Law no. 55/2014 of the 25 August 2014.
30. Article 82 of the Estatuto de los Trabajadores; Real Decreto-ley 3/2012, of 10 February, de medidas urgentes para la reforma del mercado laboral, *BOE*, no. 36, 11 February 2012, pp. 12483-12546.

agreement with greater scope. We shall limit ourselves here to agreements that derogate from the law. When a derogatory agreement is signed, the employer benefits from a system that makes fewer demands on him – while not being necessarily more favourable to employees – than is established by law. There are numerous examples of derogation. They exist in the majority of countries analysed, with the notable exception of Austria. They can be observed to have developed even in countries where the 'favourable treatment principle' is still in place, such as Slovenia. In the latter, for example, the minimum salary reform which took place in 2010 left open the possibility of negotiating company agreements which would allow the new law to be temporarily derogated, by allowing minimum salaries of less than the legal amount to remain in place.[31] Derogatory agreements can cover various aspects of employment relationships, whether in relation to salaries, regulation of working hours or part-time work.[32] More specifically, agreements that permit derogation from the system governing redundancy on economic grounds have appeared in some countries, such as the Netherlands and France. In the Netherlands, a collective agreement can allow social partners to derogate from certain aspects of the legal system and establish a special commission responsible for ruling on the legitimacy of redundancies.[33] In France, the legislator has established collective agreements that allow for major derogations from the system governing redundancy on economic grounds. For example, these include 'internal mobility agreements'[34] and 'employment maintenance agreements'.[35] Internal mobility agreements govern the geographical mobility of employees within the company. 'Employment maintenance agreements' allow for a temporary reduction in the number of employees or an increase in working hours without any increase in pay. In exchange, the employer undertakes not to make any economic redundancies throughout the duration of this agreement. These mechanisms have a point in common: even if employees overwhelmingly refuse the application of these agreements, they will be made redundant without benefiting from the regulations on collective redundancy.[36] The redundancies that are made will then be subject to a procedure that is much less onerous for the employer.

---

31. Minimum Wages Act, 'Zakon o minimalni plači', Official Journal of the Republic of Slovenia, No. 13/2010.
32. In Italy, for example, numerous possibilities of derogation from the law can be cited. For instance, there is the example of legislative decree no. 66 of 2001 regulating working time. The maximum weekly working hours fixed by law are forty-eight (including overtime). Collective agreements even at company level can calculate the maximum weekly working hours as an average over a period that could be extended up to six or twelve months if there are economic or organisational reasons to do so. In more recent legislation (Jobs Act Legislative decree no. 81/2015) in the case of short-term contracts, the law sets the percentage of the workforce on this kind of contract at 20%, but collective agreements (even at company level) can derogate and increase the percentage.
33. Article 7:671a (2) and (3) Italian Civil Code. In cases of dismissal for economic reasons, the employer, together with the trade unions, may establish by collective agreement a commission that decides on the lawfulness of the planned dismissal.
34. Articles L. 2242-17 et seq. of the French Labour Code.
35. Articles L. 5125-1 et seq. of the French Labour Code.
36. More recently still, French law has provided a new category of agreement: 'agreement for the preservation and development of employment' (Articles L. 2254-2 et seq. of the French Labour Code). The regime under this agreement is similar to the 'employment maintenance agreement'

In the countries analysed, the techniques aimed at relieving the burden of legal constraints on the employer are diverse but the incentive seems to be based on the same principles. The unions can be encouraged to sign an agreement on the basis of a promise made by the employer, for example, to maintain employment despite the company's difficulties or to encourage employee mobility in order to avoid announcing redundancies in the future. In turn, the employer may be encouraged to enter into an agreement because, if it is successful, the employer's power may be exercised in a less onerous legal framework and may, therefore, be subject to fewer demands. However, the possibility remains that these promises may not be kept and that negotiators may not achieve the result they were hoping for from the agreement signed. In other words, the incentive to enter into a collective agreement may be a source of disappointment for both employer and unions alike. The French experience offers an example of this: an 'employment maintenance agreement' could lead to results that are in direct opposition to those to which its negotiators aspired.

From the employer's side of things, the legal leeway it is granted can sometimes seriously harm the basic rights of its employees. For example, a law of 17 August 2015, removed the employer's obligation to reclassify employees subject to redundancy when they refuse the application of an employment maintenance agreement. Under this law, employers are no longer obliged to check whether another job is available and offer it to the employee before making them redundant, which in principle is set out by law for any redundancies based on financial grounds. Under Constitutional Council case law, the right to reclassification arises from the 'right to employment' guaranteed by the Constitution.[37] This exclusion from reclassification could, therefore, be the subject of an appeal on the grounds of unconstitutionality and, as a result, is very fragile. There is a case to be answered, therefore, that this reward which the employer is promised, namely the benefit of a less onerous legal regime if an agreement is reached, may in fact turn out to be disadvantageous for him. It is in cases like these that the reward can actually turn against the interests of the party that it is aimed to satisfy.

The unions, in turn, may be incited to sign such an agreement in order to maintain employment over some years, even if the company is suffering financial difficulties. An example of an agreement signed in a company located in France ('Mahle-Behr') is a good demonstration of how this mechanism can have the opposite effect to the one intended.[38] An employment maintenance agreement was signed in this company in July 2013, by the majority unions, in order to avoid the loss of *one hundred and two* jobs. However, *one hundred and sixty two* employees refused the application of this agreement. These one hundred and sixty two employees were then made

---

where employees who oppose its application can be made redundant under the same conditions. However, the agreement for the 'preservation of employment' can be signed even where there is no economic difficulty and does not contain any commitment on the part of the employer not to announce redundancies while it is in force.

37. Constitutional Council 13 January 2005, *Loi de programmation pour la cohésion sociale* [Planning Act for Social Cohesion], no. 2004-509 DC.
38. *See* on this point: P. Adam, *Le 'prodigieux' accord de maintien de l'emploi. Escapade en pays de Rouffach*, 1611 *Semaine Sociale Lamy* (2013).

redundant and were unable to benefit from the guarantees implemented in cases of collective redundancy. This is a good example of how a so-called employment maintenance agreement can result in more widespread redundancy than was initially envisaged.

The incentive can, therefore, lead to disappointment when the signing of an agreement does not give its signatories the expected advantages or, worse, produces a result diametrically opposed to the one sought. Since the reward consists of rewarding the actors – basically the employer – for reaching an agreement, a third and final means of providing an incentive for collective bargaining consists of *taxing* employers who do not negotiate.

§3.04 TAXATION

'Taxation' is very common in economists' discussions on incentives.[39] A tax is aimed at making undesirable conduct more onerous. It consists of taxing the party who does not accomplish an act expected of it. From this point of view, taxes have very close links with criminal sanctions which are also a reaction on the part of the law to undesirable conduct (theft, impediment, discrimination, etc.).

There are, however, two aspects that distinguish taxation from a criminal sanction. Unlike a criminal sanction, taxation is much more predictable in terms of *amount*. While a criminal sanction can vary depending on the judge's assessment of the severity of the offence – as compensation might vary according to the prejudice caused to a victim – taxation varies on the basis of predefined, quantifiable criteria, such as a company's work force or the percentage of its total payroll. 'Taxation' does not have the connotations that a sanction does either. Under a taxation system, undesirable conduct is not necessarily 'illegal' or 'prohibited', it is simply more costly. In terms of collective bargaining, taxation consists of making an employer pay a certain amount when he does not engage in negotiation with the unions, or when he fails to respect the agreement resulting from such negotiation. The few examples that we have managed to discover – in France and in Italy – show that taxation can either be in addition to a criminal sanction, or replace it.

Taxation sometimes seeks to augment criminal sanctions, the dissuasive nature of which is often debated. Thus French companies with at least fifty employees who have not engaged in annual collective bargaining on workforce salaries are subject to taxation,[40] in addition to any criminal sanction to which they might be subject for

---

39. See for example France, where well-known economists have proposed replacing the damages that an employer can be ordered to pay when he makes a redundancy without genuine, serious grounds for doing so, with a specific, predetermined 'tax': O. Blanchard, J. Tirole, *Protection de l'emploi et procédures de licenciement*, Report by the Economic Analysis Council, (Paris: La documentation française, 2003).
40. Article L. 2242-5-1 of the French Labour Code.

having failed to respect this obligation to negotiate.[41] In other cases, taxation completely replaces sanctions. This is the case, again in France, where companies with at least three hundred employees are subject to a financial 'penalty' when they fail to commence negotiations on the implementation of the 'generation contract'[42] aimed at boosting the employment of young people. Similarly, under Italian law, the fact of making collective redundancies when an agreement has set out alternative measures is not subject to a criminal sanction but to taxation. In this case, employers have to pay a higher social contribution in order to finance the special unemployment benefits due to workers collectively dismissed.[43]

In the European countries that we have considered, taxation is not a general trend. However, it is a good illustration of the content of an incentive-based approach. It does not find an actor who fails to negotiate or respect a collective agreement guilty of either a civil or criminal offence. It leaves it to the actors to decide what is most advantageous for them, by comparing the tax cost with the cost of negotiation or the ensuing costs of an agreement resulting from such negotiation.

§3.05 CONCLUSION

This article clarifies the diversity of the mechanisms for legally regulating employment. The negotiation of collective agreements is far from the sole option; labour laws in Europe also use incentive-based mechanisms to encourage the signing of collective agreements. This latter type of regulation constitutes a 'soft' option for achieving the signing of a collective agreement. Rather than obliging social partners to enter into collective agreements, the law is conceived such that it is rational for them to want to do so. From the point of view of the public authorities, incentive-based mechanisms offer a major advantage: they enable a result to be obtained (the signing of decentralised collective agreements) without interference in the employer's management decisions. While obliging social partners to sign agreements would be flying in the face of contractual freedom, incentives mean that such courses of action can be encouraged without the application of any constraints. Basically, this could be described as making the perspective of negotiating and reaching agreement appear more in line with the actors' interests. Signing a collective agreement does not become obligatory; it simply becomes more rational.

In the European countries that we have studied, incentives to sign collective agreements basically relate to the management of employment within a company, with a view to, or in the context of, economic difficulties, and working conditions. The most 'offensive' agreements relating to working conditions, in particular to salary and working hours, are still those rooted in financial justification. In other cases, incentives

---

41. Articles L. 2243-1 and L. 2243-2 of the French Labour Code. Failure to respect this obligation to negotiate is punishable by a fine of EUR 3,750 and a one-year prison sentence. We should, however, specify that only the fine, and smaller than the maximum possible, is pronounced by the judges.
42. Article L. 5121-9 of the French Labour Code.
43. Law No. 223/1991.

can be related to employment of certain categories (young or old) of workers. The incentive to sign collective agreements can thus be seen as a means of boosting an employment policy without forcing employers to recruit particular categories of workers. As a result, employment policies are implemented by the 'softer', but by no means less genuine, process of incentive. For this reason, the core of the incentive-based mechanisms highlighted in our study aim to encourage collective bargaining; incentives are used to support an employment policy that is implemented directly at company-level. It is, however, still necessary to bear in mind the fact that the incentive-based mechanisms that we have identified are not particularly linked to the decentralisation of collective bargaining. These incentives (facilitation, reward, taxation) could also be used in support of policy aimed at the development of collective agreements at a branch level or indeed national, inter-professional agreements.

In the European countries that we have studied, the majority of incentives favouring the signing of collective agreements are aimed at employers and employees. In this light, the signing of a collective agreement can be perceived as a condition for allowing them to benefit from certain advantages or avoid certain inconveniences. And it is to allow employees or the employer to benefit from these advantages or avoid these inconveniences, that collective agreements are indeed signed. This being the case, the policies we have studied demonstrate a considerable range of mechanisms, to the point that the recipients of the incentive are not always easy to identify. In certain cases, the incentive is aimed at employees as much as the employer. For example, French Labour Code states that 'in order to improve the professional development of employees on a fixed-term contract, a collective agreement at branch or company level can both cap the amount of compensation when the contract comes to an end at 6% [rather than 10%], while offering consideration to these employees, particularly in the form of preferential access to professional training' (Article L. 1243-9 of the Labour Code). In this case, the incentive benefits both the employer (reduction in social charges) and employees (improved professional training). However in other situations, identifying the beneficiary of the incentive is much less clear-cut. Let us take the example of the provisions of the French Labour Code on internal mobility. In order to encourage the implementation of such collective agreements, the law stipulates that employees who refuse the application of the provisions of the agreement to their employment contract may be made redundant. In this case, the law specifies that their redundancy takes the form of individual redundancy on economic grounds. The redundancy follows the individual redundancy procedure (less onerous for the employer), whatever the number of employees involved and even if, in total, they exceed the thresholds for definition as collective redundancy. Is the incentive aimed at the employee or the employer? Predetermination of the redundancy system applicable in the event of an employee's refusal to apply the agreement allows the employer to benefit from a less onerous redundancy regime. At the same time, the incentive is extended towards the employee who is incited to accept the implementation of the agreement (and thus the mobility clause), under the threat of redundancy.

Strangely, while in the European countries that we have studied, collective agreements are entered into between employers or their representatives on the one hand and union organisations on the other, very few rewards are given directly to the unions. The incentive to enter into collective agreements always seems to be aimed at employers and employees, based presumably on the supposition that this should leave them to encourage the union organisations to enter into agreements. Among the rare examples that we found was that of the Netherlands, where in practice if not in law, the employer pays the so-called *vakbondstientje* (the union bargaining subsidy) for all his employees covered by the collective agreement in question, to the trade unions that are party to it. How can this situation be explained? An initial explanation might be that providing unions with a direct incentive to sign collective agreements could give rise to an unlawful inequality of treatment between different union organisations. For example, in France, rewarding a union simply because it is more inclined than another to sign an agreement would not constitute legitimate grounds for such a disparity.[44] This argument is, however, far from sufficient in terms of explaining why unions are not rewarded in European law, on the basis of their consent to collective agreements. There are two, not mutually exclusive, hypotheses as to why this may be the case.

In the first hypothesis, the employer, in so far as he has the power to influence employment, must be the main target of these incentives. In the examples given, the reward is not given to encourage *both parties* to reach agreement, but to encourage the employer to accept the obligation to maintain employment and retain employees as an essential part of its decision-making process. In this context, the incentive appears as a means of introducing a decision that is solely the employer's into a collective agreement. Consequently, the rewards are aimed exclusively at the employer. In turn, the unions will already be encouraged to take the decision to sign the agreement by the promise made to them in relation to maintaining employment and/or salary level, without the need to promise them further reward.

According to a second hypothesis, it is necessary to admit that the role of unions would be called into question if they were acknowledged as having a vested interest in the signing of an agreement. It is in fact very difficult to reconcile the idea that unions represent the collective interests of employees with the idea that these same unions could be guided towards 'rational' behaviour by incentives, particularly those of a financial nature. Providing direct incentives to unions to enter into collective agreements would be tantamount to giving them a vested interest. This interest could potentially diverge from the professional interests of the workers that they represent, as such interests are not always convergent.

---

44. The French Court of Cassation holds that the 'principle of equality is a constitutional rule, and does not allow an employer to subsidise one representative union and not another, on the basis of whether or not they have signed a collective agreement or convention' (Cass., Soc. 29 May 2001, *Bull. civ.* V, no. 185).

CHAPTER 4
The Impact of the Economic Crisis on Collective Agreements in Poland

Łukasz Pisarczyk

§4.01 INTRODUCTORY REMARKS

The influence of the economic crisis on the collective bargaining system varies from country to country. Poland can be seen as an important example of a legal system where the economic crisis coexisted with a deep crisis of collective bargaining and indeed the whole idea of social dialogue.[1] The current situation is disquieting in terms of both industrial relations and the basic principles of the socio-economic system.

According to Article 20 of the Polish Constitution, the basis of the economic system shall be a social market economy, with freedom of economic activity, private ownership, and solidarity, dialogue and cooperation between social partners. Moreover, the Constitution guarantees freedom of association in trade unions and employer organizations (Article 59.1). Trade unions and employers/employer organizations shall have the right to bargain collectively to resolve collective disputes and to conclude collective agreements (Article 59.2).[2] In theory, collective agreements should play a

---

1. This is a result of long-lasting political, social and economic process that has led to the formation of a specific model of collective negotiations. To an extent, it was connected with the transition from a centrally planned to a market economy. Compare e.g., M. Seweryński, *Polish Labour Law from Communism to Democracy*, (Warsaw: ABC Publisher 1999); L. Florek, *Labour Law* in S. Frankowski (ed.), *Introduction to Polish Law*, 275-276 (Kluwer Law International, 2005); J. Gardawski, *20 Years of Social Dialogue in Poland* in: *Collective Labour Law*, 60 Studia Iuridica, 53 et seq. (2015); G. Goździewicz, *Collective Labour Agreements as a Fundamental Tool of Trade Union Operation* in: *Collective Labour Law*, 60 Studia Iuridica, 79 (2015); K.W. Baran (ed.), M. Wujczyk *Outline of Polish Labour Law System*, 77 (Warszawa: Wolters Kluwer 2016); L. Mitrus, Z. Hajn, *Poland* in R. Blanpain (ed.), *International Encyclopaedia of Laws: Labour Law and Industrial Relations*, 31 et seq. (Kluwer Law International 2016).
2. *See also* K. Baran, *The Autonomous Labour Law – De Lege Lata and De Lege Ferenda*, in: *Collective Labour Law*, 60 Studia Iuridica 12 (2015); and Z. Hajn, L. Mitrus, *Poland*, *supra* n. 1, p. 263. The

crucial role in the process of determining working conditions.[3] But the reality of industrial relationships in Poland is, unfortunately, different.[4] Existing collective agreements cover a relatively small group of workers. The result is a striking discrepancy between the theoretical model of social dialogue and the reality of collective agreements. Prima facie there are two main factors influencing the current status of collective bargaining in Poland. The first is common to all European countries: the economic crisis. The second is the specific development and features of social dialogue in post-communist countries. It is interesting to see how these two phenomena interact and influence the nature of the social dialogue.

It is also necessary to clarify the concept of the crisis and its frameworks. In Poland, various anti-crisis instruments had been adopted from the early 2000s (before the global crisis began). This was connected with a very difficult situation in the labour market, when the unemployment rate reached 20%.[5] The legal solutions adopted at that time are still in use. Paradoxically, the main wave of the economic crisis did not produce such negative consequences. However, to counteract any worsening of the situation, further anti-crisis legislation was developed: two special acts providing for short-time work (2009 and 2013),[6] and an amendment of the Labour Code resulting in the flexibilization of working time regulations (2013). Taking into account the specific development of the Polish labour market and employment legislation, the concept of the crisis should be understood as broadly covering the whole period 2001-2017.

§4.02 THE STRUCTURE OF COLLECTIVE AGREEMENTS IN POLAND

The Polish legislation regulates the process of collective bargaining in a fairly detailed way. The social partners may conclude collective agreements of a normative or non-normative character. The normative agreements directly influence the rights and duties of the third parties (primarily workers), covering all the employees engaged by a given employer (not only trade unions members).[7] The non-normative agreements

---

above-mentioned rules are developed by the legislation, which guarantees a broad personal and objective scope for the collective agreements. In particular, Article 77^1 LC provides that collective agreements should constitute the main instrument shaping remuneration.
3. See e.g., W. Sanetra, *Social Dialogue as an Element of Polish Socio-Economic System in the Light of the Constitution of the Republic of Poland*, in: *Collective Labour Law*, 60 Studia Iuridica 191 et seq. (2015).
4. See e.g., Z. Hajn, L. Mitrus, *Poland*, supra n. 1, p. 44.
5. The legislature introduced the institution of collective agreements that may temporarily modify (*in peius*) the conditions of work and pay. The agreements are still present in the Labour Code (the law of 26 June 1974 – the Labour Code, Journal of Laws 2014, item 1502, as amended).
6. The Laws of 1 July 2009 on Mitigation of the Economic Crisis Consequences for Employees and Entrepreneurs and of 6 November 2013 on Special Solutions Concerning the Protection of Workplaces (Official Journal 2017, item 842). *See also* L. Mitrus, *Anti-Crisis Regulations of Polish Labour Law*, 2 European Labour Law Journal, 269-275 (2010), and *Crise économique et droit du travail: l'expérience polonaise*, 2 Revue de droit compare du travail et de la sécurité sociale 50-58 (2012).
7. Collective agreements may be also concluded for workers engaged on a civil law basis (Article 239 § 3 LC).

are binding only between the parties (e.g., employers and trade unions). The employees may base their claims on civil law grounds (e.g., *pactum in favorem tertii*), which is less effective than the protections guaranteed by the labour law sources.

When it comes to normative acts, which are considered autonomous sources of labour law, the law distinguishes between typical and atypical collective agreements. Typical collective agreements, shaped by the Labour Code, are normal (regular) instruments of the social dialogue that can be utilized at any time. They are negotiated exclusively by trade unions[8] and may regulate practically all conditions of work and pay.[9] Because of their far-reaching legal consequences, the law determines specific requirements concerning the parties, the bargaining procedure and the agreement registration.[10]

Atypical agreements (accords) of a normative character supplement the system of typical agreements. They are provided for by the legislation in extraordinary situations where there is a need for a collective intervention and no room for comprehensive negotiations. Atypical collective agreements are negotiated either to protect workers (transfer of undertaking, collective redundancies) or to support the employer (the worsening of working conditions, flexibilization of working time). The law provides for a special (less complicated) procedure for negotiating atypical agreements. These are not registered, either. As a result, they constitute quite a flexible legal instrument.[11] Since the agreements influence the content of employment relationships, they can be concluded only in circumstances expressly indicated by the law.[12] Consequently, the legislation creates a closed system of normative collective agreements.

Collective agreements of a non-normative character do not require any special authorization. They can be negotiated and concluded between employers (or their organizations) and structures representing workers (primarily trade unions) at any time.

The system of collective agreements is supplemented by acts that do not constitute the result of the social dialogue *sensu stricto* but are created unilaterally by the employer (sometimes with the involvement of employee representatives).[13] Work order regulations determine mainly organizational rules, while pay regulations influence the content of the employment relationship (remuneration and other work-related benefits). In fact, they operate where there is no collective agreement and remain in

---

8. A special role is played by representative (i.e., the strongest) trade unions.
9. However, it is not entirely utilized by the social partners (G. Goździewicz, *Collective Labour Agreements as a Fundamental Tool of Trade Union Operation* in: *Collective Labour Law*, 60 Studia Iuridica 83 (2015).
10. See Z. Hajn, L. Mitrus, *Poland, supra* n. 1, pp. 266 et seq.
11. *Ibidem*, pp. 273-274.
12. See e.g., K. Baran, *The Autonomous Labour Law – De Lege Lata and De Lege Ferenda, supra* n. 2, pp. 18-19. However, this solution has not been evident (see judgment of Supreme Court of 23 May 2001, III ZP 25/00).
13. K.W. Baran (ed.), *Outline of Polish Labour Law System, supra* n. 1, pp. 106-111.

force until one is concluded.[14] Employers with at least fifty employees are obliged to issue internal regulations. Employers with at least twenty employees should produce internal regulations at the request of trade unions. In the case of employers with fewer than twenty employees, the issuing of the regulations is left to their decision.

§4.03 THE CURRENT STATE OF COLLECTIVE AGREEMENTS

Although the Constitution and the legislation guarantee an important role for collective agreements, their practical import is very limited.[15] First of all, in Poland there is no system of sectoral (industry-based) agreements.[16] The number of company-level agreements – which, being atomized, do not constitute a real alternative to sectoral or regional ones – has decreased as well. The decrease in coverage by collective agreements is due to a number of factors, including the decline in unionization and the structure of trade unions and employer organizations, as well as some legislative solutions. Company-level negotiations are deeply influenced by the requirements concerning the internal structure of trade unions. The law requires that the structure must unite at least ten members employed by a given employer. This is a prerequisite to exercising their rights – including the right to bargain collectively and to conclude collective agreements of normative character. Moreover, there is no real alternative in the form of elected bodies. Though works councils have been established in a few companies, their rights are usually limited to information and consultation. They have no right to bargain collectively. When there are no trade unions, some atypical collective agreements can be concluded with ad hoc elected representatives. However, they deal only with selected matters and usually serve as a tool to overcome economic or financial difficulties on the part of the employer. As a result, they cannot create a comprehensive system of agreements.

The decrease in coverage by collective agreements is a long-term process and cannot be associated with the economic crisis of the 2000s only. However, the crisis deepened some negative tendencies. Recently, the number of collective agreements has also decreased (i.e., no collective agreement of a multi-establishment character has been recently concluded). It would be unreasonable to predict that the end of the crisis will improve the status of the social dialogue. Industrial relations in Poland need rather profound changes. A lot depends on the social partners themselves. Some legislative amendments are needed as well.

---

14. Regulations concerning remuneration (pay) must be agreed with trade unions. But if there are no trade unions or they are unable to work out a common view, the employer issues the regulations unilaterally.
15. *See* e.g., G. Goździewicz, *Collective Labour Agreements as a Fundamental Tool of Trade Union Operation* in: *Collective Labour Law, supra* n. 9, pp. 88-90.
16. As regards the system of collective bargaining *see* Z. Hajn, L. Mitrus, *Poland, supra* n. 1, pp. 263-265.

§4.04 PERSONAL SCOPE OF COLLECTIVE BARGAINING

In the past, Polish law regulated freedom of association in a very restrictive way, limiting the categories of workers who could form and join trade unions. These rights were granted (with a few minor exceptions) to employees only. People working on the basis of civil law contracts (e.g., service contracts), as a rule, fell outside the freedom to associate in trade unions.[17] The Constitutional Court challenged this solution, declaring it inconsistent with Articles 12 and 59.1 of the Constitution.[18] There is at least some temporal coincidence between the economic slowdown and the lodging of this complaint with the Constitutional Court. The economic crisis caused the development of atypical employment patterns and intensified concerns about the protection of the most vulnerable groups of workers. The economic situation thus proved to be a stimulus in the process of reconstruction of the collective representation system.

Workers outside an employment relationship should have the right to form and join trade unions. However, the legislature has faced very serious problems during the implementation process. As a result, the amendments to the Law on Trade Unions have not yet been introduced. The main question is, who should have the right to form and to join trade unions? The Constitutional Court stated that freedom of association cannot be linked to a specific form of employment. The guarantees arising from the Constitution cover all individuals who perform work personally, and who are thus in a legal relationship with a beneficiary of the service and have collective interests that can be represented by trade unions. A separate problem is the situation of the self-employed, who are treated as entrepreneurs. The draft Law on Trade Unions guarantees them the right to join trade unions if they do not employ workers. The situation of workers carrying out economic activity at the same time is, however, more complicated. Their collective representation must be confronted with the provisions of competition law (and economic freedoms). These considerations can be extended to crowdworkers, who are usually treated as self-employed. In their case, the question arises of who the counterpart in the negotiations process should be. In all of the above-mentioned situations, the right to be covered by collective agreements should be incontestable if the self-employment is of a bogus nature.

Typical collective agreements are concluded, as a rule, for employees. Although they can also cover workers employed on a civil law basis, this is not common. Moreover, almost all the new legal mechanisms, which can be treated as response to the economic crisis, concern the employment relationship in a narrow sense. At the same time, the parties to civil law contracts enjoy a great freedom in shaping their content. This group of workers is excluded from the majority of protective standards provided for by the labour legislation (the parties may adopt solutions that are too

---

17. Such a solution was criticized by the labour law doctrine. *See* e.g., Z. Hajn, *The Right of Association in Trade Unions – the Right of Employees, or the Right of Working People* in: *Collective Labour Law*, 60 Studia Iuridica 107 et seq. (2015). *See also* D. Skupień, M. Łaga, Ł. Pisarczyk, *Recent Development in Polish Labour and Social Security Law. The Social Dialogue, Flexibility and Welfare State*, in M. Stefko (ed.), *Labour Law and Social Security Law at the Crossroads*, 200-204 (Prague: Univerzita Karlova, Právnická fakulta 2016).
18. Judgment of the Constitutional Court of 2 June 2015, K 1/13, Journal of Laws 2015, item 791.

flexible to be applied in the employment relationship). The situation may evolve if the legislature enlarges the scope of protective standards.

§4.05 THE CONTENT OF COLLECTIVE AGREEMENTS

Over the last fifteen years, the subjective scope of collective agreements has been significantly restructured. The main goals have been to guarantee greater flexibility in the employment relationship and to support employers experiencing economic or financial difficulties. The changes may be classified into three types:

(1) temporary worsening of working conditions;
(2) flexibilization of working time;
(3) short-time provisions.

The law provides for various procedures to introduce specific solutions. Sometimes they can be introduced only in typical collective agreements. Theoretically, this increases the level of protection and makes the procedure more rigid. More often, the law provides for alternative solutions. The majority of new instruments can be applied via typical or atypical agreements, depending on the social partners' preferences (atypical agreements provide more flexibility). When there are no trade unions, only atypical agreements can be concluded (with employee representatives elected according to the procedures applied by a given employer – on condition that this is allowed).

The worsening of working conditions *sensu stricto* may be achieved by means of three collective agreements:

(1) an agreement suspending the provisions of a typical collective agreement (Article 241^{27} LC);
(2) an agreement suspending the provisions of other autonomous sources of labour law, i.e., atypical collective agreements, internal regulations issued by the employer, and statutes (Article 9^1 LC);
(3) an agreement worsening working conditions arising from individual employment contracts (Article 23^{1a} LC).[19]

The suspension may concern the whole act or a part of it. During the suspension period, the employer does not apply the selected provisions.[20] The change occurs by the virtue of the law. No individual agreements or other legal actions are required.

The agreements can be concluded, if justified by the financial situation of the employer, for a period of up to three years (the conclusion of a successive agreement

---

19. *See* e.g., G. Goździewicz, *Collective Labour Agreements as a Fundamental Tool of Trade Union Operation* in: *Collective Labour Law, supra* n. 9, p. 85. The agreement suspending typical collective agreements can be concluded with trade unions only. Other agreements can be concluded with trade unions and if there are no trade unions with employee representatives elected according to the procedures applied by a given employer.
20. There is also a possibility to suspend some provisions partially. This means, in fact, a partial worsening of an element of the employment relationship.

is not excluded). They are negotiated at company level. However, the social partners may also suspend the provisions of multi-establishment agreements.[21] The agreement modifying individual employment standards refers directly to the conditions arising from employment contracts concluded with individual employees. It can therefore be criticized as a far-reaching interference in the autonomy of the will of the parties to the employment relationship.[22] The subject of the intervention can be all elements of the employment relationship, including pay, working time or additional employee rights (e.g., extra days of annual leave). The most common are provisions influencing remuneration. For example, the social partners suspend the right to premiums, bonuses, extra annual payments or severance allowances. The borderline for the worsening is statutory standards that cannot be modified *in peius*. The worsening of working conditions is not compensated, e.g., from the public funds. On the one hand, the employee bears an important part of the economic risk connected with a given activity. On the other hand, the agreements may contribute to the maintenance of workplaces.

The second important group is provisions of collective agreements leading to working time flexibilization. First, the social partners may extend reference periods for average working time norms (typically forty hours weekly). Regular calculation periods cannot exceed four months. By means of collective agreements, they can be extended to twelve months. Second, the social partners may provide for intermittent work – with a break during the working day that is not calculated as working time. Third, the collective agreements may introduce variable working hours on consecutive days (in two versions). In the first option, it is the employer who fixes the hours of commencing and finishing work. In the second case, the employer determines only the core time while the employee decides when to commence work. It is necessary to add that some other flexible solutions that can be introduced by means of collective agreements had existed before the crisis began (e.g., the possibility to extend working hours up to twelve per day, compensated by shorter working time on other days or by additional days off; or working time calculated by the number of tasks).

Finally, the collective agreements can suspend the employment relationship or shorten working hours (entailing a decrease in remuneration). When the conditions determined in the anti-crisis laws are met, there is a possibility for a partial compensation of the remuneration lost by the employee. This is paid by the employer but also from public funds. Moreover, public institutions may participate in financing professional training for workers affected by lay-offs or short-time work.[23] The anti-crisis instruments have been used on a very limited scale. Currently, due to the improvement in the labour market, public support is, as a rule, suspended; however, the legal mechanism is still present in the system.

---

21. In the latter case, the social partners suspend the collective agreement only in a part concerning the specific company (establishment), while the agreement as such remains untouched.
22. On the other hand, numerous employers are not covered by any collective regulations.
23. The main criterion is the decrease in turnover (by at least 15%). Additional requirements may be added by law.

The last problem is connected with the structure of labour law sources and the possibility of worsening conditions of work and pay that arises from the legislation or collective agreements situated higher in the legal hierarchy. Polish law leaves rather limited space for deviation from statutory standards (*in peius*). The list of legislative provisions that can be modified is closed and concerns only selected matters. During the economic crisis, the list was extended mainly when it came to working time regulations (e.g., longer reference periods). With regard to the structure of collective bargaining, the legislation allows the suspension of multi-establishment collective agreements concluded at a company level. This possibility does not play a particularly important role due to the very limited practical importance of sectoral negotiations. Collective agreements may, as a rule, improve conditions of work and pay (however, they cannot violate the rights of third parties).

§4.06 PARTIES TO THE COLLECTIVE AGREEMENTS AND THE BARGAINING PROCEDURE

The application of the mechanisms described above may be based on various procedures. Usually the anti-crisis or flexible constructions must be agreed with trade unions or (in their absence) with employee representatives elected according to the rules adopted at a given employer. This mechanism applies, *inter alia*, to the suspension of atypical collective agreements and internal regulations issued by the employer; the extension of the reference period and the introduction of flexi-time.

The employer and trade unions may conclude or amend a typical collective agreement following a general procedure regulated by the Labour Code. The economic crisis has not caused any significant changes when it comes to the composition of the parties and the bargaining procedure of typical collective agreements. As a rule, the collective agreements are negotiated with all the trade unions representing workers for whom an agreement is going to be concluded. If the trade unions cannot achieve a consensus, the bargaining procedure may be conducted if there is at least one representative organization on the trade union side (i.e., the trade unions with the strongest support).[24] Finally, the agreement must be signed by all the representative organizations that participated in the negotiations. The social partners may also opt for an atypical collective agreement, and do so more often due to the less formalized procedure involved. Such agreements are concluded with all trade unions or at least with those organizations that are deemed representative. No registration of the agreement is required.

In numerous sectors and companies, negotiations with trade unions are non-existent. To support employers affected by economic difficulties, the legislation allows for the engagement of elected representatives. When there are no trade unions in a

---

24. The criterion of representativeness at an establishment level is met by an organization that unites 7% or 10% of employees engaged by a given employer. The 7% criterion applies to trade unions that are represented in the Social Dialogue Council (the largest organization at national level). If none of the organizations meets these requirements, the organization uniting the largest number of employees is considered to be representative (Article 241^{25a} LC).

given company, atypical collective agreements can be concluded with representatives chosen according to the procedures adopted at a given employer (ad hoc representatives). In recent years, the law has enlarged the scope of matters that can be regulated by this type of agreement. Although the competences of these bodies are relatively broad, the law neither regulates the election procedure nor guarantees any protection against dismissals or other actions undertaken by the employer (representatives are covered only by general anti-discriminatory rules).[25] Paradoxically, works councils, though bodies of stable structure with strong legal protection for their members, are excluded from the bargaining procedure unless they obtain the workers' authorization (according to the procedure used in a given company to elect ad hoc representatives). As a result, the balance between social partners is not guaranteed.

In some cases, the legislation introduces a higher standard of protection and requires specific solutions to be agreed with trade unions only. Concerning the suspension of typical collective agreements, company-level agreements are suspended by their parties while multi-establishment agreements are suspended with trade unions entitled to participate in collective negotiations.

§4.07 CONCLUSIONS

The crisis enveloping the Polish economy and labour market must be seen in a broader perspective, spanning the years 2001-2017. Without doubt, it has caused significant changes in the structure and content of collective agreements. However, the changes reflect some specific features of the social dialogue in Poland, especially a significant decline in unionization and the breakdown of collective negotiations over recent years. As a result, anti-crisis instruments and flexitime solutions may be introduced by means of not only typical agreements, but also atypical ones negotiated in a special, less formalized procedure. Moreover, the majority of them can also be adopted in cooperation with elected representatives when there are no trade unions. Without doubt, the crisis fostered the development of elected bodies and the enlargement of their competences. This is, however, a dubious development because the position of elected representatives is very unstable and thus threatens the balance between the social partners. In most cases, the elected bodies are involved mainly to introduce solutions advantageous for the employers.

As regards the content of collective agreements since the beginning of the 2000s, the Polish legislature has adopted a number of legal instruments and mechanisms to overcome economic difficulties and to flexibilize the process of work. The social partners may temporarily worsen the working conditions as well as flexibilize the organization of working time. They could also introduce various forms of short-time work (temporarily suspended). The practical use of respective solutions is, however, diversified. The most popular are provisions leading to the flexibilization of working time. The social partners also make use of the possibility to suspend collective

---

25. The labour law doctrine proposes to introduce at least some election and protective standards (A. Sobczyk, *Non-Union Forms of Representation within the Collective Employee Representation System – Current Situation and Trends* in: *Collective Labour Law*, 60 Studia Iuridica 218 (2015).

agreements or internal regulations issued by the employer, while short-time work has not played any important role. The law still significantly limits the freedom of social partners.

Although the scope and nature of changes concerning collective agreements is significant, their real influence over social relationships remains very weak (in some sense symbolized by the very limited coverage of the agreements). Social dialogue in Poland is undergoing a very deep crisis. As a result, the main task for both the social partners and legislation is to reconstruct the system of collective negotiations. Without further changes, collective agreements cannot serve as an important, authentic instrument of social dialogue able to reconcile the needs of employers and workers.

CHAPTER 5
Collective Bargaining in Romania: The Aftermath of an Earthquake

Felicia Rosioru

The legislative changes adopted in the context of the economic crisis were similar to an earthquake of the social dialogue in Romania: everything was paralyzed and the victims needed time in order to recover. The measures have seek to decentralize collective bargaining but, at the same time, trade unions were weakened at company level by the adoption of new representativeness criteria, among other measures. Trade unions had to gather significantly more members and to address the courts in order to be recognized as social partners according to the new representativeness criteria; sectoral level collective bargaining was put on 'hold' for about half a year (as the Government has delayed the establishment of the relevant sectors) and, at the same time, seriously undermined, because of the new representativeness criteria, as well as of the changes in the effects of collective agreements concluded at this level. The reform of the social dialogue system in Romania was adopted having as pretext the economic crisis, but in reality they were not contingent by nature, but have been designed to become permanent features of the labour market. In this paper, we shall focus mainly on the effects of the legislative changes, linking them with the social-economic context and the historical background, as they play an important role when assessing the importance of the social dialogue system's reform.

The economic crisis has struck the European countries in different ways,[1] but the key-word of the industrial relations' reform adopted in this context was 'collective bargaining decentralisation', with new possibilities of opting-out or *in pejus* derogation at enterprise level. Sometimes decentralization was adopted by way of collective bargaining, by the social partners themselves; in other cases, opting-out possibilities

---

1. S. Laulom, E. Mazuyer, C. Escande Varniol (sous la direction de), *Quel droit social dans une Europe en crise?*, (Bruxelles: Larcier 2012).

were seen as ways of proving the social partners' capacity to manage the effects of the economic crisis.

Collective bargaining and social dialogue in general were seen as one of the means to circumvent the effects of the economic crisis, offering 'custom fit' solutions, adapted to the particular situation of a certain company and of a certain country. As a response to the crisis, the legislation adopted in many EU Member States has changed the way of adopting collectively bargained rules, establishing a different hierarchy of the sources of social (labour) law and new representativeness criteria that have to be met by the trade unions in order to render the outcome of collective bargaining more 'legitimate', and Romania was a part of the trend. The pretext was the economic crisis, and 'calling something a crisis means to frame an issue as an urgent, structural threat'; since the threat is structural, an alternative, urgent course of action seems to be necessary in order to avert the danger.[2]

As 'crisis seems to be everywhere',[3] the economic crisis turned out to be a crisis in law and institutions.[4] Romania didn't make an exception and the regulatory framework of the social dialogue constructed at national level was dismantled in this context. The legislative intervention was brutal, without involving the social partners and it has ruined the social dialogue and the system the social partners have managed to build in two decades, after the fall of the communism. Decentralization of collective bargaining to the lowest level has weakened the social acquis achieved so far by the trade unions at national and local level and affected sectoral collective bargaining. It has also lowered the standard of rights recognized so far, anchored in higher level collective agreements.

§5.01 ONCE UPON A TIME ... GENERAL TRENDS IN THE EVOLUTION OF THE COLLECTIVE BARGAINING SYSTEM IN ROMANIA

At the moment when eight new Member States in Central and Eastern Europe have joined the European Union (May 2004), the industrial relations in this group of post-socialist countries (including Bulgaria and Romania, who have joined later) were seen to have many important things in common, such as the predominance of decentralized wage bargaining.[5] However, until 2011, 'decentralisation' was not the key word for the Romanian collective bargaining system.[6]

---

2. L. Henderson, *What It Means to Say 'Crisis' in Politics and Law*, (2014) http://www.e-ir.info/2014/03/05/what-it-means-to-say-crisis-in-politics-and-law/ (accessed 17 March 2016).
3. *Ibid.*
4. A. Supiot, *A Legal Perspective on the Economic Crisis of 2008*, 149 International Labour Review 151, 153 (2010).
5. L. Funk, H. Lesch, *Industrial Relations in Central and Eastern Europe – Organisational Characteristics, Codetermination and Labour Disputes*, Intereconomics 264 (2004).
6. Al Athanasiu, L. Dima, *Dreptul muncii*, 284-287 (All Beck 2005); I. T. Ştefănescu, *Tratat teoretic şi practic de drept al muncii*, 168-172 (2nd ed., Universul Juridic 2012); Al. Ţiclea, *Tratat de dreptul muncii*, 316-325 (2nd ed., Universul Juridic 2007); M. Ţichindelean, *Dreptul colectiv al muncii*, 142-144 (Universul Juridic 2015); C.-A. Moarcăş Costea, *Dreptul colectiv al muncii*, 200-202 (C.H. Beck 2012).

The historical background shows that there were *two contradictory trends* in the evolution of the collective bargaining system in Romania during the last twenty years. *The first trend* (1991-2011), aiming to encourage social dialogue in general, collective bargaining in particular, has, up to a certain extent, a historical explanation. It was manifested after forty years of communism, when collective bargaining was rather formal and ineffective. As a result, in Romania collective bargaining was rendered compulsory, but only at company level in companies with a workforce of at least twenty-one employees (i.e., more than 24,000 companies). This trend was manifested in the context of relatively high trade-union density (similar to the unweighted average for the EU fifteen Member States), but also of structural changes in the economy, involving a high rate of company closures and company start-ups.[7]

The second trend (since 2011) aimed to 'discourage' collective bargaining, without being expressly linked to the economic crisis, but using its effect and the socio-economic context created during the crisis. Legislative measures were adopted in order to decentralize collective bargaining, seen as one of the ways to reduce the effects of the crisis, by reducing the pressure in wage-setting at company level. However, collective bargaining was 'hit' in several ways, as decentralization was combined with a higher percentage of trade union membership required in order to meet the representativeness criteria at company level and a limitation of the *erga omnes* effects of sectoral level collective agreements.

In the first part of our paper we shall highlight some aspects of the historical background that explain some of the features of collective bargaining in Romania.

[A] Collective Bargaining During the Communist Regime

The first trend was a natural reaction after the fall of communism, as in Romania, during the communist regime (1947-1989) trade union membership and collective bargaining were rather formal. All the employees were trade union members and, formally, trade union representatives were involved in decision making at undertaking level; in reality, undertakings were integrated in a centralized system and the most important decisions were taken at central level.

Trade unions were important during the communist regime, for ideological reasons. From this perspective, communism aims to replace private property and a profit-based economy with public ownership and communal control of the major means of production and the natural resources of a society. The property belonged to what we usually call the State (even if the communist doctrine says that there is no state, but a community of interests of the working class or the proletariat), who served for the well-being of the working class. Thus, as undertakings were integrated in the centralized system, formally there weren't any antagonist interests between the workers and the undertaking's representatives, as undertakings themselves served for

---

7. Funk, Lesch, *supra* n. 5, at 264.

the well-being of the working-class.[8] Collective agreements were mandatory in every state-owned company, but they have contained general, impersonal provisions, linked to the 'superior organization of work' and to the achievement of the economic goals of the 'plan' established at central level. Collective agreements were signed by the employer and the representatives of the trade union, but they had to be previously approved by the general assembly of the employees.

On the one hand, trade unions were involved to some extent in the distribution of benefits to the workforce;[9] on the other hand, during the communist regime, trade unions had stopped playing their traditional role, linked to collective bargaining and collective action. This historical background is also useful to explain why today there is a certain lack of confidence on behalf of the workers concerning the power of social dialogue and the minimization of the role of trade unions and collective bargaining.

[B] Legislative Overview of the Industrial Relations in the Democratic, Post-communist Regime

After the fall of the communist regime, two laws – adopted in 1991 and 2003, aimed at reviving pre-communist trade union traditions: collective bargaining was (and still is) mandatory in companies with a workforce of at least twenty-one employees. There was an annual obligation (that has disappeared after the reform of social dialogue) to periodically re-negotiate wages, working conditions, working time and schedules. The employer had and still has the obligation, according to the law, to start the negotiation process; in case that he fails to do so, a formal request can be addressed by the representative trade union or by the workers' elected representatives (if there isn't any representative trade union in the company, according to the legal criteria).

In 1996, Law no. 130 on Collective Agreements was adopted; thus, these agreements have regained their traditional functions. The Law on Collective Agreements has chosen to continue the tradition initiated by their first Romanian regulation, contained in a law of German inspiration, adopted in 1929.[10] Collective disputes and the ways for their resolution, including collective action, were strictly regulated by a law adopted in 1999 (Law no. 168 on Labour Disputes' Resolution), repealing a previous law adopted in 1991.

During the last decade there has been *a major reform* of social dialogue in Romania. Law no. 62/2011 on Social Dialogue has regrouped five existing laws, elaborated in different social-economic contexts: Law no. 130/1996 on Collective

---

8. In this context, collective agreements were seen to be 'essentially different' than the ones concluded in 'capitalist countries', where collective agreements were 'the legal tool (...) to fight against exploitation' – S. Ghimpu, I. T. Ştefănescu, Ş. Beligrădeanu, Gh. Mohanu, *Dreptul muncii. Tratat*, vol. I, 107 (Editura ştiinţifică şi Enciclopedică 1977).
9. Trade unions were involved in allocating resources to providing workers with holidays for themselves and their families, housing, and money when they had particular needs – R. Croucher, M. Rizov, *Union Influence in Post-socialist Europe*, 65 ILR Review 630-650 (2012) http://digitalcommons.ilr.cornell.edu/ilrreview/vol65/iss3/7/ (accessed 20 March 2017).
10. J. Moscovici, *Lege asupra contractelor de muncă*, 217-228 (Socec & Co S.A 1937); Tichindelean, *supra* n. 6, at 18.

Agreements; Law no. 109/1997 on the Organisation and the Functioning of the Economic and Social Council; Law no. 168/1999 on Labour Disputes' Resolution; Law no. 356/2001 on the Employers' Associations; Law no. 54/2003 on the Organisation and the Functioning of Trade Unions. The law on social dialogue (n° 62/2011) has also regrouped the previous legislation on the functioning of social dialogue committees organized at central and local level in the public administration authorities.

Before this major legislative change (2011), and the laws replaced by the new regulation (1996-2003), the collective bargaining system was regulated by different laws adopted in 1991,[11] after the fall of communism and the change of the political regime, but in the context of a Labour Code adopted during the communist regime (Law no. 10/1972), which was in force until February 2003.

Since 2011 there was no significant change in the collective bargaining system in Romania. However, only as a statement, in the 2011-2013 National Reform Programme, the Romanian Government considered, among the measures to achieve Euro Plus Pact[12] and to boost employment, the need to strengthen social dialogue and to render flexible the system of collective labour agreement, as well as the need to reform the legislation on social dialogue.

§5.02 SOCIAL DIALOGUE REFORM AND THE REASONS BEHIND IT

The most obvious change brought by the labour law reform (2011) consists in the decentralization of collective bargaining, giving a more prominent role to enterprise bargaining compared to sectoral or group of undertaking bargaining. Decentralization by itself might not have been such a bad idea, but the changes adopted in the field of social dialogue were in reality much more complex, as: the national collective agreement has been abolished in favour of sectoral collective agreements, but, at the same time, sectoral level collective bargaining was seriously undermined; there is no longer a compulsory agenda for negotiations; and new company level representativeness criteria were adopted for trade unions. Collective bargaining still is mandatory in companies with a workforce of at least twenty-one employees and the employer is bound to start the negotiation process.

In reality, collective bargaining was seriously undermined, as trade unions themselves were severely hit. The decentralization of collective bargaining was associated with new *representativeness criteria for the trade unions* (having to have as members more than a half of the total number of employees at company level,[13]

---

11. Law no. 13/1991 on Collective Agreements, Law no. 15/1991 on Labour Disputes Resolution, Law no. 54/1991 on the Organisation and the Functioning of Trade Unions; Governmental Decision no. 503/1991 on the Organisation and the Functioning of the Employers' Associations.
12. Even though the Pact is addressed to Member States of the EUR zone, Romania has decided to join.
13. In Romania, the existence of company level trade union is strictly related to a legal person: for setting up a trade union, at least fifteen people working for the same employer are required, whereas previously, fifteen persons working in the same branch or profession, albeit in different companies, were enough. However, 90% of Romanian companies have only nine workers or fewer and a person may only belong to one trade union at the same time. According to the ILO,

compared to the previous representativeness criteria of more than a third of the total number of the employees).[14] In addition, a collective agreement can be registered at sectoral level, producing *erga omnes* effects, only if the signatory employers' associations have as employees more than a half of the total number in that sector. If this condition is fulfilled, the collective agreement may be extended to the whole sector, on the signatory parties' demand, by decision of the Labour minister, with the approval of the National Tripartite Council.

The legislative measures were accompanied by practical impediments, as trade unions were obliged to get their company level representativeness (according to the new criteria) recognized by the courts. In addition, the shift from branch level to sectoral level company agreements – and the possibility to conclude such agreements – were delayed by the fact that the sectors defined by the Law on social dialogue (entered into force on May 2011) were established by Decision by the Romanian Government only in December 2011.[15]

As a result, even if collective agreements could, in theory, be concluded at sectoral, group of undertakings or company level, in reality, because of all the legislative changes, including the reform of the representativeness criteria, company level collective bargaining has become the usual level of collective bargaining.

[A] The Reasons Behind the Legislative Reform

The declared purpose of the 2011 legislative change was of a 'noble' and neutral nature: the need to unify terminology, the legal and procedural aspects related to social dialogue in general, to collective bargaining in particular, as the existing legal framework[16] was mainly adopted in the context of the former, 'communist' Labour Code (Law no. 10/1972).[17] The law was considered to 'ensure the efficiency of collective bargaining, as a result of the clarification of the representativeness criteria of the social partners, of collective agreements coverage and the implication of civil society in the settlement of social-economic problems'.

The new Law no. 62/2011 on social dialogue, reforming the existing collective bargaining system, was adopted without a direct or express link to the economic and financial crisis. However, in the National Reform Programme (2011-2013),[18] the

---

while a minimum membership requirement is not in itself incompatible with Convention No. 87, the Committee on Freedom of Association has stated that the number should be fixed in a reasonable manner so that the establishment of organizations is not hindered; the proportion of small enterprises in the country should be taken into account, with a view to ensuring that it will not hinder the establishment of unions in an important segment of enterprises – ILO (2011) Memorandum of Technical Comments on the draft Labour Code and the Draft Law on Social Dialogue of Romania, Geneva, 17 January 2011.

14. The unionization rate was approximately 24% in 2008.
15. The Governmental decision, establishing twenty-nine sectors, was published only on the 29 December 2011.
16. The laws mentioned *supra* n. 11, except for the law on the organization and the functioning of trade unions (Law no. 54/2003).
17. The new Labour Code was adopted in Romania in 2003 (Law no. 53/2003).
18. http://ec.europa.eu/europe2020/pdf/nrp/nrp_romania_en.pdf (accessed on 2 February 2017).

Romanian Government had admitted that the Social Dialogue Act would be promoted 'according to the commitments undertaken by Romania under the Stand-by arrangement concluded with International Monetary Fund (IMF), in order to render more flexible the system of collective labour agreement and to strengthen the social dialogue'. The industrial relations' reform indented to extend the dialogue structures at regional level, with the declared purpose of a better management of the problems; to increase the autonomy of the social partners in the negotiation process; and 'to remove the rigidities existing in the labour relations and in the wage setting in the private sector', in order to render more flexible the system of wage setting and the settlement of labour disputes.

There wasn't any official European recommendation directly addressing collective bargaining structures. There is only one statement of the Romanian Government concerning collective bargaining, in the Memorandum of Understanding signed on 29 June 2011, in the sense that: *'the Romanian Government will seek with the relevant stakeholders how to rationalize wage bargaining in the private sector'* (emphasis added).[19] However, this statement was made after the law reforming the social dialogue system was adopted (10 May 2011) and, since then, Law no. 62/2011 on social dialogue did not undergo major reforms.

There weren't any 'secret' letters either, but, as an illustration of the fact that the legal answers to the economic crisis were not contingent by nature, most of the reforms have been designed and enacted in such a way as to become permanent features of the labour market, neither the change of the political orientation of the Government, nor the relative economic stability let to the elimination of the collective bargaining decentralization tendency, initiated in 2011. Furthermore, as the Romanian Government intended to amend Law no. 62/2011 on social dialogue, in a document entitled 'Joint Comments of European Commission and International Monetary Fund (IMF) Staff on the Draft Emergency Ordinance to Amend Law 62/2011 on Social Dialogue (12 October 2012)', the Commission and the IMF have 'strongly' urged the authorities 'to

---

19. Memorandum of Understanding, signed on June 2011, p. 5. On the 6 May 2009, the Council adopted a Decision (2009/459/EC) to make available to Romania medium-term financial assistance for a period of three years. The accompanying Memorandum of Understanding, signed on 23 June 2009, and its successive supplements have settled the economic policy conditions on the basis of which the financial assistance was disbursed. The structural reform measures required by the European Community referred mainly to the need to tackle undeclared work, the establishment of a unified, simplified pay scale, through the elimination of the large majority of bonuses or rolling them in the base wage and the reform of the pensions systems. Romania has successfully implemented the programme, but, given remaining structural weaknesses in Romania's labour markets, the Council adopted a Decision (2011/288/EU) to make precautionary medium-term financial assistance available to Romania for a period of three years (http://ec.europa.eu/europe2020/pdf/recommendations_2011/csr_romania_en.pdf, (accessed 5 December 2016). The new accompanying Memorandum of Understanding was signed on 28 June 2011 and one of the conditions for financial assistance conceited in the Romanian Government's obligation to continue the reform of the labour market through the adaption of the flexicurity principle (especially to widen the situations when the use of fixed-term labour contracts is legally allowed). This Memorandum of Understanding was followed by another one, signed 6 November 2013, for precautionary financial assistance, but the only mention on the labour market reforms concerned the need to equalize the pensionable age between man and women.

limit any amendments to Law 62/2011 to revisions necessary to bring the law into compliance with core International Labour Organization's (ILO) conventions'[20] and manifested their concern about 'loosening procedures in the existing legislation that are intended to avoid the proliferation of strikes'.[21]

[B] Collective Bargaining in the Public Sector

The regulation of collective bargaining in the public sector was also partly integrated in the new law no. 62/2011 on social dialogue, as in the system financed through public funds there are employees (persons with an employment contract, in the educational or public health system, for example) and civil servants, working in the public authorities and having a special statute (regulated mainly by Law no. 188/1999). For the employees of public sector, the same rules apply as for the other employees,[22] except for the collective bargaining of wages: all the aspects related to the level and the payment of wages are established through legislation and cannot be modified by way of collective bargaining.

Most of the civil servants have the possibility to conclude collective agreements,[23] through representative trade unions or elected representatives, but the scope of such agreements is limited to working time, working conditions, professional training, health and safety at the workplace and protection of the bargaining agents (Law no. 188/1999 on the Statute of Civil Servants and Governmental Decision n° 833/2007 on the Functioning of Joint Committees and the Conclusion of Collective Agreements). The law forbids collective bargaining on wages for civil servants (as well

---

20. This 'behind-the-scenes pressure to halt the restoration of core labour rights' was strongly condemned by the International Trade Union Confederation (ITUC) – ITUC News: *IMF and EC Apply Behind-the-Scenes Pressure on Romania to Halt the Restoration of Core Labour Rights*, ITUC Press release, 21 November 2012, http://www.ituc-csi.org/imf-and-ec-apply-behind-the-scenes.html, (accessed 15 December 2016).
21. The right to strike is strictly regulated and related to collective bargaining; as a result, less social dialogue in practice means that the possibilities to declare a strike are diminished. For example, in 2015, out of 41.976 undertakings having more than 21 employees, only 35 conflicts of interests were registered (compared to only 33 out of 42,645 undertakings in 2016) and there are no clear statistics as to the number of strikes that were subsequently declared (http://www.mmuncii.ro/j33/index.php/ro/transparenta/statistici/buletin-statistic/4391, (accessed 19 March 2017).

    A strike can be declared only in cases of collective labour disputes ('conflicts of interests') that may occur in the following situations: the employer or employers' organization refuses to start the collective bargaining, while not having signed a collective agreement or the previous one having ended; the employer or employers' organization does not accept the claims made by the employees; the parties don't reach an agreement until the date agreed to end the negotiations.

    The negotiation of collective agreement is limited to sixty days, than a collective labour dispute is triggered, after prior registration to the local labour inspectorate (for company level disputes) or the Ministry of Labour (for group of undertakings and sectoral level disputes), followed by a mandatory dispute resolution mechanism (called conciliation); a strike may be declared only afterwards. For example, in 2015, out of the thirty-five conflicts of interests, nine were solved through conciliation (compared to thirteen out of the thirty-three conflicts in 2016).
22. Law no. 62/2011 is applicable for the conclusion of collective agreements – called 'contracte collective de muncă' for the employees of the public system.
23. For the civil servants, collective agreements are called 'acorduri colective'.

as for employees of the public sector). This rule was considered to be contrary to the International Labour Organization's (ILO) standards and the Government was requested to take all the steps necessary to amend the Act so as to ensure that base salaries, pay increases, allowances, bonuses and other entitlements of public service employees are no longer excluded from the scope of collective negotiations.[24] However, the restriction is still in force.

In addition, collective agreements negotiated by public servants must be concluded at undertaking (local authority) level. This rule appears to restrict collective bargaining in ministries or public institutions and such restriction, according to ILO, is not in compliance with the principle of free and voluntary collective bargaining embodied in Article 4 of Convention No. 98, ratified by Romania.[25] The level of negotiation should not be imposed by law, but it should be left to the discretion of the parties.[26] Consequently, 'public service should be able to enter into a global level negotiation with the Government, e.g., on minimum wage, pension age or entitlements, working hours, etc.'.[27]

§5.03   THE IMPACT OF THE SOCIAL DIALOGUE REFORM: THE AFTERMATH OF THE EARTHQUAKE

The legislative reforms were adopted without huge protests of the workers, as everybody had feared the potential effects of the economic crisis, coming after another important crisis acknowledged by Romania in the 1990s, after the fall of the communist regime.

There was an immediate effect of the reform of social dialogue: the decentralization of collective bargaining, giving a more prominent role to enterprise bargaining compared to sectoral bargaining led, in 2011 (when the social dialogue reform occurred) to a decrease in the number of company level collective agreements.[28]

On a longer term, the reform of social dialogue has led to contradictory effects. On the one hand, there was an increase in the number of collective agreements concluded

---

24. Effect given to the recommendations of the committee and the Governing Body – Report No 370, October 2013, Case No 2611 (Romania) http://www.ilo.org/dyn/normlex/en/f?p = 1000:50002: 0::NO:P50002_COMPLAINT_TEXT_ID,P50002_LANG_CODE:3143904,en:NO, (accessed 17 January 2017).
25. ILO (2011) Memorandum of Technical Comments on the draft Labour Code and the Draft Law on Social Dialogue of Romania, Geneva, 17 January 2011, available at: http://www.araco.org/infutile/infirmatiiue/2011/OIM_IANUARIE2011/Technical%20Memorandum%20Romania%20on%20Draft%20Labour%20Code%20and%20Draft%20Law%20on%20Social%20.pdf, (accessed 20 March 2017) (hereinafter: ILO (2011) Memorandum of Technical Comments).
26. 2006 Digest of decisions and principles of the Freedom of Association Committee of the Governing Body of the ILO, para. 988.
27. ILO (2011) Memorandum of Technical Comments, *supra* n. 25.
28. According to the National Institute of Statistics, 7,473 company level collective agreements were registered in 2011 by the Labour Inspectorates (out of which 4,209 new collective agreements and 3,264 addenda to existing collective agreements), comparing to 2010, when 7,718 company level collective agreements were registered (out of which 4,827 new collective agreements and 2,891 addenda to existing collective agreements).

at company level (according to the National Institute of Statistics).[29] But, in reality, even if the number of company level collective agreement is increasing, *collective bargaining coverage* – that is, the number of employees covered by collective agreements – is considerably lower than it was before the reform operated in 2011, as decentralization has given a more prominent role to enterprise bargaining compared to sectoral bargaining. In Romania, the annual national collective agreement has been abolished in favour of sectoral collective agreements but, at the same time, only a very limited number of sectoral collective agreements were signed. For example, in 2013, 2014 and 2017, only one sectoral collective agreement was signed each year (out of which the collective agreements concluded in 2014 and 2017 were applicable in the public sector and concluded for a year), without any such agreement having been signed in 2015 or 2016.[30]

Thus, on the other hand, one of the persisting effects of the social dialogue reform consists in an important decline in collective bargaining coverage, as employees working in companies with a workforce of less than twenty employees are, most often, totally uncovered.

In addition, because of the new company level representativeness criteria, most of the collective agreements were concluded by elected employees' representatives, deemed to be weaker, less experienced and less informed than the trade unions. The Law on social dialogue has undermined the traditional prerogatives of the trade unions, by replacing in the collective bargaining process non-representative company level trade unions with the elected employees' representatives. If there wasn't any trade union meeting the representativeness criteria at company level, employees' representatives – elected with the votes of more than 50% of the total number of employees in the company– were entitled to negotiate and to conclude collective agreements at company level. For example, 37% of the employees were represented in 2013 in the negotiation of company level collective agreements by trade unions (representing 8% of the existing companies) and 63% of the employees were represented by elected employee representatives (52% of the existing companies). The situation has led often to very diverse and 'weak' collective agreements, providing for only a limited number of rights.

---

29. In 2015, 8,702 company level collective agreements were registered (out of which 6,300 new collective agreements and 2,402 addenda to existing collective agreements). In 2014, Labour Inspectorates have registered 9,477 company level collective agreements (out of which 6,931 new collective agreements and 2,546 addenda to existing collective agreements); in 2013, 8,726 company level collective agreements were registered (out of which 6,171 new collective agreements and 2,645 addenda to existing collective agreements); in 2012, 8,783 company level collective agreements were registered (out of which 6,859 new collective agreements and 1,924 addenda to existing collective agreements). In 2016 there was an increase in the number of collective agreements concluded at company level – 9,366 – out of which 7,269 new collective agreements and 2,097 addenda to existing collective agreements, 'doubled' by the re-introduction of the representativeness by affiliation of the trade unions.
30. Before the social dialogue reform, the *erga omnes* principle was applicable for any collective agreement, concluded at any level (the national level collective agreement was applicable to all the employees and all the employers in Romania, the sectoral level collective agreement – to all the employees and all the employers in the sector, the company level collective agreement – to all the employees of the company).

Another effect of the social dialogue reform, determined by the vertical hierarchy of agreements, is that the level of rights negotiated at company level is very low, as more often there isn't any higher level collective agreement (basically, collective bargaining starts from the level of rights provided by the labour legislation). When a collective agreement is concluded, statutory employees' rights have a minimal character. Thus, collective agreements may not contain provisions setting an inferior level of rights than the one established by law and by the applicable collective agreement concluded at a higher level. The law of 2011 reforming social dialogue is not allowing lower-level bargaining outcomes to deviate unfavourably from the protection provided by a higher level collective agreements or statutory legislation. As it was before the adoption of Law no. 62/2011 on Social Dialogue, only derogation *in favorem* applies, only if this results in an *in melius* improvement in the norm, combined with the vertical hierarchy of agreements). Through collective bargaining, employees can only beneficiate of supplementary rights compared to the ones provided by higher level collective agreements (sectoral or group of undertakings level) or statutory legislation.

[A] The Impact of Decentralization of Social Dialogue on Wage-Setting Mechanisms

The decentralization of social dialogue had a significant impact on wage-setting mechanisms in the private sector in Romania. Before the reform operated in May 2011, collective agreements were concluded at national (inter-sector) level, at sectoral level and at company level. Only one collective agreement could have been concluded at each level and it had *erga omnes* effects, covering all the employees at that specific level. At national level collective agreements were always concluded and the rights they provided for had to be respected by all the employers. As a result, all the Romanian employees were covered by collective agreements and had a collectively negotiated level of rights, higher than the statutory minimum level, because of the favourability principle. The *erga omnes* effects of the collective agreements were severely restricted at sectoral level. According to Law no. 62/2011 on social dialogue, sectoral level collective agreements provide rights only for the employees of the undertakings belonging to the signatory parties (to the employers' associations having signed the collective agreement). As a result, one of the easiest ways for employers to 'escape' the legal effects of sectoral level collective agreements is to quit the employers' associations.

The situation has dramatically changed after the Law on social dialogue was adopted in 2011, as the national level collective agreement has disappeared, there wasn't any collective agreement extended at sectoral level since 2011 and company level trade unions were forced to convince more employees to become their members and to get their company level representativeness recognized by courts. Romania was one of the two countries (alongside with Ireland) where the prevalent regime has shifted from multi- to single-employer bargaining. Coordination across sectors was weakened by the fact that the national, cross-sector agreement was abolished in 2011 and wage bargaining has largely moved to the company rather than to the sector level.[31] For the moment being, there is no coordination of wage setting across different sectors.

In this context, the bargaining coverage has decreased with more than 60% since 2008. As a result, only a small proportion of employees are actually covered by a conventional minimum pay, set by the applicable collective agreement.[32] Mainly employees in large or medium-size companies tend to be covered, because of the forced shift to single-employer bargaining,[33] but the great majority of Romanian companies are small and medium companies. Even though in Romania collective bargaining is mandatory for all the undertakings having more than twenty employees, there is a significant number of companies that don't meet this criteria.[34]

According to the Romanian labour legislation, employees are entitled to benefits and extra-pay for overtime working, work in dangerous work-places or involving significant levels of physical or mental effort, night work, as well as to allowances (for domestic or foreign business trips) and other bonuses. The minimum level of such benefits is established by legislation, but higher levels of benefits are often negotiated by the social partners and inserted into the collective agreements. For example, the Romanian Labour Code establishes a minimum premium of 75% of the employee's basic hourly pay for each overtime working hour performed, but higher compensation for overtime working (up to 100% of the employee's hourly wage for each overtime working hour performed) is often negotiated and included in collective agreements. Benefits for a certain length of service or bonuses based on productivity may also be set by the collective agreements; they also often provide for transport, childcare facilities, childbirth or even holiday allowances. However, such benefits and bonuses are often negotiated by strong trade unions, not by the elected workers' representatives, who are employees of the employer they are negotiating with. A relatively recent study[35] shows

---

31. P. Marginson, C. Welz, *Changes to wage-setting mechanisms in the context of the crisis and the EU's new economic governance regime*, 3 (Eurofound 2014), http://www.eurofound.europa.eu/observatories/eurwork/comparative-information/changes-to-wage-setting-mechanisms-in-the-context-of-the-crisis-and-theeus-new-economic-governance (accessed 17 October 2016). The 2011 Social Dialogue Act, enacted by the government without consulting the social partners, abolished the national cross-sector agreement. In fact, this agreement had hitherto provided the point of reference for wage negotiations at lower levels.
32. The collective bargaining coverage rate was estimated to 35% for Romania – J. Visser, S. Hayter, R. Gammarano, *Trends in collective bargaining coverage: stability, erosion or decline?*, Issue Brief no. 1 – Labour Relations and Collective Bargaining 5 (2015), http://www.ilo.org/global/topics/collective-bargaining-labour-relations/publications/WCMS_409422/lang-en/index.htm (accessed 25 October 2016).
33. F. Rosioru, *El salario en Rumania: the myths behind the facts*, 108 Documentacion Laboral 132 (2016).
34. In December 2015, in Romania there were 41,976 such undertakings.
35. PayWell Romania: *Salariile din sectorul privat au crescut în medie cu 4,1% în 2014. Studiul confirmă tendința de scădere a tuturor tipurilor de beneficii extra salariale*, 2014, http://economie.hotnews.ro/stiri-finante_banci-18035723-paywell-romania-salariile-din-sectorul-privat-crescut-medie-4-1-2014-studiul-confirma-tendinta-scadere-tuturor-tipurilor-beneficii-extra-salariale.htm., (accessed 13 October 2016).

a decreasing trend in certain extra salary benefits, such as social benefits and allowances (meal tickets, transport), insurance benefits (life insurance, medical, private pensions' schemes), statute benefits (car, phone) or benefits related to life style (sports and recreation, childcare).

The former national (inter-sectoral) level collective agreement provided for different minimum wages, according to the level of qualifications required in order to perform the job duties (the statutory minimum wage was paid to unskilled workers, whereas highly skilled employees were entitled to a conventional minimum wage of twice the statutory minimum wage). This differentiated collective minimum wage is not of general applicability anymore, but often collective agreements set different minimum wages, according to job complexity or employee skills and qualifications.

As a preliminary conclusion, the reform of social dialogue had major effects in Romania, as besides the significant decrease in the number of Romanian employees covered by collective agreements, in many cases collective wage bargaining was absent or irrelevant, providing for a slightly higher level of wages than the statutory minimum pay and rights. The forced decentralization of collective bargaining and the criteria for the extension procedure introduced in legislation were accompanied with the replacement of the automatic continuation of collective agreements beyond expiry with the requirement of an express agreement between the parties.[36] Even if social partners stipulate clauses providing for collective agreement to continue to have effect beyond the date of expiry, such effect is legally limited to twelve month.[37]

A small step towards recentralization was made in 2014,[38] as two sectoral agreements in the public sector – for the healthcare and veterinary activities sector[39] and for the pre-university education sector[40] – were signed. However, the step towards recentralization is very small, as their provisions apply only to the bodies that have signed the agreements.

[B] Tripartite Institutions

There are several tripartite institutions, playing mostly a consultative role. One of them is the *Economic and Social Council*,[41] a public institution of national interest charged with creating the conditions for a civic dialogue between employers' associations, trade

---

36. A similar condition can be found in Estonia.
37. Such clauses providing for agreements to continue to have effect beyond the date of expiry until a new agreement is concluded can be found in several EU Member States, such as: Austria, Croatia, Denmark, Estonia, Greece, Portugal, Slovakia, Spain and Sweden (Marginson, Welz, *supra* n. 31, at 12).
38. *Developments in working life in Europe 2014*: EurWORK annual review, http://www.eurofound.europa.eu/observatories/eurwork/comparative-information/developments-in-working-lifein-europe-2014-eurwork-annual-review, (accessed 23 October 2016).
39. The collective agreement from 21 November 2013, signed between the Ministry of Health and Sanitas Federation, CNs.SAN.Asist, CNS Cartel Alfa, BNS, CNSLR Frăia and CNS Meridian.
40. The collective agreement from 13 November 2014, signed between the National Federation of Free Unions from Education, FSLI, FSI Spiru Haret and the Ministry of Education.
41. The Economic and Social Council was transformed in an institution of civil dialogue, from a social dialogue institution.

unions, entities of civil society and government. The Economic and Social Council must be consulted on the legislation that is to be adopted in the field of labour law, social protection and wages policy, among others fields of interests.

A Tripartite National Social Dialogue Committee, composed of trade unions and employers' representatives, as well as representatives of the financial and banking industry (the President of the Romanian National Bank, the President of the Economic and Social Committee), was set up by the Law no. 62/2011. This Committee, called now National Tripartite Council for Social Dialogue is coordinated by the Prime Minister, but it only acts in an advisory capacity. This Committee approves the decision to extend a collective agreement for a whole sector of activity and it is the structure where negotiations in order to establish the minimum wage take place. The National Tripartite Council for Social Dialogue is legally empowered now to establish the sectors where the collective bargaining might take place.

In addition, Law no. 62/2011 on social dialogue settles the functioning of social dialogue committees organized at central and local level in the public administration authorities, which play an important role in the tripartite dialogue.

There was dissatisfaction among the social partners when the law on social dialogue was adopted, in particular because there were no supporting impact studies for several provisions of the law and comments and observations made by the Economic and Social Council and the ILO[42] were not taken into consideration. In keeping with the spirit of the Tripartite Consultation (International Labour Standards) Convention, 1976 (No. 144), ratified by Romania in 1992, ILO has urged the Government and the relevant workers' and employers' organizations to engage in constructive dialogue on the package of reforms required to mitigate the impact of the financial crisis, which includes but is not restricted to the labour law reform.[43] The 'constructive dialogue' did not take place and the Law on Social Dialogue was adopted by the Government circumventing the normal parliamentary procedure, without any kind of real debate.

§5.04 CONCLUSIONS

The reforms operated in the field of social dialogue has left trade unions unprotected, struggling to regain their representativeness and less concerned about the new topics that arise out of the organization of the labour market, in the context of globalization and use of technology, or about vulnerable categories of workers or 'outsiders'.

The social dialogue reforms have definitely weakened trade union representation and action at all bargaining levels. They have affected the very structure of trade unions as well as their institutional means of protecting and representing workers. The introduction of the elected employees' representatives as a collective bargaining actor has weakened the trade union's existing 'monopole' in the field of collective bargaining and has lowered the quality of social dialogue.

---

42. ILO (2011) Memorandum of Technical Comments *supra* n. 24.
43. *Ibid.*

According to the ILO, the new representativeness threshold might prove to be difficult to achieve and, as a result, collective bargaining will take place primarily with workers' representatives, undermining unions established within the enterprise, situation which is not in compliance with the promotion of collective bargaining in the sense of Article 4 of Convention No. 98, nor with the Workers' Representatives Convention, 1971 (No. 135), and the Collective Bargaining Convention, 1981 (No. 154), ratified by Romania.[44]

Collective bargaining and collective agreements in Romania focus on the 'insiders', on the employees, without effectively ameliorating the situation of young workers or of the 'outsiders'. Because of the representativeness criteria set by the law, at least at company level, as trade unions represent the majority of the employees, they are mainly concerned with the protection of the interests of this majority.[45] According to ILO, the narrow definition of 'worker' which gives right to collective bargaining, according to Law no. 62/2011, 'will not capture the variety of emerging patterns of work organization through which services or goods are being produced in Romania. In some of these new work arrangements, it is increasingly difficult to establish whether or not an employment relationship exists between the parties based on the sole criteria that the work is performed under the authority of the employer. This is particularly the case where workers perform their duties with great autonomy, where the respective rights and obligations of the parties concerned are not clear, or where there has been an attempt to disguise the employment relationship by not establishing a contract of employment'.[46]

In the great majority of the cases collective bargaining doesn't contribute to the search for solutions to the issues of complex organizations. In extremely rare cases, the employer voluntarily takes the obligation, through collective agreement, not to have recourse to subcontracting companies. Transnational collective agreements are recognized in the Romanian law as the expression of a private contract that is binding only to the signatory parties. The implementation of these agreements is generally based on the parties' responsible commitment to apply the content of the agreement. There have been many transnational collective agreements applied in undertakings in Romania, but their effectiveness depends on the will of the employer.

Decentralization of collective bargaining to the lowest level has lowered the standard of rights recognized so far, anchored in higher level collective agreements. On the other hand, collective bargaining in Romania doesn't substantially contribute to the search for solutions to youth and/or senior unemployment, to precarious situation of 'outsiders', 'para-subordinate' workers or independent workers, nor for the issues of complex organizations.

---

44. *Ibid.*
45. According to the European Commission's Recommendation for a Council Recommendation on the 2015 National Reform Programme of Romania and delivering a Council opinion on the 2015 Convergence Programme of Romania (Brussels, 13.5.2015, COM(2015) 272 final), while some improvements were seen in 2014, employment and activity rates continue to be especially low among women, young people, older workers and Roma.
46. ILO (2011) Memorandum of Technical Comments *supra* n. 25.

As a reaction to the proposed legislative change, in September 2011, Romania's five trade union confederations – Cartel Alfa, BNS, CLSR-FRatia, the Democratic Trade Union Confederation of Romania and the Meridian National Trade Union Confederation – and some employers' organizations (Conpirom, the National Union of Romanian Employers and UGIR-1903) joined forces and signed a memorandum of understanding calling on the centre-right government to revive social dialogue as soon as possible in order, notably, to discuss concrete measures to prevent a possible new economic crisis. At the end of October 2011, Patrorom – an umbrella for four employers' associations: Conpirom, UGIT-1903, UGIR-1903 (Romanian employers) and the National Union of Romanian Employers – signed a social agreement with five trade union confederations (Cartel Alfa, BNS, CLSR-FRATIA, the Confederation of Democratic Unions of Romania and the Meridian National Union Confederation). This agreement lays down the foundations for bilateral cooperation (whereby they recognize each other in their respective capacity as social partner) and the rules for tripartite social dialogue. Thus, the text provides that collective agreements will be negotiated outside the framework of tripartite dialogue provided for in the Social Dialogue Act and will apply to all businesses whose representatives have signed this agreement. The signatory employers and unions have also decided to leave the Social and Economic Council until the government replaces its representatives with civil society representatives, as provided for in the new Law on Social Dialogue.[47]

However, at company level, trade unions are competing with each other, in order to gain new members and to be recognized as representative, rather than to join forces and effectively protect the essential elements of the employment relationship.

A sufficient membership base, organizational capacity to negotiate, legal recognition and the workers' confidence in the trade union are considered to be key-preconditions 'for a strong and functional social dialogue'.[48] The reform of social dialogue in Romania has left the trade unions confused, struggling to regain their traditional role, too 'busy' and unable to change their representation model and to develop new strategies in order to attract new members. At the same time, trade unions are fragmented, incapable – in the great majority of situations – to join forces in order to be stronger and more effective. To conclude the same way we have started this paper, the victims of the earthquake are recovering, but they are still confused and their convalescence is longer and more painful than it was expected... .

---

47. http://www.etui.org/Publications2/Working-Papers/The-crisis-and-national-labour-law-reforms-a-mapping-exercise (accessed 15 March 2017).
48. *Collective Bargaining in Europe in the 21st Century*, 11 (Eurofound 2015).

CHAPTER 6
The Importance of Sectoral Collective Bargaining in Austria

Elisabeth Brameshuber

§6.01 INTRODUCTION

Compared with other countries,[1] the Austrian labour law (relations) system has proved quite stable over the past decades and especially during the economic crisis. As a result, there were no major systematic changes or amendments to the Austrian labour law system in general or to the system of collective bargaining in particular.[2] One might therefore ask whether the Austrian system of collective bargaining is a 'miracle cure' for the erosion of collective labour relations. In other words, is the Austrian example a 'best practice model' that could be implemented in other countries as well? The aim of this paper is to demonstrate primarily why collective bargaining at sectoral level is so important in Austria. Therefore, §6.02 focuses on the functions of sectoral collective bargaining. Reference to current data and examples highlights that despite not having a national statutory minimum wage, there are no employment relationships with a minimum wage of less than EUR 1,000/month[3] and that currently, the vast majority of employment relationships in Austria are even covered by a minimum wage of at least

---

1. *See* the reports regarding Spain or Portugal in this volume, or the recent systematic change in German labour law, where a national statutory minimum wage was introduced in 2015.
2. *See* Franz Marhold, Klaus Poier, Paula Aschauer, Elisabeth Kohlbacher, Manuel P. Neubauer & Lisa Wewerka, *Austria*, in Marie-Cécile Escande Varniol, Sylvaine Laulom & Emmanuelle Mazuyer (eds), *Quel droit social dans une Europe en crise?* 89 et seq. (Bruxelles: Larcier 2012), which shows that apart from some minor legislative changes regarding part time employment, short-time work and educational leave, no amendments were made to the labour law system.
3. *See* the respective agreement between the leading social partners, the Austrian Economic Chambers and the Austrian trade union federation, dating from 2007, http://wko.at/bstv/Mindestlohngrundsatzvereinbarung.pdf (13 February 2017); http://www.ots.at/presseaussendung/OTS_20070702_OTS0138/hundstorfer-und-leitl-unterzeichnen-sozialpartner-vereinbarung-ueber-1000-euro-mindestlohn (13 February 2017).

EUR 1,500/month.[4] From 2020 onwards, a minimum wage of at least EUR 1,500/month shall be applicable to all employees covered by collective bargaining agreements.[5] But how does it work from a systematic legal point of view? In §6.03 we explore the functioning of the system of sectoral collective bargaining. Referring not only to the hard-law legal provisions but also to practice carried out over the past decades, it is argued that only because of that very complex system of normative rules in combination with the de-facto practices, no erosion has taken place. However, as shown in §6.04, in the event of one of these systemic elements being abolished, the whole system as we know it today would collapse. The caveat when considering whether the Austrian system or one of its components could serve as best practice model therefore lies in the fact that only the system as a whole can guarantee (relative) stability in the labour relations system.

§6.02 SECTORAL COLLECTIVE BARGAINING AS STABILISER

When referring to sectoral collective bargaining as stabiliser, one cannot avoid digging a little in the history of Austrian labour relations. When the Austrian Constitution was adopted in 1920, collective bargaining agreements already existed and their application was widespread.[6] Thus, it can be safely argued that there has been a longstanding practice leading to a common consensus between both political parties and economic players that there is no necessity for statutory national minimum wages.[7] This is displayed by the recent agreement concluded in June 2017 between the presidents of the social partners – Trade Union Federation, Economic Chambers, Chambers of Labour and Agricultural Chambers – to establish a minimum wage of EUR 1,500 in all collective bargaining agreements for all full-time employees until 2020.[8] However, this agreement was concluded under pressure of the government only, because the latter

---

4. http://diepresse.com/home/wirtschaft/economist/4793068/Gewerkschaft-will-1700-Euro-Mindestlohn (13 February 2017). Apparently, currently about 211,000 employees earn less than EUR 1,500,-/month, http://www.salzburg.com/nachrichten/rubriken/bestestellen/karriere-nachrichten/sn/artikel/211000-verdienen-weniger-als-1500-euro-im-monat-82703/ (13 February 2017).
5. http://www.proge.at/servlet/ContentServer?pagename = P01/Page/Index&n = P01_0.a&cid = 14 98701612051 (28 September 2017).
6. Franz Marhold & Michael Friedrich, *Österreichisches Arbeitsrecht*, 455 et seq. (3rd ed., Verlag Österreich 2016). *See* for the similar development in Germany and thus generally speaking, respectively, Volker Rieble, *Arbeitsmarkt und Wettbewerb*, §1122 (Springer 1996).
7. *See* the recent Eurofound-data on statutory minimum wages in the EU 2017 that shows that in twenty-two out of twenty-eight Member States, a generally applicable statutory minimum wage exists. Besides Austria, there is no general statutory minimum wage in Cyprus, Denmark, Finland, Italy and Sweden, although in the last four of these countries, the minimum wage level is de facto set in (sectoral) collective bargaining agreements; https://www.eurofound.europa.eu/observatories/eurwork/articles/statutory-minimum-wages-in-the-eu-2017?utm_campaign = Minimum + Wage + 2017&utm_medium = bitly&utm_source = CRM (accessed 13 February 2017).
8. http://www.proge.at/servlet/ContentServer?pagename = P01/Page/Index&n = P01_0.a&cid = 14 98701612051 (28 September 2017). N.B. that already in 2007, the collective partners concluded a general collective bargaining agreement applicable to all sectors of industry providing for a minimum wage of EUR 1,000. Thus, currently no employee working on a full-time basis earns less than EUR 1,000, http://diepresse.com/home/innenpolitik/5163384/Mindestlohn-wird-Hae rtetest-fuer-die-Sozialpartner?from = suche.intern.portal (accessed 2 February 2017).

had envisaged adopting a statutory national minimum wage in the case where the social partners would not agree upon such a minimum standard.[9]

Of course, sectoral collective bargaining agreements provide not only for minimum wages but also for standard employment conditions in other crucial areas, such as the length of notice periods for terminations. Yet, cartelisation of working conditions is not the only function sectoral collective bargaining agreements in Austria fulfil.[10] The particularity of the Austrian system lies in further functions, and although these are – at least in some way – also acknowledged as general functions of collective bargaining systems,[11] the Austrian labour relations system provides for a quite strong shaping of them.

[A] Functions

Generally speaking, collective bargaining agreements are supposed to guarantee just and fair employment conditions, provided that the bargaining parties are – to a certain extent – 'socially powerful'.[12] This is particularly true when comparing collectively bargained employment conditions with those laid down by individual employment contract. From a functional point of view, due to the structurally weaker position of employees, the collective bargaining agreement is deemed the better agreement: it is agreed between two relatively equal parties, so there is no need for any abuse control exercised by the state.[13]

[1] Cartelising Function

One of the functions of sectoral collective bargaining agreements is its cartelising function.[14] The first caveat lies in the fact that this must not be mistaken for a general regulatory function. It is not the purpose of the sectoral collective bargaining agreement to cater for the application of the same employment conditions in all the undertakings of one sector. The cartelising function aims at creating schematic minimum employment conditions in which all employers and employees belonging to one specific sector of industry can trust.[15] Thus, a twofold understanding of this function is necessary. On the one hand, employers legitimately expect their fellow business-owners in the sector to apply at least the employment conditions laid down in the sectoral collective

---

9. Agenda of the Austrian Federal Government 2017/2018, 10, http://archiv.bundeskanzleramt.at/DocView.axd?CobId = 65201 (accessed 2 February 2017).
10. *See* e.g., Franz Marhold & Michael Friedrich, *Österreichisches Arbeitsrecht* 457 et seq. (3rd ed., Verlag Österreich 2016).
11. Cf. for Germany e.g., Abbo Junker, *Arbeitsrecht*, paragraphs 500 et seq. (15th ed. C.H. Beck 2016), and §4a I of the German *Tarifvertragsgesetz*.
12. Günther Löschnigg in Günther Löschnigg (ed.), *AngG* I §6 paragraph 191 (10th ed., ÖGB Verlag 2016).
13. Volker Rieble, *Arbeitsmarkt und Wettbewerb*, paragraph 1211 (Springer 1996).
14. For example Franz Marhold & Michael Friedrich, *Österreichisches Arbeitsrecht*, 458 (3rd ed., Verlag Österreich 2016).
15. Volker Rieble, *Arbeitsmarkt und Wettbewerb*, §§1307 et seq. (Springer 1996).

bargaining agreement.[16] Because deviation from the sectoral collective bargaining agreement in the individual employment contract is only allowed to the employee's advantage in Austria,[17] no employer in the respective sector can adjust their production costs based on wage-cutting or reducing other employment rights provided for in the sectoral collective bargaining agreement. On the other hand, employees cannot dump their colleagues by offering their labour at a cheaper price.

Apart from that very general assessment of the cartelising function of collective bargaining agreements, sectoral bargaining in the Austrian system also leads to a certain kind of market adjustment. Although there is no relevant data available, it is widely acknowledged that wage-setting in a specific sector is not oriented towards the most productive companies in that sector, but rather the most productive of the last third. So if a given sector comprises ninety companies, with company no. 90 the most and company no. 1 the least productive, collectively agreed wages will be oriented towards the productivity of company no. 30. In this way, 'low-performing' companies perish in the long run because they cannot compete with the other companies within their sector.

As we are going to see *infra*, the near 100%[18] coverage rate does provide for a very distinct cartelising function in Austria. Thus, it is hardly surprising that there is no substantive call for a statutory national minimum wage. In addition, the strength of sectoral collective bargaining and its cartelising function strongly relies on the fact that the collective partners at sectoral level may regulate any rights and obligations deriving from the individual employment contract, as long as they do not infringe mandatory statutory provisions.[19]

The distinctness from other systems of sectoral collective bargaining, leading to a very strong formation of the cartelising function, is also depicted by the definition of a sector or a branch. In the Austrian model, a branch is defined according to the production method and not the market-outcome, i.e., the generated products. As we are going to see *infra*, this is strongly related to how businesses are registered, on the one hand, and on the other to their mandatory membership of the Economic Chambers, which are organised according to the production method. However, there is also de facto leeway regarding the setting of wages, even within collective bargaining agreements of very homogeneous sectors, as the following table of minimum wages extracted from the current (valid from 1 May 2017 onwards) collective bargaining agreement for white-collar employees in Hotels and Catering shows:

---

16. Franz Marhold & Michael Friedrich, *Österreichisches Arbeitsrecht*, supra n. 14.
17. See *infra* §6.03.
18. Maxence Brischoux, Anne Jaubertie, Christophe Gouardo, Pierre Lissot, Thomas Lellouch & Arthur Sode, *Mapping out the options for a European minimum wage standard*, 133 Trésor-Economics, 4 (July 2014), www.tresor.economie.gouv.fr/File/402604 (accessed 13 February 2017).
19. Cf. §2 paragraph 1 lit 2 of the Austrian Labour Constitution Act (Arbeitsverfassungsgesetz, ArbVG).

Chapter 6: The Importance of Sectoral Collective Bargaining in Austria   §6.02[A]

Category (First Six Years of Employment)	Vienna	Upper and Lower Austria, Burgenland, Styria, Carinthia	The Tyrol, Salzburg, Vorarlberg
0 (best)	EUR 2,128,00/ 2.250,00 (hotels)	EUR 1,965.00	EUR 2,240.00
5 (worst)	EUR 1,475.00/ 1,460.00 (hotels)	EUR 1,460.00	EUR 1,460.00

Although the Hotel and Catering sector can definitely be described as homogenous in terms of the 'production method', taking into account the productivity level in different regions can be presented as a positive example for flexibility within a rather strict system. Yet this outcome is completely up to the collective partners and not provided for by law.[20]

Another specific phenomenon is the acceptance of so-called *Istlohnklauseln*/guarantee clauses:[21] according to these clauses, which might form part of the sectoral collective agreement, annual pay rises not only apply to the collectively agreed minimum wages in the whole sector, but also to individually agreed overpayments. According to the courts, employer and employee might deviate from these clauses to the employee's disadvantage. Yet if they do not reach an agreement, the overpayment is also adjusted automatically.

Example: the collectively agreed minimum wage in sector A for 2015 is EUR 1,500. The *Istlohnklausel* in the agreement provides that individual overpayments have to be adjusted in the same nominal way as the minimum wage. Employee X gets a monthly payment of EUR 1,700. In 2016, the collective partners agree on a minimum wage of EUR 1,550. Because of the clause, employee X gets EUR 1,750 in 2016.

In this way, the cartelising function of the collective agreement is guaranteed, but at the same time, the *Istlohnklausel* allows for specific circumstances of each undertaking in the sector to be taken into account. Where one employer can afford to pay more than the collectively agreed minimums, the *Istlohnklausel* provides for an automatic guarantee of purchasing power, an important factor regarding employee satisfaction, which also leads to a relatively low level of collective action.

[2]   Peace Function

The importance of sectoral collective bargaining in Austria is also reflected in the strike statistics of recent years.[22] Overall, the strike minutes per employee[23] per year always amounted to less than one minute, with exceptions only in 2003 and 2011.

---

20. Cf. also https://kurier.at/wirtschaft/1500-euro-mindestlohn-in-der-gastronomie/246.389.427 (14 February 2017).
21. *See* for the following Franz Marhold & Michael Friedrich, *Österreichisches Arbeitsrecht, supra* n. 14, pp. 504 et seq.
22. http://wko.at/statistik/Extranet/Langzeit/lang-streiks.pdf (accessed 3 February 2017).
23. In 2015, there were on average 3,609,200 employees in Austria, http://www.statistik.at/web_de/statistiken/menschen_und_gesellschaft/arbeitsmarkt/erwerbstaetige/unselbstaendig_erwerbstaetige/index.html (accessed 7 February 2017).

Year	Participating Employees	Strike Days	Strike Minutes/Employee
2000	19.437	2.947	0.5
2001	0	0	0.0
2002	6.305	9.306	1.4
2003	779.182	.305.466	196.8
2004	30	178	0.0
2005	0	0	0.0
2006	0	0	0.0
2007	0	0	0.0
2008	0	0	0.0
2009	0	0	0.0
2010	0	0	0.0
2011	87.034	56.670	7.9
2012	1.500	563	0.1
2013	5.529	3.277	0.5
2014	5.196	3.309	0.5
2015	-	-	-

Whereas collective bargaining is supposed to contribute to collective peace in general, the Austrian example shows that a strong sectoral collective bargaining system establishes industrial peace most effectively.[24] It strengthens employers' and employees' positions to a much larger extent than bargaining at company level, simply because united employers are more powerful. Employees do not or simply cannot take strike measures against one single employer because of the peace function inherent to the sectoral collective bargaining agreement: as long as the collective agreement is valid, collective action cannot be taken legitimately.

[3] Innovation Function

The third reason why sectoral collective bargaining is so important in Austria is that it is a driver for innovation in the field of labour legislation.[25] Contrary to regular labour legislation that is particularly resistant to modification in Austria, sectoral collective agreements are the ideal arena to test whether modifications to existing rules or new regulations should be adopted. Historical milestones are the forty-hour week and the regulations regarding a mandatory five weeks of holidays. Although these regulations have now been part of general labour legislation for a long time, the collective partners in specific sectoral collective agreements first tested their provisions. Currently,

---

24. Cf. Franz Marhold & Michael Friedrich, *Österreichisches Arbeitsrecht* 457 et seq. (3rd ed., Verlag Österreich 2016).
25. *Ibidem*, p. 458; Christoph Kietaibl, Arbeitsrecht I 195 (9th ed., new academic press 2015).

whereas the federal government cannot come to an agreement regarding more flexible working time arrangements, some sectoral collective bargaining agreements have already established regimes that enable employees to take compensatory time off instead of having their wages adjusted. Thus, sectoral collective bargaining agreements allow for both more flexible bargaining conditions and an opportunity to test new regulations for a limited period, and are therefore driving innovation in the field of labour legislation.

[B]   **Stabiliser in Times of Crisis**

The Austrian system of sectoral collective bargaining and corresponding strength of the collective partners was one main factor in the Austrian economy faring reasonably well during the 2008-2010 crisis. As outlined in the study carried out during the INLACRIS I-project on *'Quel droit social après la crise'*, short-time work arrangements were established within already existing sectoral collective bargaining agreements.[26] In this way, the needs of one specific sector could be addressed without having to wait for the government and eventually Parliament to decide upon any legislative measures. As a result, and because of the flexibility of the sectoral collective bargaining agreements, hardly any legislative amendments were necessary. Thus, sectoral collective bargaining agreements are an important stabilising factor in times of crisis.

This last assessment shows that the Austrian system of sectoral collective bargaining is obviously quite stable and reform-resistant, while at the same time apparently being flexible enough to cope with unpredictable developments. In the following chapter, we are going to explore its legal foundations and look at the legislative as well as at the de facto pillars supporting the system.

§6.03   THE SYSTEM OF SECTORAL COLLECTIVE BARGAINING

The Austrian system of collective labour relations is often considered to be in breach of freedom of association,[27] above all because of the employer's mandatory membership of the Economic Chambers. However, the leading Austrian doctrine is that both the Act on the Economic Chambers and the Austrian Federal Constitution, according to which the Economic Chambers are public associations with public authority,[28] place the

---

26. Franz Marhold, Klaus Poier, Paula Aschauer, Elisabeth Kohlbacher, Manuel P. Neubauer & Lisa Wewerka, *Austria* in Marie-Cécile Escande Varniol, Sylvaine Laulom & Emmanuelle Mazuyer (eds), *Quel droit social dans une Europe en crise?* 95 et seq. (Bruxelles: Larcier 2012).
27. A mandatory membership of the employers' and employees' associations is deemed to be in breach of Article 9 paragraph 3 of the German Basic Law (Grundgesetz, GG), according to which associations must not be established by mandatory membership, but only by members joining them voluntarily, Volker Rieble, *Arbeitsmarkt und Wettbewerb* §1145 (Springer 1996). See also Abbo Junker, *Europäische Grund- und Menschenrechte und das deutsche Arbeitsrecht (unter besonderer Berücksichtigung der Koalitionsfreiheit)*, ZfA 91 (134) (2013) with further references.
28. ECtHR, 30 June 1993, Sigurjónsson./. ISL, Nr 16130/90, paragraph 31.

Economic Chambers beyond the scope of Article 11 ECHR or Article 12 CFR.[29] In addition, employers can always establish and join so-called voluntary business associations (*freiwillige Berufsvereinigungen*) that are also entitled to conclude collective bargaining agreements. The potential conflict between a collective bargaining agreement concluded by the Economic Chambers and an agreement concluded by a voluntary business association is resolved by the Labour Constitution Act (*Arbeitsverfassungsgesetz, ArbVG*). From that moment on, when an agreement concluded by the voluntary business association enters into force, the mandatory representative body (the Economic Chambers) loses its entitlement to conclude collective agreements for those employers who are members of the voluntary association.[30]

[A] Legal Background

The system of collective bargaining is laid down in the Labour Constitution Act, which was adopted in its current form in 1973 and came into force in 1974. However, not every aspect of the 'success' of the Austrian system of sectoral collective bargaining can be explained by referring to statutory law, as displayed by the de facto (and not *de iure*) bargaining monopolies of the Economic Chambers on the one hand, and the Austrian trade union federation on the other.

[1] Registration of Business

In Austria, the registration of a business is the precondition for its exercise. The registration, though, leads *ipso iure* to automatic and mandatory membership of the Economic Chambers.[31] The Act on Economic Chambers further provides for automatic membership of one of the seven industry sectors within the Federal Chamber, as well as for automatic membership of one of the trade groups, according to the respective business licence. The crucial nexus with the Labour Constitution Act lies in the fact that (1) the Economic Chambers are the statutorily provided association entitled to conclude collective bargaining agreements for the employer's side,[32] and that (2) as soon as an employer is member of the Economic Chambers or of a voluntary business

---

29. Christoph Grabenwarter & Katharina Pabel, *Europäische Menschenrechtskonvention*, §358 (6th ed. C.H. Beck 2016).
30. See §6 ArbVG: 'Wird einer freiwilligen Berufsvereinigung die Kollektivvertragsfähigkeit gemäß §5 Abs. 1 zuerkannt und schließt diese einen Kollektivvertrag ab, so verliert die in Betracht kommende gesetzliche Interessenvertretung hinsichtlich der Mitglieder der Berufsvereinigung die Kollektivvertragsfähigkeit für die Dauer der Geltung und für den Geltungsbereich des von der Berufsvereinigung abgeschlossenen Kollektivvertrages.'
31. According to §2 paragraph 2 of the Act on Economic Chambers (Wirtschaftskammergesetz, WKG): 'Zu den Mitgliedern gemäß Abs. 1 zählen jedenfalls Unternehmungen, die der Gewerbeordnung unterliegen sowie insbesondere solche, die in der Anlage zu diesem Gesetz angeführt sind'.
32. See §4 paragraph 1 Labour Constitution Act: 'Kollektivvertragsfähig sind gesetzliche Interessenvertretungen der Arbeitgeber und der Arbeitnehmer, denen unmittelbar oder mittelbar die Aufgabe obliegt, auf die Regelung von Arbeitsbedingungen hinzuwirken und deren Willensbildung in der Vertretung der Arbeitgeber- oder der Arbeitnehmerinteressen gegenüber der anderen Seite unabhängig ist.'

association that has concluded a collective bargaining agreement, the agreement applies automatically.[33] In combination with the statutorily provided outsider validity for employees, the mandatory membership of the Economic Chambers and the nexus with the Labour Constitution Act as outlined above are the main contributing factors to the nearly 100% coverage[34] of collective bargaining agreements in Austria.

However, the existing system is under pressure. The process of business registration is regarded as too complex, so the current federal government is seeking to make it more flexible, and eventually to provide for a single business licence to conduct any business; whereas under current legislation, there are more than 80 so-called regulated businesses ('reglementierte Gewerbe') and 440 so-called free businesses ('Freie Gewerbe'). Because the application of the respective collective bargaining agreement is strongly related to the prevailing business licence, the question of whether the current collective bargaining system could remain in place – and if not, how a new system under the altered circumstances of business registration just indicated could work – is most uncertain and still awaiting academic investigation.

[2]   De-facto Bargaining Monopolies

Although there are the Chambers of Labour that are the statutorily provided mandatory representation of employees, and therefore allowed to collectively bargain for the employees' side, the Austrian trade union federation has a de facto monopoly on the conclusion of collective bargaining agreements. In other words, the Chambers of Labour do not make use of their theoretical right to conclude collective bargaining agreements. Yet, the trade union monopoly is not provided for by law, but is historically grown, which makes it hard to integrate with any other system of collective bargaining.

However, this is only one of the reasons why the employees' position is deemed to be fairly strong in comparison with other countries. In contrast to Germany, for example, where it is quite usual for there to be more than one collective bargaining agreement applicable for comparable groups of employees working for the same employer,[35] such a situation has never arisen in Austria, because the Austrian trade union federation is the only organisation bargaining for the employees' side. In other words, there is no other relevant employees' association that has been granted the right to conclude collective bargaining agreements.[36] Thus, there is no competition between

---

33. See §8 paragraph 1 ArbVG: 'Kollektivvertragsangehörig sind, sofern der Kollektivvertrag nicht anderes bestimmt, innerhalb seines räumlichen, fachlichen und persönlichen Geltungsbereiches die Arbeitgeber und die Arbeitnehmer, die zur Zeit des Abschlusses des Kollektivvertrages Mitglieder der am Kollektivvertrag beteiligten Parteien waren oder später werden.'
34. Maxence Brischoux, Anne Jaubertie, Christophe Gouardo, Pierre Lissot, Thomas Lellouch & Arthur Sode, *Mapping out the options for a European minimum wage standard*, 133 Trésor-Economics, 4 (July 2014) www.tresor.economie.gouv.fr/File/402604 (accessed 13 February 2017).
35. Cf. Abbo Junker, *Arbeitsrecht*, §§571 et seq. (15th ed. C.H. Beck 2016).
36. There is the employees' association of dependent apothecaries and the recently founded trade union for employed medical doctors. However, the latter was not granted the right to conclude collective agreements because it had not fulfilled the statutorily provided criteria, the most

trade unions, guaranteeing a strong employee position that cannot be undercut by competing associations. The de facto strength of the Austrian trade union federation is reflected in the size of its membership. Of the approximately 3.6 million employees in Austria, more than a quarter are members.[37]

The de facto bargaining monopoly on the employer's side derives from the fact that there are hardly any voluntary employers' associations that (1) are granted the power to conclude collective bargaining agreements, and (2) actually make use of it if granted. Thus, because of mandatory business registration, the Economic Chambers exercise a de facto bargaining monopoly in most business sectors, too.[38]

[3] Mandatory Applicability to All Members of the Concluding Party

One particular feature of the Austrian system of collective bargaining providing for its high coverage rate is that according to § 8 paragraph 1 of the Labour Constitution Act, all members of the concluding parties of a collective bargaining agreement automatically fall under its scope, irrespective of whether they were already members when the agreement was concluded or whether they joined the bargaining party at a later point in time. In other words, the legal system provides for a de facto automatic applicability of collective bargaining agreements, without granting an 'opt-out'. The only de facto possibility for employers to 'escape' the applicability of a collective bargaining agreement concluded by the Economic Chambers and the Austrian trade union federation is (1) to establish a voluntary business association that, (2) fulfils all legal criteria to be officially granted the right to conclude collective bargaining agreements, and (3) also achieves the conclusion of a collective bargaining agreement with the trade union federation.

[4] Outsider Validity for Employees

The so-called outsider validity (*Außenseiterwirkung*) is provided for by the law itself: according to § 12 paragraph 1 of the Labour Constitution Act, those employees who are not members of the concluding party, i.e., the Austrian Trade Union Federation, are

---

important being a certain power within the groups of the employees represented; http://derstandard.at/2000030642011/Aerztegewerkschaft-darf-Aerzte-nicht-vertreten (accessed 7 February 2017).

37. In 2015, 1,196,538 employees were members of the Austrian trade union federation, http://www.oegb.at/cs/Satellite?blobcol=urldata&blobheadername1=content-type&blobheadername e2=content-disposition&blobheadervalue1=application%2Fpdf&blobheadervalue2=inline%3B+filename%3D%22Mitgliederbewegung_seit_1945.pdf%22&blobkey=id&blobnocache=false&blobtable=MungoBlobs&blobwhere=1342611866772&ssbinary=true&site=S06 (accessed 7 February 2017).

38. Franz Marhold & Michael Friedrich, *Österreichisches Arbeitsrecht* 437 (3rd ed., Verlag Österreich 2016).

automatically bound by the collective bargaining agreement applicable to their employer.[39] Although one might conclude that this outcome could be a violation of the state's monopoly on establishing generally binding law, the Austrian Constitutional Court's (Verfassungsgerichtshof, VfGH) line of argumentation shows that the Constitution is not violated. In other words, as long as the outsider validity is provided for by the legislator, and as long as the parties to the employment relationship may also deviate from the applicable collective bargaining agreement (to the employee's advantage), the state's monopoly in creating generally binding law is not violated.[40]

The reason for outsider validity being provided for by law is the Austrian legislators' realisation that especially without provision for statutory minimum wages, there was a need for equal treatment and protection of all employees, irrespective of their membership of the concluding party to the collective bargaining agreement.[41] In this way, employees are protected from wage dumping by their colleagues who are not members of the concluding party.[42] As a result, outsider validity only leads de facto to advantageous outcomes for the employees – and thus does not violate the Constitution.[43]

Compared with other legal systems, for example the German one, where the application of a collective bargaining agreement to an employee who is not member of the concluding party is guaranteed by so-called *Bezugnahmeklauseln* (reference clauses),[44] Austrian outsider validity provides for an application of a collective agreement without the need to declare its application in the individual employment contract. This outcome benefits the strong position of the only bargaining party for the employees' side, the Austrian trade union federation, and although one might argue that outsider validity means that trade union federation membership rates are rather low, the opposite is in fact the case. Membership rates are at around a quarter of all employees.[45]

[5] Deviation from the Collective Bargaining Agreement Only to the Employee's Advantage

According to § 3 of the Labour Constitution Act, deviation from the collectively bargained employment conditions in the individual employment contract or by company agreements (so-called *Betriebsvereinbarungen* concluded between one single

---

39. §12 paragraph 1 of the Labour Constitution Act: 'Die Rechtswirkungen des Kollektivvertrages treten auch für Arbeitnehmer eines kollektivvertragsangehörigen Arbeitgebers ein, die nicht kollektivvertragsangehörig sind (Außenseiter).'
40. Cf. Rudolf Strasser in Peter Jabornegg & Reinhard Resch (eds), *Kommentar ArbVG*, §12 paragraph 7 (Manz 2012); Christian Holzner, 'Legitimationsprobleme' der Satzung?, 7 (11) DRdA (1994).
41. *Ibidem*,10 et seq.
42. Rudolf Strasser in Peter Jabornegg & Reinhard Resch (eds), *Kommentar ArbVG*, §12 paragraph 2 (Manz 2012); Hans Floretta, *Die Differenzierung nach der Gewerkschaftszugehörigkeit im deutschen Tarifvertragsrecht*, 1 (15) DRdA (1968).
43. Cf. Theodor Tomandl, ZAS 14 et seq. (1995).
44. Abbo Junker, *Arbeitsrecht* paragraphs 538 et seq. (15th ed. C.H. Beck 2016).
45. See *supra* §6.03[A][1].

employer and the relevant works council) is only possible where it is to the employee's advantage. Apart from that rather general feature, the distinct feature of the Austrian system lies in the court-acknowledged possibility to include the already mentioned 'Istlohnklauseln' in sectoral collective agreements. According to these clauses, which are part of the sectoral collective agreement, annual pay rises apply not only to the collectively agreed minimum wages in the whole sector, but also to individually agreed overpayments. According to the courts, employer and employee might deviate from these clauses to the employee's disadvantage, as long as the collectively agreed minimum wages are not undermined. Yet if they do not reach an agreement, the overpayment is also adjusted automatically.[46]

[B] **Critical Assessment**

[1] No Sectoral Bargaining: No Cartelising

One case recently decided by the CJEU[47] shows that as soon as there is more than one collective bargaining agreement applicable in one rather homogeneous sector, the system falls apart. In the 1990s, the peak Austrian employers' organisation, the Austrian Economic Chambers, and the Austrian trade union federation had concluded two separate collective agreements for the aviation sector, one for Austrian Airlines and one for Tyrolean, the latter being the subsidiary of the former. In addition, there was another collective agreement for Lauda Air, which was then the third aviation company in Austria. Over the years, the Austrian Airlines collective agreement proved to be too costly, especially because of rather generous company pension payments, automatic pay increases and automatic adaptation to inflation. Because neither side's representatives could agree upon a less expensive (to the employers) collective agreement within Austrian Airlines and because the collective agreement applicable at Tyrolean was much cheaper from the employer's point of view, the parent company, Austrian Airlines, decided to take the curious step of transferring its business to its subsidiary in order to apply the cheaper collective agreement.[48] The outcome of the dispute before the CJEU was to the employer's disadvantage and shows that the co-existence of several collective agreements in one homogenous sector might easily lead to unwelcome results. The employer's defeat in the courts gave the employee's side much more leverage when bargaining for a new collective agreement (at last), enabling it to exert a lot of pressure over the employer's side.

Another conflict decided by the Austrian Supreme Court of Justice (*Oberster Gerichtshof, OGH*) regarding the applicability of different collective agreements in one homogeneous sector – banking – reveals that the existence of more than one collective bargaining agreement in one sector leads, when strictly sticking to the provisions of the Labour Constitution Act, to apparently undesirable outcomes. Specifically, there

---

46. See already under §6.02[A][1].
47. Case C-328/13, ÖGB, 11 September 2014, EU:C:2014:2197.
48. Cf. Elisabeth Brameshuber, *Balancing vs. Preservation of Rights under the Acquired Rights Directive*, 45 ILJ 443 (2016).

existed two collective agreements concluded with the Austrian trade union federation by two different voluntary business associations, respectively. Several banking institutes were members of these voluntary business associations. At one point, one banking institute decided to change memberships. As a result, the other collective agreement became applicable, which was less advantageous for the employees regarding their wages. If the provisions of the Labour Constitution Act had been applied strictly, this would indeed have been the correct outcome. However, the *OGH* decided that the national provisions regarding a transfer of business had to be applied by analogy, resulting in the application of the new collective agreement – but also in preservation of the wage level according to the collective agreement concluded by the 'old' voluntary business association. According to the *OGH*, any other outcome would have been contrary to the employees' justified trust in the stability of their wages.[49]

This last example shows that in the end, from a systemic point of view, only the application of a single collective bargaining agreement in one sector can possibly prevent disputes over wages. It also shows that – at least when applying the provisions of the Labour Constitution Act – the Austrian system of sectoral collective bargaining might not guarantee wage stability in the event of employers (and employees) deciding to make use of their right to freedom of association. Yet even the Labour Constitution Act itself undermines the cartelising function of the sectoral collective bargaining agreement to some extent: the statutory provision for the collective bargaining power of public bodies/foundations under public law means there is a specific collective agreement for entities such as the Austrian Broadcasting Corporation (*Österreichischer Rundfunk, ORF*). Although this is advantageous for the ORF, as the relatively good employment conditions mean journalists are eager to work there, it is to the disadvantage of all other competitors in the TV and radio market. Due to the lack of public funding, they cannot afford wages as high or employment conditions as generous as those granted to *ORF*-employees.

[2]   Deviation to the Employee's Advantage: Another Threat to the Cartelising Function?

On the one hand, the use of the so-called *Istlohnklauseln* guarantees the employees' purchasing power, yet on the other it can harm economically weak employers in particular. Since it is up to the parties to the individual employment contract to arrange for deviations from the *Istlohnklausel*, these clauses might harm employers in economically difficult periods: it is quite obvious that employees will not voluntarily agree to a lower rise in wages than provided for by the collective agreement and the *Istlohnklausel*. Thus, it is up to the employer's initiative to settle for a lower rise in wages. However, the balancing act between competing with the other employers in the sector and trying to keep employees by granting the same rise in payments as those other employers is not easy. Therefore, it is not at all surprising that in Germany the validity

---

49. OGH 9 ObA 128/04w ecolex 2006/95 = DRdA 2006, 149 = ZAS 2006/41 (Winkler) = SZ 2005/169 = DRdA 2006/42 (Grillberger).

of comparable so-called *Garantieklausel/Effektivklausel* is also highly contentious because of their threat to the cartelising function of collective agreements.[50]

[3] The Difficulty of Defining a Sector

Recent developments show that the Austrian system of sectoral collective bargaining is more fragile than expected prima facie, threatening its peace function especially. In 2012, for the first time there were six collective bargaining agreements instead of one for the rather inhomogeneous metal sector.[51] Originally, the six different trade groups within the metal branch had decided to bargain together for one general collective agreement. Before 2002, there was even a seventh member of that bargaining group, representing the electro and electronic-industry employers. However, that employer's trade group decided to bargain its own collective agreement, resulting in a very distinct collective bargaining agreement when compared with the general one for the metal sector, especially regarding its structure. It was one of the first collective bargaining agreements that had overcome the anachronistic division between blue-collar and white-collar workers (which is still upheld in many statutes and collective bargaining agreements).

On the eve of the annual bargaining round on wages in 2012, the remaining six trade groups forming the employer's side decided to break apart and to bargain separately for the six different groups of businesses within the metal sector. In the end, though, the current wage levels in the metal sector have proved to be more or less the same. Thus, it is not quite apparent why the bargaining-group was dissolved, although productivity in the foundry-sector, for instance, is much lower than that in the metal industry.

One of the underlying questions was and remains how a sector should be defined. Generally speaking, there are two possible methods, one relying on the productivity of a group of businesses, the other on their production methods. Defining a sector according to the productivity level or the outcome of the working process does not fit into a system where the applicability of a collective bargaining agreement strongly depends on the business registration and therefore the production method. This is illustrated by the example of textile fabrics, produced on the one hand by businesses that belong to the trade group of the textile industry, and on the other by businesses that, according to their registration, belong to the trade group of the chemical industry. As can be imagined, the collective bargaining agreement for the chemical industry is much more advantageous for the employees because of its higher wage levels, but possibly creating a mismatch regarding the competition between the different employers. In other words, those employers that are members of the chemical industry trade

---

50. Peter Löwisch & Volker Rieble, *Tarifvertragsgesetz*, §1 paragraphs 2160 et seq. (4th ed. C.H.Beck 2017).
51. *See* for the currently applicable agreements https://www.wko.at/Content.Node/branchen/oe/Arbeitsrecht--Kollektivvertraege--Bildung--Sozialrecht/Sozialpolitik_und_Arbeitsrecht,_Sozialpolitik_und_Kollekti.html (accessed 7 February 2017). *See* for the following also Franz Marhold & Elma Osmanovic, *Ausstieg eines Fachverbandes aus einer Kollektivvertrags-Verhandlungsgemeinschaft*, ASoK 202 (2012).

group have to compete on wages with those employers that are members of the textile industry trade group, the latter needing to pay much lower wages than the former.

Solutions to overcome fragmentations within sectors have already been presented supra, one being the possibility of including so-called *Istlohnklauseln* in collective bargaining agreements. By including an *Istlohnklausel* in a collective bargaining agreement, collective wage increases also apply to individually agreed overpayments, unless the single employer agrees with the single employee that this wage increase should not take place. Another solution might be having one general collective bargaining agreement for one sector but adjusting the wage tables to a region's productivity level, as seen within the collective bargaining agreement for Hotels and Catering.

§6.04 SECTORAL COLLECTIVE BARGAINING: 'BEST PRACTICE MODEL'?

As the previous chapters have made clear, the Austrian system of sectoral collective bargaining is fairly complex, both from a legal as well as from a de facto point of view. Although the current system works quite well, with a collective bargaining coverage of nearly 100%, making appeals for a national statutory minimum wage rather redundant, attempts to copy only some features of the Austrian system should be watched most critically. Only the system as a whole with its legal and factual particularities has proved to guarantee relative peace, cartelised wages and innovative solutions for emerging problems.[52] In other words, it is most crucial to take into account the whole legal and factual system when assessing whether some particularities could serve as 'best practice model'. As the German example shows, mandatory membership of the Economic Chambers as provided for in Austria would be deemed unconstitutional under German law. Yet, as we have seen, that mandatory membership is one of the main pillars of the Austrian system, although it appears hardly exportable.

§6.05 CONCLUSION

It was the aim of this paper to show that up until the present, the Austrian system of sectoral collective bargaining has proved to be quite successful. It leads to a cartelising of wages, with hardly any sector of industry currently offering a minimum wage of less than EUR 1,500/month for a full-time position. The regulatory function of the cartelised wages should not be underestimated either, leading to a de facto perishing of low-performing companies in the long run. By bargaining the wages and working conditions for one sector rather than just a single employer, the employer's position especially is reinforced, thus leading to relatively low strike rates. In this way, the Austrian system provides for a very distinct peace function. Another important feature

---

52. Cf. Stephan Kampelmann, Andrea Garnero and François Rycx, *Minimum wages in Europe: does the diversity of systems lead to a diversity of outcomes?* ETUI 2013, 7 http://www.etui.org/Publications2/Reports/Minimum-wages-in-Europe-does-the-diversity-of-systems-lead-to-a-diversity-of-outcomes (accessed 7 February 2017).

is its innovation function, which was particularly visible during the crisis of the past few years where important decisions to stabilise the labour market were taken at the level of sectoral collective bargaining. Although current political developments are threatening the system's stability, it seems highly unlikely that it is going to change in the near future. So far, there has been hardly any in-depth research on what alternatives to the current system would and should look like. Thus, although some features of the Austrian system are deemed to be the 'incarnation' of everything that under say German law would be regarded as unconstitutional,[53] the system of sectoral collective bargaining seems to be a valid way of regulating employment relations.

---

53. Abbo Junker, *Europäische Grund- und Menschenrechte und das deutsche Arbeitsrecht (unter besonderer Berücksichtigung der Koalitionsfreiheit)*, ZfA 2013, 91, 134 with further references. Junker even calls it *Teufelswerk* – devil's work.

Chapter 7
The Revival of Sectoral Collective Bargaining: The Portuguese Experience

Teresa Coelho Moreira

§7.01 INTRODUCTION

[A] The Crisis in Portugal

The financial crisis that hit the global market in the middle of 2008 gave way to the sharpest contraction of the European economies since the Great Depression, a crisis that has resulted in widespread job losses and social hardship.[1] During the 2008-2009 financial and economic crisis, most EU Member States experienced a major economic downturn that led to a sharp deterioration in their labour markets. At EU level, the unemployment rate increased to a historically high level.[2]

As in some other European countries, the Portuguese economy had and still has a severe problem of growth. Portugal was hit hard by the global crisis and unemployment hit record levels but, fortunately, the unemployment rate has been declining in the last few months.[3]

Portugal was subjected to a bailout programme from May 2011 to May 2014, which led to legislative measures in the area of employment legislation and the labour market, as in the area of economic policy generally, it had to ensure compliance with several obligations foreseen in the *Memorandum of Understanding*, signed in May 2011 between Portugal, the European Commission, the International Monetary Fund and the

---

1. As Alain Supiot wrote in 2010, (*A legal perspective on the economic crisis of 2008*, Vol. 149, No. 2, International Labour Review, 151 (2010), 'the global financial meltdown in the autumn of 2008 was but a symptom of deeper underlying trouble, ultimately a crisis in law and institutions'.
2. European Commission, *Proposal for a Council Recommendation on the integration of the long-term unemployment into the labour market*, COM (2015) 462 final, 2015, p. 2.
3. Being 10.5% in November 2016.

European Central Bank.[4] The *MoU* set the tone for a new social dialogue agreement, signed on 18 January 2012 by the government and the majority of social partners – one of the two trade union confederations and the employers' associations – called *Growth, Competitiveness and Employment Commitment*.[5] This established a wide range of economic policies, active labour market policies and measures relating to labour laws, unemployment benefit and industrial relations.

The increase in unemployment in Portugal was largely driven by low hirings, caused by a *perfect storm* of austerity measures, economic uncertainty, weakened external demand and downward wage rigidities. Such an extreme economic environment prompted a substantially weakened labour demand, particularly in terms of new hires.

Portugal has successfully completed a demanding adjustment programme under conditions of strong fiscal constraints, high unemployment and accelerated reform. Securing equitable, high-quality education and jobs are essential planks in building a strong foundation for further growth and social well-being for the people in Portugal.

[B] The Right to Negotiate

Collective bargaining is an employee's fundamental right, consecrated in Article 56 no. 3 of the Portuguese Constitution. According to this article, collective bargaining is a right that can only be exercised by trade unions and which has to be assured by law, determining a trade union monopoly on the workers' side as far as collective bargaining is concerned. As a result, workers' councils have no collective bargaining capacity in Portugal.

From 2012, the workers' councils were given, in Article 491 no. 3 of the Portuguese Labour Code, a chance to negotiate collective agreements at company level, within legally defined and rather restrictive terms. Such terms included a delegation-like empowerment by trade unions granted in the context, and stated in the text, of a collective agreement of broader scope and a company size threshold of 150 or more workers. Since these company-level collective agreements are believed to either adjust or develop broader collective agreement discipline, their contents will comprise only the designate subjects where such tasks are deemed necessary.[6] However, it must be noted that most firms in Portugal are SMEs and, therefore, the costs to employers of negotiating a company-level agreement are high.

Trade unions are also entitled, according to Article 56 of the Constitution, to participate in the creation of labour legislation, to express their opinion on any of the government's economic or social plans, and to participate in the management of social security institutions and company restructuring procedures.

---

4. This can be seen and followed in http://ec.europa.eu/economy_finance/eu_borrower/mou/201 1-05-18-mou-portugal_en.pdf (accessed February 2017).
5. At http://www.ces.pt/concertacao-social/acordos (accessed February 2017).
6. Joana Vasconcelos, *Economic Crisis and Labour Law Reforms in Portugal*, in ISL&ISSL European Regional Congress, 10 (2014).

On the employers' side, the freedom to set up employers' associations was introduced in 1975 by Decree-Law 215-C/75, although no reference was made to them in the Constitution. These provisions can be found in the Portuguese Labour Code from Article 440 onwards, regulating the freedom of association of both employers and employees as if they were equal.

Trade unions have the exclusive legal right to call strikes and to sign collective agreements.

[C]   **The Traditional Tripartite Concertation**

Portugal has a long tradition of social dialogue between the government and representatives of both employers and employees – especially at the highest level of representation. This dialogue consists of regular consultations and active participation by the social partners in approving new legislation on employment and industrial relations, as imposed by the Portuguese Constitution, and in formulating the tripartite agreements concluded regularly over the years at the Standing Committee on Social Concertation. It is important to note that in Portugal many subjects are discussed beforehand in the Social Concertation Standing Committee. The main tasks of this committee are to foster dialogue and social concertation so as to enter into agreements, offering opinions on restructuring and socioeconomic development policies, as well as their implementation; to provide solutions for the proper functioning of the economy, taking into account their social and labour impact; to regularly appraise the evolution of the country's social and economic situation; and to appraise legislation projects concerning social and labour matters – namely labour law, employment policies, vocational training, social welfare, tax and public administration policies, including active labour market policies.[7]

From the mid-1970s onwards, collective bargaining developed largely according to the *favor laboratoris* principle, interpreted in the most traditional form. Collective agreements were seen as instruments planned only to improve legal provisions that were considered the minimum standard of labour protection, and a collective agreement in force could only be replaced by a more favourable one. Collective agreements therefore had the tendency to be more protective than the law and remained in force for a long time.[8]

The Labour Code of 2003 adopted new stipulations on the relationship between law and collective agreements, allowing for the latter to establish less favourable conditions than those prescribed by the law. In addition, it adopted a set of provisions intended to favour the regular replacement of the old collective agreements by new ones. But there was a huge fall in the number of collective agreements following these provisions and later on, in the Labour Code of 2009, a partial restoration of the previous provisions in this area. Since 2009 the general principle has remained the same: collective agreements can establish less favourable conditions than those prescribed by

---

7. See for more information http://www.ces.pt/ (last consulted in January 2017).
8. All this information can be seen in Maria Do Rosário Palma Ramalho, *Portuguese labour law and industrial relations during the crisis*, in ILO Working Paper, 10 (2013).

law, but there are some issues – such as, *inter alia*, equality and non-discrimination, personality rights, limits to the duration of working period – that can only be established in a more favourable way than the law.[9]

However, concerning the relationship between law and employment contracts, the principle continues to be the same – *favor laboratoris*, interpreted in the most traditional way – as it is for the relationship between collective agreements and employment contracts, according to Article 476 of the Portuguese Labour Code.

§7.02 SECTORAL COLLECTIVE AGREEMENTS IN PORTUGAL

In Portugal, collective bargaining has traditionally taken place at the sectoral or multi-employer levels, with collective agreements extended to non-parties to the agreement to fill the gap caused by the low level of union membership in Portugal – i.e., less than 20%. Despite the general principle that they apply only to the members of the trade union or of the employers' association that signed the agreement based on the affiliation principle, in practice they are applied to non-affiliated workers and employers, because the law has allowed the administrative extension of those agreements by extension ordinances and there is a strong tradition of the use of this tool. This administrative extension of collective agreements makes it possible for a large proportion of the labour force to benefit from collective agreements without belonging to the organizations that signed them.

However, over the past few years these collective bargaining arrangements and practices have undergone significant changes.[10] Even so, despite these changes, in the second semester of 2015 and in 2016, there was again a significant increase in the number of extension ordinances.

Of course, one has to understand that this tradition has its roots in the type of enterprise that exists in Portugal. There are many SMEs with large numbers of low-skilled workers, so the sectoral collective agreements tend to offer more protection to unskilled workers. Also, as the ILO[11] points out, it tends to offer more inclusive labour protection for vulnerable categories of workers, such as migrants, those in non-standard forms of employment or working in small firms. It can also help to establish minimum standards for working conditions in an industry or sector, taking these out of competition.

On the other hand, in Portugal, as a rule, there are no legal criteria to assess how representative trade unions are. As collective agreements may be extended to employers and employees that are not represented or affiliated respectively by employers' organizations or trade unions through administrative procedures, the government has

---

9. Article 3, No. 3, of Portuguese Labour Code.
10. However, it is important to notice that in these cases, the sharp decline in collective bargaining activity and coverage was not the direct result of employer resistance to collective bargaining or declining membership in unions, but rather the result of policy-induced changes reversing support for collective bargaining.
11. *Tackling the jobs crisis in Portugal*, Studies On Growth with Equity (ILO 2014) http://ilo.org/wcmsp5/groups/public/---dgreports/---dcomm/documents/publication/wcms_228208.pdf (accessed 20 July 2017).

Chapter 7: The Revival of Sectoral Collective Bargaining §7.02

a discretionary power to extend the personal scope of collective agreements even when the signatories of that collective agreement may be insignificant, having only a very small number of members.[12] That is why the *Memorandum* established that the Portuguese government should define clear criteria to be followed for the extension of agreements and commit to them and 'the representativeness of negotiating organizations and the implications of the extension for the competitive position of non-affiliated firms will have to be among these criteria'.

Regarding the restriction of extension ordinances, the *MoU* set the goal of defining criteria for issuing them that took into account the representation of the parties to collective bargaining agreements and their consequences to companies not covered by the collective bargaining agreement.[13]

After the third regular revision on 15 May 2012, it was established that the extension of collective bargaining agreements signed by employers' associations representing less than 50% of the workers in that sector would no longer be possible; however, even if that limit was reached, the government should always assess the consequences for the competitiveness of companies in that sector.

Council of Ministers Resolution no. 90/2012 of 31 October defined the following criterion for the issuing of extension ordinances: the employer that had signed the collective bargaining agreement should have in its service at least 50% of the workers in that sector of activity, within the envisaged geographic, personal and professional scope, except if the request for extension excluded micro, small and medium companies.

This decision had two important effects: a significant reduction in both collective labour regulation instruments and the number of workers covered, leading to wages and working conditions being increasingly determined by direct negotiation between employers and individual workers.

All social partners were against these changes in the extension ordinances. The CIP – Confederation of Portuguese Business – declared that:

> For good or for evil, our collective bargaining coverage is closely connected with the extension ordinances. [...] Our response to the new regulation, as employers, was obvious: as soon as collective bargaining implies an extra set of obligations and changes to what is established in the general law, and as soon as there are companies under such rule and others that are not, considering the impact of this asymmetry on competitive loyalty, what is the expected reaction? Companies withdraw from the association. Companies withdraw from the agreement. It is fairly obvious. Therefore this measure was clearly a source of disaggregation. [...] And later the implementation of the condition that small and medium companies make up at least 30% of the employers' organization that signed the agreement: so now we turn around the logic of workers' representativeness? Is there any

---

12. Maria Do Rosário Palma Ramalho, *Tratado de Direito do Trabalho – Parte III – Situações Laborais Coletivas*, 225 et seq. (Coimbra: Almedina 2012); António Monteiro Fernandez, *Direito do Trabalho*, 661 et seq. (16th ed. Coimbra: Almedina 2012); Pedro Romano Martinez, *Direito do Trabalho*, 1125 et seq. (7th edition, Coimbra: Almedina 2015); Bernardo da Gama Lobo Xavier, *Collective bargaining in Portugal*, in *Collective Bargaining in Europe*, (Spain MTSS 2004).
13. 'Define clear criteria to be followed for the extension of collective agreements and commit to them'.

justification for this utter deviation from the original requirement? Perhaps the official explanation was decentralization, but in fact it has nothing to do with it. It was the conviction that collective bargaining was a tool used by the big companies dominating the associations to wipe out the small ones.

On the workers' side, the CGTP-IN – the General Confederation of Portuguese Workers-National Interunion – said:

> What some call decentralization is to our mind dismantlement. [...] This entails contradictory aspects, even for employers. Because an agreement is a commitment between the parties, power is shared and a commitment must be achieved. If power is not shared, one of the parties imposes on the other, of course. In many sectors, employers themselves have an interest in this commitment in order to regulate the market in which companies operate. On the other hand, the representative organizations do not want to lose power to the companies in their activity sector. Employer confederations know this, they feel the need to tackle it; at the same time, they know that certain changes in the regulation result in workers being further unprotected. Thus they go on accepting this situation.

The other workers' confederation, the UGT – General Union of Workers – asked:

> Are there a higher number of agreements published? No. At this moment, they are at a minimum. [...] We must demand and push for more collective bargaining, push for the publication of more agreements, and bring extension ordinances back to the way they were before the tripartite agreement. [...] The struggle for the regulation of the labour market, the struggle against unfair competition: this is what extension ordinances exist for! To promote the equality of circumstances among actors working in the same branch of the economy. The government paid heed to the IMF and now it is time to undo what was done. This is our opinion and also the opinion of the employers.[14]

This new situation also led to a change in the predominant type of collective agreement. The traditionally preponderant sectoral top-level branch and professional agreements (CCT and ACT), gave way to company-level agreements which also led to a decrease in the number of workers covered. The number of employees covered by collective agreements fell from almost 1.9 million in 2008 to some 246,643 in 2014.[15] These developments show the difficulty that social partners were facing in reaching agreements during the crisis.

However, the low density of employer association membership led to concerns that the 50% representativeness criterion was too strict, and so, after the adjustment programme in 2014, Council of Ministers Resolution no. 43/2014 of 27 June created different criteria aimed at ensuring the representativeness of the parties. This change was necessary given paragraph 27 ('Labour Market Institutions') of the Letter of Intent of 26 May 2014, submitted by the Portuguese government to the International Monetary Fund, highlighting the policy steps to be taken in the months ahead and providing that the Government 'will encourage wage developments consistent with

---

14. Maria Da Paz Campos Lima and Manuel Abrantes, *DIADSE – Dialogue for Advancing Social Europe – Country Report: Portugal*, 24-25 (March 2016).
15. These data are in http://www.dgert.msess.pt/wp-content/uploads/2016/01/IRCT-publicados-2014.pdf (accessed February 2017).

productivity, including by making collective bargaining more dynamic and fostering decentralization of wage bargaining'. The government's immediate priority in this area was to adjust the criteria for the extension of collective agreements, taking into account the representativeness of micro-, small- and medium-sized enterprises in the various sectors and maintaining the aim of the previous reform under the programme.

This resolution was enacted after the end of the adjustment programme and adopted to introduce flexibility into the principle for issuing extension ordinances. Therefore, the employer need only comply with one of the following criteria: to have in its service at least 50% of the workers of that sector of activity, within the envisaged geographic, personal and professional scope; or its associates must include at least 30% of micro, small and medium companies.

According to Article 100 of the Portuguese Labour Code, micro, small and medium-sized enterprises are defined as firms employing less than 250 employees. Since this is likely to be the case for the large majority of employer associations, this mainly represented a return to the situation before 2011.

However, this decision by the Portuguese government was criticized by the IMF in January 2015 because they said that this option would 'undermine the progress towards a more dynamic and inclusive system of collective bargaining'.[16] Also the European Commission[17] in December 2014 wrote that this option 'is likely to hinder efficient wage adjustment at firm level. This measure represents a major setback in the reform of collective bargaining in Portugal.'

We have our doubts about this, though. In our opinion, the new principle can allow a significant increase in the issuing of extension ordinances, without this meaning a return to the past, when extension ordinances were issued on a case-by-case basis and almost automatically.[18] Maybe collective bargaining can be more dynamic thanks to these amendments, because new contracts have been negotiated. The new option of extending agreements to the whole sector aims precisely at fostering improved collective bargaining.

As the ILO[19] noted, a new approach to collective bargaining was needed. It was not a question of moving back to where the system was before the crisis, because that earlier system, among other limitations, was too focused on wages, with not enough attention devoted to skills development, mobility and competitiveness. Instead, the challenge was to build an environment that allowed wages and working conditions to move in line with productivity while supporting job recovery.

These new criteria have resulted in a pick-up in the number of extensions issued in 2015 and 2016.

---

16. IMF Country Report No. 15/21, p. 12.
17. *Occasional Papers 208*, p. 30.
18. In the same sense David Carvalho Martins, *Labour Law in Portugal between 2011 and 2014*, in ISL&ISSL European Regional Congress, 25 (2014).
19. *Supra.*

Figure 7.1 CA and Extension Ordinances from 2011 to 2016[20]

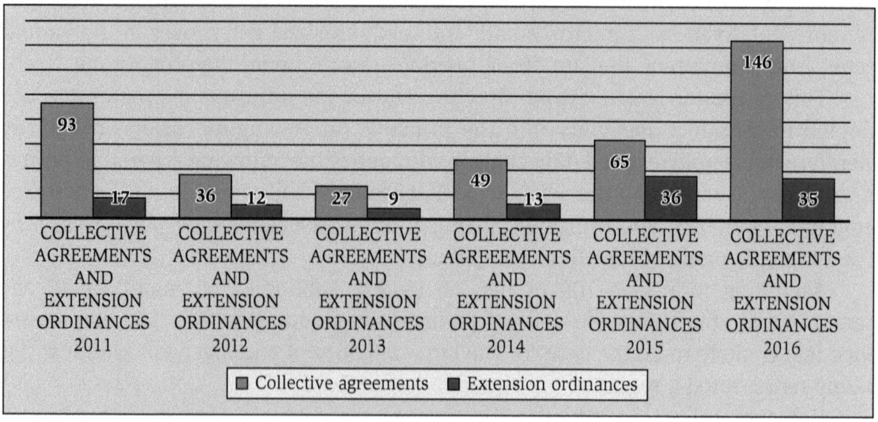

	COLLECTIVE AGREEMENTS AND EXTENSION ORDINANCES 2011	COLLECTIVE AGREEMENTS AND EXTENSION ORDINANCES 2012	COLLECTIVE AGREEMENTS AND EXTENSION ORDINANCES 2013	COLLECTIVE AGREEEMENTS AND EXTENSION ORDINANCES 2014	COLLECTIVE AGREEMENTS AND EXTENSION ORDINANCES 2015	COLLECTIVE AGREEMENTS AND EXTENSION ORDINANCES 2016
Collective agreements	93	36	27	49	65	146
Extension ordinances	17	12	9	13	36	35

Source: Data from DGERT.

Due to these changes, collective bargaining is slowly picking up. According to very recent data, 2015 saw an increase in the collective agreements at sectoral level and the same happened in 2016. Also, the total collective labour regulation instruments recorded an increase of 17.1% over the same period when compared with 2014. There has been also an increase in the number of workers covered because of the number of extension ordinances approved. From 2014, the number of agreements signed and workers covered by those agreements increased after the substantial decline observed in recent years. In contrast to the situation in 2014, when company-level agreements constituted the majority of newly signed collective agreements, in 2015 most new agreements were signed at sectoral level and evidence shows that most company-level agreements are renegotiations of contracts already in force, typically in larger firms.

Table 7.1   The Evolution of Collective Agreements at Sectoral Level[21]

	2008	2009	2010	2011	2012	2013	2014	2015	2016
Number of CCT Sector Agreements	172	142	141	93	36	27	49	65	69

---

20. These data are in http://www.dgert.gov.pt/relacoes-de-trabalho/contratacao-coletiva/dados-sobre-a-contratacao-coletiva (accessed February 2017).
21. These data are available at http://www.dgert.gov.pt/relacoes-de-trabalho/contratacao-coletiva/dados-sobre-a-contratacao-coletiva (accessed February 2017).

Chapter 7: The Revival of Sectoral Collective Bargaining §7.02

	2008	2009	2010	2011	2012	2013	2014	2015	2016
Number of ACT – Multi employer	27	22	25	22	10	19	23	20	19
Number of AE company agreements	97	87	64	55	39	48	80	53	58
Total number of Collective Agreements	296	251	230	170	85	94	152	138	146
Number of extension ordinances	137	102	116	17	12	9	13	36	35
Workers covered (thousands)	1849.8	1397.2	1407.1	1242.2	404.8	241.5	246.6	568.9	749.348

Source: DGERT.

Figure 7.2   Workers Covered by CA from 2009 to 2016[22]

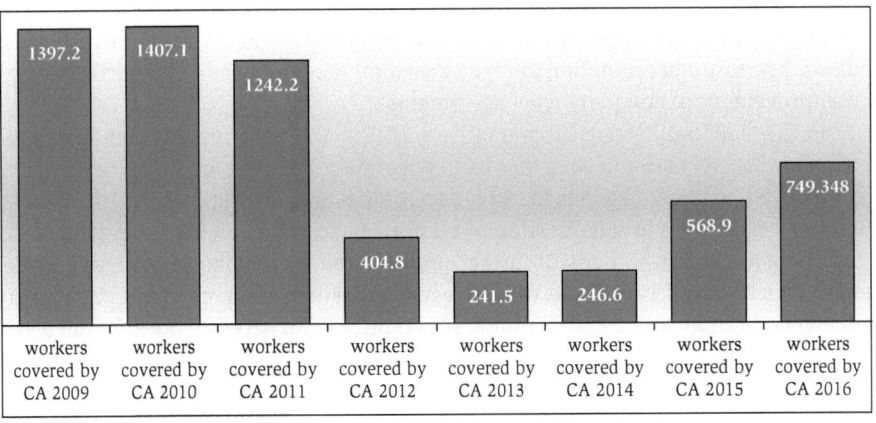

Source: DGERT.

---

22. These data are available at http://www.dgert.gov.pt/relacoes-de-trabalho/contratacao-coletiva/dados-sobre-a-contratacao-coletiva (accessed February 2017).

In Portugal, there is evidence that the collective bargaining system remains highly centralized. This reflects both the tradition of centralized social dialogue and structural factors in the Portuguese economy, including the small average firm size and the consequent low diffusion of workers' councils.

We also have to see the implications of the *MoU* – and after the *MoU*, the changes – because the measures introduced in line with *MoU* requirements had a differentiated impact on collective bargaining developments and the reduction of labour costs. The measures regarding decentralization, such as the company-level negotiations with non-union worker representatives, did not have any impact, because collective agreements of this type were not signed.

The most significant and negative impact on collective bargaining resulted from freezing the minimum wage and introducing stricter criteria for the extension of collective agreements.

§7.03 THE NEW POLITICAL CYCLE

On 26 November 2015, following the 4 October general election, a Socialist Party government came to power, supported by the far left parties, the Communists, the Greens and the Left Bloc. This was the result of an unprecedented alliance – the first since the birth of democracy in Portugal four decades ago – that defeated the short-lived, twelve-day minority government of the centre-right appointed after the election. The basis of the left alliance was to 'turn the page on austerity'.

The government programme showed its commitment to enhance collective bargaining in the public sector, including on wages and working time. It also more generally indicated an approach to collective bargaining that favoured inclusiveness and stability, through promotion of regular sectoral bargaining and extended coverage and improvement of company-level agreements.

In the National Reform Programme for 2017,[23] the government intends to have new policy measures in this area that would change collective bargaining rules. There are, however, no concrete plans to foster decentralization. On the contrary, the general intention seems to be in the direction of reinforcing sectoral collective bargaining.

The government intends to further promote the extensions of collective agreements, which would contribute to this result by issuing clear new criteria, namely about when to enact them, and by promoting co-ordination between the different levels of collective bargaining.

The government is also exploring options for changing the rules regarding the expiry and survival of collective agreements. However, as the European Commission[24] pointed out, any changes that would imply a prolongation of the survival period could in practice reduce the incentives of social partners to negotiate, and have a negative impact on the capacity of firms to adjust to new economic conditions.

---

23. Law No. 41/2016, 28 December.
24. Institutional Papers 36, September 2016, p. 26.

§7.04 CONCLUSION

The changes in the collective bargaining legal framework during the period of financial assistance did not promote organized decentralization but a dramatic erosion of sector bargaining and coverage by collective agreements. This situation has been changing in the last couple of years and now the intention is to relaunch sectoral collective agreements, because collective agreements and social dialogue are essential to maintain the principle that *work is not a commodity*.

CHAPTER 8
The Spanish Example

Yolanda Maneiro Vázquez & José María Miranda Boto

§8.01 COLLECTIVE BARGAINING REGULATION IN FORTY YEARS

The Spanish democratic system of collective bargaining was established in 1980, with the first version of the *Estatuto de los Trabajadores* (ET, Workers' Statute), which nonetheless clearly drew on the system of the Franco regime that preceded it.[1] In 1994, a major reform took place, giving more competences to collective bargaining and thus limiting the role of state legislation.[2] From that date, there was no further reform until the crisis arrived. Then there were two major reforms in 2011 and 2012, the first under a Socialist government, the second a Conservative one.[3]

After several months of negotiations between trade unions and employers' organisations, by the end of May 2011 an agreement had proved unreachable. The Socialist government therefore decided to act unilaterally and on 10 June it passed *Decreto-Ley*[4] 7/2011, embodying urgent measures for the reform of collective bargaining. From a technical point of view, it is remarkable that seven and a half of the eighteen pages that made up the regulation amounted to explanatory preamble, seeking to justify the reform and its procedures. No mention was made of the crisis, but rather of the need for systemic re-structuring and optimisation. Remarkably, it was one

---

1. F. Valdés Dal-Ré, *La negociación colectiva, entre tradición y renovación*, (Granada: Comares 2012).
2. J. Rivero Lamas, *Estructuras y contenidos de la negociación colectiva en la Ley 11/1994 (una aproximación interpretativa)*, 43 Documentación laboral, 35-92 (1994).
3. For a broader perspective on the reforms during these years, see M. Espín Sáez et al., *Spain*, in M. Stefko (ed.), *Labour Law and Social Security Law at the Crossroads*, 242 et seq. (Prague: Charles University 2016).
4. A *Decreto-Ley* is an action taken by the Government with the status of an Act of Parliament which must be validated by Parliament after it is passed and can only be used in case of extreme and urgent need.

of the few regulations in Spain to discuss the combination of flexibility for companies and security for employees that is commonly referred to as 'flexicurity'.[5]

General elections in November 2011 brought a change of government. One of the new administration's first measures was a labour reform that was introduced in February 2012, in its first three months, as *Decreto-Ley* 3/2012, and subsequently converted into Act 3/2012. This paper will mainly analyse the changes initiated by that piece of legislation,[6] as they represented a profound reform of the system.

Before considering the essential elements of this reform, it should be pointed out that prior to adopting this legislation in 2012, the trade unions and employers' organisations had finally reached a state-level agreement known as the 'Agreement towards Employment and Collective Bargaining 2012-2014' (AENC, in its Spanish acronym), drawing on a well-established tradition.[7] As the government itself acknowledged, *Decreto-Ley* 3/2012 contained measures that were clearly inimical to this agreement between the social partners, which meant implementation of the AENC was blocked de facto. A new AENC, nonetheless, was signed for the period 2015-2017.[8]

Hence, ignoring the agreements signed by the social partners, the reform enacted in 2012 introduced several changes in three aspects, with the stated objective of 'making collective bargaining an instrument rather than an obstacle in adapting employment conditions to specific circumstances in the enterprise'. Those three aspects were, first, increasing the possibilities to 'opt out' from statutory collective agreements (Article 82.3 ET) at the level of the enterprise; second, granting the company agreement a partial priority over the sectoral agreement (Article 84.2 ET), and thus dispensing with the social partners' authority to specify a suitable negotiation structure; and thirdly, introducing a temporary limitation on the 'extended validity' ('ultraactividad') of collective agreements (Article 86.3 ET) to avoid the forced extension of their content. Later, *Decreto-Ley* 20/2013 allowed for the non-enforcement of collective agreements in the sphere of public administrations at the unilateral will of the administration.

Decreto-Ley 3/2012 and the measures it contained have been strongly criticised both by law academics and by the courts, with doubts arising about whether they are constitutional. Nevertheless, the Constitutional Court upheld the validity of the reform in several decisions (STC 119/2014,[9] STC 8/2015,[10] among others). On the other hand,

---

5. J. M. Goerlich Peset, *La flexiguridad en la reforma laboral de 2012*, 13 Teoría y derecho: revista de pensamiento jurídico, 91-104 (2013).
6. For a global perspective of both reforms, see J. M. Miranda Boto & R. Rodríguez Contreras, Spain, in Marie-Cécile Escande Varniol, Sylvaine Laulom, Emmanuelle Mazuyer (eds), *Quel Droit Social dans une Europe en crise?*, 151 et seq. (Bruxelles: Larcier, 2012).
7. S. Canalda Criado, *Las funciones de los acuerdos interconfederales frente a la situación actual de la negociación colectiva*, Revista General de Derecho del Trabajo y de la Seguridad Social, 44, (2016).
8. J. Cruz Villalón, *El diálogo social en España y las aportaciones del III AENC*, 25 Gaceta sindical: reflexión y debate, 55-72 (2015).
9. A. Martín Valverde, *La reforma del mercado laboral de 2012 se ajusta a la Constitución: análisis de la sentencia del Tribunal Constitucional 119/2014, de 16 de julio (BOE, 15 de agosto)*, 12 Actualidad laboral, 1 et seq. (2014).
10. I. García-Perrote Escartín, *La constitucionalidad de la reforma laboral de 2012. Comentario a la STC 8/2015, de 22 de enero*, 105 Revista española de derecho constitucional, 239-283, (2015).

the International Labour Organisation's Committee on Freedom of Association in March 2014 settled the complaint raised by several Spanish trade unions against this regulation and against RDL 20/2012, criticising such reforms in view of ILO Conventions 98 and 154.

'Rationalization', 'economic growth' and 'flexibility' were the shibboleth of the reforms. *Decreto-Ley* 3/2012 even referred to 'flexicurity' as its final aim. To quote verbatim, 'collective bargaining should be a tool, and not an obstacle, in adapting the working conditions within the enterprise'. Furthermore, one of its goals was 'facilitating the adaptation and other working conditions to productivity and company competitiveness', and helping 'decentralization' of collective bargaining. Thus, economic logic, and not protection of workers, was the basis of these reforms.

§8.02 SOURCES AND OUTCOMES OF THE REFORMS

The measures described in this paper do not all arise exclusively from the ideologies of the governing parties. There is no doubt that many of them were promoted from the outside, with the European Commission playing its part. Through Commissar Rehn, the Commission was a strong promoter of the austerity measures implemented. With regard to other driving forces of these reforms, there was strictly speaking no memorandum in Spain similar to the one in Portugal. However, a secret letter from the ECB dating from 2011 was published by former President Rodríguez Zapatero in 2013 and declassified in December 2014 by the ECB. In it, we can read verbatim:

> a) The wage-bargaining reform bill adopted by the Spanish government on 10 June 2011 should more effectively strengthen the role of company-level agreements, with a view to ensuring an effective decentralisation of wage negotiations. During the forthcoming parliamentary process, the law should be amended in order to reduce the possibility of industry-level agreements (at national or regional level) limiting the applicability of company-level agreements. b) Furthermore, we remain very concerned that the government has not taken any measures to abolish inflation-adjustment clauses. Such clauses are not an appropriate feature for labour markets inside a Monetary Union as they are a structural obstacle to the adjustment of labour costs and thereby contribute to hampering competitiveness and growth. We encourage the government to take bold and exceptional steps to exclude the use of such clauses in view of the current crisis.

It is clear that the great lines of reform had been drawn in Frankfurt and not in Madrid.

The impact of these reforms has been smaller than expected, as will be shown in subsequent paragraphs of this report. The most successful tool of the reforms, perhaps, has been the possibility of opting out. It was rigorously employed in 2013 (2,512 times, affecting 1,59,550 workers), but with reducing frequency nowadays (548 times up to March 2015, affecting 18,097 workers).[11] Company level bargaining has not had the expected development, at all.

---

11. http://mcaugt.org/documentos/14/doc14094.pdf (accessed 6 August 2017).

The main actors in the task of mitigating its effects have been the judges of the social jurisdiction, the specific branch of the Spanish judiciary charged with the application of labour law. They have built huge obstacles to the application of the new legislation, whenever possible. The European Social Charter is showing itself a powerful tool for lower courts to use in avoiding the reforms.[12] Nonetheless, these rulings can be challenged in higher courts, so only time will confirm if this tactic has been effective.

§8.03 THE PUBLIC SECTOR: THE DEMISE OF COLLECTIVE BARGAINING

As pointed out in our previous INLACRIS research, social dialogue has been completely halted within the context of the general administration of the state.[13] This kind of measure was explicitly justified in the subsequent *Decreto-Ley* 20/2012 on the grounds that 'the current economic situation and the need to reduce the public deficit without affecting the effectiveness of essential public services makes it necessary to improve the efficiency of the public administrations in the use of public resources, with the aim of contributing to the achievement of the essential objective of budget stability, resulting from the constitutional framework and the European Union'.

Particularly worrying was the amendment to Article 32 of the Basic Statute of Public Employees (EBEP) inserted by *Decreto-Ley* 20/2012. That provision now reads: 'The fulfilment of collective agreements and agreements affecting staff members shall be guaranteed, except when exceptionally and on serious grounds of public interest resulting from a substantial change in economic circumstances, the governing organs of the public administrations suspend or modify the fulfilment of collective agreements or agreements already signed in such manner as is strictly necessary to safeguard the public interest'.

In other words, the real effectiveness of collective bargaining is now made dependent on a decision by the public administration itself. Public power, and not collective autonomy, becomes the *ultima ratio,* creating an immediate option to depart from agreements, thus making hard-pressed public employers very happy. There is no procedure specified beyond the simple provision of information to the workers' representatives. The extent to which this provision complies with Article 37 of the Spanish Constitution is now a matter for the courts responsible for overseeing its implementation. In any event, challenges to decisions of this kind appear to have to been brought before the administrative courts as they are seeking to reverse the actions of a governmental organ within the public administration. This is likely to increase the time taken for a judgment to be reached and, hence, to reduce the immediacy of any resolution.[14]

---

12. C. Salcedo Beltrán, *La aplicabilidad directa de la Carta Social Europea por los órganos judiciales*, I Trabajo y Derecho, 27-52 (2016).
13. J. M. Miranda Boto, *Some Observations on Public Employment in Europe*, Vol. 5, 3-4 European Labour Law Journal, 255-266 (2014).
14. At the time of finishing this paper, four years after the reform, no decision has yet been taken.

Similarly, as far as working time is concerned, Article 50 EBEP is amended to provide for paid annual leave of twenty-two working days (not counting Saturdays as working days) or the corresponding pro rata entitlement in the event of less than full service in the previous year. In the same way, both in relation to public servants and staff employed under contract to the public administration and its dependent and associated bodies, the 2012 reform declares as 'suspended and without effect' all agreements and pacts concerning special leave days for personal reasons, holidays and days additional to personal days, or others of a similar nature.

Finally, the new version of Article 48 EBEP, inserted by *Decreto-Ley* 20/2012, should be mentioned, as it has standardised the rules on additional leave entitlements for public employees, in particular reducing the number of days of personal leave 'for special reasons' to three. All improvements obtained through collective bargaining are also suspended and deemed to have no effect.

Thus, there has been a general change in the way EBEP rules are formulated. Whereas previously they were considered basic rules that could be improved on or adapted by the different parts of the public administrations, under the new regime they have become uniform rules of an absolute nature for all public employees. The former possibilities of establishing supplements or variations have now been eliminated. In other words, the previous formulation in terms of simple or 'relative' mandatory law has been replaced by a different type of provision more typical of absolute mandatory law, which permits no alteration or improvement whether by a statutory or collectively agreed route.

§8.04 THE AGENTS OF COLLECTIVE BARGAINING: THE DOUBLE CHANNEL

Since 1985, no changes have taken place concerning this issue. Workers' representation is, perhaps, the most stable part of Spanish labour law. As a result of history and the clash of political circumstances, the Spanish representation system is based on a double channel.

On the one hand, there is the so-called legal representation, established in the *Estatuto de los Trabajadores*, that we can mainly summarise as works councils ('comités de empresa') and staff representatives ('delegados de personal'). Both of them represent all the employees in an establishment, including all types of contract relationship.[15] As they represent establishments, and not whole companies, the classic principle of 'unity of company' is no longer in force, and different establishments within the same company can have different agreements. On the other hand, the Supreme Court has ruled that a single works council cannot bargain on behalf of the others ('principle of correspondence').

On the other hand, there is the so-called trade union representation (*representación legal*), based on the *Ley Orgánica de Libertad Sindical* (LOLS, or Organic Act on

---

15. J. Cabeza Pereiro, *Comité de empresa*, in *Diccionario internacional de derecho del trabajo y de la seguridad social*, 213-217 (Valencia:Tirant lo Blanch, 2014).

Trade Union Freedom). Its main manifestations are the trade union sections within the enterprise, voluntary in their creation and only representing their own members.[16] Both bodies have legitimacy to bargain, according to Article 87 ET, and have the same competences and powers when doing so. Since the reform of 2011, trade unions have priority in bargaining, if they represent the majority of posts in the works council. Thus, both channels are clearly interlinked. In any event, case law has ruled that *hybrid* bargaining bodies are not possible. In order to negotiate an agreement for a company with multiple establishments, trade union sections have been shown by case law to be the most suitable body.

In the vast majority of cases, works councils have a very close bond with trade union organisations. In fact, the Spanish trade union model is based more on representation through the works council structure than on membership. However, as EIRO highlights, in sectors with high union membership – for example the automobile or chemical industries – the works councils, though remaining unionised, lose much of their 'prominence'. In these cases, the protagonists of trade union activity and organisation within enterprises are the workplace sections of the different unions, marshalling their own members.

Trade union members predominate within the works councils, as they are the source of legitimacy to obtain the category of 'most representative' trade union.[17] This is a legal status in Spain conferring many legal privileges, guarantees and access to public funding. Nonetheless, individual workers can be members of works councils and thus participate in collective bargaining (though that is not the rule).

Above company level, the only bargaining agents recognised by Spanish law are trade unions. On the employers' side, for this type of agreement, only organisations have the right to bargain. At these higher levels of bargaining, in order to respect the rules of the *Estatuto* and thus have general efficacy, it is necessary to achieve certain majorities. Any trade union holding 10% of the posts in works councils or staff representatives of a given geographical and functional scope can bargain, as well as those trade unions with 'most representative' status. It is necessary to have at least 50% of all representatives to conclude a valid collective agreement. For employers' organisations, the rate is calculated by taking into consideration the number of employees within the scope of the agreement.

§8.05 STRUCTURE OF COLLECTIVE BARGAINING: FROM BRANCH TO COMPANY

The predominance of sectoral agreements in a context of intense business fragmentation has been a defining characteristic of the Spanish bargaining structure, giving

---

16. A. Merino Segovia, *Sección sindical*, in *Diccionario internacional de derecho del trabajo y de la seguridad social*, 1933-1937 (Valencia: Tirant lo Blanch 2014).
17. J. L. Monereo Pérez, *La mayor representatividad sindical como eje del sistema de relaciones laborales en España*, 10 Revista derecho del trabajo, 283-327 (2016).

priority to intermediate levels of negotiation and province-level agreements especially.[18]

In this context, prior to the reform introduced by *Decreto-Ley* 7/2011, Article 84 ET ensured the enforcement of any existing agreement, which could not be affected 'by the content of agreements with a different scope' unless otherwise stated in a cross-industry agreement reached according to Article 83.2 ET. However, the trade unions and employers' organisations legitimised negotiation of a collective agreement in accordance with Articles 87 and 88 ET and could 'negotiate agreements that affect the contents of agreements held at a higher level' than that of the enterprise so long as such a decision was backed by the majority required to establish a negotiating body for the corresponding level (Article 84 ET, second paragraph). In such a case, a number of issues considered strategic to the labour balance in a sector or branch of activity could not be negotiated at lower levels.[19]

The aforementioned *Decreto-Ley* 7/2011 introduced significant changes in this regard, granting priority to company agreements on a number of issues essential to the management of employment contracts. However, it maintained governance of industrial relations by trade unions and employers' organisations by allowing them to agree (in state-level or regional industry agreements) on other rules regarding the structure of negotiation, thus limiting the priority implementation of company agreements. Furthermore, it created a new level of bargaining – that of the 'group of enterprises'.[20] This had existed for several years, based on case law,[21] but the reform was consecrated in the *Estatuto de los Trabajadores*. It is not really relevant, as it is focused on a very specific situation, amounting to between 10% and 20% of agreements above company level.

On this basis, the 2012 reform introduced the imperative rule for all purposes, unalterable by any agreement reached by the autonomy of the negotiating parties. Thus, absolute priority was given to company agreements (and the agreement in a group of enterprises) over the state-level, regional or lower level sectoral agreements on issues such as the basic wage and supplementary payments, or compensation for overtime,[22] specific payment schemes for shift work, working time and work time

---

18. J. R. Mercader Uguina, *La estructura de la negociación colectiva*, 76 Temas laborales: Revista andaluza de trabajo y bienestar social, 113-134 (2004).
19. J. Cruz Villalón, *Texto y contexto de las reformas de la negociación colectiva 2011 y 2012*, in *Reformas estructurales y negociación colectiva: XXX Jornadas Universitarias Andaluzas de Derecho del Trabajo y Relaciones Laborales*, 17-76 (Sevilla: CARL 2012).
20. H. Ysàs Molinero, *Derecho de negociación colectiva y grupos de empresa: comparación de sus rasgos principales en España y en Francia*, 51 Justicia laboral: revista de Derecho del Trabajo y de la Seguridad Social, 63-75 (2012).
21. R. Menéndez Calvo, *Las estructuras empresariales complejas: los grupos de empresas*, in *La Negociación Colectiva en España: Una mirada crítica*, (Valencia: Tirant Lo Blanch 2006).
22. E. E. Taléns Visconti, *Cuestiones en torno a la preferencia aplicativa del Convenio de Empresa en materia salarial*, 183 Nueva revista española de derecho del trabajo, 149-172 (2016).

distribution,[23] shift work schemes and annual planning of rest periods, etc.[24] Case law from the Supreme Court has recently declared that agreements below company level do not enjoy this particular position of privilege.[25] On the other hand, the Supreme Court has also indicated that this preference does not mean exclusivity. All these issues can be negotiated at other levels than company, in the absence of a company level regulation. Furthermore, the issues that enjoy preference must be interpreted in a restrictive manner.

Thus, the major reform in these years has been the shift of power from the sectoral agreement to the company agreement. The Spanish legislative tradition in these matters was the pre-eminence of the sectoral agreement. Since 2012, as stated above, the company agreement has had preference. However, according to the data provided by the employers' organisations, this option is not being really used in Spanish enterprises. Their size makes conducting collective bargaining difficult and the fear of legal problems usually stops employers from using this tool. As pointed out by law academics, having such a structure is a problem as most enterprises are small-scale (nine out of ten Spanish enterprises have ten employees or fewer), so there is usually no representation to negotiate a company agreement.

§8.06 THE LEGAL EFFECTS OF COLLECTIVE AGREEMENTS: THE OPTING-OUT AND *ULTRACTIVIDAD*

The general efficacy (*erga omnes*) of collective agreements is still the rule in Spanish labour law, for those agreements bargained according to the rules of Title III of the *Estatuto*. Nonetheless, some critical, minority voices in the legal academy and in the employers' confederations are asking for a change on this. No political party has yet dared to accept these proposals, as they would find a hostile reception from trade unions and perhaps from a large part of the employers.

However, the possibility of opting out from an existing collective agreement has been greatly strengthened by the most recent reforms, to the detriment of general efficacy. Legislation nowadays offers the possibility of amending the employment conditions established in an agreement, especially concerning wages, by means of agreements reached at the company level, based on exceptional causes and through a more or less formal procedure. Act 35/2010 of 17 September regarding urgent measures to reform the labour market was the first response to the economic crisis in the sphere of labour law. It significantly accelerated and simplified opting-out procedures in those cases where an enterprise's situation could be damaged as a result of a wage scheme forged through collective agreement.

---

23. M. Navas-Parejo Alonso, *Salario y jornada: entre la prioridad temporal del convenio sectorial y la preferencia aplicativa del convenio de empresa*, 176 Nueva revista española de derecho del trabajo 317-330 (2015).
24. A. Domínguez Morales, *La prioridad aplicativa del convenio colectivo de empresa: una mirada comparada Italia y España*, 105 Documentación laboral, 141-159 (2015).
25. A. B. Muñoz Ruíz, *La prioridad aplicativa del convenio colectivo de ámbito inferior a la empresa respecto al convenio de sector: dificultades y propuestas de solución*, 9 Trabajo y derecho: nueva revista de actualidad y relaciones laborales, 116-126 (2015).

Similarly, *Decreto-Ley* 3/2012 went further in this legal flexibilisation by enlarging the scope of the grounds on which opting out was possible to include most employment conditions, and by establishing a looser regulation of the economic, technical, organisational or productive reasons justifying the opting-out process.[26] Economic causes are deemed sufficient when business figures show a negative economic situation: for instance, current or expected losses or a continuing loss of income level or sales.[27] In any case, a decrease will be considered to be continuing if it takes place over two consecutive quarters. It should be pointed out that since the amendment introduced by Act 35/2010, legitimacy to negotiate an opt-out agreement has been extended to the workers' representatives authorised to negotiate an *erga omnes* applicable collective agreement and, in the absence of such representatives, a council appointed ad hoc and made up of three members, who can be company workers or members of trade unions with representation in the sector to which the company belongs.[28]

Lastly, it should be pointed out that the opting-out procedure includes a consultation period. The reform established that if such a period ends without agreement or without the parties submitting voluntarily to procedures to settle such differences, compulsory arbitration is enforced by the National Consultative Commission on Collective Agreements.[29]

The second great change in the reform of 2012 was the radical modification of *ultractividad*, the survival of the collective agreement after its termination, thus overcoming the legal void that occurs during the process of collective bargaining, encouraging the parties to regulate employment conditions anew in the corresponding sphere.

Traditionally, labour legislation in Spain sought to protect the stability of collective agreements. This conservationist approach was primarily articulated through legal references contained in Article 86 ET, according to which whenever a collective agreement ceased to have force, a new stage of negotiations was started with the aim of signing a new agreement. During this time, enforcement of the so-called legal content of the agreement was guaranteed (i.e., all provisions establishing and regulating working and employment conditions at the negotiating level of the agreement). The reform undertaken by *Decreto-Ley* 7/2011 opened up the autonomy of the negotiating parties, making the extended validity of the agreement a subsidiary issue.

The earthquake came in 2012. The extended validity of agreements was severely limited by the reform, which established that 'one year after a collective agreement has been contested without a new agreement or arbitration decision being reached, the

---

26. C. Martínez Moreno, *Impugnación de medidas de modificación sustancial de condiciones de trabajo y de inaplicación de convenios*, 4 Derecho de las Relaciones Laborales, 323-345 (2016).
27. J. M. Goerlich Peset, *Régimen de la negociación colectiva e inaplicación del convenio colectivo en la reforma de 2012*, (Valencia: Tirant lo Blanch, 2013).
28. P. Nieto Rojas, *Comisiones Ad Hoc y reorganización productiva empresarial: una solución para las empresas sin representación legal de los trabajadores*, in R. Escudero Rodríguez, (dir.), *La negociación colectiva en las reformas laborales de 2010, 2011 y 2012*, 57-86 (Madrid: Cinca 2012).
29. N. Mendoza Navas, *Los procedimientos de inaplicación de condiciones de trabajo al amparo de las decisiones de la Comisión Nacional Consultiva de Convenios Colectivos*, 74 Revista de derecho social, 61-86 (2016).

former agreement will no longer be enforced unless otherwise agreed. In such case, the applicable collective agreement at a higher level will be implemented'.[30]

One of the main concerns among academics and social partners once the reform was passed was that limiting the enforcement of an agreement would lead to a void in negotiation. This could place a large number of workers in a situation where no collective agreement was applicable once the date arrived when 'generalised decline' was possible (8 July 2013, one year after Law 3/2012 entered into force).[31]

As an immediate remedy, the social partners signed an Interconfederal Agreement establishing that 'before such term comes to an end, the negotiating parties must commit to continue negotiating, guaranteeing that the collective agreement will continue to be enforced during the duly-agreed duration of the process'. Later on, several court decisions have allowed the continuation of legal clauses in collective agreements that contained their own validity scheme prior to the reform. In any case, as pointed out by several authors, this mechanism must be understood in a context of norms that aim to regulate collective bargaining in Spain (Articles 37.1 and 28.1 Spanish Constitution) in accordance with its true structure.[32]

A remarkable ruling by the Supreme Court (22 December 2014) was the pioneer in the interpretation of the new Article 86 ET. According to that article, one year after the end of the validity of a collective agreement, the higher-level agreement enters into force. The problem raised in that ruling was the situation where there was no higher agreement. The enterprise had answered the question by applying the legal provisions, including those on wages. The Supreme Court ruled, in a very polemical decision (with two dissenting opinions from six Magistrates out of fourteen), that the working conditions existing in a collective agreement should effectively become contractual conditions in the situation described.[33]

§8.07 CONTENT AND PARAMETERS OF COLLECTIVE AGREEMENTS

The contents of collective bargaining have not changed in their essentials since 2007. That year, compulsory bargaining on gender and reconciliation issues was imposed in

---

30. C. Martínez Moreno, *Revisitando as regras sobre a vixencia e a ultractividade do convenio colectivo*, 1-1, Revista Galega de Dereito Social – 2ª etapa: (RGDS), 79-120, (2016).
31. S. Olarte Encabo, *La ultractividad de los convenios colectivos antes y después del 8 de julio de 2013. Debate doctrinal y primeras interpretaciones judiciales*, 12 Relaciones laborales: Revista crítica de teoría y práctica, 215-236 (2013).
32. C. Martínez Moreno, *La vigencia del convenio colectivo estatutario, problemática general y análisis en particular de la ultractividad*, in José Luis Monereo Pérez (dir.), *El sistema de negociación colectiva en España. Estudio de su régimen jurídico*, 587-625 (Cizur Menor: Thomson Reuters Aranzadi, 2013).
33. Luis Enrique de la Villa Gil, Antonio Ojeda-Avilés, Manuel Carlos Palomeque López, Elías González-Posada Martínez, José Ignacio García Ninet, *Reflexiones acerca de la sentencia del Pleno de la Sala de lo Social del Tribunal Supremo de 22 de diciembre de 2014, sobre ultractividad de los convenios colectivos*, 40 Revista General de Derecho del Trabajo y de la Seguridad Social, (2015).

Chapter 8: The Spanish Example §8.07

all collective agreements applying to more than 250 workers.[34] In fact, collective bargaining in Spain lacks creativity and is mainly governed by inertia. Contents repeat themselves throughout the years, even in the case of derogated norms.

The only real innovation in the parameters of collective bargaining came with Act 20/2007, on the Statute of Independent Work ('*Estatuto del trabajo autónomo*'). That created the possibility of 'professional interest agreements' for TRADEs. TRADEs are 'economically dependent, autonomous workers' ('*Trabajadores autónomos económicamente dependientes*'), truly independent workers, at least 75% of whose income comes from a single customer.[35] Between 2007 and 2011, thus in the first years of the crisis, a reduced number of these agreements was negotiated. According to one of the best academic law papers on this subject,[36] the most important were: Panrico (a bread company), with independent drivers; DSV Road Spain, SAU, also with drivers; the association of basketball clubs, with referees; Lozano Transportes, SAU, again with drivers; Sertrans Catalunya, S.A., idem. As they do not have to be published officially, it is hard to know the reality of these agreements. In any case, it is clear that they were not a resounding success. That is the same conclusion for nearly the whole of Act 20/2007.

---

34. R. Menéndez Calvo, *Estudio de la reforma de 2010 desde la perspectiva de género: clasificación y promoción o ascensos en la negociación colectiva*, in R. Escudero Rodríguez, (dir.), *La negociación colectiva en las reformas laborales de 2010, 2011 y 2012*, 361-382 (Madrid: Cinca 2012).
35. H. Álvarez Cuesta, *El régimen profesional del trabajador autónomo económicamente dependiente: análisis de los últimos pronunciamientos judiciales*, 10 Actualidad laboral, 4 et seq. (2014).
36. M. A. Castro Argüelles, *Los acuerdos de interés profesional: un balance de la negociación llevada a cabo al amparo del estatuto del trabajador autónomo*, 29 Anales de derecho, 34-80 (2011).

PART II The Contents of Collective
    Agreements: Old and New Issues

A Wages

CHAPTER 9
Decentralisation of Wage Setting Mechanisms and Statutory Minimum Wage: Towards the End of Sectoral Collective Bargaining?

Piera Loi

§9.01 WAGE-SETTING MECHANISMS UNDER THE NEW ECONOMIC GOVERNANCE

This paper discusses some central issues raised by changes in wage-setting mechanisms, and particularly collective bargaining, due to EU interventions during the economic crisis. The INLACRIS research on decentralisation of collective bargaining[1] has shown that, directly or indirectly, EU institutions and especially the new economic governance have been determinant in reshaping the role and functions of collective bargaining in EU Member States, generally driving it towards a clear decentralised model (even if there are some exceptions).[2]

We will see that the decentralisation of collective bargaining in wage setting can be considered a general phenomenon boosted by the economic crisis in many EU countries. Even if the collective bargaining decentralisation process was already regarded as a possible way out from the crisis in different countries, responding to company needs and market competition,[3] the strong EU interventionism towards

---

1. *See* in this volume Part. 1.
2. This is confirmed by other comparative research on the same issue. See e.g., S. Clauwaert & I. Schömann, *The Crisis and National Labour Law Reforms: A Mapping Exercise*, 2012.04, ETUI working paper, (Brussels: ETUI 2012) (available at: http://www.etui.org/Publications2/Working-Papers/The-crisis-and-national-labour-law-reforms-a-mapping-exercise, accessed July 2017).
3. See the National reports K. Nebe, M. Maul Sartory, *Germany*; J.M. Miranda Boto & R. Rodrìguez Contreras, *Spain*; M.C. Escande-Varniol, *France*; A. Koukiadaki & L. Kretsos, *Greece*; T.

decentralisation of collective bargaining aimed at attaining its austerity objectives – as the only crisis exit strategy – is capable of producing serious side effects in national industrial relations systems. It is particularly in wage setting that the pressure towards decentralised collective bargaining can be seen as an attack on the cornerstones of national collective bargaining systems.[4] We will see that before the crisis and the establishment of the new European economic governance, the general picture of wage setting through collective bargaining was dominated by co-ordinated or multi-employer collective bargaining, with some clear exceptions such as the UK, traditionally described as a single-employer collective bargaining system. Since the crisis, the picture has dramatically changed: with a few exceptions (such as Belgium) still anchored to the prevalence of sectoral or inter-sectoral collective bargaining in wage setting, the generality of Member States have moved towards a system of wages bargained by decentralised collective agreements, even if that is within different models of organised or disorganised decentralisation (see *infra*).

At the same time, it should be underlined that in many Member States, with some exceptions, a statutory minimum wage has been introduced. The question to analyse is how these two phenomena, decentralisation of wage setting and the introduction (or confirmation) of statutory minimum wages, can affect the functions and very survival of national/sectoral collective bargaining – or more generally of multi-employer bargaining.

The first issue to be addressed is the function of multi-employer bargaining as an alternative model to single-employer bargaining and as some scholars have pointed out, decentralisation of collective bargaining is one of the different forms taken by the marketisation process in Europeanisation.[5] Marketisation is described as the extension of markets in any area of life and includes processes like flexibilisation and deregulation.[6] Normally this process produces two opposite consequences: gains in efficiency, and losses and damages, that are not simple by-products occasionally created by market functioning. Some gain from the operation of the market, while others bear the negative effects of it – and the calculation of these negative externalities cannot be ignored.[7] Seen from the negative externalities perspective, the marketisation process is an expression of the flexicurity agenda, and the frequent inability of Member States to guarantee worker security during the crisis can be described as a negative externality that the crisis has revealed. At the same time, other kinds of negative externalities can be produced when a labour market does not function as such. When, for example, labour costs are too high, prices tend to increase, and this may lead to a loss of

---

Gyulaváry, *Hungary*; P. Loi, *Italy*; J. Unterschütz, *Poland*, in M.C. Escande-Varniol, S. Laulom & E. Mazuyer (sous la coordination de), *Quelle droit social dans une Europe en crise?*, (Bruxelles: Larcier 2012). In all these countries the authors report a more or less extensive phenomenon of decentralisation of collective bargaining as a strategic exit from the crisis.
4. A, Dufresne, *The Trade Union Response to the European Economic Governance Regime. Transnational Mobilisation and Wage Coordination*, 2 Transfer, 143 (2015).
5. C. Crouch, *Introduction: Labour market and Social Policy after the Crisis*, Transfer, 15 (2001).
6. *Ibid.*, p. 8.
7. *Ibid.*, p. 8. C. Crouch suggests the use of the Coasian approach in considering the negative externalities produced by the functioning of the labour market as for pollution, environmental damage and man–made climate change.

business; or when an incompetent worker cannot be dismissed because dismissal legislation makes it very difficult to dismiss him/her, this may impede other skilled workers from applying for the same job, and so on.[8] In other words, these kinds of negative externality are normally produced by the labour market, and they need to be calculated and balanced. The most relevant negative externality produced by the market is the insecurity suffered by workers and their families, due to current or future job losses and income reduction.[9] Of course, not all workers suffer the same level of insecurity. Similar conclusions have been reached by other researches that has adopted the risk perspective, highlighting the fact that workers have been exposed in different ways to the negative effects of the crisis itself, with the risks produced by the functioning of labour markets – and, indirectly, by the financial market – being borne by some workers but not by others.[10] The question is how to get this negative externality calculated and balanced. Collective bargaining, especially during the economic crisis, has demonstrated the capacity to address negative externalities produced by the functioning of the market, as well as playing an important role in moderating the impact on employment of the dramatic downturn in economic activity.[11] The techniques to maintain employment through collective agreements have been very different: agreements on short-time working, freezes in basic pay, suspension of pay premiums, and so on.[12] Empirical research has tried to demonstrate that this securisation function against the marketisation process was mainly guaranteed by multi-employer bargaining systems, especially at the onset of the economic crisis. When it was clear that the crisis was not a contingent one, employers found it easier to impose wage moderation and increased flexibility without offering employment securities. The second phase of the crisis is characterised by the need to decentralise collective bargaining in multi-employer bargaining systems, with the increased use by decentralised collective agreements of clauses opting out from higher levels of collective agreements. In the short term, employers asked for more marketisation, better served by a single-employer bargaining system.[13] In other words, single-employer collective bargaining, especially if referring to wage setting, better serves company needs for flexibility than employee needs for security and, from the economic analysis of law, does not calculate or internalise negative externalities.

---

8. *Ibid.*, p. 9.
9. P. Marginson, M. Keune & D. Bohle, *Negotiating the Effect of Uncertainty? The Governance Capacity of Collective Bargaining Under Pressure*, 1 Transfer, 38 (2014).
10. P. Loi, *Risk: A New Paradigm to Face Market Challenges*, 5 ELLJ, 390 (2014).
11. P. Marginson, M. Keune & D. Bohle, *Negotiating the Effect of Uncertainty? The Governance Capacity of Collective Bargaining Under Pressure*, supra n. 9, p. 38.
12. V. Glassner & M. Keune, *The Crisis and Social Policy: The Role of Collective Agreements*, 4 International Labour Review, 351 (2012).
13. P. Marginson, M. Keune & D. Bohle, *Negotiating the Effect of Uncertainty? The Governance Capacity of Collective Bargaining Under Pressure*, supra n. 9, p. 50.

§9.02 CHANGES IN WAGE-SETTING MECHANISMS AND EUROPEAN ECONOMIC GOVERNANCE

Decentralisation of collective bargaining was a feature of some industrial relations systems even before the crisis, so the new economic governance has accelerated a process that was already on its way, pushed by market principles and the need to overcome losses in productivity. Nonetheless it is a widely held opinion[14] that European economic governance has pushed the process of decentralisation of collective bargaining to its maximum and has produced dramatic changes in collectively bargained wages in a number of Member States. The first question that could be raised in relation to these changes is how any kind of intervention by EU institutions in a European legal framework where the question of pay is totally excluded from EU competencies could be considered legitimate under Article 153(5) TFEU. The same question could be raised in relation to freedom of association, excluded from EU competencies by the same Article 153(5) TFEU, recognised as a fundamental right by Articles 12 (freedom of association) and 28 (right to collective bargaining) of the EU Charter of Fundamental Rights. From this point of view, any EU intervention aiming, directly or indirectly, to alter the hierarchy between regulatory collective sources could be deemed to violate Member State competencies under Articles 153(5) TFEU and 28 of the Charter of Fundamental Rights. That is not to mention other international labour sources such as the European Social Charter Articles 5 (right to organise) and 6 (right to bargain collectively) or the ILO conventions nos. 98/1947 and 87/1948. It is worth remembering that the fundamental right of freedom of association is interpreted by the ILO conventions primarily as a freedom 'from' the state, or we could say from a supranational organisation of states like the EU, so that 'public authorities shall refrain from any interference which would restrict this right or impede the lawful exercise thereof' (Article 3 of ILO Convention concerning Freedom of Association and Protection of the Right to Organise, 1948, no. 87).

However, ascertaining a violation of EU treaties or of the international sources by European institutions is not an easy task if we stick to a formalist interpretation of legal norms, since many of the regulatory sources forming part of the new economic governance are on the one hand based on intergovernmental treaties and, on the other, soft law mainly in the form of recommendations.

As we all know, European economic governance comprises a set of acts whose effectiveness on Member State regulatory sources was defined, at least in its first phase, under the Stability and Growth Pact (SGP), and not linked to their mandatory nature, following the regulatory model of open co-ordination. The economic crisis exposed the

---

14. See G. Van Gyes & T. Schulten (eds), *Wage Bargaining under the New European Economic Governance. Alternative Strategies for Inclusive Growth*, 11 et seq. (Brussels: ETUI 2015); P. Marginson & C. Weltz, *European Wage Setting Mechanisms Under Pressure: Negotiated and Unilateral Change and the EU's Economic Governance Regime*, 4 Transfer, 429 et seq. (2015); A, Dufresne, *The Trade Union Response to the European Economic Governance Regime. Transnational Mobilisation and Wage Coordination*, supra n. 4, p. 143; P. Marginson, M. Keune & D. Bohle, *Negotiating the Effect of Uncertainty? The Governance Capacity of Collective Bargaining Under Pressure*, supra n. 9, pp. 48 et seq.

weaknesses of this model and led to the introduction of the European Semester in 2011,[15] an annual economic coordination cycle through which the European Commission analyses economic and structural reforms of Member States and subsequently address a set of recommendations to them, aiming to align their policies with the economic objectives set at EU level. A stricter economic co-ordination was set up in 2011 with the so-called Six Pack, five Regulations and one Directive, setting the new economic governance. The Six Pack contains a system of early warnings for Member States not in line with the stricter economic constraints. Member State economies are monitored by the Commission, which analyses their plans for sound public finances (Stability and Convergence Programmes [SCPs]) and for reforms and measures towards smart, sustainable and inclusive growth (National Reform Programmes [NRPs]). An assessment of Member States' Stability and Convergence Programmes and National Reform Programmes is made by the Commission following economic and financial indicators, in order to verify compliance with targets defined in the Europe 2020 strategy. In case of non- compliance, the Commission proposes country-specific recommendations (CSRs), which are formally adopted by the Council.

European economic governance has produced a massive unprecedented intervention in collectively bargained wages. It is primarily via the Country Specific Recommendations –part of the European Semester – that the European institutions, the European Commission and the Council in particular, have exerted a major influence on Member State wage-setting mechanisms and social policies in general.[16]

In some cases, these interventions have been realised through non-institutionalised and soft instruments: it is widely recognised[17] that changes in wage setting in countries receiving financial assistance from the Troika are directly dependent on government measures imposing changes to adapt to Troika requests. Although it is not the aim of this paper to evaluate the pros and cons of the economic effects of EU interventions on economic growth and their utility as exit strategy from the crisis, we share the view that the crisis in Europe has been erroneously interpreted as a crisis of competitiveness, which is why wages have been seen as the core adjustment variable for 'internal devaluation', in order to restore competitiveness through a reduction in labour costs.[18] EU institutions' heavy interventions have been channelled, in many cases, towards the structure of collective bargaining, the main instrument of

---

15. The European semester has been modified by the Treaty on Stability, Coordination and Governance in the Economic and Monetary Union (TSCG), the fiscal component of which is the Fiscal Compact, entered into force on 1 January 2013. It is an Intergovernmental Treaty signed by the Member States of the Eurozone and other eight Member States. It is not an EU Treaty and does not amend the existing EU treaties but its implementation involves using the EU institutions, part of EU law. The Fiscal Compact complements and reinforces the Six Pack, five Regulations and one Directive setting the new economic governance. Later, the so-called Two Pack entered into force (2013), aiming to strengthen fiscal and economic surveillance.
16. See the overview on country specific recommendations 2011-2012, 2012-2013 and 2013-2014.
17. See P. Marginson & C. Weltz, comparative report, *Changes in Wage Setting Mechanisms in the Context of the Crisis and the EU's New Economic Governance Regime* (Eurofound 2014).
18. See G. Van Gyes & T. Schulten (eds), *Wage Bargaining under the New European Economic Governance. Alternative Strategies for Inclusive Growth*, supra n. 14, p. 9.

wage regulation, heavily affecting the current and future architecture of the industrial relations systems of the Member States addressed by EU interventions.

§9.03 SOFT AND HARD INTERVENTIONS OF EU INSTITUTIONS ON NATIONAL WAGE REGULATORY SOURCES

As we have seen in the preceding paragraph, the techniques used by the EU institutions to modify national wage-setting mechanisms have been elaborated in order to bypass two main obstacles: the lack of any formal competence at EU level in the treaties as far as wages or the right of association and collective bargaining are concerned. Both issues are, in fact, excluded from EU competences by Article 153(5) TFEU.

The types of intervention differ based on the more or less serious imbalance problems of the Member State involved. Through the new economic governance, EU interventions in wage-setting mechanisms are institutionalised, but in other cases the intervention of EU institutions in Member States' policies have been realised through non-institutionalised, but largely effective, procedures. We refer to procedures such as direct requests from the European Central Bank. Though differing in form, the requests were more or less similar: to enhance the role of firm-level collective bargaining in wage setting. The cases of Italy and Spain are revealing of the overall strategy. In the famous 'secret' letter sent on 29 September 2011 by Jean-Claude Trichet and Mario Draghi,[19] the European Central Bank asked the Italian government (Berlusconi was the President of the Council of Ministers at the time) to implement fundamental reforms of the labour market and the pension system in order to restore the investors' confidence. The series of suggested reforms were all supposed to follow the flexicurity policy. The most invasive intrusion of the ECB was in the area of the collective bargaining system, with the 'suggestion' of allowing firm-level agreements to tailor wages and working conditions to firms' specific needs and to increase their relevance with respect to other layers of negotiation. Clearly enough, the ECB declared its preference for decentralised collective bargaining in the matter of wage setting, since that enables it to tailor wages to firms' specific needs. From this point of view, the idea behind the decentralisation of collective bargaining in wage setting could not be clearer: it is a way of guaranteeing rapid adaptation to the functioning of the market, following the logic of marketisation behind the flexicurity agenda.

Another 'secret' letter was sent by the ECB in 2011 and published by the then President Rodríguez Zapatero in 2013. The precise requests of the ECB, as far as wage setting, were as follows:

> a) The wage-bargaining reform bill adopted by the Spanish government on 10 June 2011 should more effectively strengthen the role of firm-level agreements, with a view to ensuring an effective decentralisation of wage negotiations. During the forthcoming parliamentary process, the law should be amended in order to reduce the possibility of industry-level agreements (at national or regional level) to limit the applicability of firm-level agreements. b) Furthermore, we remain very concerned that the government has not taken any measures to abolish inflation-

---

19. Published by the Corriere della Sera on 5 October 2011.

adjustment clauses. Such clauses are not an appropriate feature for labour market inside a Monetary Union as they are a structural obstacle to the adjustment of labour costs and thereby contribute to hampering competitiveness and growth. We encourage the government to take bold and exceptional steps to exclude the use of such clauses in view of the current crisis.

Moreover, in this case, the ECB's vision in relation to wage-setting mechanisms is clear enough: wages are seen as labour costs hampering competitiveness (the reference to growth in this case seems more of an embellishment than a real conviction, given the wage restriction policies pursued by EU institutions). Once again, the paramount instrument suggested is to let the collective agreement at enterprise level prevail over the sectoral collective agreements.

Following these suggestions, the Spanish reform of 2012[20] gave absolute priority to company agreements (and agreements in groups of undertakings) over state-level, regional- or lower-level industry agreements on issues such as the basic wage and wage supplements, payment or compensation for overtime, and specific payment schemes for shift work. These provisions have been criticised, since the size of most undertakings in Spain is very small (nine out of ten Spanish undertakings have ten employees or fewer) and no workers' representation to negotiate a company agreement is present.[21]

In Italy some years before the ECB letter, the tendency towards decentralisation of collective bargaining was inaugurated by an inter-sectoral collective agreement signed in January 2009 by the most important employers association (Confindustria) and two out of the three most representative union confederations: Cisl and Uil. The left-wing CGIL union confederation did not sign the agreement. The most controversial part of the January 2009 agreement is the possibility of introducing at decentralised level 'opting-out clauses' to cope with a territorial or enterprise crisis or to foster economic growth and employment creation. These clauses can derogate from both the economic and normative parts of national sectoral agreements.[22]

This is definitively the part of the agreements that was most influenced by the crisis context and represents the most important reason for the CGIL's refusal to sign the agreement. The 2009 agreement was confirmed by subsequent agreements in 2011, 2013 and 2014, which faced the question of the representativeness of the contracting agent. If a derogatory agreement at enterprise level is to produce effects, it has to be signed by representative actors. That is why the more recent inter-sectoral agreements deal with the question of representativeness,[23] which has been rather explosive since

---

20. Decreto Ley no. 3/2013 The 'opting out' from national collective agreements is regulated by Article 82.3 ET, increasing the possibilities to opt out from such agreements by enterprise collective agreements; enterprise collective agreements have partial priority over the industry-based agreement (Article 84.2 ET), thus eliminating the authority of social partners to specify a suitable negotiation structure; another provision establishes a temporary limitation on the 'extended validity' ('ultra-actividad') of collective agreements (Article 86.3 ET) to avoid the forced extension of their content.
21. See Y. Maneiro Vázquez & J.M. Miranda Boto, in this Volume, Part 1, Chapter 8.
22. Point 16 of the January 2009 agreement.
23. The importance of the question of the representativeness of the agent of derogatory agreements at enterprise level is demonstrated by the French solutions. The Law of 14 June 2013 reinforced

the Fiat case demonstrated the weakness of the industrial relations system in Italy in the face of the flexibility needs of that kind of multinational enterprise. The question of the representativeness of the agent of derogatory agreements at enterprise level is demonstrated by the French solutions. The Law of 14 June 2013 reinforced the role of enterprise collective agreements: the reduction of wages or the increased duration of work could be decided in agreements on professional and geographical mobility exchange.

The EU institutions have addressed their suggestions on wage setting to another group of Member States through formalised *country-specific recommendations* and *memoranda of understanding*.

The philosophy of EU institutions in giving more or less strict indications to Member States on wage policies is clearly illustrated in the DG ECFIN Report on 'Labour Market Developments in Europe 2012'. This document contains a list of measures that, following the employment-friendly ideology of the EU institutions, should be adopted in wage setting:

- Statutory and contractual minimum and collective minimum wages via tripartite agreements: enacted measures decrease statutory and contractual minimum wages/tripartite agreements decrease the indicative wage threshold for lower-level wage negotiations beyond past records, or remove/decrease non-wage emoluments.
- Government interventions, tripartite agreements, and other measures on wage- bargaining mechanisms. Enacted measures, governmental interventions or tripartite agreements.
- decrease the bargaining coverage or (automatic) extension of collective agreements.
- reform the bargaining system in a less centralised way, for instance by removing or limiting the 'favourability principle', or introducing/extending the possibility to derogate from higher-level agreements or to negotiate firm-level agreements.
- result in an overall reduction in the wage-setting power of trade unions.
- Performance-related pay: enacted measures increase the share of the variable component (dependent on workers' productivity/performance) on employees' wages or the share of company profits and bonuses.[24]

The picture of techniques used by the EU institutions to drive the wage-setting decentralisation process should be completed by analysing the case of Member States under international bailout programmes. The governments of a group of six countries

---

the role of enterprise collective agreements: the reduction of wages or the increased duration of work could be decided in agreements on professional and geographical mobility exchange, but it was the law of August 2008 that established the representativeness rules. *See* C.Nicod, P-E. Berthier, F. Debord & S. Laulom, *French National Report*, Inlacris Budapest Seminar, 2015 and Ch. Vigneau in this volume, *infra*.

24. European Commission, *Labour Market Developments in the European Union*, European Economy 104 (5/2012). Available at http://ec.europa.eu/economy_finance/publications/european_economy/2012/pdf/ee-2012-5_en.pdf (accessed July 2017).

Chapter 9: Wage Setting Mechanisms and Statutory Minimum Wage   §9.03

(Greece, Hungary, Portugal and Romania, and Ireland and Latvia) have signed memoranda of understanding with the Troika (European Commission, European Central Bank and International Monetary Fund).[25]

The other countries have received precise indications in the country-specific recommendations (CSR) within the context of the European Semester (France, Belgium, Italy, Slovenia, Bulgaria and Finland). The memoranda of understanding have either exerted a direct intervention on the wage structure through wage freezes, especially in the public sector, or cuts in minimum wages (see the example of Greece and Portugal), or an indirect intervention in the structure of collective bargaining. The same set of interventions seeking changes in collective bargaining structures and wage-setting arrangements are contained in the CSR, and are surely aimed at rendering wages more responsive to market conditions. They can be summarised as follows: a first set of measures aimed at decentralisation of collective bargaining means the ending of collective bargaining at national level in Romania, with the reduction of extension mechanisms and the applicability of sectoral collective agreements only to signatory parties (e.g., Romania, Greece); the introduction of opting-out clauses in the national/sectoral collective agreements or the predominance of enterprise-level collective agreements over higher levels (Greece, Spain); the abolition of the favourability principle (Greece); new criteria on trade union representativeness (Romania) and on the representativeness criteria validity of company-level agreements (Italy), and the possibility of opting-out from law and national collective agreements (Italy).[26]

As we have seen among European institutions, there is a dominant view circulating on wages, which is strictly linked with the dominant view on the reasons behind the crisis. The economic crisis is seen as a crisis of cost competitiveness and the cures identified by EU institutions are all in the direction of eliminating or reducing this loss of competitiveness. At the same time, wages are considered the major causes of this loss since in deficit countries they are too high and imbalances are the results of unit labour cost developments.

Economic and sociological literature strongly criticises this narrow concept of competitiveness, focussed exclusively on labour costs and confining wages to being a cost factor, completely ignoring their role in domestic demand[27] and most of all neglecting their constituting a fundamental right, defined by international sources and constitutional provision in various Member States. Besides that, the evidence about the impact of collective bargaining structures on macroeconomic performance in general, and on aggregate employment and unemployment, is considered inconclusive in much

---

25. The EBC was not formally part of the bailout programme in the case of Romania, which is not a Eurozone country.
26. European Commission, *Labour Market Developments in Europe*, supra n. 24, p. 51.
27. T. Müller, T. Schulten & S. Zuckerstätter, *Wages and Economic Performance in Europe*, in G. Van Gyes & T. Schulten (eds), *Wage Bargaining under the New European Economic Governance. Alternative Strategies for Inclusive Growth*, 259 et seq. (Brussels: ETUI 2015).

of the research.[28] What is clear, instead, is that these policies have produced dangerous by-products in the whole collective bargaining system.[29]

§9.04 WAGE SETTING BETWEEN LAW AND COLLECTIVE BARGAINING

Wage setting is at the core of any collective bargaining system. In all EU Member States, the first experiences of collective bargaining are linked to pay setting and no longer left to the arbitrary rules of the individual employment contract, given the power imbalances between the two parties to the employment contract. At the same time, the determination of wages has generally been excluded from statutory regulation, at least until the advent of national constitutions or the International Charter of Fundamental Rights, which establishes very general principles such as equality of pay, a sufficient wage and so on. In spite of the enduring differences between legal systems, we can say that, generally speaking, wage setting is left to the agreement of collective actors, between statutory and individual regulation. Nonetheless, in many EU countries legislation on the minimum wage has been introduced, in some cases a long time ago and in others quite recently, to guarantee minimum wages to categories excluded from collective bargaining coverage.

Modern industrial relations and labour law systems somehow maintain these features of their origins: labour law and wage regulation are still a matter for collective bargaining. An historical analysis of the evolution of wage determination would be beyond the scope of this paper, but it is important to bear in mind that setting wages is one of the key functions of collective bargaining in industrial relations systems, aimed at protecting workers against the risk of losing purchasing power and guaranteeing them security of pay. But in the context of the economic crisis and under the pressure of market needs, enterprises are pushing towards a marked differentiation and flexibilisation of pay mechanisms, also through decentralisation of collective bargaining. In this new context of greater wage insecurity, in order to guarantee more security to workers, a possible solution could be the imposition of a statutory minimum wage. The introduction of a statutory minimum wage has multiple aims, but it is generally recognised that combating poverty, aggravated by wage insecurity, is one of the most important.[30]

---

28. M. Keune, *Wage Flexibilisation and the Minimum Wage*, in European Commission (ed.) *Industrial Relations in Europe* 2010, 128 (Luxembourg, 2011); critics also by T. Schulten & T. Müller, *A New European Interventionism? The Impact of the New European Economic Governance on Wages and Collective Bargaining*, in David Natali & Bart Vanhercke (eds), *Social Developments in the European Union* 190 et seq. (2012).
29. See e.g., the countries where decentralisation in wage setting has been driven by CSR or memoranda of understanding that produced a dramatic reduction in the number of collective agreements (see the case of Portugal, Spain and the case of Italy and France).
30. J. Addison & L. Blackburn, *Minimum Wages and Poverty*, vol. 52 no. 3 Industrial and Labor Relations Review, 393 et seq. (1999); the aim of reducing the wage differentials and the booster effect on economic growth should not be underestimated E. Hein, A. Truger & T. Van Treek, *The European Financial and Economic Crisis: Alternative Solutions from a (Post-) Keynesian Perspective*, 9 IMK Working Paper (2011).

The necessity of determining wage uniformity by a collective agreement for all workers performing a certain job entails the construction of the principle that wages set by collective agreements cannot be reduced and modified *in pejus* by the employment contract. This is the cornerstone of the inderogability of collective agreements by individual parties to the employment contract rule, a declination of what Otto Khan Freund called collective power.[31] If the aim of a collective agreement was originally to set wages (see the *tariff vertrag* that was the first kind of collective agreement), other negotiation issues were gradually added to collective bargaining. The same concept of inderogability is linked at higher level to the necessity of not modifying the wages set by higher-level collective agreements, and then applied in similar terms to the relationship between collective agreements and individual employment contracts.

The aim of the EU interventions is first of all to open a breach in the whole construction and then to dismantle it. Before the crisis, the majority of Member States had a centralised wage-setting system controlled by sectoral collective bargaining. A centralised, collectively bargained wage-setting system needs institutional and legislative support to be effective. One of the most important pillars is the favourability principle, avoiding any deviation from the collectively bargained clause by the individual parties to the employment contract being considered legitimate. Another principle, established by law or by collective agreements, is the principle of hierarchies between different levels of collective agreements.

The principle of the inderogability (and thus the favourability) of the higher levels of collective bargaining is either discouraged or strongly opposed. In the short term, given that the aim of the EU institutions was to regulate wages in EU Member States (paradoxically lacking any competence in treaties), and that wages in Member States are predominantly regulated through collective agreements, it was necessary to reshape the structure and functions of collective bargaining in most countries.

The amplitude of the EU interventions in collective bargaining structures is clarified by the list of measures indicated by the Troika with regard to collective bargaining,[32] and comprising:

- the abolition or termination of national collective agreements;
- facilitation of the derogation of firm-level agreements from sectoral agreements or legislative provisions, for instance through opening or hardship clauses, or by generally giving firm-level agreements priority over (cross-)sectoral agreements;
- suspension of the favourability principle, relating to the relationship between sectoral and company agreements;
- introduction of more restrictive criteria for the extension of collective agreements;
- reduction of the continuity of application of expired collective agreements;

---

31. O. Kahn Freund, *Labour and the Law*, 17 (London: Stevens & Sons, 1983).
32. Well summarised by T. Schulten & T. Müller, *A New European Interventionism? The Impact of the New European Economic Governance on Wages and Collective Bargaining*, supra n. 28, p. 196.

- extension of the possibility for non-union employee representatives to conclude collective agreements at company level.

It is a common fear that all these measures will inevitably 'weaken trade union representation and action at all bargain levels'.[33]

Another important issue to analyse is the relationship between collective agreements and the law. It is important to understand if any change in the relationship between these two regulatory sources has intervened, since in many cases wage setting through decentralised collective agreements is conducted in countries where a statutory minimum wage already exists.

In many countries, collective bargaining has traditionally been supported by legal provisions[34] following the auxiliary legislation model. But this is not the only scheme. The complexity of the relationship between law and collective agreements in different legal systems cannot be summarised in this paper, but we can surely describe this complex relationship as a continuous process of delegating regulatory functions from the law to the collective agreements.[35] In general, the delegating function process is from the law to the sectoral or national collective agreements, in which the law recognises the solidarity function, i.e., the capacity to balance advantages and disadvantages for all the workers involved.

Besides, that is not an uncommon phenomenon, boosted by the recent interventions of the EU institutions, and involving the legitimation of the enterprise collective agreement to derogate the law *in pejus* too. From this point of view, a very controversial intervention can be seen in Italy, with the enactment of Law no. 148/2012, whose Article 8 provides that in a vast number of issues (ranging from dismissal and atypical forms of employment to wages and so on), enterprise collective agreements can be signed also derogating *in pejus* from legal provisions. The principle of the predominance of enterprise collective agreements over the law can therefore be used for wage setting, too. From this point of view, enterprise collective agreements can be regarded as the instrument for dismantling the securities established by the law. These considerations bring another set of questions: what are the relationships between decentralised wage setting and the existence of a statutory minimum wage, when the principle of the predominance of enterprise collective agreements over the law is also determined in wage setting?

---

33. S. Clauwaert & I. Schömann, *The Crisis and National Labour Law Reforms: A Mapping Exercise*, supra n. 2, p. 14.
34. F. Traxler, *Collective Bargaining in the OECD: Developments, Preconditions and Effects*, European Journal of Industrial Relations, 207 et seq. (1998); P. Marginson, *European Wage Setting Mechanisms Under Oressure: Negotiated and Unilateral Change in the EU's Economic Governance Regime*, Transfer 433 (2015).
35. See A. Lo Faro, *Finzioni e funzioni della contrattazione collettiva comunitaria* (Milano: Giuffrè 1997).

§9.05 WAGES BETWEEN LEGAL AND COLLECTIVE SOURCES AND A STATUTORY MINIMUM WAGE: SOME COMPARATIVE REMARKS

Wage dynamics in most EU countries are governed by collective bargaining.[36] Traditionally collective agreements are the principal regulatory source of wages in almost all EU Member States, but we should not underestimate the role of law in wage regulation. First, many international and European legal sources contain general principle on wages that signatory Member States should respect. For example the Community Charter of Fundamental Social Rights for Workers, adopted by the EU in 1989, even if not a mandatory instrument, contains the principle that every job must be paid a fair remuneration (Title 1 [5]). The 1961 'European Social Charter' of the Council of Europe provides 'the right to a fair remuneration sufficient for a decent standard of living...' (Article 4). The principle of fair wages is also provided in many written constitutions of EU Member States such as Belgium, Italy, Spain, Portugal and the Czech Republic, as well as in the federal constitutions of several German states. In order to guarantee the right to decent or fair wages, the states can set minimum wages, so it is important to distinguish between the concepts of a decent wage and a minimum wage by saying that they normally but not necessarily coincide, since the latter could be higher than the former. Following ILO Conventions no. 26 in 1928 (*Agreement on Minimum-wage fixing machinery*) and no. 131 in 1970 (*Convention concerning Minimum Wage Fixing, with Special Reference to Developing Countries*), all states should undertake a system of minimum wages to cover all groups of wage earners, and this system should have the force of law and not be subject to abatement.

These ILO conventions do not preclude any form of regulation, but establish that the level of the minimum wage should be determined 'in agreement or after full consultation with the representative organisations of employers and workers concerned'.

In the majority of EU Member States, there is a statutory minimum wage applicable to all sectors. The exceptions are represented by Italy, Austria, Cyprus, Denmark, Finland and Sweden, where no statutory minimum wage exists. Germany was traditionally included among the states with no statutory minimum wage, but recent reforms, starting from January of 2015, have introduced it.[37] Recent research highlights the fact that the introduction of a statutory minimum wage in Germany has triggered debates about the minimum wage across Europe, in particular in the Member States that do not have one.[38] This debate is strictly linked to the features of the industrial relations system, to the role and functions of sectoral collective bargaining, or to the decentralising tendencies in collective bargaining; and we think that, even if it is not always explicit in the debates, any position on the pros and cons of a statutory

---

36. For a general overview see T. Schülten et al., *Theses for a European Minimum Wage Policy* (Brussels: Etui 2006).
37. For a comment on the reform after one year see M. Amlinger, R. Bispinck & T. Schulten, *The German Minimum Wage: Experiences and Perspectives after One Year*, 28 WSI-Report (1/2016).
38. See E. Melegatti, *Il salario minimo legale. Aspettative e prospettive*, 13 et seq. (Torino: Giappichelli 2017).

minimum wage has an indirect effect on the structure and functions of collective bargaining.

In Italy, the German case has surely triggered a certain debate. First of all, some scholars think that sectoral collective agreement inderogability is a totem of old left-wing parties and unions that should be dismantled. Consequently, what should be changed is minimum wage setting, today left to the sectoral collective agreements,[39] which should instead be left to collective agreements at company level. The same critical position towards the supremacy of sectoral collective agreements seems to underlie the policy adopted by the Renzi government in seeking to introduce a statutory minimum wage in the reform known as the Jobs Act. In the event, the government decided not to implement the statutory minimum wage for the time being because of strong criticism from the trade unions.[40]

In the majority of Member States, the law has a specific role in determining the wage level under which is not possible to contract. In other countries, minimum wages are set by collective agreements, which are extended by law to all wage earners and declared generally binding.

What are the implications of the introduction of a statutory minimum wage for the structure of collective bargaining so modified after the crisis? The answer to this question should be contextualised in the more recent situation, where a process of decentralisation of collective bargaining in wage setting has been activated in different Member States, and should take into account different variables. Even before the crisis, many authors pleaded for the introduction of a statutory minimum wage at European level, as the only instrument capable of halting the proliferation of low and poverty-level wages throughout Europe, guaranteeing the principle of dignity at work and blocking the race to the bottom created by internal social dumping, not to mention the pressure of international markets.[41]

First, it is relevant if any co-ordination of collective bargaining exists, and whether multi-employer bargaining (in the form of either a sectoral or an inter-sectoral agreement) or a single-employer agreement predominates. A second consideration is whether the collective bargaining decentralisation process can be classified, following a Traxler framework analysis,[42] as an organised or disorganised decentralisation. In organised decentralisation systems, the marketisation is controlled, since the space of second-level negotiation is created and regulated within the framework of multi-employer agreements.[43] Countries in western and southern Europe belong to the first

---

39. P. Ichino, *Contro il totem dell'inderogabilità del contratto nazionale*, available in http://www.pietroichino.it/?p=37409.
40. See M. Biasi, *Il salario minimo legale nel 'Jobs Act': promozione o svuotamento dell'azione contrattuale collettiva?* 241 WP CSDLE Massimo D'Antona 30 2015).
41. T. Schülten et al., *Theses for a European Minimum Wage Policy* (Düsseldorf, Zurich, Paris, 15 April 2005); T. Shülten, R. Bispink & C. Schäfer, *Minimum Wages in Europe*, 369 et seq. (Brussels: ETUI, 2006).
42. F. Traxler, *Farewell to Labour Market Associations?*, in C. Crouch & F. Traxler (eds), *Organised Industrial Relations in Europe? What Future?*, 3 et seq. (Aldershot: Avebury 1985).
43. P. Marginson, M. Keune & D. Bohle, *Negotiating the Effects of Uncertainty? The Governance Capacity of Collective Bargaining Under Pressure*, supra n. 9, p. 39.

model, whereas the UK – and more recently, Poland and Hungary – belong to the second model.

As for wages, the collective bargaining decentralisation process implies a tendency to marketisation that means enterprises need to adapt their wage levels to market fluctuations. For workers, this inevitably means more uncertainty and less wage security.

The fact that in many Member States a statutory minimum wage exists (see the recent introduction of a statutory minimum wage in Germany), whereas in others (e.g., Italy and the Nordic countries) it does not, is linked to various factors such as the historical reluctance or agreement of social partners to accept interference by the legislator in regulating wages or a high level of coverage. One of the key factors is the level of coverage of collective agreements and the existence of rules underpinning the collective agreements considered legally binding, or alternatively the existence of other mechanisms such as judicial interpretation. In Italy, for example, the binding nature of sectoral collective agreements on all employers (even those who are not members of the employers' association signing the collective agreement) with regard to wages is guaranteed by a judicial interpretation of Article 36 of the Italian Constitution.[44] From this point of view, the role of the judiciary is fundamental in guaranteeing, at least for wages, an extension mechanism to sectoral collective agreements that would not otherwise be generally applicable. If no collective agreement is applicable (because the employer is not affiliated to the signatory employer's association) and the employee thinks that their salary is far below the level of any sufficient salary guaranteed by Article 36 of the Constitution (which gives any employee the right to have a sufficient and proportionate salary), they can sue their employer pursuant Article 36 Const. The judge has to decide on the question of what the sufficient level of wages to be recognised to the employee is, and in the majority of cases will make reference to the minimum wage set by sectoral collective agreements. Through this judicial interpretation, a high level of coverage of collective bargaining in wage setting is guaranteed. Although in principle the *erga omnes* extension of collective agreements is guaranteed only for minimum wages set by sectoral collective agreements, this limited extension mechanism produces a spill-over effect on sectoral collective agreements as a whole, since employers are keen to apply it not only to wages but also to other issues such as working time or job assignments. It is undeniable that the key judicial role, via the interpretation of Article 36 of the Constitution, has been the most important instrument in supporting a wage-setting mechanism established by sectoral collective agreements in the absence of legal extension mechanisms.

In this framework, we should analyse the recent attempt by the Italian legislature to launch a different system of wage setting. In 2014, the Renzi government proposed the introduction of a statutory minimum wage in sectors not covered by any collective agreements signed by the comparatively most representative unions at national level (Article 1, section 7, lett. g, of Law no. 183/2014). It is worth pointing out that this measure was definitively repealed in the final text of the law, mainly because of the

---

44. See T. Treu, *Article 36*, in G. Branca (eds), *Commentario della Costituzione*, 72 et seq. (Roma: Rapporti Economici, I 1979), Roma.

opposition of social partners, but it is still important to analyse the proposal since it shows how the introduction of a statutory minimum wage is perceived by social partners. Although in theory the statutory minimum wage should have been applied only in sectors not covered by any collective agreement signed by representative unions, some research demonstrates that in Italy the 440 sectoral collective agreements guarantee a high de facto coverage and that the impact of this provision would have been very low (which sectors are 'not covered'?). The opposition to the proposal expressed by Italian unions was in reality related to the loss of the authority of collective bargaining in wage setting. It is not surprising that a similar argument has been expressed by the Nordic unions in industrial systems characterised by the absence of a statutory minimum wage and high levels of coverage of collective agreements.[45] In these countries, the debate has focused on whether the minimum wage is a competitor to the collective agreements or whether it supports them in areas with a low degree of coverage.[46]

Germany is one of the most interesting cases to analyse, since a statutory minimum wage has been introduced quite recently, and more generally because of its wage policy and job creation during the crisis. Besides that, the German wage-setting model is considered very influential, especially in Nordic countries, and recent research highlights the impact of the German model on Nordic wage bargaining systems.[47]

The traditional legal abstentionism on the minimum wage has lasted for a very long time in Germany, at least de facto. Although some legislation on the issue has existed since 1952, wage setting is left to centralised collective agreements (at Federal and Lander level) in the form of *Lohntarifvertrag*. Minimum wages have been guaranteed for many years to workers not covered by collective agreements either by judicial interpretation of §138 BGB, which considers invalid any contractual clause contrary to the principle of moral codes, or by orders extending collective agreements to the whole sector.[48]

The choice of introducing a statutory minimum wage has been determined by the growing proportion of low-income earners, especially in hotels and restaurants, agriculture and forestry, the retail trade, the food industry and other service sectors not covered by collective agreements or collective agreements guaranteeing minimum wages under the level of EUR 8.50 per hour.[49] The level of collective agreement

---

45. L. Eldring & K. Alsos, *European Minimum Wage: A Nordic Outlook*, Norway, 2012 available in http://www.dev.world-psi.org/sites/default/files/fafo_report.pdf, pp. 71 et seq.
46. *Ibid.*, p. 81.
47. S.K. Andersen, C.L. Ibsen, K. Alsos, K. Nergaard & P. Sauramo, *Changes in Wage Policy and Collective Bargaining in the Nordic Countries – Comparison of Denmark, Finland, Norway and Sweden*, in *Wage Bargaining under the New European Economic Governance*, in G. van Gyes & T. Schulten (eds), *Wage bargaining under the new European Economic Governance*, 139-168 (Brussels: European Trade Union Institute 2105).
48. A. Seifert, *L'emploi décent. Le débat sur un salaire minimum en Allemagne*, in AA. VV., *Droits du travail, emploi, entreprise. Mélanges en l'honneur du Professeur François Gaudu*, 48 (Paris: LGDJ 2014).
49. M. Amlinger, R. Bispinck & T. Schulten, *The German Minimum Wage: Experiences and Perspectives after One Year*, supra n. 37, p. 6.

coverage in Germany started to decline after the reunification process. This phenomenon, together with the representativeness crisis in both employer's associations and unions, has led to a situation where entire sectors are not covered by any collective agreement – or, in other cases, to the expansion of collective agreement derogation *in pejus* for wages. That is why new legislation on a minimum wage set by law was adopted in 2014, with the support of all unions.[50] What is worth underlining is precisely this union support for legislation, which is part of a wider reform aiming to strengthen collective bargaining and the union role in wages.[51] It provides that before the government redefines the minimum wage level (initially fixed at EUR 8.50 per hour), a proposal should be made by a tripartite commission with a union as a member.

The German case is interesting because we could say that minimum wage setting through legislation has not been interpreted as an attack on collective union autonomy. This depends very much on the context of industrial relations in Germany, characterised by a quite high union density rate, and on the fact that the legal minimum wage is defined by the government through a social concertation procedure. That preserves the union role in wage setting and, in some ways, reduces the risks of union under-representation in wage setting in certain sectors.

The case of Greece is interesting from another point of view, since legislation on the minimum wage was enacted during the economic crisis in applying the second memorandum of understanding signed with the Troika for 2011-2012, with the aim of reducing the minimum wage level in the private sector, so as to reduce labour costs.[52]

Traditionally, the minimum wage in Greece was set by a confederation agreement valid *erga omnes*. Since 2012,[53] it has been set by legislation and more recently by governmental decree, considerably lowering the minimum wage level. What is worth underlining is that, in setting minimum wages, these pieces of legislation have not only lowered the minimum wage level, but also established criteria not previously taken into account by collective agreements. These criteria are the economic situation of the country, enterprise productivity, the unemployment rate and so on. In other words, even though we can say that collective bargaining is a system aimed at finding equilibrium between opposing economic interests, the system of industrial relations has been significantly affected by EU interventions during the crisis, with a significant shift towards enterprise collective bargaining in order to facilitate management control over the bargaining outcomes, and consequently reduce labour costs.[54] Since Greece (together with Romania, Poland and Hungary) is classified as a country with weak or

---

50. M. Corti, *La nuova legge sul salario minimo in Germania: declino o rinascita della contrattazione collettiva?*, in 3 Dir. Lav. Merc. (2014).
51. The whole reform is called *Gesetz zur Stärkung der Tarifautonomie.*
52. See M. Yannakourou & C. Tsimpoukis, *Flexibility Without Security and Deconstruction of Collective Bargaining: The New Paradigm of Labor Law in Greece*, 35 Comp. Lab. Law & Pol. J. 337 et seq. (2014).
53. Law no. 4093 of 2012 and Law no. 4172 of 2013.
54. G. Economakis, V. Funzaru & I. Zisimopoulos, *The Economic Crisis and Industrial Relations: Greece and Romania in Comparison*, 2 EAST-WEST Journal of Economics and Business, 54 (2016).

non-existent articulation mechanisms of collective bargaining across levels,[55] the effect of the disorganised decentralisation of collective bargaining is that the collective bargaining system is 'in a state of collapse',[56] due also to the fact that the Greek economy is dominated by micro- and small enterprises, which does not favour the development of large-scale collective bargaining at enterprise level.[57] As a consequence, the significant reduction of collective bargaining coverage has legitimated and required statutory intervention in minimum wage setting, which has meant, in a disrupted and fragmented system of industrial relations and collective bargaining, a further reduction of collective powers.

§9.06 CONCLUSION

The effects of a statutory minimum wage could be very different in countries characterised by an ongoing or stable process of decentralisation of collective bargaining from those characterised by a form of co-ordinated collective bargaining.

It is not possible to give a single answer to the question of whether the statutory minimum wage supports collective agreements or whether it is a competitor capable of undermining their strength, since it depends on a multiplicity of variable elements and above all on the level at which a minimum wage is fixed. For example, the statutory minimum wage in France is higher than the minimum rates in several collective agreements. Here, there have been indications that the national statutory minimum wage has served to reduce bargaining frequency. That is why the introduction of a statutory minimum wage could reduce this driving force of wages set by sectoral collective agreements, and also dramatically lessen the coverage level and necessity itself for sectoral collective bargaining.

Finally, even if in times of decentralisation of collective wage bargaining and in the context of the economic crisis, statutory minimum wages might have an important role in providing a floor, there is no clear evidence that they could have much impact on the reduction of low pay and growing inequalities. That is why there should be careful evaluation of the opportunity of introducing statutory minimum wages in countries characterised by a disorganised decentralisation of collective bargaining with no co-ordination at sectoral level. In the medium term, this could imply support for collective actors in wage setting, but over the longer term it could reinforce their loss of authority in wage setting, especially at sectoral level, which could be very difficult to reverse. The German model, from this point of view, represents an attempt to reduce the risk of a loss of union authority in wage setting, since any statutory minimum wage

---

55. P. Marginson, *Coordinated Bargaining in Europe: From Incremental Corrosion to Frontal Assault?*, European Journal of Industrial Relations, 97 (2014).
56. A. Koukiadaki, I. Tavora & M.M. Lucio, *The Reform of Joint Regulation and Labour Market Policy During the Crisis: Comparative Project Report*, University of Manchester, 6 (2014) available at: https://research.mbs.ac.uk/european-employment/Portals/0/docs/SDDTEC/Comparative%20report- final%20version%20Koukiadiki_Tavora_MartinezLucio.pdf.
57. G. Economakis, V. Funzaru & I. Zisimopoulos, *The Economic Crisis and Industrial Relations: Greece and Romania in Comparison*, supra n. 54, p. 66.

Chapter 9: Wage Setting Mechanisms and Statutory Minimum Wage §9.06

should be defined through procedures of information and consultation of collective actors.

Another important issue under discussion, which has to be taken into account in a future European regulatory framework, is how to combine the tendency to decentralise collective bargaining on wage setting with the opportunity to co-ordinate wages at European level,[58] even if this does not necessarily imply the need to have a statutory minimum wage in each Member State. The pros and cons of a European minimum wage are under discussion, and European trade unions do not all share the same opinion on the issue,[59] but finally the ETUC in its 'Social compact for Europe' (June 2012) advanced the idea that in the countries where trade unions consider it necessary, the statutory minimum wage should be increased. That means the choice of having a statutory minimum wage is finally in the hands of trade unions, which should be capable of analysing their forces and capacity through the traditional instrument of collective bargaining and action, to defend workers' interests in setting wages.

---

58. A. Dufresne, *The Trade Union Response to the European Economic Governance Regime. Transnational Mobilisation and Wage Coordination*, supra n. 4, p. 149.
59. *See* the different opinion at the ETUC Athens Congress in May 2011.

CHAPTER 10
Measures of Wage Moderation in Times of Crisis: The Example of Belgium

Fabienne Kéfer

The influence of the crisis on state interventionism in Belgian collective bargaining can be observed in various fields, such as flexibility[1] for example. Wage moderation also lends itself particularly well to the demonstration, since a government intervention mechanism set up in 1996 was only activated from – and due to – the economic crisis and has been continuously in use over the past eight years.

To facilitate the demonstration, it is first useful to describe the institutional setting of collective bargaining. It will then be possible to show that, without calling into question the bargaining framework, the economic crisis has disrupted its usual functioning.

§10.01 ARCHITECTURE OF THE BELGIAN MODEL OF SOCIAL DIALOGUE

Compared with social dialogue in other Western countries, the Belgian model appears highly institutionalised and coordinated; it is based on permanent structures for dialogue. Social dialogue in Belgium is also characterised by a high level of membership of representative organisations: the unionisation rate is almost 52% of the working population. It is estimated that 76% of employers are members of an employer organisation.[2]

---

1. See on this subject, Opinion No. 2008 of 7 December 2016 of the National Labour Council in Belgium on the draft bill concerning feasible and manageable work, available in French at http://www.cnt-nar.be/AVIS/avis-2008.pdf.
2. E. Léonard and F. Pichault, *Belgique: l'adaptation d'un 'modèle' de concertation sociale*, in D. Andoleatto, and S. Contrepois (dir.), *Syndicats et dialogue social. Les modèles occidentaux à l'épreuve*, 55 (Brussels: Peter Lang, 2016).

The Belgian model of social dialogue was forged just after the Second World War. In 1944, a Draft Agreement of Social Solidarity was concluded between employer and employee representatives. It was a true founding text for a comprehensive system of social security and social dialogue. As soon as the country returned to independence, the parties 'agreed to ask the Government to take a series of emergency measures to repair the misery suffered by the large mass of salaried workers during the Occupation and to pave the way for a renewed movement of social progress arising from both the economic development of a pacified world and an equitable distribution of income from increasing production. These emergency measures are mainly aimed at the wage system, since implementing a comprehensive system of social security for workers relies on national cooperation and restoring or implementing joint collaboration methods between employer and employee organisations. Although these measures are definitive in principle, so as to increase the material and moral well-being of workers and establish peaceful relations between workers and their employers, based on justice, they will be initially provisional in nature due to their urgency. The legislative chambers will be asked to give them definitive status as soon as possible'. This definitive status was quickly provided in the following years.

The institutional framework appears sophisticated. Belgian law promotes social dialogue at several levels. To simplify matters, we shall only mention some of the levels and bodies of negotiation and dialogue here.

At the top is the National Labour Council.[3] Its members are delegates from the largest employer and employee organisations. Its scope of action extends over various industry sectors and over the entire country; its collective labour agreements deal with industrial relations problems of general interest to all companies in Belgium.[4] At multi-industry level, there is also the Central Economic Council[5] and the High Council for Prevention and Protection at Work[6] which fulfil advisory roles.

At the next level (industry sectors), joint committees have been set up. These have multiple areas of expertise, each with a scope of action for a sector previously defined by royal decree.[7]

---

3. Organic Act of 29 May 1952 of the National Labour Council (*M.B.*, 31 May 1952).
4. Article 7 of the Law of 5 December 1968 on collective employment agreements and joint committees (*M.B*, 15 January 1969).
5. Established by the Act of 20 September 1948 on the organisation of the economy, it comprises some fifty full members presented jointly by trade unions and employer organisations, in addition to three experts (Article XIII.2 of the Code of Economic Law and Order of the Regent of 28 December 1948 fixing the number of members of the Central Economic Council and determining the conditions of their presentation). Its role is to bring to the attention of the legislative chambers, Council of Ministers, one or more ministers or any other federal public body, either on their own initiative or at the request of these authorities and in the form of written reports, all opinions or proposals concerning problems relating to the national economy. These opinions or proposals are adopted by consensus. In the absence of consensus, the opinion contains the different points of view expressed by its members (Article XIII.1).
6. Established by Royal Decree of 27 October 2006, the Higher Council for Prevention and Protection at Work consists of an equal number of representatives from employer, employee and civil servant representative organisations. It has a broad advisory role in the field of health, safety and well-being at work.
7. For example, the clothing industry employee sector or the food industry employee sector, etc.

At the company level, negotiation and dialogue take place within the works council and trade union delegation. The works council is a joint body whose employee representative delegation is constituted after internal employee elections. A works council should only be set up in companies that usually employ an average of at least one hundred workers.[8] If this threshold is not reached, the employer is not obliged to set up a works council. The employer may be required to allow a trade union delegation to operate if one or more employee organisations so request. The status of this delegation is determined by means of collective agreements adopted by the National Labour Council[9] and by the joint committee to which the company in question is affiliated. An employer's obligation to allow a trade union delegation to operate is subject to having a minimum number of employees; this number varies from one business sector to another.

Belgian law is characterised by a certain trade union pluralism. Freedom of association allows the creation of multiple professional organisations. This said, only those labelled as being representative (which requires a certain number of conditions to be met[10]) are entitled to a seat on the above-mentioned bodies. In tangible terms, only three trade union organisations fall into this category.[11]

One of the prerogatives of employee representative organisations is the conclusion of collective agreements; these can be concluded at different levels of social dialogue: i.e., at the National Labour Council, joint committee or company level. Where an employer is bound by a collective agreement, it applies to all employees, whether or not they belong to a representative trade union organisation. The hierarchy of collective agreements is regulated by law according to a pyramid scheme.[12] A company collective agreement cannot override a sectoral collective agreement; a sectoral collective agreement cannot contravene a multi-industry collective agreement. The French *principe de faveur* does not exist in Belgian law. Nevertheless, in the vast majority of cases, a collective agreement sets out a minimum level of workers' rights and it is permitted for other norms of lower rank (an individual or collective agreement) to expand these rights.

By way of illustration, the wage setting process is based predominantly on collective bargaining. A multi-industry agreement[13] guarantees a minimum monthly wage for adult workers in full-time employment. In each industry sector, joint committees conclude collective agreements which set the minimum wage according to

---

8. Article 2 of the Act of 28 July 2011 determining the applicable threshold for establishing works councils or renewal of their members at the time of internal employee elections in 2012 (*M.B.*, 31 August 2011). This act supersedes Article 14, §1 of the Act of 20 September 1948 on the organisation of the economy (*M.B.*, 27 September 1948).
9. Collective Labour Agreement No. 5 of 24 May 1971 concerning the status of trade union delegations of company staff (available in French at http://www.cnt-nar.be/Cct-liste.htm).
10. Article 2, §4 of the Organic Act of 29 May 1952 of the National Labour Council.
11. These three organisations are the General Confederation of Christian Trade Unions, the General Federation of Labour of Belgium and the General Confederation of Liberal Trade Unions of Belgium.
12. Articles 10 and 51 of the Act of 5 December 1968.
13. Collective Labour Agreement No. 43 of 2 May 1988 (available in French at http://www.cnt-nar.be/Cct-liste.htm).

job function, degree of qualification required, professional experience, etc., by placing this amount above the minimum guaranteed monthly income. Sectoral collective agreements are also responsible for automatically indexing wages to the price index.[14] Indexing is generally organised via sectoral collective agreements, using variable methods. Companies can also sign collective agreements that provide for higher compensation than set by the sectoral collective agreement. The place given to autonomy of individual will is very limited: contractual clauses must be compatible with the minimum amounts agreed collectively – or risk being declared null and void.[15]

Alongside these bodies, whose composition, rules of operation and powers are defined by law,[16] there is an informal body called the *Groupe des Dix* [Group of Ten] which plays a key role in coordinating social dialogue. Since the 1960s, a practice exists whereby the Group of Ten concludes 'cross-sectoral agreements' (*accords interprofessionnels*) every two years.[17] These agreements, which aim to ensure that the fruits of economic growth are shared while promoting the country's economic development, cover a variety of areas: working hours, flexibility, wage increases, employee training, etc. These agreements have no legal value. They nevertheless influence a large part of sector based bargaining content as they morally commit the signatories. These signatories subsequently negotiate, in joint commissions, collective agreements that comply with the minimum conditions agreed within the Group of Ten. On the trade union side, this mode of operation based on a common multi-industry basis, makes it possible to improve employee protection in sectors where trade unions are weaker and would not obtain such benefits if they were negotiated just at the sectoral level. For their part, employers gain peaceful industrial relations.[18]

This is how bipartisanship has been established at every level of the economy. Social partners meet in full autonomy when they want, to discuss subjects agreed among themselves. State authorities do not interfere in the process except to provide a legal framework for dialogue and the outcome of its agreements, namely collective agreements. The government also provides significant logistical support. The chairs of the National Labour Council and joint committees are civil servants, as are official conciliators, veritable 'mine-clearers' of social conflict. Social partners also participate in the joint management of the main social security institutions and are involved in developing the country's social and economic policy. No bill on industrial relations law

---

14. This link is generalised. It is not imposed by a governmental norm but is the outcome of collective bargaining.
15. Article 11 of the Act of 5 December 1968.
16. With a nuance for trade union delegation, as indicated above.
17. M. Capron and P. Reman, *Flexibilité: vers un modèle belge?*, nos 7-8 La revue nouvelle 54 (2006); E. Léonard, and F. Pichault, *Belgique: l'adaptation d'un 'modèle' de concertation sociale*, supra n. 2.
18. On several occasions, this practice has experienced periods of difficulty and even suspension (J. Vilrokx, *De interprofessionele arbeidsverhoudingen in België in de jaren '90: een keerpunt*, Liber amicorum R. Blanpain, 503-506 (Bruges: Die Keure, 1998); I. Cassiers, and L. Denayer, *Concertation sociale et transformations socio-économiques en Belgique, de 1944 à nos jours*, in E. Arcq, M. Capron, E. Léonard, and P. Reman, *Dynamiques de la concertation sociale*, 88 (Bruxelles: CRISP 2010).

is adopted without turning to the Group of Ten and consulting the National Labour Council.

Multi-industry social dialogue has been 'deadlocked'[19] since 2008. The cross-sectoral agreement concluded on 22 December 2008 only emerged after very difficult negotiations. It was not been possible to conclude any other agreement of this kind during the eight following years. State authorities have, for this reason, been required to intervene directly in areas which until then were the realm (if not exclusively, at least chiefly) of the collective bargaining process. The government has thus repeatedly adopted binding measures in the wage setting process aimed at controlling the rise in payroll costs, considered a handicap for Belgian firms vis-à-vis their competitors in neighbouring countries. These measures, which are part of a government policy in accordance with the expectations of European institutions,[20] have almost always been accompanied by strong protests from trade union circles decrying, among other things, that the traditional model of social dialogue was being called into question. An unjustified intrusion into the right to collective bargaining was unsuccessfully claimed before various courts in the country. We can nevertheless note that state authority intervention helped to 'unlock' collective bargaining that had broken down at multi-industry level, enabling it to continue at lower levels.

§10.02 IMPACT OF THE CRISIS ON THE STATE'S ROLE IN COLLECTIVE BARGAINING

Collective bargaining had already been placed under supervision by the State in the past, owing to the economic crisis after the first oil crisis. The dramatic increase in production costs which were directly or indirectly indexed to oil prices jeopardised the competitiveness of Belgian firms, not only because of an increase in the cost of energy, but also because the labour costs were linked to increases in the consumer price index, including oil. The export-focused Belgian economy encountered serious under-employment problems. As of 1976, State authorities adopted several measures to control pay: wage or wage indexing freezes, or both at the same time.[21] A competitiveness standard was released in support of the Belgian franc's devaluation in 1982:

---

19. M. Capron, B. Conter, and J. Faniel, *Belgique. La concertation sociale interprofessionnelle grippée*, 141 *Chroniques internationales de l'IRES*, 3 et seq. (2013).
20. Recommendation of the Council of 13 May 2015 on the national reform programme of Belgium for 2015 and with regard to the Council opinion on the stability programme of Belgium for 2015 COM(2015)252.
21. Act of 30 March 1976 on economic recovery measures (*M.B.*, 1 April 1976); Act of 23 December 1980 on precautionary and transitional measures for the moderation of all incomes (*M.B.*, 25 December 1980) and Act of 10 February 1981 on the adjustment of income moderation (*M.B.*, 14 February 1981); Act of 2 February 1982 attributing certain special powers to the King (*M.B.*, 4 February 1982) and Royal Decrees No. 11 and 180 (*M.B.*, 18 January 1983); Act of 11 April 1983 on fiscal and budgetary provisions (*M.B.*, 16 April 1983) and Royal Decree No. 278 (*M.B.*, 7 April 1984); Act of 22 January 1985 on adjustment containing social provisions (*M.B.*, 24 January 1985).

labour costs could not increase higher than the weighted average of Belgium's seven main trading partners.[22] As of 1987, wage negotiations regained their freedom.

This freedom nevertheless proved to be impaired; the concept of supervising the wage setting process persisted. While before the oil crisis cross-sectoral agreements aimed to achieve social progress and share the results of growth, agreements concluded from 1986 onwards were designed to support corporate competitiveness.[23]

On a technical level, the Act of 6 January 1989 on safeguarding the country's competitiveness,[24] which gave a legal framework to the competitiveness standard, set out the criteria and procedure for social partners to assess competitiveness.

Each year, the competitiveness standard was negotiated by social partners in the Central Economic Council.[25] Assessment of this standard took account of different factors, including payroll costs. A comparison was made with Belgium's seven main trade partners. The government then convened social partners to discuss the change in this competitiveness. Whatever the attitude of social partners, the Act allowed the government to take the measures it deemed necessary if it considered that competitiveness was still under threat.[26] It could, in particular, lay down the framework within which any agreement on changes to employee earnings was to be concluded.

This has produced a new wage freeze in 1994-1995.[27,28]

Belgium's entry into the monetary union deprived the authorities of the possibility of making macroeconomic adjustments by adjusting exchange rates and interest rates, rendering the mechanism of the 1989 Act obsolete in certain respects. To prevent the loss in competitiveness having a very negative effect on employment rates, the choice was made to implement a policy to control payroll costs.[29] In the eyes of social partners, the 1989 Act also presented several disadvantages including only being able to intervene *after the event*, to correct deviations in the economy. A wage setting

---

22. The choice of these partners and their weighting was based on the International Monetary Fund's model for World Trade. To calculate labour cost increases in the seven countries, the Commission of the European Communities was used as the source for EEC countries and the OECD for other countries (Article 34 of the Law of 11 April 1983).
23. M. Capron, B. Conter and J. Faniel, Belgique. *La concertation sociale interprofessionnelle grippée*, supra n. 19, p. 5.
24. *M.B.*, 31 January 1989.
25. On this body, *see supra*.
26. When Parliament finds by vote that competitiveness is threatened, the King may, within two months following the vote, take by decree deliberated in the Council of Ministers, measures he deems necessary for safeguarding or restorating competitiveness (Articles 8 and 10).
27. B. Nyssen, *La modération, pour trois ans, des revenus du travail salarié*, Orientations 109 et seq. (1994).
28. Furthermore, a new index has been adopted as an instrument of wage indexation: the health index. It is obtained by subtracting certain products from the consumer price index basket, namely alcoholic beverages, tobacco, petrol and diesel (the effects of certain contributions and taxes are also excluded). Since, individual or collective agreements providing for wage indexation must refer to this index (Article 2 of the Royal Decree of 24 December 1993 implementing the Act of 6 January 1989 on safeguarding the country's competitiveness (*M.B.*, 31 December 1993), confirmed by the Act of 30 March 1994).
29. *See* image *in* E. Doutrepont, *Formation salariale et concertation collective en Belgique*, 54 (Bruges: La Charte, 2009), illustrating the fact that the employment rate in Belgium is directly dependent on the difference between the cost of Belgian labour and that of neighbouring countries, who are also our main competitors.

process based on anticipating declining competitiveness seemed more preferable to social partners.[30] Despite the government's conciliatory approach, they were nevertheless unable to agree on the procedure. Therefore, an act, the general content of which was negotiated with social partners, helped to break the gridlock in discussions. Thus the emphasis was placed on the preventative nature of wage negotiations in the Act of 26 July 1996 (on the promoting employment and *preventive* safeguarding of competitiveness).[31] The main given concern proposed was job preservation, and even new job creation.[32] The method employed was a system which, by coordinating social dialogue,[33] tended to control wage increases and prevent the average hourly payroll cost from rising faster in Belgium than in neighbouring countries. To this end, the act restored greater autonomy to social partners at the same time as regulating this autonomy. Every two years, a margin of increase in payroll costs (hereinafter: margin) is determined by representative organisations at multi-industry level. Negotiations on wage cost increases subsequently carried out at lower levels cannot exceed this margin. Contrary to what was provided for by the Act of 1989, it is only when social partners cannot agree amongst themselves that the Government can set the margin. In addition to or in exchange for wage moderation, social partners are also supposed to provide for 'adequate measures in favour of employment'.[34]

[A] Description of the Mechanism[35]

[1] Procedure

Negotiations between social partners are preceded by bi-annual reports drawn up jointly by two multi-industry social consultation bodies (Central Economic Council and National Labour Council) on 'employment and payroll cost increases in Belgium and in reference Member States'. Only three of these reference Member States remain: Germany, France and the Netherlands.[36] Added to this is a 'new economic and social monitoring tool',[37] namely a technical report from the Central Economic Council, published each year on 30 September on 'maximum margins available for the increase on payroll costs, based on the last two years' growth, as well as expected increases in

---

30. Hearing of the President of the Central Economic Council, *Doc. Parl.*, Chambre, 1995-1996, no. 49-609/9, pp. 210 and 212; *Doc. Parl.*, Senat, 1995-1996, no. 1-386/4, p. 11.
31. *M.B.*, 1 August 1996.
32. *Doc. Parl.*, Chambre, 1995-1996, no. 49-609/1, pp. 1 et seq. and no. 49-609/9, p. 205; R. Plasman, M. Rusinek, F. Rycx and I. Tojerow, *La structure des salaires en Belgique*, November 2007, p. 61, available in French at https://www.researchgate.net/publication/4800931_La_structure_des_salaires_en_Belgique.
33. *Doc. Parl.*, Senat, 1995-1996, no. 1-386/4, p. 16; E. Doutrepont, *supra* n. 29, pp. 56 et seq.
34. This obligation derives from Article 9, §3 of the Law of 26 July 1996.
35. The description is of the law in force in February 2017. A draft bill is currently being debated in the House of Representatives with a view to adapting the process involving mainly technical issues.
36. I. Cassiers and L. Denayer, *Concertation sociale et transformations socio-économiques en Belgique, de 1944 à nos jours*, *supra* n. 18, p. 90.
37. Article 5, al. 1 of the Act of 26 July 1996.

payroll costs in the reference Member States. A distinction is made between expected inflation and the margin for wage increases in real terms'.[38]

Then, by 31 October, social partners must have concluded an agreement which contains measures for employment in addition to the margin,[39] based on these various reports. This agreement must, according to Article 6, sit within a 'cross-sectoral agreement'. It is not explicitly required to subsequently transpose this into a multi-industry collective agreement. Undoubtedly riding on this ambiguity, social partners have chosen not to entrust negotiations, including setting the margin, to the National Labour Council but to the informal Group of Ten body.[40]

If no agreement is concluded within two months of the technical report, or more specifically 'in the absence of consensus', the government attempts mediation and, failing this, sets the margin itself.

During bilateral negotiations, we have seen that social partners have the capacity to side-line the government by concluding an agreement on the margin, regardless of its content. The government is not able to oppose an agreement between social partners; it can only compensate for the absence of an agreement. Furthermore, when the government sets the margin itself, it cannot adversely affect the indexation and scale increases resulting from sectoral agreements.[41]

Once this margin has been established, collective agreements are concluded at industry or company level during the first year of the period covered by the cross-sectoral agreement, in order to set payroll cost increases for a two-year period.[42-43]

[2]   Content of the Cross-Sectoral Agreement

The cross-sectoral agreement covered by the Act of 1996 must contain two parts, one relating to the margin for payroll cost increases and the other relating to employment measures. The second part will not be discussed here.

What should be decided at multi-industry level is not wage increases but the margin for 'increases in payroll costs'. This margin is defined as 'the nominal increase

---

38. Article 4, §1 of the Act of 26 July 1996.
39. Article 6, §1 of the Act of 26 July 1996. The State Council had denounced, in vain, the pleonastic nature of this expression (*Doc. Parl.*, Chambre, 1995-1996, no. 49-609/1, p. 43).
40. I. Ficher, *L'accord interprofessionnel a-t-il une place parmi les sources de droit du travail?Les sources du droit revisitées*, vol. 2, 419-420 (Bruxelles: Presses de l'Université Saint-Louis, 2012).
41. Article 7 of the Act of 26 July 1996.
42. Article 8 of the Act of 26 July 1996.
43. In the autumn of the first of the two years of application, the Central Economic Council will draw up its technical report which, if the payroll cost trend in Belgium is higher than that observed among neighbouring countries, can result in the obligation to apply a predefined corrective mechanism in the cross-sectoral agreement and in sectoral collective agreements. On observing any of these forecasts, social partners apply the corrective mechanism. Failing this, the State again plays the role of mediator and, if this fails, may itself impose the correction margin (Articles 11-13 of the Act of 26 July 1996).

in the average payroll cost per worker in the private sector, expressed as equivalent full time wages [...]'.[44,45]

The margin is defined generally, as an average for the whole private sector. The same margin is applicable to all business sectors, whatever their performance level or exposure to international competition.[46] This is therefore a macroeconomic concept. It is not a percentage or amount that necessarily needs to be allocated.[47] It is a framework for wage bargaining, a budget for sectors and companies to negotiate wage increases and other social benefits in turn, whether they are one-off or recurrent, or subject to social security contributions.

Since the cross-sectoral agreement covers increases in payroll costs and not wage increases, a reduction in employers' social security costs provides room for increasing wages without exceeding the margin and affecting competitiveness.[48] This can however weaken a job stimulation policy by reducing social contributions.[49]

What the act doesn't say is at what level compliance to the margin is required. At the private sector level as a whole? At the business sector level? At company level or even for each individual worker?[50] All interpretations have been defended, but it is most often conceded that compliance with the margin set in the cross-sectoral agreement[51] is required at the company level.

According to Article 6, §2, the margin does not affect indexation and scale increases, terms within which the act includes wage increases resulting from normal promotions or individual job category changes. Even when the margin is set at 0% by a cross-sectoral agreement or by royal decree, indexation and scale increases are maintained. It can be quite the opposite if the legislator itself makes an exception to this principle by organising an index jump, as he did in 2015.[52]

---

44. Article 2 of the Act of 26 July 1996. The wage increase in Belgium and in reference Member States is based on OECD data and forecasts.
45. Payroll costs include not only gross salary, but also bonuses, holiday pay, guaranteed wages in the event of sickness, meal vouchers, employer contributions, etc. Some compensatory benefits are excluded from the concept of payroll costs, in particular beneficiary shareholdings (Article 10 of the Act of 26 July 1996).
46. V. Bodart, L. Jacquet, and B. Van der Linden, *Salaires et norme salariale en Belgique*, no. 6 Regards économiques, 2-3 (2002).
47. E. Doutrepont, *supra* n. 29, p. 72.
48. Hence in 2016, parallel to the margin set at 0.8%, the cost of employee social contributions decreased due to the reduction in the basic rate of employers' social security contributions from 32.40% to 30% as of 1 April 2016. This was in the context of a *tax shift* and increase in the number of workers entitled to a target group reduction (Articles 14 and 21 et seq. of the Act of 26 December 2015 on measures to strengthen job creation and purchasing power).
49. V. Bodart, L. Jacquet, and B. Van der Linden, *Salaires et norme salariale en Belgique*, supra n. 46, pp. 10 and 11.
50. This latter opinion is notably defended by H. Takaert and D. Casaer, *De loonnormering voor de periode 1999-2000: illusie of realiteit ?*, Orientaties 56 (2000).
51. Not. O. Debray, *Les mesures de modération salariale*, Orientations 123 (1997); W. van Eeckhoutte and V. Neuprez, *Compendium social. Droit du travail*, t.2, no. 2567, 1373, (Diegem, Kluwer 2015-2016). This is also the Belgian government's viewpoint (http://www.emploi.belgique.be/defaultTab.aspx?id=14406).
52. Article 2 to 2*quater* of the Law of 23 April 2015 on the promotion of employment, *M.B.*, 27 April 2015.

[3] Impact of the Economic Crisis

Wage determination was overseen in this way, practically without a hitch until 2008. Negotiations were formalised by a cross-sectoral agreement[53] almost every time.[54] It must be said that, in several respects, social partners took liberties with the law. While the margin was designed by the 1996 legislator as a limit to be imposed on sectors in wage bargaining and to which employers had to comply under the threat of repressive sanctions, in most cases, the cross-sectoral agreements classed the margin as indicative, hence giving social partners in joint committees the freedom to negotiate wage increases beyond the margin. It was more like a message of prudence in wage negotiations than a legal norm.[55]

It has also been observed that while the margin must be established uniformly for the private sector as a whole, for the period 2001-2002, social partners have provided for two different margins, the highest being for the most successful sectors over the previous two years.[56]

This practice contributed to undermining the effectiveness of the Act of 26 July 1996. For it to be established that the margin has been exceeded and therefore infringed, the margin must be a true limit. Yet since it was declared 'indicative' by the authors of the agreement, it was conceptually impossible to declare an infringement.[57] The low effectiveness suffered by the Act of 26 July 1996 for a dozen or so years can also be explained in part by the difficulty in sanctioning ignorance of the Act through civil sanctions. The sanction of invalidity is difficult to manage, whether for collective or individual agreements.[58] Null and void, reduced to exceeding the margin,[59] can only be invoked once it has been established, at the end of the two-year period, that the average payroll cost per worker has increased; meanwhile, and unless the illegality of the wage increase is wildly obvious (which is not frequent), the employer is obliged to pay the benefits prescribed by collective or individual norms requiring the employer to do so.[60]

---

53. The texts are available in French at http://www.cnt-nar.be/Accord-interpr.htm.
54. Social partners were unable to reach an agreement in the first period after the law came into effect; it was a Royal Decree of 20 December 1996 which fixed the margin for the years 1997 and 1998 (*M.B.*, 31 December 1996, p. 32357). There was no cross-sectoral agreement in 2005-2006 but the government preferred not to take action to determine the margin, giving free rein to sector specific negotiations.
55. V. Bodart, L. Jacquet, and B. Van der Linden, *Salaires et norme salariale en Belgique*, supra n. 46, p. 9; E. Doutrepont, supra n. 29, p. 58; K. Magerman, *De maximale marge voor loonkostenontwikkeling voor 2011-2012*, Orientaties, 173 (2011); I. Ficher, *L'accord interprofessionnel a-t-il une place parmi les sources de droit du travail?*, supra n. 40, pp. 426-427.
56. V. Bodart, L. Jacquet, and B. Van der Linden, *Salaires et norme salariale en Belgique*, supra n. 46, p. 3.
57. Until March 2007, there was only one report which was not followed up. *Doc. parl.*, Chambre, 2006-2007, no. 51-3059/001, p. 248. There does not appear to have been other subsequent cases.
58. J. Vanthournout and P. Humblet, *Loonmatiging en de loonnorm 2011-2012*, 99-104 (Gand: Story Publishers, 2011).
59. M. De Vos, *Loon naar Belgisch arbeidsovereenkomstrecht*, 218-227 (Anvers: Maklu 2000).
60. The government has found that refusing to grant the surplus accorded by royal decree to be an effective way of ensuring compliance with the margin in sectoal collective agreements (P. Humblet, *Het IPA: exponent van het tripartisme ?*, Nouvelle Revue du travail, 53 (2012).

Since the 2008 economic crisis, the negotiation process has ground to a halt. Negotiations for the 2009-2010 cross-sectoral agreement began at the end of 2008. This agreement only came into being because the government decided to put a significant sum on the negotiating table to promote it. The (tiny) margin of increase was declared mandatory and identical for all... but at least there was an agreement.

During the three following periods, covering 2011-2016, social partners were unable to find common ground, despite state mediation.[61] As provided for by law, the state authorities have taken over responsibility. The government could have refrained from doing so – intervention was not compulsory – but it preferred to take action because of the difficult economic situation. Two royal decrees were adopted, on 28 March 2011 and 28 April 2013,[62] setting mandatory and uniform margins for all sectors. The first decree set the margin at 0.3% for 2011 and 2012, increased (where applicable) by indexation and scale increases, stating that it was 0% for the year 2011 and 0.3% for the year 2012. In the second decree, the margin was 0% for the years 2013 and 2014, increased (where applicable) by indexation and scale increases. For 2015-2016, it is a law[63] rather than a royal decree (for technical reasons) that set the margin at 0% for 2015 and 0.8% for 2016.[64]

Once this margin was established by state authorities, wage bargaining was able to resume at industry and/or company level.

It can therefore be observed that the economic crisis led to a freeze in collective bargaining. Government intervention in the negotiation of wages made it possible to unblock the situation thanks to an interventionist mechanism invented long ago but which only needed to be used after the economic crisis of 2008.[65]

On a more ad hoc basis, the state authorities – via an Act of 23 April 2015[66] – organised a 2% index jump, paralysing all collective labour agreements related to linking wages to the price index for some months. The aim of this act was to reduce the wage gap that had widened with neighbouring countries through wage indexation, something not done in these reference Member States (or at least not in the same way) and which has always been maintained since the Act of 26 July 1996 came into effect.[67]

---

61. The 2011-2012 draft agreement, drawn up by the Group of Ten was rejected by the trade unions. Two years later, trade union organisations refused to start negotiations because the government had established a narrow framework in advance. For 2015-2016, the Group of Ten's draft agreement was rejected by one of the trade union organisations and accepted by the others and by employer organisations. The Act of 28 April 2015 follows this draft agreement.
62. *M.B.*, 1 April 2011 and 2 May 2013.
63. Law of 28 April 2015, establishing the maximum margin for payroll cost increases for the years 2015 and 2016 (*M.B.*, 30 April 2015).
64. The 0.8% margin is 0.5% of gross payroll increased by 0.3% of net payroll (Article 2 of the Act of 28 April 2015).
65. Putting aside the very first period after the act came into force; it was a Royal Decree of 20 December 1996 which set the margin for 1997 and 1998.
66. Act of 23 April 2015 on stimulating employment, *M.B.*, 27 April 2015.
67. National Bank of Belgium, *Indexation en Belgique: ampleur, nature et conséquences pour l'économie et alternatives possibles*, 28 June 2012; V. Bodart and F. Shadman, *Indexation et compétitivité en Belgique*, 107 Regards économiques, 4 (2013).

[B] Legality of State Intervention

State intervention in wage negotiations is criticised, notably in trade unions circles for unjustified interference with the right to freedom of association: collective agreements should be able to freely regulate the wages and their growth. By not endowing social partners with exclusive jurisdiction to decide the amount of remuneration and by allowing the state authorities to do so themselves, could Belgian law have infringed the right to collective bargaining consecrated by supra-legislative norms, such as the Constitution and Law of the Council of Europe in particular?[68]

Article 6.2 of the (Revised) European Social Charter aims to ensure the effective exercise of the right to collective bargaining. For the European Committee of Social Rights, state intervention in determining wages is likely to undermine this right. However, 'in order to remedy a particularly serious economic situation, a government should be able to set certain limits to collective bargaining, particularly where wage increases are concerned. However, the Committee wished to emphasise that such restrictions should be imposed only after extensive consultation of all the parties concerned, notably trade unions and employers' associations, and that they should be of an exceptional kind and of limited duration.[69] Furthermore, they should not be imposed unless it has been proved that no other measures can produce the same effects without recourse to such government intervention'.[70]

The law of some countries was declared non-compliant with Article 6.2 by the Committee because restriction came into force without prior extensive consultations and resulted in full suspension of negotiations (Iceland)[71] or because application of the law was not linked to a particularly serious economic situation and was not limited to a short period of time (The Netherlands).[72]

However, the Belgian situation, as from application of the Act of 26 July 1996, has been declared compliant with Article 6.2. of the Charter by the Committee in its conclusions of 5 December 2014.[73]

---

68. One might also want to examine compliance with Article 12 of the Charter of Fundamental Rights of the European Union, Article 8 of the International Covenant on Economic, Social and Cultural Rights, and Convention No. 98 and Convention No. 154 of the ILO. On the regime prior to the Act of 1996, see International Labour Conference, 76th session (Geneva 1989): Report of the Committee of Experts on the Application of Conventions and Recommendations, Report III (Part 4A), p. 276 and Q. Detienne's study, *La Belgique et les conventions internationales du travail*, J.T.T., 335 (2014).
69. The restriction must be limited to 'the time needed to return to a normal situation in which the exercise of the right to collective bargaining would again be fully ensured' (European Social Charter, Committee of Independent Experts, Conclusions XII-1, 1988-1989, pp. 129-131).
70. European Social Charter, Committee of Independent Experts, Conclusions IX-1, 1985, pp. 55-56 and Conclusions XII-1, 1988-1989, pp. 127-129.
71. European Social Charter, Committee of Independent Experts, Conclusions XII-1, 1988-1989, pp. 127-129.
72. European Social Charter, Committee of Independent Experts, Conclusions XII-1, 1988-1989, pp. 129-131.
73. European Social Charter (Revised), European Committee of Social Rights, Conclusions 2014, Belgium, p. 24 (available in French at http://hudoc.esc.coe.int/fre/?i=2014/def/BEL/6/2/FR).

The right to engage in collective bargaining with the employer and conclude collective agreements is also derived from the right to freedom of association consecrated by Article 11 of the European Convention on Human Rights. This is one of the lessons of the *Demir and Baykara v. Turkey* judgment.[74] According to the Council of State of Belgium, restricting this right by a royal decree, setting the margin and excluding a significant part of negotiations from collective bargaining, is compliant with Article 11.2 of the Convention. It is provided for by a law; it pursues a legitimate aim and could be deemed necessary in a democratic society. All in all, it is proportionate to this purpose; government intervention is subsidiary, has an impact for only two years and leaves a margin of negotiation for collective bargaining at sector and company level. The state authorities have used their leeway to ensure the competitiveness of the Belgian economy, the protection of which falls 'within the context of protecting the rights and freedoms of others, notably the right to work and to a decent standard of living'.[75]

The Constitutional Court holds the same opinion. With more specific regard to the proportionality between the measure and the objective it aims to achieve, the Court draws its inspiration from the view of the Committee on Freedom of Association, a supervisory body of the International Labour Organisation. A restriction must be applied as an exceptional measure, limited to what is indispensable, it must not exceed a reasonable period of time and must be accompanied by appropriate safeguards to protect workers' standard of living. In any event, such a restriction on collective bargaining must be preceded by negotiations with employee and employer organisations with a view to seeking agreement among social partners. There must also be guarantees that collective bargaining on non-monetary issues can take place.[76] After insisting on the fact that, every two years, negotiations on payroll cost increases are left primarily to social partners while state authorities only act on a subsidiary basis to compensate for the lack of an agreement, the Court found that the act[77] gives plenty of opportunity for collective bargaining.[78]

With respect to the Act of 23 April 2015, which neutralises up to 2% sectoral collective agreements organising wage indexation, the Court ruled that the state authorities therefore had the right to veto what the social partners had decided whenever interference in the right to collective bargaining is done with a legitimate aim under Article 11 of the European Convention on Human Rights. This legitimate aim is to encourage company competitiveness by reducing the wage gap between Belgium and neighbouring countries and keeping public expenditure within reasonable limits. The Court also ruled that it seemed necessary in a democratic society to move towards

---

74. Eur. court D.H. (Grand Chamber), 12 November 2008, *Demir and Baykara c. Turkey*, §154; Eur. court D.H. (Grand Chamber), 9 July 2013, *Sindicatul Păstorul cel Bun c. Romania*, §135.
75. C. E., 27 September 2013, no. 224.863; C. E., 13 February 2015, no. 230.207.
76. B.I.T., *La liberté syndicale*, Recueil de décisions et de principes du Comité de la liberté syndicale du Conseil d'administration du BIT, 5th ed., Geneva, §§999, 1024 and 1027, 214 (2006).
77. In this case, it was a matter of reviewing the constitutionality of the Act of 28 April 2015.
78. C.C., 1 December 2016, no. 152/2016, B. 11.

the pursuit of legitimate objectives. In other words, the interference should not infringe on the right to collective bargaining.[79]

[C] Conclusion

In Belgium, the land of consensus and surrealism, social dialogue has flourished as almost nowhere else in Europe. Even the wage moderation system is backed by social dialogue. Social partners, who must submit biennially to a certain level State constraint by negotiating a margin for payroll cost increases for the next two years, are free to set this margin when they reach an agreement. State authorities may not oppose their agreement. The system's framework, bodies set up on an autonomous basis and encouraged by public authorities, was not undermined by the crisis in 2008. Nevertheless, social dialogue has proved difficult since then. The deadlock in negotiations at cross-sectoral level has led to increased interventionism by the government in the decision-making process for wage increases. However, one observes a two-fold movement, that may appear paradoxical. On the one hand, wage negotiations are placed under governmental control. On the other, this interventionism makes it possible to revive social dialogue. Once the margin has been set by the government, social partners who failed to reach an agreement at multi-industry level, regain the power to negotiate new wage benefits at sector and company levels within the limits of the margin, based on their specific characteristics.

The current deadlock begs the question: is it temporary? Linked to the crisis? Will collective bargaining return to its usual operating mode once the storm has passed? Despite the criticism elicited by this attempt at tripartism, a common desire between state powers and social partners to preserve social dialogue subsists fundamentally.[80] Through it, both State and employers have secured peaceful industrial relations. 2014 and 2015 – when the government implemented an austerity policy with little or no discussions with social partners – were marked by widespread industrial movements. State intervention in what forms the very basis of social dialogue, namely wages, despite apparently serving the interests of employers, is also criticised by them as it deprives them of a bargaining tool with employee organisations.

One can imagine that, as was the case during the 1980s, 'the recurrent intervention of the State [will], for a limited time, [allow] social dialogue to cross this period of turmoil and then try to adapt to a transformed context'.[81] The survival of the Belgian model of collective bargaining is linked to the ability of its stakeholders to adapt to new issues and challenges and their aptitude 'to actively redefine a joint vision of economic

---

79. C.C., 13 October 2016, no. 130/2016, B. 27 and 28.
80. Without a doubt, the 'Michel' government in place since 2014 (centre-right coalition) is marked by a lesser sensitivity to the functioning of social dialogue. But this cannot be considered a general trend among the state authorities.
81. This is a paraphrase – out of its chronological context – from I. Cassiers and L. Denayer, *Concertation sociale et transformations socio-économiques en Belgique, de 1944 à nos jours, supra* n. 18, p. 92.

and social progress'.[82] The signing of a cross-sectoral agreement at the beginning of 2017 opens the perspective, with a touch of optimism, for a return to 'Belgian-style' dialogue.

---

82. I. Cassiers and L. Denayer, *Concertation sociale et transformations socio-économiques en Belgique, de 1944 à nos jours*, supra n. 18, p. 92; E. Léonard and F. Pichault, *Belgique: l'adaptation d'un 'modèle' de concertation sociale*, supra n. 2, p. 75.

CHAPTER 11
Decentralized Collective Bargaining: A Solution to Economic Crisis? – The Case of Turkey

Kübra Doğan Yenisey & Berrin Ceylan Ataman

§11.01 INTRODUCTION

Recognition of collective labour rights as fundamental rights does not spare collective agreements from a critique that considers collective agreements as a source of labour market rigidity with a negative impact on efficacy.[1] The general assumption is that workplace/enterprise level collective bargaining gives more flexibility to the firm than branch level through the implementation of anti-crisis measures and the increase of company competitiveness.

Decentralized collective bargaining devolves the focus of decision making over wages and working hours downwards to the individual enterprise.[2] The literature shows an ongoing discourse from the 1980s onwards about the decentralization of collective bargaining. Many authors have observed the shift from industry-level to lower-level (i.e., company or plant) collective agreements due to the economic situation.[3] The economic crisis in 2008 and the political support given by the European

---

1. S. Hayter (ed.), *Introduction, The role of Collective Bargaining in the Global Economy: Negotiating for Social Justice,* (ILO and Edward Elgar 2011), 7-10.
2. J. Visser, *Wage Bargaining Institutions – from crisis to crisis,* 488 Economic Papers, (European Commission 2013), 23.
3. For example C. Crouch, *Industrial relations and European state traditions,* (Oxford Universiy Press, 1993) 260 et seq.; T. Treu, *General Report, Procedures and Structures of Collective Bargaining at the Enterprise and Workplace Levels,* 7 Comp. Lab. L., 219 (1986); H. C. Katz, *The Decentralization of Collective Bargaining: A Literature Review and Comparative Analysis,* Industrial and 47, Labour Relations Review, 3 (1993); R. Blanpain, *Recent trends in collective bargaining in Belgium,* 123 Int. Lab. Rev, 319.

institutions and International Monetary Fund to the reform of national collective bargaining models have once again made decentralization a current issue. The point of interest is the efficacy of the collective bargaining system.[4] Thus, the level of collective bargaining, among other issues, is presumed to affect the content and outcomes of collective agreements.

Turkey originally had a multi-level bargaining model like many European countries, but shifted from two-level to one-level bargaining in 1982, leaving the workplace as the only level at which a collective agreement could be concluded. With such a decentralized system, our research question is to examine how this model reacts during an economic crisis. We believe that the case of Turkey can shed interesting new light on the question of whether the decentralized model per se brings flexibility to the system. If that is not the case, the reasons for rigidity need to be explained.

After summarizing the Turkish legislative framework for collective bargaining, this interdisciplinary study will analyse, using the data set we have collected, the wage increase rates and working time clauses while comparing the relevant enterprise- and group-level collective agreements. Finally, we will discuss the possible explanations relating to our main questions.

§11.02 LEGISLATIVE OVERVIEW OF TURKISH COLLECTIVE BARGAINING SYSTEM

[A] Historical Evaluation

The Turkish collective bargaining system was mainly based on the French model in the 1960s.[5] The legal structure comprised two levels: workplace and industry. Under this now abolished system, both plant unions and industrial unions were authorized to conclude collective agreements under the condition that the union had a majority in the workplace. Furthermore, the federation or industrial union, representing the majority of employees working in the industry, was authorized to conclude industry-level collective agreements. Although the principle of favour was applicable, the implementation of two different collective agreements at the same workplace caused many legal problems.[6]

From the 1970s, the increase in oil and energy prices caused a general increase in prices and foreign debt in the Turkish economy. The sharp antagonism between unions' and employers' interests resulted in high number of industrial conflicts before

---

4. P. Marginson, C. Welz, *European wage setting mechanisms under pressure: Negotiated and unilateral change and the EU's economic governance regime*, 21(4) Transfer, Vol. 21 (4), (2015), 429; N. Braakmann, B. Brandl, *The Efficacy of Hybrid Collective Bargaining Systems: An Analysis of the Impact of Collective Bargaining on Company Performance in Europe*, MPRA Paper No. 70025, posted 16 March 2016 00:21 UTC, https://mpra.ub.uni-muenchen.de/70025.
5. The Constitution of 1961 guaranteed for the first time trade union freedoms, the right to collective bargaining and the right to strike. It was in July 1963 that special acts (Act No. 274 and Act No. 275) governing trade unions, collective bargaining, the right strike and lock-outs were adopted by the Parliament.
6. *See* T. Esener, *İş Hukuku*, (Ankara 1978), 425 et seq.

the 1980s. Strikes and the wage levels in collective agreements were among the factors blamed for the economic crisis. With the economic measures taken on 24 January 1980, there was a transition from a planned import substitution system to a liberal economy, with structural changes inserted according to the policies of the World Bank and IMF.[7] After the military coup d'état, a new legal framework for trade union and collective bargaining was set up by Acts Nos 2821 and 2822,[8] both of which received harsh criticism from the ILO's supervisory bodies.[9]

Pursuant to criticism of these two Acts, Act No. 6356 on Trade Unions and Collective Bargaining was adopted on 18 October 2012. The preamble of this new Act is based on two fundamental considerations: the need for new legislation responding to the necessities of a democratic society; and a desire to bring the unions and collective bargaining legislation into line with ILO Conventions Nos 87 and 98, as well as Articles 5 and 6 of the Revised European Social Charter and EU principles, moving the collective bargaining system forward. In addition, the legislature aimed to facilitate the conclusion of agreements by providing solutions to some practical problems. Economic motivations did not play a role in this reform.

Regarding the bargaining level, in response to the complexities arising from a multi-level collective agreement model, the legislature adopted a simpler, one-level model in 1982 and maintained this system in 2012. Collective agreements were to be concluded at one level: the workplace. There are thus no industry- or upper-level collective agreements in the system.

[B]   **Mandatory Decentralized Model**

[1]   Industry Level Unionism and Collective Agreements at the Workplace Level

Aiming to enforce trade unionism, the legislature obliged unions to be established at the industry level in 1982. This compulsory industrial unionism resulted in a considerable reduction in the numbers of trade unions before and after 1982.[10] Owing to their weakness, plant and craft unions were prohibited even after the reform in 2012. The system therefore requires both employer and labour unions to be organized at the industry level, though to negotiate at the workplace level.

---

7. For further details *see* H. Saygın, M. Çimen, *Turkish Economic Policies and External Dependency*, (Cambridge Scholars Publishing 2003), 5 et seq.
8. Act No. 2821 on Trade unions and Act No. 2822 on Collective agreements, strike and lock-out, OJ. 7.5.1983, No. 18040.
9. K. Dogan Yenisey, *On the way to attaining a free exercise of trade unions rights and free collective bargaining- The case of Turkey*, in *An Era of Human Rights, Legal Essays in Honour of Jo Carby-Hall*, (Barmarick Pub. 2006), 213-249.
10. The first Act No. 274 on trade unions enabled trade unions to decide on their own structure. The number of trade unions increased significantly, so there were 912 trade unions (including inactive unions) at either plant or industry level in 1978: B. Uçkan, *Türkiye'de Sendikalararası Rekabet*, (İstanbul 2002), 79-80. According to the most recent Ministry of Labour statistics, the number of trade unions was about 150 in July 2016.

Act No. 6356 restricts collective bargaining to three types – workplace, enterprise and group collective agreements.[11] The main bargaining unit is the workplace. If an undertaking has several workplaces in the same branch of industry, only one collective agreement – called an 'enterprise collective agreement'– can be made (Article 34/2 of Act No. 6356). Thus, 'enterprise' has a specific definition for the purpose of collective bargaining. It should be noted that the scope of an enterprise agreement might be different from that of a company agreement, while a company may have several workplaces established in different branches of activity.

In order to compensate the need for an industry-wide collective agreement, the legislature enables unions to have a group collective agreement, concluded between a labour union and an employers' union, to cover the workplaces and enterprises established in the same branch of industry belonging to more than one employer (Article 34/3 of Act No. 6356). The parties to a group agreement are the labour union, organized in their workplaces, and the employers' union, whose members are the employers of workplaces covered by the agreement.

[2] Bargaining Parties and Their Competency

A collective agreement shall be concluded between two competent parties: a labour union and an employers' union – or an employer not affiliated to a union. Since there is no legal regulation of works councils, the authorized union is the workers' sole representative in the workplace.

Act No. 6356 provides two preconditions for recognizing the competence of a labour union for a collective agreement (Article 41 of Act No. 6356):[12] first, the labour union must have as members a minimum of 1% of workers engaged in the industry wherein the union is active. The statistics published by the Ministry of Labour and Social Security in January and July of each year are to be used to determine the representation of 1% of employees in the branch of activity. The labour union, satisfying the first precondition, should also represent as members more than half of the workers in the workplace. All workers, including sales personnel in the field and those employed on a part-time, on call, temporary or seasonal basis, are taken into account when determining the majority status of the labour union.

If an enterprise agreement is intended, the trade union should represent 40% of the workers on the basis of all its workplaces, regardless of the number of members it has in each individual workplace. If there is more than one labour union representing 40% or more of workers in the enterprise, the labour union with the largest number of members shall have the competency to conclude a collective agreement.

---

11. *See* N. Çelik, N. Caniklioğlu, T. Canbolat, *İş Hukuku Dersleri*, (29. Bası, (İstanbul, 2016) 736; C. Tuncay, F. B. Savaş, *Toplu İş Hukuku*, (5. Bası, Beta Yayın. 2016) 210 et seq.; M. Sur, *(İş Hukuku, Toplu İlişkiler,* (Ankara, 2017), 268 et seq.
12. *See* N. Çelik, N. Caniklioğlu, T. Canbolat, *supra* n. 11, 755 et seq.; C. Tuncay, F. B. Savaş, *supra* n. 11, 232 et seq.; M. Sur, *supra* n. 11, 279 et seq.

With regard to a group agreement, where different workplaces belonging to different employers are concerned, the labour union must meet the majority condition in each workplace/enterprise separately.

§11.03 WAGE SETTING AND WORKING TIME CLAUSES IN ENTERPRISE AND GROUP COLLECTIVE AGREEMENTS

[A] Data and Methodology

In order to see the outcomes of such a decentralized collective bargaining model, we analysed wage increase rates and working time clauses in enterprise and group collective agreements. An enterprise collective agreement is taken as an example of one-level single-employer, and a group agreement is an example of one multi-level employer bargaining model. Since there is no industry-level bargaining, group agreements replace the functions of centralized bargaining.

Collecting the data was a difficult part of the research, as social partners do not readily share collective agreements with the public because of strong rivalry between unions. We could only obtain collective agreements through an official authorization by the Ministry of Labour and Social Security.[13]

We selected collective agreements from the metal industry due to its strong bargaining tradition. In addition, it is the only sector where we could find both group and enterprise collective agreements concluded regularly over a ten-year period. In order to eliminate possible sectoral factors from our analysis, we also checked other enterprise collective agreements from the petroleum, chemicals, rubber, plastics and medicines industry.

Nevertheless, we should mention some limits of our research. First, wage increases are shown as 10-12 steps by seniority in the group collective agreements. Thus, the wage growth rates vary from 3% to 12%. As it is impossible to calculate the wage increase for each step, the median is considered. Second, in most cases, nominal wages were not given in the collective agreement. In this respect, the 'fixed' (i.e., non-percentage) wage increase could not be reflected in the percentage wage increase. Third, in the metal sector, wage increases are expressed as inflation multiplied by a coefficient, but as no information is given about this coefficient, we could not calculate the wage increase in these cases.

Considering the limits of our data, we conducted research interviews with officers from labour and employers' unions to better understand their background policy during negotiations.

As an example of a decentralized model, we analysed twenty-three different enterprise collective agreements covering 2005-2017; and as an example of a centralized model, thirteen group collective agreements concluded covering 2002-2014.[14]

---

13. We are extremely grateful to the Ministry of Labour and Social Security for the authorization that enabled us to obtain collective agreements.
14. With respect for unions' disclosure policies, we prefer not to mention the real names of the bargaining parties to collective agreements.

[B] Wage Increase Rates

The wage increase rates in enterprise and group collective agreements concluded with the same trade union may give an idea about the impact of the collective agreement's level.

Case 1: B (Labour union)-A (Company) ↔ B-M (Employers' union)

YEAR	B-A ENTERPRISE CA(%)	B-M GROUP CA(%)
2004		5.26
2005	13	6
2006	14	14.5
2007	10	5
2008	13.40	10
2009	0.00	3.6
2010	6.5	7.7
2011	8.4	5
2012	3	10
2013	7.9	8.5
2014	8.4	4.75

Case 1:B (Labour union)-A (Company) ↔ B-M (Employers' union)

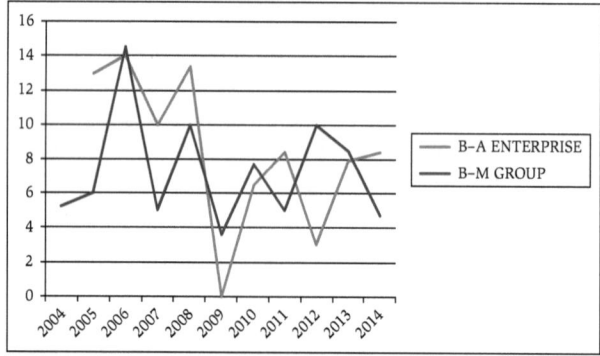

Case 2: T (Labour union)-R (Company) ↔ T (Labour Union)-M (Employers' union)

	T-R ENTERPRISE (%)	T-M GROUP (%)
2004		
2005		5.6
2006	11	7.4
2007	9.65	3.8
2008	12.8	9.6
2009	10,06	8.2
2010	5.4	9.3
2011	6.4	16.8
2012	12	3.8
2013	6.16	12.7
2014	12	11

Case 2: T (Labour union)-R (Company) ⟷ T (Labour Union)-M (Employers' union)

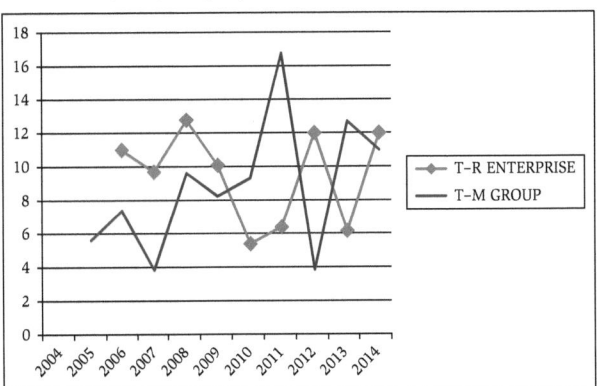

In both cases, there is a slowdown in wage increase rates after 2008. In 2009, wages at firm level decreased by 2.74 points compared with 2008, whereas the decrease at group level is only 1.40 points. This result can be interpreted as a sign that decentralized collective bargaining provided flexibility in the crisis period. However, the following years do not confirm this observation. The reason for there being no wage increase at the enterprise level in 2009 (Case 1) may be explained by the structure of the collective bargaining, regardless of the crisis. Furthermore, the high wage increase during the economic crisis years can also be explained by the fact that collective agreements are made for two or three years.

Table 11.1 Frequency of the Years That the Firm Level Wage Increase Is Superior (x) or Very Close (~) to the Group Wage Increase Level for Case 1 and Case 2 (2004-2014)

	2004	2005	2006	2007	2008	2009	2010	2011	2012	2013	2014
Case 1	ND*	x	X	x	x		~	x		~	x
Case 2	ND	ND	X	x	x	x			x		x

*No Data.

With some exceptions, the wage increases at firm level are higher than the group or almost equivalent. Thus, the Turkish experience does not confirm the initial hypothesis that the decentralized model ensures wage flexibility. In other words, the case data does not show a meaningful relationship between wage flexibility and the level of collective bargaining. However, the slowdown of wage increases after 2008 is obviously related to the economic crisis in both centralized and decentralized agreements.

Case 3: CI (Labour union)-E (Company) ↔ CI (Labour union)-M (Employers' union)

Years	CI-E Enterprise CA (%)	CI-M Group CA (%)
2005	10	7.32
2006	6	10.00
2007	9.65 x K	9.65
2008	8.39 x K	
2009	10.06 x K	
2010	150 TL (S)	
2011	6.4 x K	
2012	10.45 x K	
2013	130 TL (S)	
2014	9.4	

Case 3: CI (Labour union)-E (Company) ⟷ CI (Labour union)-M (Employers' union)

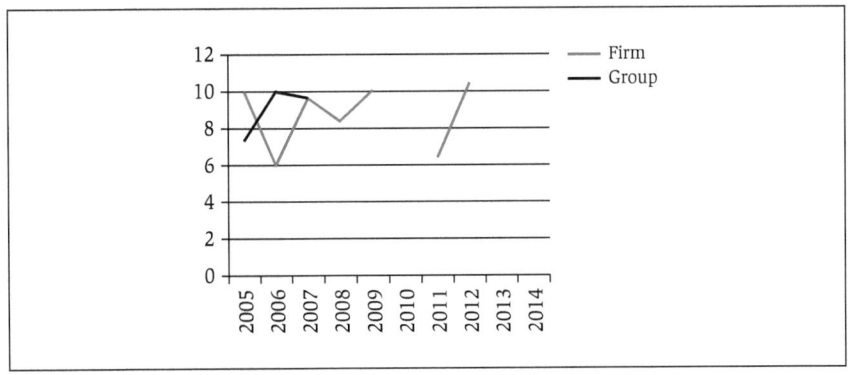

Case 4: PI (Labour union)-P (Company) Enterprise CA

Years	PI-P (%)
2005	18.34
2006	5.3
2007	9.65
2008	10.39
2009	10.06
2010	12
2011	6.4
2012	12.45
2013	12.5
2014	7.4

Case 4: PI (Labour union)-P (Company) Enterprise CA

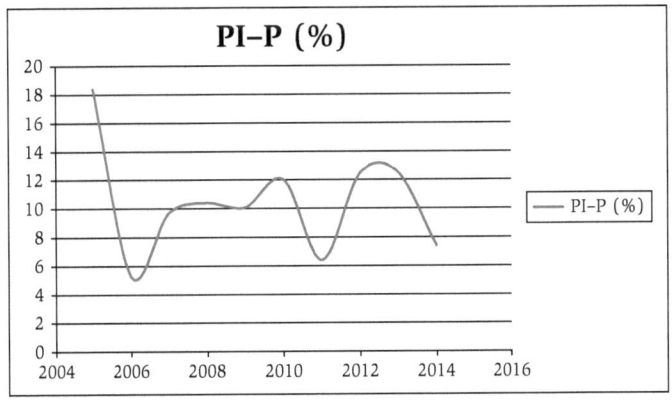

Case 5: PI (Labour union)-U (Company) Enterprise CA

YEARS	PI-U Enterprise CA (%)
2005	10
2006	8
2007	
2008	8
2009	12
2010	8
2011	24
2012	11
2013	19
2104	11

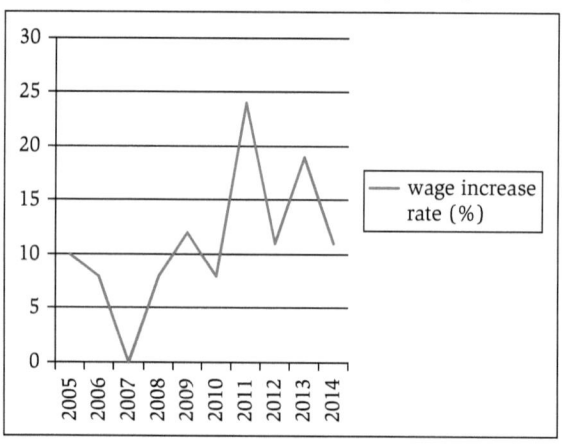

Case 5: PI (Labour union)-U (Company) Enterprise CA

Regarding Case 3, Case 4 and Case 5, we should first clarify that there is no significant data to compare the firm level collective bargaining with the group. At the enterprise level, the significant interpretation is that wage growth slows down in post-crisis years. A recovery is observed in 2011, with the pre-crisis level being reached again. This is because 2011 was general election year in Turkey.

Since inflation is taken into consideration in all collective agreements, real wages seem to be protected.

Table 11.2 Inflation Rate in Turkey (2004-2015)

Years	2004	2005	2006	2007	2008	2009	2010	2011	2012	2013	2014	2015
Inflation rate (%)	9.32	7.72	9.65	8.39	10.06	6.53	6.40	10.45	6.16	7.40	8.17	8.81

Source: Turkstat.

The low sensitivity of collective bargaining to the crisis should not mean that the economic crisis of 2008 did not affect the Turkish economy. It is in 2009 that the global crisis hit the Turkish economy: GDP fell sharply, by 4.7%. Given Turkey's 50% export to the EU, the decline in external demand has led to a reduction in production, which has in turn led to a decrease in the level of employment. It can therefore be said that the European financial crisis has turned into an employment crisis in the Turkish economy. As a result, the unemployment rate increased dramatically to 14%, an increase of three percentage points on the previous year.[15]

Under these circumstances, we can conclude that both centralized and decentralized collective bargaining protects workers' rights relatively, since wage levels have not decreased significantly despite the crisis. The annual earnings of workers in the firms covered by a collective agreement are around 60% more than those not covered by a collective agreement.[16] Nevertheless, because of the low level of the effective unionization rate (9.7%),[17] one third of unionized workers are outside the scope of collective bargaining, and collective bargaining coverage is only 4.6%.

Employment structure is among the reasons for the low rate of unionization, considering that of those employed in 2015, 20.6% were employed in agriculture, 27.2% in industry and 52.2% in the service sector. Of those who were employed in 2015, 66.3% were regular or casual workers (wage earners), 4.4% employers, 16.9% self-employed and 12.4% unpaid family workers. The employment rate is 46%, of

---

15. S. Erdogdu, "Küresel krizin istihdama etkileri ve kriz karşıtı işgücü piyasası önlemleri", *Siyaset Yönetim*, Cilt: 5, Sayı (2010): 12, 142-167.
16. Monthly average income in 2014 is 2319 TL, which is more than twice the minimum wage (891TL). The minimum wage in 2016 is 1300 TL (EUR 450). For more information about the wage structure in Turkey, see O. Tezgel, *An Assessment on Minimum Wages in Turkey From an Inequality Perspective During the 2000s*, in Berrin Ceylan Ataman & Risa Lieberwitz (eds) *Employment and Equity*, (ILO Publications, Ankara- Geneva 2015), 133-150.
17. Unionization with collective bargaining.

which 65% is male and 27.5% female.[18] This structure shows that the number of workers benefiting from a collective agreement is quite limited.

Furthermore, unions face considerable difficulties with unionization. It should be underlined that the single-employer bargaining model creates strong incentives to pursue anti-union policies, which is not the case with the multi-employer bargaining model.[19] In certain countries with industrial collective agreements, there is a default wage structure. However, as in the UK and USA,[20] in Turkey the alternative to negotiated wage setting is the non-unionized market. Since the legislation and individual employment contracts are the primary sources, the alternative to a collective agreement is the individual employment contract. In that case, there is no need to explain why employers again resist unionization so strongly.[21] The fact that some other employers in the industry are also subject to the same working conditions may mitigate their hostile attitude towards unionization.[22]

[C] Working Time Clauses

Starting from the 1990s, flexibility on working time assumed priority in employers' demands. Under the abrogated Labour Act No. 1475, weekly working time should have been distributed equally over the working days of the week. Work beyond the daily working hours was qualified as overtime and should have been compensated by the overtime tariff. In 2003, Labour Act No. 4857, based on the model of EU Directive 93/104, implemented a balancing period opportunity, allowing weekly working time to be distributed over the days of the week in different forms on condition that daily working time must not exceed eleven hours in any case. Within a given period of two months, the average weekly working time must not exceed forty-five hours. This balancing period may be increased up to four months by collective agreement (Article 63/II of Act No. 4857). This is one of the few examples in legislation for derogation *in pejus* by a collective agreement. In addition, the definition of overtime was amended so that the work above the normal weekly forty-five hours of work is deemed overtime and compensated at the overtime tariff.

We tried to see, firstly, whether social partners implement balancing periods in collective agreements; and second, we wondered whether there is a difference between enterprise and group agreements relating to working time regulations.

---

18. Turkstat 2015.
19. F. Traxler, B. Brandl, *The economic impact of collective bargaining coverage*, The role of Collective Bargaining in the Global Economy: Negotiating for Social Justice, (ILO and Edward Elgar, 2011) 239.
20. D. Card, S. de la Rica, *Firm-level contracting and the structure of wages in Spain*, Vol. 59, No. 4, Industrial and Labour Relations Review, (2006) 573, 588-589.
21. F. Traxler, *Bargaining (De)centralization, Macro Economic Performance and Control over the Employment Relationship*, 42:1 British Journal of Industrial Relations, (2003) 7.
22. *Ibid.* 7-8.

Chapter 11: Decentralized Collective Bargaining §11.03[C]

Case 1: B (Labour union)-A (Company) ↔ B (Labour union) -M (Employers' union)

Validity period of collective agreements	Enterprise CA	Group CA	Working time clauses	Degree of flexibility
1.1.2005-28.2.2007 1.3.2007-28.2.2009 1.3.2009-28.2.2012 1.3.2012-28.2.2015 1.3.2015-28.2.2017	B-A		45 h. 'equal division to working days'	Rigid than the law
1.9.2002-31.8.2004 1.9.2004-31.8.2006 1.9.2006-31.8.2008 1.9.2008-31.8.2010 1.9.2010-31.8.2012 1.9.2012-31.8.2014		B-M	Ex. 2002-2004 Reference to Labour Act	Neutral

Case 2: T (Labour union)-R (Company) ↔ T (Labour union)- M (Employers' union)

Validity period of collective agreements	Enterprise CA	Group CA	Working time clauses	Degree of flexibility
1.1.2006-31.12.2007 1.1.2008-31.12.2009 1.1.2010-31.12.2011 1.1.2012-31.12.2013 1.1.2014-31.12.2015 1.1.2016-31.12.2017	T-R		Weekly max. 42.5 h. Daily max. 8.5 h. Division is left to employer	Degree of flexibility
1.9.2004-31.8.2006 1.9.2006-31.8.2008 1.9.2008-31.8.2010 1.9.2010-31.8.2012 1.9.2012-31.8.2014		T-M	45 h. Labour Act	Neutral

Case 3: CI (Labour union)-E (Company) ↔ CI (Labour union)-M (Employers' union)

Validity period of collective agreements	Enterprise CA	Group CA	Working time clauses	Degree of flexibility
1.1.2005-31.12.2006	CI-E		Weekly 45 h. Daily max. 7.5h 'Equal division,	Rigid than the law
1.1.2007-31.12.2009 1.1.2010-31.12.2012			Labour Act	Neutral

Validity period of collective agreements	Enterprise CA	Group CA	Working time clauses	Degree of flexibility
1.1.2013-31.12.2015 1.1.2016-31.12.2018			Shifts	Degree of flexibility
1.9.2004-31.8.2006 1.9.2006-31.8.2008		CI-M	Labour Act	Neutral

Case 4: PI (Labour union)-P (Company) Enterprise CA

Validity period of collective agreements	Enterprise CA	Working time clauses	Degree of flexibility
1.1.2005-31.12.2006 1.1.2007-31.12.2009 1.1.2010-31.12.2012 1.1.2013-31.12.2015	PI-P	45 h. Labour Act	Neutral

Case 5: PI (Labour union)-U (Company) Enterprise CA

Validity period of collective agreements	Enterprise CA	Working Time clause	Degree of flexibility
1.2.2010-31.1.2012 1.2.2012-31.1.2014 1.2.2014-31.1.2016	PI-U	Weekly max. 40 h. Starting and ending hours are regulated	Rigid

In none of these collective agreements does there exist a regulation about a balancing period that will decrease the overtime payments of the employers. Furthermore, social partners are satisfied by reference to the relevant provisions of the Labour Act in the group agreements. As a whole, with regard to working time clauses, enterprise collective agreements provide more rigid clauses than legislative provisions. In Case 1, social partners keep the abrogated mode of equal daily working time and defined overtime as work above 7.5 hours per day.

Therefore, social partners seem unwilling to include working time flexibility in collective agreements. This confirms Glassner and Keune's observation that short-time working arrangements and provisions for working time regulations are more widespread in countries where multi-employer bargaining exists.[23]

---

23. V. Glassner, M. Keune, *The crisis and social policy: The role of collective agreements*, Vol. 151, No. 4, *ILR*, (2012) 357-358; 360-361.

§11.04 OTHER POSSIBLE FACTORS

Decentralization is assumed to bring required flexibility to companies during times of crisis. However, our findings do not totally confirm this assumption. There are surely factors other than the bargaining level to induce such a result.

[A] Power Relations and the Size of Companies

The difference in power relations between industry unions and local trade unions may have an impact on the difference in content between enterprise and group collective agreements.[24] However, under Turkish law, the parties to both types of agreement remain the same. Both workers' and employers' unions can only be established at industry level. Therefore, the power relations between the bargaining parties have no impact on wage increases or rigid working time regulations.

Unions in Turkey might be expected to lose their bargaining power because of the decrease in union density – 11.5% as of July 2016.[25] Nevertheless, even if union density is decreasing at the industry level, trade unions have an absolute majority in workplaces and 40% of workers as members in enterprises to negotiate. They are therefore quite strong at the bargaining table.

The size of companies may have an impact on the wage setting clauses: in an enterprise collective agreement, social partners consider the financial power of the single employer, whereas group agreements cover many employers of different sizes. Therefore, the actors may feel obliged to consider the smaller-sized employers when fixing wage increases. The relation between the nature of the earnings and the size of the companies may be among the factors that explain different levels of wage increases. We have no data to verify this assumption. However, in our interviews with unionists, they confirm such a policy. Nevertheless, if the size of company plays a role in wage setting, it is harder to explain the rigidity of working time in enterprise collective agreements by the size of company.

[B] Union Rivalry

The insights from our interviews show that union rivalry as an important factor in explaining the different attitudes of the same trade union in enterprise and group agreements. One of the characteristics of Turkish trade unionism is inter-union rivalry.[26] More than 90% of the trade unions are affiliated to three main confederations, namely Türk-İş, DİSK and Hak-İş, in accordance with their political views. Thus, the deep political divisions among confederations pass through to unions in the same industry. Furthermore, the majority condition in small bargaining units increases this rivalry. In addition, trade unions' main income is membership fees. Workers who do

---

24. A. R. Cardoso, P. Portugal, *Contractual Wages and the Wage Cushion under Different Bargaining Settings*, Vol. 23, No. 4, *Journal of Labour Economics*, (2005), 875 et seq.
25. For union density statistics see https://www.csgb.gov.tr/media/3400/2016_temmuz_6356.pdf.
26. Uçkan, *supra* n. 10, 123 et seq.

not gain any monetary advantage from a collective agreement are not willing to pay fees to their unions. Unions get membership fees once they conclude a collective agreement. Otherwise, they risk losing their members. Therefore keeping the majority in the workplace is also economically important for unions. These legislative particularities of the collective bargaining system provoke the rivalry among unions.

Moreover, this rivalry makes the use of legal extension mechanisms extremely difficult. Although the legislation enables the extension of a collective agreement concluded by a labour union with the highest number of workers as members in the branch concerned (Article 40 of Act No. 6356), in practice very few extensions exist.

We believe that such a hostile atmosphere holds back unions from applying certain adjustments that the enterprise needs during a crisis. Thus, in our interviews, some unionists said that if an enterprise was in danger of being closed down, trade unions would make some sacrifices in terms of wage moderation. Nevertheless, even in that case, these agreements would be kept confidential, for fear of any written document being captured and abused by rival unions.

[C] Unions Approach to Flexibility

Although the role of collective agreements as a means of flexibility is underlined in the literature,[27] this opinion has no echo in practice. Flexibility is perceived by unions as a deregulation process in favour of employers. In none of the collective agreements that we analysed did we encounter provisions relating to the balancing period. In the absence of an industry-level collective agreement, the workplace/enterprise collective agreement is the most prevalent factor in evaluating the performance of unions. Unions trying to avoid their members going to rival unions refrain from such derogations.

§11.05 CONCLUSION

A general overview reveals that decentralization does not bring flexibility per se. The legal structure of collective bargaining, as well as the industrial relations culture, determines how the bargaining system works.

Neither union rivalry nor the perceived flexibility of social partners is related to the level of collective bargaining. However, one-level, single employer bargaining model with a majority condition in small bargaining units leads unions to concentrate on the welfare of their members in the workplace. If union rivalry is intrinsic in the industrial relations system, unions adopt upward wage policies and a more rigid attitude towards flexible working time. Moderate achievements by a collective agreement risk being used by rival unions.

Moreover, the coverage of collective bargaining is an essential part of industrial democracy. Collective agreements play an important role in determining social policy

---

27. M. Ekonomi, *Türk İş Hukukunda Esnekleşme Gereği'*, *Çalışma Hayatında Esneklik*, (İzmir 1994), 74-76.

in highly coordinated multi-level bargaining systems. In countries with a single-employer collective bargaining model, collective agreements lose their institutional role.[28] The literature shows that shifting from a multi- to a single-employer collective bargaining model in the UK and New Zealand means that the unions have lost a massive amount of control over their employment conditions. Nevertheless, in countries where the multi-employer collective agreement model is dominant and organized, certain bargaining issues are delegated to the plant level.[29] A one-level decentralized model risks weakening the collective bargaining system and supporting growing earnings inequality.[30]

The Turkish experience confirms these observations. In the absence of extension practice, one-level small bargaining units are associated with narrow coverage and result in a reduction of the functions of collective agreements as an institution. The primary activity of Turkish unions has always been concluding collective agreements and wage settlements have always been the crucial item.[31] However, we believe that the one-level bargaining model strengthens bread-and-butter unionism.

Even if unions are established at the industry level, they have no legal tools to regulate working conditions at the upper levels, sectoral or national. Therefore, social partners play a role in the formation of social policies and legislative acts, but lack binding regulatory devices. Issues such as migration and young or old employees do not find any place in collective agreements. This result endorses the observation that countries with a narrow or narrowing bargaining agenda are also those with weak multi-level or coordinated bargaining systems.[32]

Another point of interest is that economic concerns have not played any role in the reform movement of 2012. During the 1970s, high union wage demands and large-scale strikes were alleged to be the reason for increasing unemployment and economic problems.[33] Even if economic motivations played a role in the 1982 reform, we would underline the importance of other reasons such as the aim of calming down conflict-based industrial relations and simplifying the complicated legal process. However, although Turkey has suffered many economic crises – in 1994, 1999, 2001 and 2009 – it is interesting to observe that during the last thirty years collective agreements have not been considered either among the reasons for, or the solutions to, the economic crisis. This result is also related to the narrow coverage of collective agreements.

---

28. V. Glassner, M. Keune, *The crisis and social policy: The role of collective agreements*, supra n. 23, 369.
29. F. Traxler, *Bargaining (De)centralization, Macro Economic Performance and Control over the Employment Relationship*, supra n. 21, 19.
30. F. Traxler, B. Brandl, *The economic impact of collective bargaining coverage*, supra n. 19, 248-249, 250.
31. M. Kutal, *Türkiye'de Toplu İş Sözleşmesi Düzeninde Ücret Politikası*, in *Türkiye'de İşçi-İşveren İlişkileri*, (İstanbul, 1974) 33 et seq.
32. Eurofound, *Collective bargaining in Europe in the 21st century*, (Publications Office of the European Union, 2015) 36-37.
33. T. Dereli, *Türkiye'de Sendikacılığın ve Toplu Sözleşme Düzeninin Ekonomik ve Sosyal Etkileri, Uluslararası Deneyimlerin Işığında Türkiye'de Endüstri İlişkileri*, (İstanbul, 1977) 153 et seq.. T. Dereli, *Labour Law and Industrial Relations in Turkey*, in R. Blanpain (ed) *International Encyclopedia of Laws*, (Kluwer Law International, 2012) 47-48.

To conclude, the role of collective agreements as an institution determining social policies has depended upon many circumstances related to the legal and sociological culture of each system. The bargaining level is one of the variables. Turkey is among the countries that have shifted from a quasi-multi-level bargaining model to one-level bargaining. At the time (1982), a possible risk arising from the decentralization trend – that of reducing the scope, effectiveness and coverage of collective agreements, particularly in countries with a relatively weak trade union structure – was underlined.[34] The one-level single-employer experience of Turkey shows that the 'collective voice'[35] evanesces and collective agreements do not bring the required flexibility to workplaces. If it is not possible to consider the level of collective agreement as solely responsible for the actual situation, it is clear that the decentralized model has an impact on it. In the dialectic conflict over the bargaining level,[36] it seems time for a rethink about the multi-level bargaining model for Turkey.

---

34. T. Treu, *General Report, Procedures and Structures of Collective Bargaining at the Enterprise and Workplace Levels*, supra n. 3, 230.
35. S. Hayter, *Introduction, The role of Collective Bargaining in the Global Economy: Negotiating for Social Justice*, supra n. 1, 9.
36. F. Traxler, *Bargaining (De)centralization, Macro Economic Performance and Control over the Employment Relationship*, supra n. 21, 1, 19, 20.

B Working Time

CHAPTER 12
Negotiating Working Time in Times of Crisis

Łukasz Pisarczyk

§12.01 INTRODUCTION

Recent decades have brought significant changes in the structure of the employment relationship. The evolution has been necessary to adjust the rights and duties of both employer and the employee to the changing social, technical and economic environment. Employment has had to become more flexible, with working time regulations playing a very important role in the process of flexibilisation.[1] Consequently, this part of the labour law has undergone visible modifications. The process was invigorated by the economic crisis. On the one hand, further flexibilisation may be treated as a price that employees have to pay to maintain their employment.[2] On the other hand, the protective dimension of working time standards should not be overlooked.[3] Moreover,

---

1. C. Lang, S. Clauwaert, I. Schömann, *Working time reforms in times of crisis*, 6 (Brussels: European Trade Union Institute 2013), underline that working time is treated as a key adjustment mechanism applied in the labour market reforms, predominantly to satisfy employer's needs for cost reductions and greater flexibility.
2. The (temporary) worsening of working conditions may contribute to the improvement of the employer's position and the protection of workplaces (e.g., B. Hepple, *Four Approaches to the Modernisation of Individual Employment Rights* in R. Blanpain, M. Weiss (eds) *Changing Industrial Relations & Modernisation of Labour Law. Liber Amicorum in Honour of Professor Marco Biagi*, 184-185 (Kluwer Law International, 2003).
3. The right to reasonable working hours may be treated as a fundamental employee right guaranteed by the main international documents and conventions. Article 24 Universal Declaration of Human Rights provides that everyone has the right to rest and leisure, including reasonable limitation of working hours. According to Article 7 International Covenant on Economic, Social and Cultural Rights, everyone has the right to leisure and reasonable limitation of working hours, as well as remuneration for public holidays. Article 2 European Social Charter obliges the Parties to provide for reasonable daily and weekly working hours and for public holidays with pay; the working week should be progressively reduced to the extent that the

the protection of the employee must be seen not only from the perspective of the employee's health and safety, but also from that of his/her privacy (work-life balance or life-long learning).[4]

Collective agreements have played a major role in the process of flexibilisation, so it is necessary to consider the influence of the economic crisis on collective agreements in the area of working time. The starting point is the analysis of statutory provisions concerning working time (as they determine the room for the social partners). The next step is the practical consequences of the crisis in the area of collective agreements. The spheres to be examined are parties to agreements, levels of negotiations and, last but not least, the content of collective agreements.[5]

§12.02 WORKING TIME: THE SOCIAL DIALOGUE AND THE LEGISLATION

The reforms of working time occur at various levels. In many countries, they are inspired by legislative intervention.[6] However, the legislative level is usually not sufficient to restructure working time. Working hours are inseparably connected to the functioning of companies and specific establishments. The legislator's initiatives must be accompanied by the social partners' activity. In some cases, the legislation creates merely a legal framework for collective agreements; in others, the social partners are allowed to modify the legislative standards. At the same time, an extension of the autonomy of the parties to the employment relationship (employer and employee) may threaten the equilibrium and lead to domination by the employer.[7] Moreover, in some cases statutory intervention was preceded by an agreement of social partners concluded, for example, at the national level. As a result, collective agreements must be a key element of working time reconstruction. The consent of the social partners

---

increase of productivity and other relevant factors permit. When it comes to the EU standards Article 31.2 Charter of Fundamental Rights declares that every worker has the right to limitation of maximum working hours, to daily and weekly rest periods. Finally, one should not overlook the standards arising from the ILO's conventions.

4. Such an approach is sometimes questioned. The Member States and the employers expect the extension of working time (without compensation) to increase the competitiveness of the European economy (C. Lang, S. Clauwaert, I. Schömann, *Working time reforms in times of crisis*, supra n. 1, p. 14).
5. The analysis is based on general surveys and articles as well as a number of national reports (Austria, Hungary, the Netherlands, Poland, Portugal and Romania). Poland is a characteristic example of a country with developed statutory regulations and underdeveloped collective agreements. To an extent, it is a heritage of the socio-economic system existing in Poland (and other countries of central and eastern Europe) before 1989. On the one hand, there was no room for autonomous and independent negotiations of the social partners. On the other hand, the state offered relatively high level of protection for workers (M. Seweryński, *Polish Labour Law from Communism to Democracy*, 24-25 and 119 et seq (Warszawa: Dom Wydawniczy ABC,1999). The protection was adjusted to the nature of the then-existing system.
6. In recent years the majority of European countries have modified their working time regulations to achieve greater flexibility (compare C. Lang, S. Clauwaert, I. Schömann, supra n. 1, p. 7).
7. The involvement of the social partners with a relatively strong negotiating position can be seen as an element of the protection (e.g., F. Gamillscheg, *Kollektives Arbeitsrecht*, Bd I, *Grundlagen, Koalitionsfreiheit, Tarifvertrag, Arbeitskampf und Schlichtung*, 11 (München: Beck 1997).

becomes particularly important when the organisation of working time modifies the paradigm of the employment relationship (as with e.g., work on call or zero-hours contracts). Finally, in some states where the level of legislative intervention is relatively low collective agreements are in fact the main instrument of change in the field of working hours (e.g., the Nordic countries).[8]

As a result, the social partners decide on the level of flexibility within the work organisation. Moreover, in some countries the social partners actually initiated the process of change (e.g., concluding national agreements providing for anti-crisis instruments). In these cases, the legislation establishing the legal framework for collective bargaining follows the results of a social dialogue (usually conducted at the national level).[9]

European countries vary significantly as regards working time statutory regulations. Some of them (Austria, France, Germany, Hungary, the – relatively flexible – Netherlands, Poland, Portugal and Romania) refer to the traditional model of protection based on maximum daily and weekly working hours determined by the law. This may limit the role of the social partners. However, the legislation may introduce various opening clauses enabling the extension of daily or even weekly working hours. Moreover the system of derogations concerning working time may be supplemented or even replaced by a "suppletive" method where "the law is only intended to govern a situation in the absence of collective agreement" (France)[10]. At the same time, there are Member States such as the United Kingdom in which protection is based on daily and weekly rest periods as well as maximum weekly norms of working hours. Such a solution is, of course, much more flexible. The social partners have more freedom when it comes to the organisation of working hours. Their collective agreements may improve the protection of workers by establishing norms of working time (to limit the managerial power of the employer) as well as introducing various forms of working hours organisation.

It is necessary to underline that the social partners may also be limited by the standards arising from EU law (rest periods, maximum working time, reference periods, night work)[11] and implemented by the national legislation or collective agreements. Without doubt, a very important role is played by the definition of working time adopted in *acquis communautaire*. Working time covers every period during which the employee is obliged to remain at the employer's disposal (on the

---

8. Compare C. Lang, S. Clauwaert, I. Schömann, *supra* n. 1, p. 8.
9. *See* M. Tiraboschi, S. Spattini, *Anti-crisis Labour Market Measures and their Effectiveness between Flexibility and Security* in T. Davulis, D. Petrylaite (eds.) *Labour Market of 21st Century: Looking for Flexibility and Security*, 193 (Cambridge Scholars Publishing, 2011) and C. Lang, S. Clauwaert, I. Schöman, *supra* n. 1, p. 22. For instance France resigned from the 'working more to earn more policy' and shifted to the application of short-time mechanism'.
10. See in this Volume, Ch. Vigneau, Part II Chapter 13, *Negotiation working time in time of crisis: the 'El Khomri Law'*.
11. Directive 2003/88/EC of the European Parliament and of the Council of 4 November 2003 concerning certain aspects of the organisation of working time (OJ L 299, 18.11.2003, pp. 9-19), hereinafter referred to as 'directive'.

employer's premises).¹² These periods cannot be excluded from working time or calculated in a special way that is less favourable than working time *sensu stricto*.¹³ This definition influences the subjective scope of collective negotiations.

The relationship between the legislation and collective agreements has become more complicated because of the breakdown of collective negotiations in some countries (a phenomenon is that particularly visible in central and eastern Europe). There are a number of reasons for the weakness of the social dialogue. First, the social partners, including trade unions, are undergoing a deep crisis that is even more dangerous than in the countries of the 'Old Union'.¹⁴ Second, the 'New Union' is lacking in appropriate infrastructure and background. For more than forty years in central and eastern Europe, there were no conditions for developing genuinely autonomous collective negotiations.¹⁵ As a result, there is no comprehensive system of collective agreements. Third, the tension between employers and trade unions is sometimes very strong, paralysing constructive and fruitful social dialogue. Fourth, legislators have made some mistakes. In some countries, they strongly influence the structure of social partners (mainly trade unions).¹⁶ Moreover, the room left for the social partners to regulate working conditions is usually more limited than in western countries. To an extent, it is reminiscent of the former system in which state tended to control all aspects of the economy. Consequently, the potential of collective agreements cannot be fully exploited. As a result, the majority of the eastern European countries have not established a network of branch or regional agreements. Company-level dialogue is usually more animated, but the coverage of collective agreements remains very limited. Collective agreements are being replaced by other legal instruments, including internal acts and instructions issued by employers, as well as individual employment contracts. These instruments, contrary to typical collective bargaining, do not guarantee a necessary balance between management and labour. Therefore, in many cases they cannot be used as an effective instrument to restructure working time (the scope of flexible solutions that can be introduced in this way being limited).¹⁷

---

12. See the judgments of the Court of Justice of 3 October 2000, in the case C-303/98, *Sindicato de Médicos de Asistencia Pública (Simap) v. Conselleria de Sanidad y Consumo de la Generalidad Valenciana* and of 9 September 2003, in the case C-151/02 *Landeshauptstadt Kiel v. Norbert Jäger*.
13. Judgment of the Court of 1 December 2005 in the case C-14/04 *Abdelkader Dellas and Others v. Premier ministre and Ministre des Affaires sociales, du Travail et de la Solidarité*.
14. Apart from the decreasing number of trade union members, one can also observe weaker mobilisation to conduct collective actions (G.P. Cella, T. Treu, *National Trade Union Movements* in R. Blanpain (ed) *Comparative Labour Law and Industrial Relations in Industrialized Market Economies*, 419 (Kluwer Law International 2004).
15. *See* more M. Seweryński, *Polish Labour Law from Communism to Democracy*, supra n. 5, pp. 122 et seq.
16. In Poland the law requires the trade unions to establish company structures which are necessary to enjoy basic rights.
17. Polish law provides for internal regulations concerning the organisation of work. They must be issued by employers with at least fifty employees. Any employer of twenty or more workers is obliged to issue the regulations on request of the trade unions. By means of internal regulations, it is possible to introduce the extension of daily working hours, flexible working time (without working hours), shift work or the extension of yearly limit of overtime work. However, it is not

Finally, the crisis has exposed the need for state intervention. Although the state cannot force the social partners to conclude collective agreements,[18] it can oblige them to launch negotiations (e.g., on specific matters) and, to an extent, influence their conduct.[19]

To summarise, it is necessary to underline the importance of collective bargaining in remodelling working time. However, collective agreements cannot be seen in isolation from statutory standards and state activity. In many countries, legislation determines the room left for the social partners. Moreover, the state can support and encourage social dialogue, which is particularly important in times of economic crisis. Above all, legislators may enlarge the sphere of autonomy, a result that can be achieved by means of various instruments. The legislation may step back, leaving space for autonomous negotiations (the case of countries safeguarding only rest periods). But even in the traditional model, the approach to working time may become more flexible. The legislator may resign (at least partially) from the employee privilege principle that allows so-called opening clauses, thus enabling the departure *in peius* from the statutory standards as well as from the guarantees set up by the collective agreements further up the hierarchy of labour law sources. This opens possibilities for give-and-take bargaining. Concessions can be made to agreements concluded at various levels (company or sectoral). Moreover the state may even change the nature and role of statutory standards and their relationship to collective agreements (a "suppletive" role and the retraction of the law in favour of collective agreements)[20]. At the same time, legislation can be inspired by social partners.

Analysis of the domestic systems leads to the conclusion that the crisis has caused perceptible changes in the area of working time.[21] They may either modify rights and duties of the parties in a direct way,[22] or empower the social partners to restructure the system. Usually there is a combination of various solutions. Changes that have occurred in some countries may be described as profound.[23]

---

possible to introduce reference periods longer than four months, intermittent work or variable working hours. The above-mentioned solutions must be accepted by trade unions in collective agreements. For work rules, *see* more M. Włodarczyk in: *Outline of Polish Labour Law System*, ed. K.W. Baran, 109-110 (Wolter Kluwers 2016).

18. Such a provision would contradict the freedom of association and the autonomy of the social partners.
19. Compare G.J. Bamber, P. Sheldon, *Collective Bargaining: Towards Decentralization?* In R. Blanpain (ed) *Comparative Labour Law and Industrial Relations in Industrialized Market Economies*, 543 (Kluwer Law International 2004).
20. See in this Volume, Ch. Vigneau, Part II Chapter 13, *Negotiation working time in time of crisis: the 'El Khomri Law'*.
21. Compare C. Lang, S. Clauwaert, I. Schömann, *supra* n. 1, p. 7.
22. An example is amendments concerning public holidays. Some national legislators limited the number of bank holidays, extending the total amount of work.
23. See in this Volume, Ch. Vigneau, Part II Chapter 13, *Negotiation working time in time of crisis: the 'El Khomri Law'*. In Portugal, the legislation introduced profound changes in working time to the Labour Code from 2009 and the amendments in 2012. The new laws enabled greater working time flexibility and reduction of overtime. At the same time, they undermine the balance of working and family life, and allow for extremely extended working days and weeks. The Polish reform that took place in 2013 also had very serious consequences.

§12.03 LEVELS OF NEGOTIATIONS AND PARTIES TO COLLECTIVE AGREEMENTS REGULATING WORKING TIME

In the majority of Member States, working time may be regulated at both levels, sectoral and plant. However, the provisions on working time vary from the majority of other provisions of collective agreements (e.g., concerning remuneration).[24] In some spheres, it is rather difficult to introduce comprehensive solutions concerning whole sectors or branches. Some aspects of working time are strictly connected with the organisation of work in specific companies or establishments. Consequently, sectoral agreements may refer only to general aspects of working time, while more detailed issues are regulated at company or plant levels. However, sectoral negotiations that guarantee equilibrium between the parties may play a role when it comes to deviations from the main statutory standards (e.g., number of working hours, including short-time work, overtime compensation).[25] The solutions can usually be considered a genuine compromise between management and labour, while company negotiations may be dominated by the employer (and may, moreover, provoke a conflict between the parties). In recent years, the importance of company-level agreements has increased even further. An important example of this is the French reform in 2016 that was subject to public opposition, which allowed company-level accords to modify certain key elements of working time (it significantly changed the relationship between branch and company level agreements – in favour of company level agreements).[26]

To summarise, there is a potential division between sectoral and company (plant) negotiations: between modifications of working conditions *sensu stricto* by sectoral (branch) agreements and organisation of working hours by company (plant) agreements (one can observe a growing role of company-level negotiations). Sectoral agreements may also empower company-level ones to regulate some aspects of working time. Deviations from this model may be justified by the real situation of the social dialogue, national tradition or potential of the social partners – i.e., under some conditions, the legislation may allow the extension of working hours at company level. In some countries company-level agreements may even become the main source of

---

24. In Austria, some collective agreements at sectoral level contain provisions which pass on the power to establish alternative schemes for the distribution of working time to the employer and workers' representatives at company level via plant–level agreements. This is permitted unless otherwise provided by law. It is not in the law, but it would be both levels, as long as the statutory maximums are taken into account. In Portugal, sectoral collective agreements define more favourable rules than those set by the law, including working time adaptability and the possibility for concentrated schedules, which can then be further specified at company level. In Romania, some solutions are introduced at plant level – e.g., uneven work time within the forty hour work week, as well as during the compressed working week, negotiated by means of company-level collective agreement; and the application of short-time work. The Polish law does not determine the level of negotiations. Sectoral dialogue is, however, almost non-existent. Working time is regulated at the plant level (in a collective or even in individual way).
25. On positive and negative consequences of the dialogue conducted at various levels, see more G.J. Bamber, P. Sheldon, *Collective Bargaining: Towards Decentralization? supra*, pp. 543-545.
26. The El Khomri law (2016) concerned such issues as the duration of working time (daily and weekly) and overtime work. *See* in this Volume, Ch. Vigneau, Part II Chapter 13, *Negotiation working time in time of crisis: the 'El Khomri Law', supra*.

working time standards.[27] National agreements are another phenomenon that, in many countries, have influenced legislation and more detailed negotiations between employers and employee representatives.[28]

Briefly stated, working time is regulated mainly at the plant level. It is related to the nature of working time provisions. The economic crisis has not inverted this tendency. Moreover, one can observe the growing number of provisions of company agreements increasing the flexibility of the process of work. There is, however, also a role to be played by agreements concluded at higher levels.

The composition of the social partners depends mainly on the negotiation level. Sectoral, branch or regional agreements are concluded mainly with trade unions. Employers are usually represented by their organisations. An exceptional solution is representation by economic chambers based on obligatory membership (Austria).

The structure of company dialogue is more complicated. The competences to act on behalf of workers are divided between trade unions and elected bodies. When it comes to trade unions, the law may formulate additional criteria to influence negotiations (France) – also the area of working time (representativeness). The position of elected bodies varies from country to country. Work councils sometimes enjoy autonomous rights in the field of working time. For instance, elected bodies may be involved in determining working time schedules. Sometimes elected representatives may regulate certain aspects of working time (e.g., the number of working hours) if they are empowered to do so by collective agreements (as in Austria and Germany).[29] Various solutions can be combined. In other countries (e.g., Poland and Romania), elected bodies may negotiate some aspects of working time when there are no trade unions. Moreover, the legislation in some countries provides for less formalised types of representation. British law recognises workforce agreements on working time concluded with representatives elected by employees or workers. Polish law also accepts agreements concerning working hours with ad hoc elected representatives (when there are no trade unions).[30]

Finally, in some countries in which the social dialogue undergoes a serious crisis, one can observe the development of unilateral acts issued by the employer. The right

---

27. See in this Volume Ch. Vigneau, Part II Chapter 13, *Negotiation working time in time of crisis: the 'El Khomri Law'*.
28. *See* e.g., V. Glassner, M. Keune, *Crise et politique sociale: la rôle des accords collectifs*, 4 Revue Internationale du Travail, 388 (2012).
29. Company agreements concluded with elected bodies are considered to be sources of labour law but are situated lower than traditional (typical) collective agreements. See e.g., §7 the German law on Working Time.
30. If workers are not represented by trade unions, collective agreements concerning selected aspects of working time are concluded with employee representatives elected according to the rules determined at a given enterprise (establishment). The potential scope of the regulation is relatively broad. It covers the extension of calculation periods (up to twelve months) or even the limitation of working hours connected with a decrease in remuneration (currently suspended). The law does not regulate the election procedure of representatives. Ad hoc representatives do not enjoy any protection against dismissal or other actions undertaken by the employer. As a result, the regulation does not guarantee a balance between social partners and may lead to the destruction of the traditional model of social dialogue.

to regulate working time by means of such instruments can be derived from organisational prerogatives of the employer. In some cases, they emerge from consultation with employee representatives. The involvement of bodies representing workers may strengthen the protection. However, internal regulations issued by the employer constitute a challenge to the system of collective bargaining. The legislation should determine the scope of solutions that can be introduced only with the consent of employee representation. Another alternative for collective agreements are individual contracts concluded with employees (workers).[31] Although they offer greater flexibility, they do not safeguard the equilibrium and protection that can be achieved thanks to collective accords.[32]

To summarise, the natural tendency for working time to shape its organisation at company (or even plant) level has been strengthened by the economic crisis. Many aspects of working time (including the number of working hours) are regulated by the social partners within companies. The crisis also caused some changes in the structure of employee representation. The legislators had to confront the growing importance of collective negotiations with the crisis of the trade union movement. As a result, employees are more and more often represented by elected bodies[33] (also created ad hoc). This applies to all aspects of collective bargaining, but is particularly visible in the area of working time (while some other aspects of the employment relationship may be devoted to trade unions only).

§12.04 CONTENT OF COLLECTIVE AGREEMENTS

Provisions of collective agreements relating to working time can be divided into two groups.[34] First, collective agreements may regulate the number working hours (daily and weekly working time as well as the number of days off). Second, the subject of collective bargaining is the organisation of working hours. It covers a wide range of issues including reference periods, schedules and patterns of working time. Provisions of an organisational nature play a very important role in the process of the flexibilisation of working time. The main idea is to adjust the working hours for specific days, weeks or months to the employer's current needs. Thanks to this adjustment, the

---

31. British law recognised opting out of the forty-eight hour working week (Reg. 5 the Working Time Regulations 1998). There are also further modifications that can be introduced by means of relevant agreements: 'relevant agreement', in relation to a worker, means not only a workforce agreement which applies to him, any provision of a collective agreement which forms part of a contract between him and his employer, but also any other agreement in writing which is legally enforceable as between the worker and his employer (Reg. 2(1)).
32. As a rule, the employer shall (wherever possible) allow workers to take an equivalent period of compensatory rest.
33. This tendency had already been observed before the crisis (M. Biagi, M. Tiraboschi, *Forms of Employee Representational Participation* in R. Blanpain (ed) *Comparative Labour Law and Industrial Relations in Industrialized Market Economies*, 466 et seq. (Kluwer Law International 2004).
34. C. Lang, S. Clauwaert, I. Schömann, *Working time reforms in times of crisis*, supra n. 1, p. 7, distinguish three main tendencies: (1) allowing employers to extend working time duration; (2) allowing employers to shorten time duration; and (3) allowing the employers to accommodate the allocation of working hours according to their needs.

employer may accumulate working hours when they are needed, avoiding overtime in times of slowdown. The total number of working hours may remain unchanged, so the economic interests of employees are not affected. However, the process of work becomes less predictable. As a result, it is more complicated for workers to reconcile professional and private life. It should be stressed that numerous flexible solutions, which in the past constituted a new element of the system, are becoming typical of the instruments used by the social partners.[35] Collective agreements may also regulate other aspects of working time, such as remuneration for overtime or Sunday work.

The economic crisis raises questions about the length of the working day and week. One might expect the worsening of the economic situation to invert the previous trend and lead to an increase in working hours. However, it is necessary to distinguish between extension *sensu stricto* and balancing working hours. Both may be introduced by means of collective agreements. At the same time, one can observe an apparently opposite phenomenon of reducing the number of working hours (but, with a corresponding reduction in pay).

An extension *sensu stricto* is an extension of weekly working hours that affects the total amount of work. The increase in working hours can be accomplished by legislation (e.g., the Portuguese public sector extended from thirty-five to forty, then reduced again to thirty-five hours) or by means of collective agreements. In many countries this is not allowed. The extension is considered to be a modification *in peius* that would contradict the employee privilege principle. However, it influences the scope of collective bargaining, as the parties are very limited when it comes to give-and-take techniques. Only in some countries (e.g., France) do social partners have some possibilities to extend working hours in a strict sense.[36]

A more common solution, which cannot be treated as an extension *sensu stricto*, is the increase of daily working hours balanced by a shortening of working time on other days, with the average weekly norm maintained (e.g., Austria, Germany,[37] Poland, Portugal and Romania). Domestic legislation quite often determines the conditions of the extension – e.g., work of a specific nature. In Poland, collective agreements may extend daily working hours up to twelve if justified by the nature of the work. In special cases, an extension to sixteen (readiness to work) or even twenty-four hours (security staff) is possible.[38] The application of flexible working hours can be treated as a long-term trend observed already before the crisis, which acted as a stimulus to this tendency.

---

35. C. Lang, S. Clauwaert, I. Schömann, *Working time reforms in times of crisis*, supra n. 1, p. 29. The tendency could be deepened by the economic crisis.
36. The social partners may increase a weekly limit of working hours. It is also possible to increase the daily limit (to twelve hours). The El Khomri law empowered company-level agreements to introduce such modifications. See in this Volume, Ch. Vigneau, *infra*.
37. §3 the law on working time allows the extension of daily working time to ten hours (balanced in the reference period). Moreover, in cases justified by the nature of work (e.g., readiness to work), working time may be extended beyond ten hours (§7): it is reserved for collective agreements or company agreements (under the collective agreement authorisation).
38. These solutions can be applied not only in collective agreements but also in internal regulations issued unilaterally by the employer.

One of the most popular methods of rescuing workplaces during the economic crisis is short-time work.[39] The idea of short-time work is to reduce working hours and to diminish the remuneration. The extreme form of reducing working time is the suspension of the employment relationship for a specific period (usually part of a year), leading to a reduction in working hours in a broader perspective. Short-time work is intended to support the employer and to enable it to overcome economic difficulties. The aim is to avoid – or at least to limit – redundancies. In recent years, the importance of short-time work has increased significantly. In the majority of Member States, short-time systems have been developed as in Germany and Poland. They have even been introduced (or allowed) in the countries where such solutions had not previously been provided or had been evaluated sceptically before the crisis e.g., the Netherlands.[40] As a rule, short-time work is introduced by means of collective agreements. The law may establish additional formal requirements or protective standards concerning the conditions of work, as well as provide for support granted to workers affected by the shortening. Because of the consequences of short-time work, the legislator's intervention is particularly important.

The shortening of working hours raises a question about the paradigm of the employment relationship. An important part of the economic risk is borne by the employee. This is particularly evident in the case where the employment relationship is suspended. The protection of the workplace itself cannot be treated as a sufficient and only recompense. The legislator should take into account the role of remuneration and the social consequences of shorter working hours. Problems caused by the recession cannot be solved by the parties to employment contract or even by the social partners only, so short-time work is usually supplemented by public support. The idea is to compensate at least a part of the remuneration lost by the employee. The support can be financed directly from various sources, e.g., the state or local budget, or from social security.[41] In some countries there are special funds created by the contributions paid by the employers, for example.[42] Finally, it is important to stress that short-time work provokes numerous doubts and questions. The extent to which it can improve the situation on the labour market is highly disputable.[43] It also interferes with the functioning of the economy and, last but not least, it is expensive, involving special payments for affected workers. Not surprisingly, its practical meaning in many

---

39. *See* more C. Lang, S. Clauwaert, I. Schömann, *Working time reforms in times of crisis, supra* n. 1, pp. 20 et seq.
40. Compare V. Glassner, M. Keune, *Crise et politique sociale: le rôle des accords collectifs, supra* n. 25, pp. 386-394.
41. Compare M. Tiraboschi, S. Spattini, *Anti-crisis labour market measures and their effectiveness between flexibility and security, supra* n. 9, p. 196.
42. The finest example of the application of short-time is Germany. In Austria, the Employment Promotion Act (2009) made it possible to conclude short-time work agreements for a maximum duration of eighteen months where a company faces economic difficulties. The French law on short-time work was enacted in 2013 on the basis of a transsectoral collective agreement.
43. *See* more C. Lang, S. Clauwaert, I. Schömann, *Working time reforms in times of crisis, supra* n. 1, pp. 22-23, referring to the objections against the instrument discussed: e.g., the negative influence of short-time work on the situation of so-called outsiders (non-employees). Supporting 'insiders' (employees), the countries cannot invest enough in efficient labour market policies.

countries is rather limited.[44] However, it is still treated as an important anti-crisis instrument.

One of the most popular provisions referring to working time is stipulations concerning reference periods. Reference (calculation) periods do not affect directly the number of working hours. They are, however, very important for organising working hours in a rational (efficient) way.[45] The legal framework of reference periods is determined by EU law. As a rule, reference periods should not exceed four months. They can be extended in cases justified by the character of the work. The directive also allows the extension by means of collective agreements. Numerous Member States have made use of this option.[46]

Another sphere regulated by collective agreements is working time schedules (for allocation of working time).[47] The determination of working days and hours has been traditionally treated as a part of the organisational power of the employer. There are, however, various forms of involvement of bodies representing workers, e.g., consultation or even acceptance. Schedules of working time may constitute a part of establishment (company) regulations. Some elements of schedules of working time are determined by company agreements or other collective agreements. Regulating schedules of working time by means of collective agreements increases the level of stability and predictability. Collective regulations usually leave the necessary room for the employer. Moreover, they may introduce more flexible solutions that go beyond the organisational prerogatives of the employer. Examples of such solutions are variable working hours and accounts of working time, which make it possible to avoid overtime and to reduce employment costs.

---

44. Such a situation occurred in Poland. Short-time work was introduced by the special Anti-Crisis Law (2013) that applies to those employers undertaking commercial activities who experience a deterioration in their financial situation (according to a set of specific criteria). The law provided for suspension of the employment relationship (economic lay-off) and the shortening of working hours. The application of both instruments was accompanied by a system of subsidies paid from a special public fund. Due to very complicated application criteria, the practical impact of the anti-crisis packages was very limited. Currently, due to the improvement in the labour market, public support is suspended; however, the legal mechanism is still present in the system. A contrary example is Germany, where short-time covered a large number of workers and was one of the most important anti-crisis instruments. Moreover, Germany was regarded as the leading Member State in terms of dealing with the crisis (C. Lang, S. Clauwaert, I. Schömann, *Working time reforms in times of crisis*, supra n. 1, pp. 20-21).
45. See e.g., International Labour Office, *Hours of work: from fixed to flexible? [International Labour Conference, 93rd Session 2005]*, Geneva 2005, p. 81.
46. Austria: maximum one year; can be extended by means of collective agreements. Hungary: four or six months; can be extended up to 12 months. Germany: collective agreements may introduce different reference periods than those determined by the law. Romania: can be extended by collective agreements for up to 6/12 months. United Kingdom: extended by means of collective agreements or workforce agreements from 17 to 52 weeks (for objective or technical reasons or reasons concerning the organisation of work). In Poland as a rule, reference periods cannot exceed four months; collective agreements may extend reference periods up to 12 months (the law adopted in 2013 to increase the level of flexibility). Longer reference periods cannot be introduced by means of regulations adopted by the given employer.
47. See C. Lang, S. Clauwaert, I. Schömann, *Working time reforms in times of crisis*, supra n. 1, p. 24.

One can observe a variety of solutions concerning variable working hours provided for by collective agreements. The first option is varying the hours of work commencement on different days (determined by the employer). The second is allowing variable working hours to be combined with employee needs, the employer setting up only core time and leaving a part of working hours for the employees.[48] The third is letting collective agreements resign from traditional working hours and introducing task-oriented employment.[49]

A special form of the organisation of working hours is work time banks (accounts). These allow the accumulation of hours of work to be used when justified by the employer's needs (though there can be also a part of working hours dedicated to the employee). Working time banks (accounts) may be introduced by means of typical collective agreements or agreements concluded with work councils (in Austria, Germany, the Netherlands and Portugal).[50] In some countries (Portugal), they have been allowed or developed in connection with the economic crisis. Some Member States (Poland and Romania) still do not accept this form of work process flexibilisation (or they are highly controversial). On the one hand, due to the lack of equilibrium between the social partners and a level of uncertainty, working time accounts can be evaluated as a threat for employees and their private time. On the other hand, the resignation from this construction significantly reduces the flexibility of the work process. A compromise solution would be the application of a working hours account on conditions agreed with appropriate employee representation (i.e., trade unions). One can also consider further restrictions. The prerequisite can be the existence of an opening clause in multi-establishment (sectoral) agreement.

Another serious problem is on-call work and zero hours contracts that can be regarded as particularly disadvantageous for workers. Due to the lack of a stable number of working hours, the employees bear an important part of economic risk, thus modifying the paradigm of the employment relationship. However, in some countries such terms can be introduced by means of individual employment contracts or collective agreements. In Austria, work on call can be allowed via collective agreements.[51] Some countries do not accept the organisation of work without a set number of working hours. The above-mentioned constructions belong to the most disputable ones.

---

48. Compare F. Marhold, M. Friedrich, *Österreichisches Arbeitsrecht*, 99-100 (3rd ed., Verlag Österreich 2016).
49. Austria: flexitime (flexible daily starting and ending times) is introduced by means of plant-level agreement. Poland: flexible working hours, including task-orientated employment, may be introduced by means of collective agreements (but also in an individual way – at the employee's request).
50. Working time accounts are used to a broad extent in Germany, where they are treated as an important form of the flexibilisation of the work process. In Austria, collective agreements may allow for time credits to be carried over to the next reference period. The date must be determined within four weeks or time credit use is to be granted within thirteen weeks. Otherwise, a worker may either determine the date of use autonomously, provided that he/she observes a notice period of four weeks and the date does not conflict with any compelling operational requirements, or claim cash compensation.
51. In Austria, sectoral collective agreements can permit on-call duty to be agreed for thirty days within a period of three months.

Collective agreements negotiated and concluded during the economic crisis also concern other aspects of working time. Worth mentioning are the concentration of working hours in Portugal, or various provisions referring to overtime work, such as collective agreements that may increase the number of extra hours (Austria and Poland)[52] or limit the compensation payable for overtime work (France).[53] Conversely, they may also limit the use of overtime. Collective agreements (company agreements) may modify night-time hours and introduce (in specific instances) modifications concerning Sunday work, as in Germany. In some countries, collective agreements can also introduce intermittent working time – with a break not included in the working time in Poland. Sometimes collective agreements (workforce agreements) may modify the application of rest periods (the United Kingdom.).[54]

Finally, working time flexibility must be confronted with other tendencies and policies (e.g., work-life balance or life-long learning). The new approach to working time is important to mitigate the consequences of the crisis. At the same time, it may seriously influence the employee's private life. Working hours may become longer and the process of work less predictable, making it harder to reconcile professional and family life. These consequences should be taken into account by the social partners when they reframe the organisation of working time in collective agreements.

§12.05 CONCLUSIONS

The economic crisis is a phenomenon that has significantly influenced various aspects of the social dialogue. The same applies to the regulation of working hours in collective agreements. However, the idea of restructuring working time had appeared and been developed before the crisis began. The process of flexibilisation of working hours has been going on for some decades now.

As a rule, the economic crisis has not changed the structure of bodies representing workers in negotiations concerning working time. There are, however, a few exceptions. Some Member States have introduced new requirements concerning trade unions involved in negotiations. Another phenomenon is the growing importance of elected bodies, whose role is particularly important in the area of working time. It concerns above all the countries where trade unions are undergoing a serious crisis. Apart from stable bodies, the legislation refers to ad hoc representation.

Negotiating working time has been always delegated to specific establishments and companies. The economic crisis has only deepened this tendency. It concerns particularly the provisions referring to working time that are strictly connected with the

---

52. In Austria, the law allows a maximum of five overtime hours per week; collective agreements may extend this number up to ten for workers who work in restaurants, bars, the hotel business, transport or communication. In Poland, the yearly maximum of working hours may be extended above the level of 150 hours (provided for by the law).
53. According to the 'El Khomri' Law the compensation for overtime work could be reduced to 10%.
54. Regulation 23 the Working Time Regulations 1998 provided that a collective agreement or a workforce agreement could modify or exclude the application of regulations concerning rest periods and breaks. As a rule, the employer shall (wherever possible) allow workers to take an equivalent period of compensatory rest.

functioning of specific plants. In some cases, the domestic laws entitle only multi-establishment (sectoral) agreements to regulate selected issues. Such a solution may be justified by their nature and/or by the need to guarantee an appropriate position for employee representation. Some countries are going even further and changing the whole structure of collective agreements and their relationship to statutory standards (increasing the role of social partners).

The economic crisis has also entailed some consequences in the content of collective agreements. These are visible mainly in the sphere of working time organisation. The provisions of collective agreements are intended to flexibilise working time, to organise work in a more efficient way, and to improve the situation of the employer. The extension of reference periods, or annualisation of working time, has proved very popular. More and more often, collective agreements introduce atypical organisation of working hours. The finest example is working hours accounts which over recent years have been developed or even introduced in some countries. When it comes to the length of the working day and week, collective agreements play an important role in various forms of balancing daily working time. A separate problem is systems of short-time work that have been developed in almost all European countries. They must be treated as a typical anti-crisis instrument usually introduced on the basis of collective agreements. Their application is, however, very controversial; their usefulness and effectiveness questioned.

The economic slowdown encouraged some tendencies that had been observed earlier (annualisation of working hours, flexible schedules of working time, short-time work). Flexible solutions are deployed in a more consequent way and to a broader extent. Some of them are becoming a normal element in the organisation of working time. Moreover, there are countries such as France, Poland and Portugal where the scope and nature of changes is more serious and significant. The scale of changes depends on a number of factors, including the economic situation of a country, the actual role of collective agreements (in some countries the economic crisis coexists with the breakdown of collective negotiations), the position of trade unions, and other political scenarios.

CHAPTER 13
Negotiating Working Time in Time of Crisis: The 'El Khomri Law'

Christophe Vigneau

Working time is a founding theme in labour law. The history of labour law is often presented in terms of reductions to working time or access to paid leave. Changes to working time have long been analysed as an expression of social progress supported by labour law that is required to protect employees. Studies also show that changes have never occurred without debate and conflict.[1]

Working time law is therefore an indicator of a conception of labour law and social policies. Working time, its planning and subsequent reduction, were initially conceived as a way of protecting the bodies and health of workers. This is still the conception in European law. Yet the objectives of legislators have actually varied significantly throughout history. Employment policy has recently made the organisation of working time an instrument central to the flexibility granted to employers as part of the attempt to reduce unemployment. The issue of working time is now also linked to the protection of private and family life in a context in which new information and communication technologies are emerging.[2]

Reductions in working time have always been an integral part of wide-ranging labour law reforms that include compensatory measures in favour of companies within the framework of policies to reduce unemployment (overtime options, a multi-week or annual calculation of working time, ability to apply flat-rate pay agreements in hours or days).

Working time is one of the areas in which legislative intervention has been most intense over the last twenty years, through an increasing number of reforms of varying

---

1. P. Fridenson & B. Reynaud, *La France et le temps de travail*, (Paris: Odile Jacob, 2004); I. Leray, *La réduction du travail pour tous: la loi du 23 avril sur les huit heures*, in J.P.Le Crom (Dir.), *Deux siècles de droit du travail*, 117 (Paris: Ed de l'Atelier, 1998).
2. A. Supiot, *Temps de travail: pour une concordance des temps*, Dr. soc. 957 (1995).

scope. The method used was first that of derogation from branch agreements, allowing collective negotiations of a branch or company to derogate from legal provisions, including derogations that were not favourable to employees.[3]

Combined, in terms of discussion, by the active promotion of social dialogue as a means of regulation, these reforms have gradually made collective branch agreements, followed by collective company agreements,[4] major sources of legal derogation as regards the length and planning of working time. As such, working time law has become a key lever in the flexibility and individualisation of working conditions.

More recently, the legislative authority has turned to another method of organising sources with respect to the length and planning of working time. Setting aside that of derogation, the legislative authority now favours a suppletive method. It was this rationale that was enshrined in the law of 20 August 2008 on revitalising social democracy and the reform of working time.[5] Under this reform, the law plays, with regard to many aspects of regulating working time, no more than a suppletive role with respect to collective agreements. Furthermore, collective company agreements prevail over branch-wide agreements.

This new method of organising sources established a double suppletive role. First, the law is only intended to govern a situation in the absence of a collective agreement and second, the branch-wide agreement only applies in the absence of any collective company agreement.

The law of 8 August 2016 on Labour, Modernisation of Labour Relations, and Securement of Career Paths, known as the 'Labour Act' ('*Loi Travail*') or the 'El Khomri Law' according to the name of the Employment Minister in charge of the bill, fully demonstrates this dual suppletive role, which it enshrines and generalises with respect to the length and planning of working time.

This enshrinement and generalisation involve a new arrangement of sources introduced by the Labour Law, emphasising both the retraction of the law promoting collective negotiation and the primacy of company agreements (§13.01) over branch-wide agreements (§13.02).

§13.01 RETRACTION OF THE LAW IN FAVOUR OF COLLECTIVE AGREEMENTS

The Labour Act of 8 August 2016 on Labour, Modernisation of Labour Relations and Securement of Career Paths establishes working time on the basis of three types of rules, namely rules of public policy, the scope of collective negotiation and suppletive provisions.

This architecture, which has its flaws and approximations, is systematic in its reform since it covers each area of working time. Although it generally applies on the

---

3. Y. Chalaron, *L'accord dérogatoire en matière de temps de travail*, Dr. soc. 355 (1998).
4. A. Jobert, *La négociation collective du temps de travail en France depuis 1982*, Dr.soc. 367 (2010).
5. F. Canut, *Temps de travail: le nouvel ordonnancement juridique*, Dr. soc., 379 (2010); M.Grévy, *Où en est le temps de travail?*, D. Ouv., 192 (2009); M.Véricel, *La loi du 20 août 2008 relative au temps de travail: une loi de revanche?* RDT, 574 (2008).

basis of existing laws, in other words without changing the content of rules, this new organisation raises serious questions, which are of increasing pertinence since the legislator is envisaging this triptych as a model for other areas of labour law.[6]

Through this segmentation, the Labour Law redefines the respective authority and scope of legal and collective agreement sources. The most noticeable aspect is the retraction of the law as the source of working time rules in France. While this development may not have started with the law of 8 August 2016, it takes on a new form and aspect within French law.

The first category of rules, called 'public policy' rules by the law of 8 August 2016, transforms this notion in labour law.[7] Up to this point, all labour law rules were deemed to be public policy rules and therefore essential. There is however a distinction between absolute and relative public policy rules, with the latter admitting derogations when favourable for employees. It is also worth noting that the distinction between absolute and relative public policies is not established in accordance with axiological criteria. Absolute public policy rules do not necessarily include wording that affirms the most essential values of law or the most eminent values within the hierarchy of norms. The distinction lies in the extent of the imperative nature of the rule with regard to individual and collective wishes. For a significant majority of these wishes, legal norms in labour law generally come under public policy defined as 'relative'[8] and qualified as 'social' by French doctrine in order to account for a relativity conceived *pro operaio*.[9] This conception of legislation relating to labour law is enshrined in French law under Article L. 2251-1 of the Labour Code, under which, first, '*a collective labour agreement or convention may contain provisions more favourable to employees than those of legal provisions in force*', whilst going on to specify that such agreements 'cannot derogate from public policy provisions of these laws and regulations.' The benefit for employees, correcting the imperative nature of norms, thus determines, under this article, the extent of the range of collective wishes in their relation with labour law legislation.[10]

The Labour Act partially retracts this conception, by expressly defining and identifying certain rules as being 'public policy' rules. This is a significant change, since it is the first time the legislature has applied this qualification to certain norms. It is however difficult to establish the criteria and scope of such a qualification. It is important to highlight that with respect to public policy rules, the field of collective

---

6. F. Favennec-Héry, *Nouvelle articulation des normes: la durée du travail comme terrain d'expérimentation*, 1293 Semaine Juridique Social (2016).
7. G. Loiseau & L. Pecaut-Rivolier, G. Pignarre, *L'ordre public social a-t-il un avenir?*, Dr. soc., 886 (2016).
8. T. Revet, *L'ordre public dans les relations du travail*, in *L'ordre public à la fin du XXème siècle*, 45 (Paris: Dalloz, 1996).
9. Serious reservations have however been expressed with respect to applying these rules to the category of public policy rules. Such an application could only be implemented at the price of distorting the notion of public policy (G. Couturier, *L'ordre public de protection, heurs et malheurs d'une vieille notion neuve*, in Etudes J. Flour, 114 (1979) or of derogation (A. Jeammaud, *Le principe de faveur. Enquête sur une règle émergente*, Dr. soc., 119 (1999).
10. On 'social' public policy, F. Canut, *La notion d'ordre public en droit du travail*, 27 et seq. (Paris: LGDJ, 2007).

negotiation is not established on the basis of derogations in accordance with criteria of benefit. Generally speaking, the scope of collective negotiation is not considered to be a forum for improving public policy rules. Indeed, in some cases, rules qualified as public policy consist of wording with no derogations, which brings them closer, according to the standard distinction, to absolute public policy. This includes provisions covering the definition of notions such as working time, night work, call-out time and break times. As well as being the case for employee agreements on flat rate calculations of working time.

There are admittedly areas in which the articulation can be presented on the basis of criteria of benefit, such as break times,[11] but this is not at all the general framework governing the relationship between public policy rules and the scope of collective negotiation. Lastly, in other situations, a standard mechanism of *in peius* derogation can be found within the limits stipulated by law, such as in the matter of daily maximum working hours, which collective negotiations can increase from ten to twelve.[12] Consequently, qualifying certain legal provisions as being public policy does not enable us to draw any conclusions other than that of their imperative effect on collective and individual wishes. As such, public policy provisions counter those envisaged as 'suppletive' under the law.

The most important new aspects of the Labour Act of 8 August 2016 is, without doubt, the enshrinement of suppletive law with respect to working time.[13] Indeed, in many aspects, the law stipulates provisions for which the imperative nature ceases to apply in the presence of a collective agreement norm. This mechanism, which featured in the law of 20 August 2008[14] is not new in relation to working time, but the systematisation of this suppletive role vested in legislation in working time law is without precedent. Legal provisions are no longer to be considered as susceptible to collective agreement improvements, but rather to be applied solely if no collective agreement is reached. Collective negotiation is no longer confined to the role of improving the law but can, more radically, set the law aside with no consideration as to whether the outcome is beneficial or not for employees. The suppletive mechanism renders the rule of benefit inoperable since it is not a question of articulation, but rather of substitution. The rationale of the suppletive law with respect to collective agreements is gradually replacing that of collective agreement derogations. Such an approach obviously has an effect on the imperative nature of legislation in labour law.

---

11. Under the rule set out in Article L. 3121-16 of the Labour Code and included in the 'public policy' category, in cases where daily working time is six hours or more, employees must have a minimum break of twenty consecutive minutes. Article L. 3121-17 of the Labour Code, which is included in the 'scope of collective negotiation' category, stipulates that a company or site convention or agreement or, failing that, a branch convention or agreement, may set a longer break time.
12. Articles L. 31218 and L. 3121-19 of the Labour Code.
13. G. Borenfreund, *Quel ordonnancement des sources du droit du travail? – Les rapports de l'accord collectif avec la loi et le contrat de travail*, 781 RDT (2016); F. Canut & F. Géa, *Le droit du travail, entre ordre et désordre – A propos de la « loi travail » du 8 août 2016*, 1038 Dr. soc. (2016).
14. F. Canut, *Temps de travail: le nouvel ordonnancement juridique*, supra n. 5, p. 379; M. Grévy, 'Où en est le temps de travail?, supra n. 5; M. Véricel, *La loi du 20 août 2008 relative au temps de travail: une loi de revanche?*, supra n. 5.

Indeed, if we examine the substantive scope of suppletive law in the Labour Law, there is no doubt that this has largely taken over from imperative law. Working time rules now mostly fall within the scope of collective agreements. The reform of 8 August 2016 thus accentuates a movement of primacy conferred upon collective negotiation over the law as the source of working time legislation with a new aspect relating to the suppletive character of the law.

Subsequently, the new architecture of sources relating to working time as regards provisions of public policy, the area of collective negotiations and suppletive provisions results in a two-fold weakening of the law. First, it affects the authority of the law in the field of working time and working time planning by conferring a suppletive,[15] and therefore ancillary,[16] character upon it in a number of areas. Among these, for illustrative purposes, we can quote increased pay for overtime at rates of 25% and 50%, which now comes under suppletive[17] provisions, with a collective company or site agreement or, failing that, a branch agreement being able to lower this rate to 10%.[18] In addition, suppletive provisions sometimes refer back to regulatory powers or even the unilateral decision of an employer.

Second, this weakening of the law in terms of authority is coupled with retraction in terms of scope by the extent of the scope left to collective negotiation. Indeed, aside from public policy rules and suppletive legal provisions, the law sets out the 'scope of collective negotiation' for each aspect of working time law. In this respect, no issue escapes from collective negotiation, whether involving maximum working time, minimum rest time, paid leave or changes to working time. The law of 8 August 2016 merely delegates regulation of certain aspects of working time, in which it does not intervene or intervenes solely in a suppletive role, to labour relation stakeholders.

In certain circumstances, a collective agreement is the condition for introducing changes to working time. Such is the case when a system of calculating working time is put in place on the basis of an annual flat rate of working days or hours[19] or intermittent work.[20] Under the heading of 'scope of collective negotiation', the legislative authority specifies, in a number of areas, the field and content of collective agreements, for example as regards overtime,[21] changes in working time over a one-week period,[22] annual flat rates of working days or hours[23] or night work.[24] However, under the law of 8 August 2016, it is primarily the responsibility of the company agreement to set out working time rules.

---

15. M. Bonnechère, *L'articulation des normes*, 67 Dr. Ouv. (2017).
16. F. Canut & F. Géa, *Le droit du travail, entre ordre et désordre*, Dr. soc., 1038 (2016).
17. Article L. 3121-36 of the Labour Code.
18. Article L. 3121-33 1) of the Labour Code.
19. Article L. 3121-63 of the Labour Code.
20. Article L. 3123-33 of the Labour Code.
21. Article L. 3121-33 of the Labour Code.
22. Article L. 3121-44 of the Labour Code.
23. Article L. 3121-63 of the Labour Code.
24. Article L. 3122-15 of the Labour Code.

§13.02 PRIMACY OF COMPANY AGREEMENTS OVER BRANCH AGREEMENTS

The other key change introduced by the law of 8 August 2016 lies in the primacy conferred upon company or site agreements over branch agreements.

As regards this aspect, the Labour Act, rather than a breakthrough, should be seen as a legislative movement towards normative decentralisation that was already well under way. Indeed, through successive reforms, the French legislative authority has gradually extended the fields in which company agreements prevail over branch agreements. In this respect, the law of 20 August 2008 on revitalising social democracy and the reform of working time was already clearly part of this trend as regards working time.

From a political point of view, it is clear that the response to the economic crisis takes the form of decentralising collective negotiation to the level of companies, or even lower, down to site level. From a legal standpoint, two different methods are used to achieve this end.

The primacy of company agreements over branch agreements is a result first of retracting the rule of benefit in the articulation of these collective agreement sources. Abandoning the rule of benefit between collective agreement sources and in particular between the branch and the company, goes back to the law of 4 May 2004 on lifelong professional training and labour relations.[25]

Since this reform, company agreements may derogate from branch agreements in an unfavourable way for employees, except currently on specific subjects (minimum wages, classifications, supplementary collective guarantees, prevention of hardship, equality between men and women in the workplace and the mutualisation of funds for professional training) for which the rule of benefit continues to govern inter-agreement relations. The legislation has however left it open to branch negotiators to insert a clause on other subjects re-establishing the rule of benefit with respect to company negotiations.

The importance of the change, or even the rupture, brought about by this new method of ordering collective agreement sources, as set out in Article L. 2253-3 of the Labour Code, should not be overlooked. Although branches were permitted to insert lock-in clauses with respect to the company, the changes initiated by the 2004 reform caused an upheaval in French labour law which, historically, granted a predominant role to the branch with the aim of standardising labour norms between companies.

On this subject, it is interesting moreover to quote the new Article L. 2232-5-1 of the Labour Code introduced by the law of 8 August 2016. Indeed, this provision contains a paragraph three which states that the mission of the branch is to '*regulate competition between companies within its scope of application*'.

Under paragraph two of the same article, it is stated that the mission of the branch is to '*define, through negotiation, the subjects on which company agreements and conventions may not be less favourable than the agreements and conventions concluded*

---

25. M.-A. Souriac, *L'articulation des niveaux de négociation*, Dr. soc., 579 (2004).

at branch level, excluding subjects for which the law provides for primacy of the company convention or agreement'. The field of collective negotiation thereby gives labour relation stakeholders the possibility of producing rules that could be qualified as falling within 'collective agreement public policy'[26] which certainly raises serious questions.[27]

Through this wording, the legislative authority, as provided for by Article L. 2253-3 of the Labour Code, leaves the option for branch negotiation to reintroduce the rule of benefit with respect to company negotiation. However, the wording does specify that this option granted to social partners does not cover subjects for which the legislator has introduced suppletion of the branch in relation to the company.

Yet this is precisely what the law of 8 August 2016 does, relegating the branch collective agreement to a suppletive role in respect of company collective agreements as regards working time and thus opening up the possibility of social dumping.[28]

All this demonstrates that the legislative authority, even if it leaves the option for a collective autonomy to reintroduce a rule of benefit in relations between the branch and the company, has employed a far more radical method of collective agreement and normative decentralisation by means of suppletion.[29] Indeed, in the Labour Act, the decentralising rationale proceeds by conferring only a subsidiary role upon collective branch agreements with respect to the collective company agreement. Introduced with respect to working time by the law of 20 August 2008,[30] this mechanism was significantly extended to cover the entire area by the Labour Law of 8 August 2016. To quote the legal formula sanctioned by these two reforms, the collective branch agreement only applies 'in the absence' of any collective company or site agreement. It is precisely this aspect that is often denounced as an 'inversion of the hierarchy of norms'. The law of 20 August 2008 and the law of 8 August 2016 thereby introduced a change in method, as the articulation of collective agreement sources was replaced by suppletion of one in respect of the other. There is indeed an inversion in the hierarchy insofar as the collective branch agreement is superseded by the collective company agreement.

This primacy of the collective company agreement over the branch agreement applies to most working time rules (paid leave, overtime pay and compensation, working time planning over a maximum period of one year, working flat rate hours or days, introduction of a call-out system, intermittent work or night work). There are admittedly situations in which the collective branch agreement retains a predominant and imperative role with respect to company negotiation, but, under the law of 8 August 2016, this has become exceptional in relation to working time. We can cite the example of night work, where the law maintains the exclusive competence of an

---

26. J.D. Combrexelle, *La négociation collective, le travail et l'emploi*, Rapport au Premier ministre, 88 (France Stratégie, 2015).
27. P.-Y.Verkindt, *A propos de la notion d' « ordre public conventionnel*, 1751 Semaine Sociale Lamy, 5 (2017).
28. F. Canut & F. Géa, *Le droit du travail, entre ordre et désordre*, supra n. 16.
29. H. Tissandier, *Les rapports entre accords collectifs*, RDT, 794 (2016).
30. M. Grévy, *Où en est le temps de travail?* D. Ouv. 192 (2009); M.Véricel, *La loi du 20 août 2008 relative au temps de travail: une loi de revanche?*, RDT, 574 (2008); F. Canut, *Temps de travail : le nouvel ordonnancement juridique*, supra n. 5.

extended branch agreement to cover an increase in the number of night hours worked for enabling an employee to be considered a night worker.[31] Similarly, the introduction of an equivalence system[32] or the option of modulating the increased rate of overtime pay for part-time workers to a maximum of 10% remains the competence of an extended branch agreement.[33]

These few exceptions cannot conceal the gradual removal of the role and authority of the branch by recent reforms in French labour law. Combined with retraction of the law, this trend is doubtlessly the most distinctive feature of the reforms undertaken by the legislative authority in time of crisis. In the French legal tradition characterised by the central role of law and structuring the branch, this is a significant change. The company has undoubtedly become the level favoured by the legislator for collective negotiation and defining work norms, to the detriment of the branch.

This can be seen moreover in the law of 8 August 2016 which, in relation to working time, whilst favouring the company over the higher level of collective negotiation, allows for a centralising movement at company level with respect to lower levels. Indeed, the Labour Law introduces a new provision enabling a company agreement to substitute *'for stipulations with the same object of agreements or conventions concluded at an earlier or later date in sites included within the scope of said agreement'* (Article L. 2253-6 of the Labour Code). Here, the legislator sets out the central and centralising role it grants to the company, which can become an area for locking in site negotiations. In the same centralising spirit, the Labour Act also allows for a group agreement to take precedence over company or site collective conventions and agreements signed at an earlier or later date (L. 2253-5 of the Labour Code).

Under recent reforms relating to working time therefore, the company, whether in the form of a group or not, becomes the central negotiation area for collective agreements envisaged as the primary source for creating labour standards.

---

31. Article L. 3122-16 of the Labour Code.
32. Article L. 3121-14 of the Labour Code.
33. Article L. 3123-21 of the Labour Code.

C New Issues

CHAPTER 14
Work-Life Balance in Collective Agreements

Barbara Kresal

§14.01 INTRODUCTION

Better reconciliation of work and family responsibilities is one of the most important preconditions for achieving greater gender equality. Work-life balance measures form part of gender equality policies. From the decent work perspective, they improve the quality of working life in general. If not designed carefully to address both women and men, i.e., working parents, they can contribute to unequal opportunities and to gender segregation in the labour market instead of making it more inclusive.

New challenges in this area emerge, such as the ageing population and the need to care for older family members, or equality of different family patterns; and certain challenges persist, such as active fatherhood or more women in leadership positions.

The recent crisis and its effects may provide a new perspective on this issue. On the one hand, the crisis has had a major impact on industrial relations in European countries, reshaping the structures and functioning of social dialogue and collective bargaining,[1] and on the other hand, families have been significantly hit by the crisis.[2]

In many European countries, the crisis has shifted the policy focus away from reconciliation issues and work-life balance, while funding in this area has been

---
1. *See*, for instance, N. Bruun, K. Lörcher, I. Schömann, *The Economic and Financial Crisis and Collective Labour Law in Europe* (Oxford and Portland, Oregon: Hart Publishing, 2014); M.A. Moreau (ed.), *Before and after the economic crisis: What implications for the 'European Social Model'?* (Cheltenham Northampton: Edward Elgar, 2011); A. Broughton, C. Welz, *Impact of the crisis on industrial relations* (Dublin: Eurofound, 2013); E. Voss, K. Schöneberg, R. Rodriguez Contreras, *Collective bargaining in Europe in the 21st century* (Dublin: Eurofound, 2015); and many others.
2. D. Ahrendt, S. Blum, C. Crepaldi, *Families in the Economic Crisis: Changes in Policy Measures in the EU* (Dublin: Eurofound, 2015).

reduced, the rights of working parents limited or even cut, and the social partnership model weakened.[3]

However, work-life balance remains high on the EU agenda, at least at the declarative level. There are numerous EU strategic documents addressing the issue and in 2015, the European Commission started a new initiative on work-life balance,[4] in which the role of social partners was also emphasized.[5] It is worth mentioning that this initiative considers the work-family balance predominantly as an issue of employment policy (the main challenge to be tackled is how to improve women's participation in the labour market), which is a rather narrow and limited perspective.

In 2005, the European social partners identified supporting work-life balance as one of the four priorities – along with addressing gender roles, promoting women in decision-making and tackling the gender pay gap – in their Framework of Actions on Gender Equality.[6] In this document, they emphasize that social partners also have a responsibility to promote gender equality, including work-life balance measures, which can be addressed through their actions at different levels and by the use of different instruments, one of them being collective bargaining. Actions at national, sectoral and/or company levels, in accordance with national industrial relations practice, are mentioned as an effective tool in this regard.[7]

It is therefore useful to analyse the national responses of social partners to work-life balance issues in order to find out whether developments in collective bargaining during the crisis have had an impact in this area as well.

Do social partners address in their collective bargaining the challenges that working parents and caregivers face, and do they include work-life balance measures in collective agreements? If so, to what extent do they address new challenges in this area? What are the recent trends? Have any new initiatives, new solutions or innovative work-life balance measures been introduced into recently negotiated collective agreements in different European countries?

A comparative study on this issue could show some relevant characteristics, recent trends as well as differences between the countries. To that end, a survey based on a questionnaire has been conducted as part of the INLACRIS project,[8] with

---

3. European Institute for Gender Equality, *Reconciliation of work, family and private life in the European Union – Policy review* (Luxembourg: Publications Office of the EU, 2015), 39-46.
4. European Commission, *New start to address the challenges of work-life balance faced by working families* (Brussels, 2015) Online: http://ec.europa.eu/smart-regulation/roadmaps/docs/2015_just_012_new_initiative_replacing_maternity_leave_directive_en.pdf. (accessed 7 August 2017).
5. European Commission, *Second-stage consultation of the social partners at European level on possible action addressing the challenges of work-life balance faced by working parents and caregivers,* C(2016) 2472 final, 12.7.2016 (Brussels, 2016). More on http://ec.europa.eu/justice/gender-equality/economic-independence/economic-growth/index_en.htm (accessed 7 August 2017).
6. https://www.etuc.org/sites/www.etuc.org/files/framework_of_actions_gender_equality_01030 5-2_2.pdf (accessed 7 August 2017).
7. *Ibid.*
8. Project *Collective bargaining developments in time of crisis* (INLACRIS) (funded by the EU, No. VS/2014/0532; coordinated by the University Lumière Lyon 2, CERCRID-UMR), 2014-2016.

Chapter 14: Work-Life Balance in Collective Agreements §14.01

country-specific reports prepared by national experts from nine countries[9] and the main findings gathered in the following chapters.

The role of social partners and collective agreements in the area of work-life balance in different countries depends on many factors, such as:

- the characteristics of a particular national system of industrial relations, taking into account the general features of collective bargaining in that country, including trade union density, collective bargaining coverage rate and other indicators;
- the level of statutory rights for parents and caregivers;
- the functioning and characteristics of the labour market, in particular the participation rate of women and men in employment, the level of occupational gender segregation and other aspects of gender inequalities in professional life;
- the provision of public childcare and other social services in the country;
- the overall cultural, social and economic framework within which a particular national social welfare model is defined, as well as the relationship between public and private sphere, between paid work and (predominantly unpaid) care work, and the division of gender roles in the society.

For instance, the fact that collective agreements in a particular country do not include many work-life balance measures could mean that social partners are not aware of the importance of such measures, or that trade unions' negotiating power is not strong enough, or that collective bargaining in general is weak in that country; or, on the other hand, that the statutory level of rights for working parents and caregivers is already rather high, that public childcare is well-organized, that general regulation of workers' rights is so employee- and family-friendly that no special measures for working parents (or not many of them) are needed. It could also mean that care work in a particular country is still mainly familiarized and that there is still a strong division of gender roles, with low participation of women in paid employment.

Due to limited space, it is not possible to present a detailed analysis of all interrelated aspects, allowing for an overall comparative analysis, contextualization and better understanding of differences and similarities between the countries.[10] Rather, the aim of this contribution is to give an overview of recent developments in collective bargaining as regards its content, by way of examples from different countries and their respective approaches to work-life balance as an issue in collective agreements.

---

9. Eight EU Member States – Portugal (prepared by T. Coelho Moreira), France (S. Laulom), Hungary (T. Gyulavári), Austria (F. Marhold), Spain (Y. Maneiro Vázquez/J. M. Miranda Boto), Romania (F. Rosioru), the Netherlands (N. Gundt), Slovenia (B. Kresal) – and Turkey (K. Dogan Yenisey). National reports were written in Spring 2016.
10. Some basic labour market and gender equality indicators as well as characteristics of collective bargaining for the EU countries covered by this survey are gathered in the Annex, at the end of the contribution.

§14.02 FRAMEWORK AGREEMENTS ON WORK-LIFE BALANCE AND GENDER EQUALITY

The importance of work-life balance and gender equality issues for social partners can be expressed by way of concluding a special (framework) agreement or similar basic document specifically addressing these issues. The European social partners expressed their attitude in this regard by concluding the Framework of Actions on Gender Equality (2005).

Only in France are intersectoral (framework) agreements on gender equality, work-life balance or on the quality of working life in general a well-established practice, whereas such framework agreements on work-life balance do not exist in any other country covered by the survey.

In France, there has been a long tradition of involving the social partners in the promotion and implementation of gender equality. Statutory obligation to annually negotiate on these issues was introduced into the French Labour Code in 1982, and later modified and reformulated several times. It applies to sectoral and company (or group of companies) level. According to the Labour Code, company-level negotiations on equality should, among other things, focus on work-life balance (Article L.2242-8 of the Labour Code).

In 2004, the first national intersectoral agreement on gender equality and gender balance in workforce composition was concluded between the main social partners at national level.[11] No specific paragraph was devoted to work-life balance, but the agreement contained various relevant provisions (e.g., on motherhood and women's careers). In 2013, a national intersectoral agreement addressing the quality of working life and professional equality was concluded.[12] It explicitly installs a better work-life balance at the heart of the quality of working life. The first part of the agreement deals with well-being at work in general, the second with gender equality at work, and the third with work-life balance. It is a framework agreement to guide collective bargaining at sectoral and company level. At least it reveals that the issue is acknowledged by social partners.

In Spain, the Third Framework Agreement on Employment and Collective Bargaining of 2015[13] contains a special chapter on equal treatment and equal opportunity (Chapter II, point 6 – *Igualdad de trato y oportunidades*); however, no special attention is given to work-life balance.

---

11. Accord National Interprofessionnele du 1er mars 2004 relatif à la mixité et l'égalité professionnelle entre les femmes et les hommes (http://www.lexisnexis.fr/pdf/DO/mixite.pdf) (accessed 7 August 2017).
12. Accord National Interprofessionnel du 19 juin 2013, Vers une politique d'amélioration de la qualité de vie au travail et de l'égalité professionnelle (https://www.cfdt.fr/upload/docs/application/pdf/2013-07/ani_du_19_juin_2013_sur_la_qualite_de_vie_au_travail.pdf) (accessed 7 August 2017).
13. III Acuerdo para el Empleo y la Negociación Colectiva, 8.6.2015, http://www.ugt.es/Publicaciones/III_AENC_empleo_negociaci%C3%B3n_colectiva_2015_2016_2017_UGT.pdf. (accessed 7 August 2017). It was signed by the main employers' organizations (CEOE and CEPYME) and the two main trade unions (CCOO and UGT) and establishes a framework for all subsequent collective bargaining in Spain.

In Slovenia, the main social partners at national level are engaged in different projects tackling the issues of gender equality and work-life balance, one of them being the project 'Reconciliation of Professional and Family Life in Collective Agreements: Role of Social Partners in the Promotion of Gender Equality (GEQUAL)',[14] with the objective of strengthening collective bargaining on work-life balance measures. Among other instruments, a framework collective agreement on work-life balance and gender equality was foreseen as one possible option; however, so far no such agreement has been concluded.

In Portugal, there is a special type of agreement on gender equality, covering issues such as the protection of maternity and paternity rights and the reconciliation of work and family life, which the employers sign with the CITE (*Comissão Para a Igualdade no Trabalho e no Emprego* – Commission for Equality at Work). This is not an intersectoral or framework agreement signed between trade unions on one side and employers' organizations on the other. Rather, the employers sign the agreement with the CITE, which is a tripartite body composed of the representatives from public administration and the main trade unions and employers' confederations.[15] In January 2016, a forum of thirty-eight enterprises signed such an agreement with the CITE.

Although there are no framework collective agreements dealing specifically with work-life balance measures in Austria, it should be noted that there are many initiatives and projects at the national level that promote gender equality and work-life balance.[16] All these examples are either unilateral or government initiatives, which may be supported by the social partners but are not part of their collective bargaining or social dialogue structures.

§14.03 WORK-LIFE BALANCE MEASURES IN SECTORAL AND COMPANY LEVEL COLLECTIVE AGREEMENTS: TYPICAL ISSUES

In France, various issues of work-life balance are very often regulated by collective agreements at sectoral, company and group level. Some companies have concluded specific agreements on this issue. The most common provisions deal with: parental, maternity or paternity leave (such as an extension of maternity and/or paternity leave, or improvements to the benefits system and social protection during leave); part-time working; working time and working time organization (e.g., when organizing working time, employers are encouraged to take into account their workers' family responsibilities and both male and female workers' requests to go part-time or to have some

---

14. The project GEQUAL (http://www.institut-delo.com/S40300/GEQUAL?Language = en accessed 7 August 2017) was financed within the Norwegian Financial Mechanism Programme (http://norwaygrants.si/).
15. CCP (Portuguese Retail and Services Confederation), CIP (Confederation of Portuguese Industry), CGTP-IN (General Confederation of Portuguese Workers-National Trades Union), UGT (General Workers' Union).
16. For instance, the network 'Companies for Families', which issues the 'Commitment Certificate' to companies with a family-oriented personnel policy; the '*Berufundfamilie Index*', which offers a self-evaluation tool for companies to measure their family friendliness via a short, anonymous and free test; the 'State Prize for the most family-friendly employer', which is a part of the Government's National Plan for Employment.

flexibility in the organization of their working time, as in the publishing sector, where workers can ask to work at home one day a week for personal reasons, such as maternity or illness, meeting only during normal working hours); teleworking; child care; and more recently, the 'right to disconnect'.[17]

In Spain, large companies (over 250 employees) are obliged to have an equality plan that includes measures aimed at avoiding any type of gender discrimination. These plans are normally agreed and signed under the same terms as collective agreements, thus underlining the importance of social dialogue in the introduction of equality measures. Usually, such company-level collective agreements provide for more beneficial conditions than basic statutory regulation. Such collective agreements typically address the rights to (longer-paid) maternity and paternity leave, breastfeeding breaks, part-time work due to parenthood, additional reasons for paid absence from work (e.g., a doctor's appointment or supporting a dependent person). Some agreements provide for more flexibility in exercising these rights (for instance, family-related absence from work could be used in the part-time form), regulating different working-time flexibility formulas, offering the possibility of teleworking etc.[18]

In Austria, collective agreements contain a variety of provisions aimed at improving the reconciliation of work and family life. Some of those provisions are more, some of them less far-reaching, but the most typical issues dealt with can be summarized as follows: working time (flexi-time with/without core time, shift swaps, part-time hours); job sharing, family-friendly annual leave planning; teleworking/home office; family friendliness as a management task and part of human resource development (family-friendly objectives, special emphasis on executive education and in leadership assessment); sabbaticals; training (educational leave and part-time, unpaid leave for educational purposes); remuneration components and financial support (grants and gifts for personal occasions, use of employer infrastructure, employee loans, emergency funds, discounts for tickets to leisure events); childcare (day-care centres, childcare on a day before or after a national holiday, flying nannies, taking children to work); parenthood (marginal) employment during maternity leave; fathers in part-time work and 'daddy weeks'; and taking care of close relatives (family hospice, filial leave and part-time filial leave).[19]

In Romania, too, collective agreements include different work-family balance measures. Most of them are related to working time – for instance, flexible working time, paid absence from work for personal reasons such as a marriage in the family, the illness of a family member (parents, wife/husband, children, brothers and sisters), the death of a family member, a birth in the family etc. Unpaid leave is regulated by some collective agreements, as is the right to refuse a change of work location for certain

---

17. The report on collective bargaining from June 2014 (Ministère du travail, de l'emploi et du dialogue social, *Bilan et Rapport, La Négociation collective en 2013* (Paris, 2014).
18. A. Corral, *Spain: State of play regarding work–life balance and working time in companies* (Dublin: Eurofound, 2015), online: http://www.eurofound.europa.eu/es/observatories/eurwork/articles/working-conditions-industrial-relations-law-and-regulation/spain-state-of-play-regarding-work-life-balance-and-working-time-in-companies (accessed 7 August 2017).
19. A. Mertinz, *Familienfreundlichkeit im Betrieb aus Arbeitgebersicht*, 3 Ecolex, 224 (2015) online: https://rdb.manz.at/document/rdb.tso.Llecolex20150335 (accessed 7 August 2017).

personal reasons, such as caring for a child or for other (sick or older) family members, or being a single parent. Collective agreements also improve protection against dismissal in the event of collective lay-offs: the personal situations of employees have to be taken into consideration, with single parents the last to be dismissed. Some other measures in collective agreements concern financial support during maternity leave, provision of child-care facilities etc. According to some collective agreements, the employer is obliged to pay the difference between statutory maternity benefit (85%) and 100% remuneration.

In Portugal, equality issues and work-life balance measures do not represent an important aspect of collective bargaining. There are some collective agreements containing provisions on this topic, mainly concerning equal pay, or that simply copy statutory provisions on parental leave and assert the principle of non-discrimination. In practice, there is little new content in this regard in collective agreements, as compared with the rights guaranteed by legislation.

In Slovenia, collective agreements at sectoral and company level include work-life balance measures. Since the rights of working parents are already regulated quite extensively and in detail by the legislation, the role of collective agreements is not as important in this area as it is in some others. The majority of work-life balance measures in collective agreements address working time (adjustment of working time for male and female working parents, part-time work, exemptions for workers with family responsibilities from the obligation to work overtime, on Sundays, at night etc.), annual leave (additional days for workers with children), paid absence from work for different family-related reasons (e.g., birth), additional unpaid leave for family or similar matters, as well as work location provisions (exceptions to changes of work location for workers with family responsibilities, offering home/teleworking alternatives).

In 2015, research[20] was conducted, within which the so-called Work-Family Balance Index was developed, comprising thirteen indicators:

(1) Balanced gender representation in social dialogue.
(2) Special measures for women in leadership positions.
(3) Reduction of working time (general reduction of full-time working hours).
(4) Restrictions for overtime work.
(5) Family-friendly organization of working time.
(6) Location of work (home-work, change of work location).
(7) Annual leave (family-friendly practices).
(8) Family-related absence from work.
(9) Special measures when the child enters primary school/kindergarten.
(10) Return from parental leave.
(11) Measures for workers who care for their older family members.
(12) Measures for promoting active fatherhood.

---

20. K. Kresal Šoltes, B. Kresal, *Analiza kolektivnih pogodb v Sloveniji* ['Analysis of collective agreements in Slovenia'] (Ljubljana: Inštitut za delo pri PF UL, 2015). English abstract online: http://www.institut-delo.com/P/PDF/Analysis_abstract.pdf (accessed 7 August 2017).

(13) Pay (addressing differences in pay related to family responsibilities).

Using a sample of twenty sectoral collective agreements, the inclusion of work-family balance aspects in the existing collective agreements was analysed. The research confirmed that to date, collective agreements in Slovenia had included a modicum of work-family balance measures, but that an integrated and systematic approach was missing.

Similarly, in the Netherlands, collective agreements[21] include some work-family balance measures, but they are not numerous, since many rights for working parents are already guaranteed by the legislation. Sectoral collective agreements usually[22] include the following measures under the heading 'work-life balance' (*werk en privé*): different kinds of leave for specific purposes, such as caring for a sick child or husband, calling the plumber to fix the washing machine, adoption or parental leave. Sometimes the agreements contain specific rights concerning education and training, a personal budget or the possibility to work according to a personal schedule. The main differences between the sectors are whether or not some of the specific forms of leave are paid, and if so, to what extent (varying from 20%-100%).

In Hungary, collective agreements, which are predominantly concluded at the company level, do not pay any special attention to the issue of work-family balance.

In Turkey, traditionally only different family benefits such as wage supplements are regulated by collective agreements (a special payment for marriage, for childbirth, for the care of each child, for the education of each child etc.),[23] whereas there are no other work-family balance provisions in collective agreements. It seems that this is because the responsibility for the family is still borne by women in the eyes of both the legislator and the social partners.

Table 14.1   Typical Issues

	Work-Family Balance Measures in Collective Agreements? Typical Issues
Portugal	Not a very important issue. Usually, agreements just copy statutory provisions on parental leave and assert the principle of non-discrimination, so there is little new content in this regard in collective agreements.
Austria	Yes, very common. Working time, job sharing, family-friendly annual leave planning; teleworking/home office; family friendliness as a management task and part of human resource development; sabbaticals;

---

21. The usual bargaining level is sector/branch or, in case of big players, the enterprise itself (e.g., Shell, Philips, Unilever).
22. Examples are taken from collective agreements concluded in the following sectors: care, teaching/public sector, banking and chemical/technical industry.
23. The national report raises some doubts as to whether that kind of provision in collective agreements is actually designed to provide for a better work-family balance.

	Work-Family Balance Measures in Collective Agreements? Typical Issues
	training; grants and gifts for personal occasions, use of employer infrastructure, employee loans, emergency funds, discounts for tickets to leisure events; childcare (day-care centres, childcare on a day before of after a national holiday, flying nannies, taking children to work); parenthood (marginal) employment during maternity leave; fathers in part-time work and 'daddy weeks'; taking care of close relatives (family hospice, filial leave and part-time filial leave).
France	Yes, very common. Parental, maternity or paternity leave (improvements in relation to the statutory level of rights); working time; part-time hours for both men and women, home- and teleworking; childcare; and more recently, the 'right to disconnect'.
Romania	Yes. Working time (flexible, paid family-related absence, unpaid leave etc.), work location exceptions, protection in collective lay-offs, financial aid, payment during maternity leave, childcare facilities.
Slovenia	Yes, to a certain extent. Measures in relation to working time (annual leave in particular), paid and unpaid absence from work for different family-related reasons, change of work location, home- and teleworking.
Spain	Yes, especially in large companies (over 250 employees). They must have an equality plan, normally agreed and signed as collective agreements. Typical issues: longer paid maternity or paternity leave, breastfeeding breaks, part-time working, additional reasons for paid absence from work, more flexibility in exercising family-related rights; working time flexibility, teleworking.
Netherlands	Yes, to a certain extent. Different kinds of leave for family-related purposes (e.g., caring for a sick child), education and training, a personal budget, the possibility to work according to a personal schedule. Significant differences (20%-100%) between the sectors as regards payment during such absence.
Hungary	No special work-family balance measures.
Turkey	No special work-family balance measures. Only various pay supplements and family benefits are regulated by collective agreements.

§14.04 RECENT DEVELOPMENTS DURING THE CRISIS

During the crisis, collective bargaining in many European countries faced significant changes. Many countries experienced strong pressures towards the lowering of wages and reducing of workers' rights. Employees' rights in the renegotiated collective agreements have been weakened, with open clauses being introduced and legislation broadening the possibilities for collective agreements to regulate *in peius*. The question is whether this has been perceived by social partners as an opportunity to introduce new topics into collective bargaining: for instance, instead of higher wages, other possibilities, such as better work-life balance, may be offered to employees. It is therefore interesting to analyse whether any new work-family balance measures have been introduced into collective agreements during the crisis, and if so, within what context.

In France, no new work-family balance measures have been detected during the crisis. This period has been perceived by social partners as unfavourable for negotiating new rights in this area. Even if new flexibilities on working time, for example, are introduced, the company's needs are emphasized, not the workers' choices.

In Spain, too, the crisis has not been seen as an opportunity for introducing the new work-life balance measures into collective agreements. The report on work-life balance developments in Spain reveals that many agreements are just a set of good intentions with no real bite and that work-life balance policies have deteriorated under the current legal framework.[24]

Similarly, in Slovenia, no new work-family balance measures have been introduced into collective agreements recently. Some collective agreements renegotiated during the crisis even reduced the level at which gender equality and work-life balance aspects were integrated in collective agreements.

In Austria, there have been intensive legislative developments in this area in recent years. However, these cannot be ascribed to the crisis, at least not entirely, since they would likely have been introduced anyway.[25] They include, for example, educational leave,[26] family hospice leave (or part-time family hospice leave),[27] filial leave (or part-time filial leave)[28] and amendments to part-time working due to parenthood.[29]

Since these rights are regulated quite specifically by the statutes, there is not much room for collective agreements to regulate them more in detail. Nevertheless, some collective agreements do contain provisions that regulate certain aspects of maternity and paternity leave (these periods have to be taken into account as time of employment for the purposes of calculating paid leave, anniversary bonuses or steps

---

24. A. Corral, *supra* n. 18.
25. F. Marhold et al. *Autriche/Austria*, in M.-C. Escande Varniol, S. Laulom, E. Mazuyer, P. Vielle(eds.) *Quel droit social dans une Europe en crise?*, 89 (Bruxelles: Larcier, 2012).
26. Educational leave grants the employee a training allowance paid by the Employment Market Service (AMS) in case of twenty hours of training per week while temporarily suspending work without continuation of payment. An employee is eligible for this programme after an employment duration of at least six months and remains insured within the social security system during his/her educational leave.
27. Employees are entitled to care for terminally ill family members, their life partners as well as their severely ill children living in the same household for a fixed period and to either stay off work completely or reduce their working hours.
28. Since 2014, employees have been able to agree with their employers on filial leave (*Pflegekarenz*) for a maximum period of three months in order to care for their parents in old age. For the period of employment interruption, filial leave benefit is paid in the same way as unemployment benefit.
29. From 1 January 2016, some amendments have applied to the right of parents to work part-time until the child's seventh birthday, i.e., the main condition is a working time reduction of at least 20% as well as a minimum of twelve working hours per week once the part time period is concluded. Deviations from these provisions are possible if agreed on between the employer and the worker.

for advancement in salary). Family hospice leave is regulated by some collective agreements as well.[30]

The so called 'Free time options' (*Freizeitoptionen*)[31] were negotiated by collective agreements in the electrical, electronics, mining and iron producing industry in 2014 and, most recently, in the iron and metal processing industry.[32] Such a free time option gives workers an opportunity to choose between an increase in salary and an extended entitlement to paid leave.

Collective agreements that offer *Freizeitoptionen* either foresee the conclusion of a works agreement for companies where a works council exists or the conclusion of an individual agreement and the consent of collective bargaining parties.[33] In the case of the iron and metal processing industry, for example, the negotiated solution offers a choice to the workers: either a 1.4% salary increase or an entitlement of two hours fifteen minutes of additional free time per month in the case of full-time employment.

During the crisis, there have been no important developments in this area in Portugal or the Netherlands, and no new work-family balance measures have been introduced into collective agreements in Hungary, Romania or Turkey.

§14.05 NEW AND OLD CHALLENGES

[A] Special Work-Family Balance Measures as a Response to the Ageing of Population

Collective agreements can address new (and old) challenges and introduce new, innovative work-life balance measures, which are so far lacking in the legislation. One such challenge is the ageing of population. In the area of work-life balance, new measures for workers who care for their older family members are needed.[34]

In France, the response to the ageing of population was the introduction of the 'generation contract' in 2012; however, this does not specifically address work-life balance measures, with the aim being rather to increase the employment participation of both younger and older workers and enhance intergenerational skills transfer. In Spain, this issue has also been more or less overlooked so far by the social partners. Although the sixth state-wide Framework Collective Agreement for workers who

---

30. See the collective agreement for commercial workers and trades workers as an example, https://www.wko.at/Content.Node/branchen/oe/Arbeitsrecht-und-Kollektivvertrag/KV-Ang-2016---Text-ohne-Markierung.pdf .
31. K. Lang, *Die Freizeitoption als kollektivvertragliches Gestaltungsinstrument*, AsoK 295 (2015). See also M. Krenn, *Austria: Free time option in collective agreements* (Dublin: Eurofound, 2015), online: https://www.eurofound.europa.eu/observatories/eurwork/articles/working-conditions-industrial-relations/austria-free-time-option-in-collective-agreements (accessed 7 August 2017).
32. http://derstandard.at/2000024639155/Metaller-verhandelten-Nacht-durch (accessed 7 August 2017).
33. http://www.kollektivvertrag.at/kv/elektro-u-elektronikindustrie-ang (accessed 7 August 2017).
34. See, for instance, J.-M. Jungblut, *Working and caring: Reconciliation measures in times of demographic change* (Dublin: Eurofound, 2015); and many others.

provide care services for dependants was signed in 2012, neither the Third Framework Agreement on Employment and Collective Bargaining from 2015 nor collective agreements include such special provisions for workers who care for their older family members. In Slovenia, hardly any collective agreements address the needs of these workers explicitly, though one sectoral collective agreement (electrical industry) provides for the adjustment of the working time of employees who take care of an older family member. There are no special provisions in this regard in collective agreements in Austria, Romania, the Netherlands, Hungary, Portugal or Turkey.

[B] Special Measures in Collective Agreements That Promote Active Fatherhood

It is generally accepted that active fatherhood should be promoted.[35] The question is what the social partners and collective agreements can do in this area.

In France, recent trends show that social partners are slowly taking their share of responsibility in the promotion of active fatherhood as well.[36] The authors analyse 165 agreements on occupational gender equality. In almost all agreements, there are provisions on work-family balance. Most of them address the situation of women, since the employer does not have any influence on the choices of the organization of family life (considered as a private question or one to be addressed by state policy). However, in some agreements, a new conception of the role of the company appears where the agreement might try to influence the share of family responsibilities. Some agreements reaffirm that family leave may be taken by both parents. Some also organize specific information on their rights for the fathers. Finally, others contain specific rights for fathers, in the form of a rule about paternity leave (full wage compensation and/or the extension of paternity leave guaranteed by the legislation). The maintaining of full wages during paternity leave is now widespread in collective agreements in France.

In Spain, the 2007 Equality Law granted the right to paternity leave, separate from maternity leave and holidays, for a period of thirteen days, extendable through a collective agreement. According to the Ministry of Employment and Social Security, the majority of collective agreements (84.5%) include improvements in parental leave rights; however, just a meagre 0.48% of collective agreements grant working fathers extended paternity leave.[37]

---

35. *See*, for example, J. Cabrita, F. Wohlgemuth, *Promoting uptake of parental and paternity leave among fathers in the EU* (Dublin: Eurofound, 2015); and many others.
36. *See*, for instance, a report from 2011: F. Fatoux, R. Silvera, *La place des hommes dans les accords d'entreprise sur l'égalité professionnelle* (Paris: ORSE, 2011), online: http://www.orse.org/fichier/2881.
    See also, ORSE, CNIDFF, *Promouvoir la parentalité auprès des salariés masculins, un enjeu de l'galités professionnelle*, Guide d'appui pour les entreprises (Paris, 2008).
37. http://www.seg-social.es/prdi00/groups/public/documents/binario/129741.pdf (accessed 7 August 2017).

In Slovenia, the vast majority of sectoral collective agreements provide for additional paid paternity leave, i.e., paid absence from work for a father when a child is born. Fathers have a statutory right to thirty days' paid paternity leave, which is financed out of the social insurance scheme. Collective agreements usually add one or two days, whereby the payment of 100% compensation for these additional days is borne by the employer. Collective agreements do not so far provide for any other measures specially designed to promote fathers' engagement in family responsibilities.

In Austria, collective agreements have introduced so-called daddy weeks/month, a right for fathers which adds additional days to statutory paternity leave (to be used during the period of absolute work prohibition for the mother, i.e., eight weeks prior and after giving birth). The exact stipulations differ depending on the relevant collective agreement.[38] In the Netherlands as well, some collective agreements offer more than the two statutory days of paternity leave and make the leave (partly) paid. Daddy-days are a regular phenomenon in the Netherlands. Some collective agreements in Romania provide for additional paid paternity leave as well, though there are no other special measures to promote active fatherhood. There are no such special measures at all in either Hungary, Portugal or Turkey.

[C] Special Measures in Collective Agreements Supporting Women in Leadership Positions

In France, there are some measures in collective agreements that address the so called glass ceiling. Besides provisions dealing with other aspects of the glass ceiling, there are provisions in some collective agreements stating that managers should take workers' family life into consideration when organizing working time.[39] According to the Spanish Workers' Statute (Article 17.4), collective bargaining may establish measures of positive action to favour the access of women to all occupations and positions; however, only very few collective agreements actually provide for such affirmative action measures.[40] Similarly, in Slovenia, only very few collective agreements address this issue, and even in those, there are scant provisions, mainly dealing just with equal access to training and promotion, and with the corresponding monitoring obligation. In Austria, the employer has to consult the works council to implement measures relating in particular to hiring practice, training and career development, targeting the reduction of an existing under-representation of women in the total number of employees, as well as measures aiming at better reconciliation of professional activity with family and other care responsibilities of workers.

---

38. *See* http://www.kollektivvertrag.at/kv/banken-und-bankiers-ang, http://www.kollektivvertrag.at/kv/babe-private-bildungseinrichtungen-ang, http://www.kollektivvertrag.at/kv/fonds-soziales-wien-ang as examples (accessed 7 August 2017).
39. For instance, the national agreement on metalwork concluded on 8 April 2014.
40. E. Sanz Berzal, *Análisis de los convenios colectivos estatales a través de la Hoja Estadística de convenios: Una perspectiva de género* (Madrid: CCOO, 2013), online: http://www2.ccoo.es/comunes/recursos/1/doc157502_Analisis_de_los_convenios_colectivos_estatales_a_traves_de_la_Hoja_Estadistica_de_convenios__Una_perspectiva_de_genero..pdf (accessed 7 August 2017).

There are no such special measures in collective agreements tackling the glass ceiling and work-life balance for women in leadership positions in Portugal, the Netherlands, Hungary, Romania or Turkey.

Table 14.2 What Kind of Special Work-Life Balance Measures?

	Ageing of Population (Caring for Older Family Members Etc.)	Active Fatherhood	Women in Leadership Positions
Portugal	NO	NO	NO
Austria	NO	YES, some measures	YES, in some works council agreements
France	YES	YES, some measures	YES
Slovenia	YES, very few	YES, some measures	YES, very few
Spain	NO	YES, some measures	YES, in some collective agreements
Netherlands	NO	YES, some measures	NO
Romania	NO	YES, some measures	NO
Hungary	NO	NO	NO
Turkey	NO	NO	NO

§14.06 OTHER ISSUES

There are many other relevant issues to be analysed within the framework of work-life balance – differences in pay stemming from family responsibilities that are one of the (important) reasons for the existing gender pay gap, for instance, or the gender balance in social dialogue and collective bargaining institutions and processes.

It is interesting to compare whether there are any special measures in collective agreements (or on the agenda for collective bargaining) which address the existing gender pay gap from the point of view of family responsibilities: monitoring or any other measures which intend to identify and/or potentially reduce, eliminate differences in pay stemming from family responsibilities. Apart from France,[41] Spain and to a certain extent Slovenia, the countries in the survey do not report any special measures in collective agreements in this regard. Nevertheless, gender balance in social dialogue structures is important, since the composition of the negotiators may have a direct and indirect impact on the content and the outcome of collective

---

41. Businesses employing fifty or more staff have to produce a written annual report – a comparative analysis in terms of recruitment, training, qualifications, pay, working conditions and work-life balance supported with relevant statistically based indicators. This report is an essential instrument of the negotiation. There are provisions in collective agreements, such as the neutralization of the consequences of maternity or parental leave on the position of workers, and particular attention to part-time work that should not penalize workers' careers, etc.

bargaining processes. The survey showed that these issues are not addressed by collective agreements at all.

§14.07 CONCLUSION

It can be concluded that, in general, the period of crisis was not perceived by social partners as an opportunity to develop and introduce new work-life balance measures in collective bargaining. Collective bargaining in the countries surveyed has not been characterized by any significant developments in the area of work-life balance in recent years. Some positive examples can be observed – for instance, in Austria, Spain and to some extent in Slovenia – whereas in France, there is a long tradition of involving the social partners in matters of gender equality and work-life balance.

It is important to stress that the overall evaluation of the situation in a particular country as regards the role of collective agreements in regulating work-family balance measures has to be carried out with considerable sensitivity. As already pointed out in the introduction, the general features of industrial relations and collective bargaining in a particular country, the level of statutory rights for parents and caregivers, the organizational models of care services and other supportive institutions, as well as the general cultural, social and economic framework, have to be taken into account when analysing work-life balance measures in collective agreements and comparing different national solutions in this area. Findings can sometimes be misleading and/or misunderstood.

Last but not least, the relationship between the general regulation of labour relations and special work-family balance measures is an especially delicate issue. If the general level of workers' rights were high enough and working conditions in general took into account of the wider interests and needs of (all) the workers, than there would be less need for special measures specifically designed for workers with family responsibilities. The absence of (numerous) special work-life balance measures in such a case would not mean that social partners do not pay any attention to this issue or that the workers have difficulty reconciling their professional and family life. Above all, family responsibilities in such a case would not be perceived as an obstacle to finding or remaining in employment, since employers would not be 'burdened' by numerous additional rights and special measures related only to workers with family responsibilities.

However, as long as the general regulation of working conditions, including all aspects of working time and work organization, is not such as to offer to (all) workers an employee-friendly – i.e., at the same time a family-friendly – working environment, then the absence of adequate special measures for better reconciliation of work and family life hinders workers with family responsibilities from participating fully and on an equal basis in professional life without the risk of being discriminated against and treated less favourably in comparison with other workers. And if the majority of such workers are still predominantly women, then there are also gender inequalities, in professional as well as in private/family life.

There is room here too for the social partners and collective agreements to fill the 'work-life balance gap' by including to a greater extent in collective bargaining various measures for better reconciliation of work and family life which address all working parents, women and men, and all different (new) forms of employment.

ANNEX: LABOUR MARKET, GENDER EQUALITY AND COLLECTIVE BARGAINING – SOME FIGURES

	1	2	3 (2-1)	4	5	6	7	8	9	10
	Employment rate of women aged 20-64 (full-time equivalent), 2014	Employment rate of men aged 20-64 (full-time equivalent), 2014	Gender gap (percent. points), 2014	Gender pay gap, unadjusted, 2014	Formal childcare, 2015 (0-3 years)	Formal childcare, 2015 (3- comp. school age)	Share of part-time empl. (women), 2014	Employment rate difference parents vs. nonparents (with and without children under 12), 2010 women / men (approx.)	Dominant level of coll. bargaining (Visser, 2015)	Collective bargaining coverage (Visser, 2015)
France	59.1	71.9	12.8	15.5	41.7	93.6	30.8	-9 / +8	sectoral	96%
Portugal	60.5	69.3	8.8	14.9	47.2	89.9	14.8	-3 / +10	sectoral/ company	68%
Slovenia	60.3	70.9	10.5	7.0	37.4	90.9	14.9	+2 / +13	sectoral	89%
Spain	48.1	63.0	14.9	14.9	39.7	92	25.6	-7 / +9	sectoral	57%

	1	2	3 (2-1)	4	5	6	7	8	9	10
Netherlands	47.6	74.7	27.1	16.1	46.4	90.7	76.9	- 5 / + 6	sectoral	84%
Romania	55.7	72.7	17.0	4.5	9.4	58.2	11.1	- 5 / + 5	company	35%
Hungary	58.3	72.6	14.3	15.1	15.4	89.1	8.7	- 27 / + 6	company	23%
Austria	55.1	75.5	20.4	22.2	22.3	85.3	46.9	- 12 / + 5	sectoral	99%

Sources: 1, 2, 3. European Union, *Equality between women and men 2015* (Luxembourg: Publications Office of the EU, 2016), 49-51;
4, 5, 6. Eurostat databases (http://ec.europa.eu/eurostat);
7. European Union, *Employment and Social Developments in Europe 2015* (Luxembourg: Publications Office of the EU, 2015), 337-456.
8. Miani, C., Hoorens, S., *Parents at work: men and women participating in the labour force* (Brussels: Rand Europe, European Union, 2014), 5.
9, 10. European Union, *Industrial Relations in Europe* (Luxembourg. Publications Office of the EU, 2015), 29-31 (Source: ICTWSS database, Visser, 2015).

CHAPTER 15
Older Employees, Extended Working Lives, and Collective Bargaining

Jenny Julén Votinius

§15.01 INTRODUCTION[1]

The ageing of Europe's population will have fundamental implications for the labour market. Starting from legislation and policies on EU and national level, this article argues that collective bargaining may considerably contribute to the prolongation of working lives, due to its unique ability offer tailor-made solutions. When it comes to older employees, this ability is particularly important, as the ageing workforce is a group that is characterized by an unusually high level of heterogeneity.

For labour law, the ageing population in Europe has brought to the fore questions on age discrimination and ageism, along with a pressing need to enable and encourage employees to stay longer in the labour market before retiring. Collective bargaining for older employees takes place within a legal and policy framework where the ban on age discrimination in EU law and the agenda for active ageing in EU policy forms an important part of the background. As regards age discrimination, EU law feeds into national legislation in a very direct and specific way – not least through the CJEU's case law on the Equal treatment (framework) directive 2000/78/EC. This is in contrast with the policy agenda on active ageing; although this agenda is strongly promoted by the EU, almost all the details are left to the Member States.

Drawing on labour market research and using national examples of collectively bargained solutions to promote longer working lives, the article shows that effective strategies to meet the challenges of an ageing workforce can translate into collective

---

1. This article is written within the Norma Elder Law Research Environment (www.jur.lu.se/elderlaw) funded by Ragnar Söderberg's Foundation and The Marianne and Marcus Wallenberg Foundation. I am grateful to all the INLACRIS members who have contributed with valuable information on the national situations and with feedback on the manuscript.

agreements and thus become a part of the everyday life in the workplace. The article claims that there is an important unused potential in collective bargaining for targeting the situation of older workers, and suggests that it would be rational for both employers and trade unions to increase their engagement in the area of collective bargaining for older employees.

§15.02 THE GREYING WORK FORCE OF EUROPE[2]

The demographic development of Europe, just like the rest of the world, is characterized by a growing population, longer lifespans, and decreased birth rates.[3] The demands associated with an ageing population involves a changing economic situation.[4] Along with the increased demand for services such as medical care, senior housing and elder care, an increasingly smaller share of the population is becoming responsible for supporting more and more people.[5] In this setting, where society is presented with major challenges, the promotion of longer working lives becomes of crucial political importance. There is a need to make people stay longer on the labour market, both to support themselves and to continue their financial contribution to the societal systems.

In the political discourse on the ageing work force, as well as in policies and actions directed towards older employees in the European context, the older workers are primarily understood as those who are in the early end of their working life. The Active Ageing Index, launched by European Commission and the United Nations Economic Commission for Europe (UNECE), takes into account people from the age of 55.[6] Also the case law of ECJ on age discrimination reflects the idea that the critical age with regards to employment is the period starting in the early end of a person's working

---

2. Below, §15.02-§15.04 partly draw upon my previous research published in J. Julén Votinius, *Age Discrimination and Labour Law in Sweden*, in A. Numhauser-Henning & M. Rönnmar (eds), *Age Discrimination and Labour Law. Comparative and Conceptual Perspectives in the EU and Beyond* (Alphen aan den Rijn: Kluwer Law International, 2015); J. Julén Votinius, *Intersectionality as a Tool for Analysing Age and Gender in Labour Law*, in S. Manfredi & L. Vickers (eds), *Challenges for Active ageing. Equality Law and the Workplace* (Palgrave Macmillan 2016), and J. Julén Votinius & M Rönnmar, *Intergenerational Aspects of Elder Law: Conflict, Solidarity – or Ambivalence*, in A. Numhauser-Henning & M. Rönnmar (eds), *Elder Law: Evolving European Perspectives*, (Edward Elgar, 2017).
3. European Commission, *The 2015 Ageing Report: Underlying Assumptions and Projection Methodologies: European Economy 8* (Publications of the European Union 2014). The most aged populations are in the developed countries. In developing countries, population ageing has begun rather recently; W. Thompson, *Population*, 34 American Journal of Sociology 959 (1929); J.C. Caldwell, *Demographic Transition Theory* (Springer 2006) 307f. *World Population Ageing 2013* (United Nations 2013).
4. For a broader picture of the challenges associated with the ageing population, *see* S. Harper, *The Challenges of Twenty-First-Century Demography*, In C. Torp (ed.), *Challenges of Ageing. Pensions, Retirement and Generational Justice* (Palgrave Macmillan 2015). Cf W. Lutz, W. Sanderson & S. Scherbov, *The coming acceleration of global population ageing*, 451 Nature 716 (2008).
5. Within the EU today, there are 29 persons aged 65 and over per 100 persons of working age (15–64 years). In 2030 this number is expected to be 39, and in 2050 it is expected to be 49 (Eurostat 2015).
6. The index was launched in 2012 in the European Year for Active Ageing and Solidarity between Generations. European Centre Vienna *Active Ageing Index Concepts, Methodology and Final*

life; the case law mainly concern employees from the age of just above 50 years of age and older.[7]

The heterogenty of the group referred to as older employees cannot be stressed enough. The diversity that this group displays is vast and could almost be described in terms of polarization. In that respect, the older employees diverge from all other groups in the labour market. An important share of persons in high or top positions in society are persons who would be defined as older employees – may it be in politics, in management or in working life. On a more general level, the older employees forms an important part of what has been described as the well protected insiders of the labour market, that is persons who hold a permanent employment, high level of employment protection, accrued rights and privileges based on seniority, and, consequently, a precedence of position over other employees.[8]

But this is only one side of the coin. On the other side, quite oppositely, older employees form a precarious group in the labour market.[9] In this group, we find the largest number of people with outdated competences, people with age related health problems and people with disabilities caused by a long and hard working life. Here we also find the unemployed persons who have the most severe difficulties to get an employment. For a person who have reached the age of 50, unemployment implies a serious risk of never returning to working life. Moreover, older employees are at the highest risk of exposure to ageism and age discrimination. Research has shown that older women employees are one of the groups of workers that are at the highest risk for precarious work within the EU, before groups such as interns, apprentices, women in general, older workers in general, and women who are pregnant or returning from maternity leave.[10] In 2013, AGE Europe noted that age is quickly becoming the most commonly perceived disadvantage in the labour market, and that this particularly applies to older women 'who are among those most affected by the crisis and one of the groups most likely to lose their job and be unable to find new employment'.[11]

Results. Methodology Report Submitted to European Commission's DG Employment, Social Affairs and Inclusion, and to Population Unit, UNECE (Vienna, 2013).

7. Cases C-144/04 *Werner Mangold* (52 years), C-152/11 *Odar* (54 years), C-447/09 *Prigge* and case C-286/12 *Commission v. Hungary* (60 and 62 years respectively), cases C-499/08 *Ingeniørforeningen i Danmark*, C-411/05 *Palacios de la Villa*, C-388/07 *Age Concern*, C-45/09 *Rosenbladt*, the joint cases C-159/10 and C-160/10 *Fuchs* and *Köhler*, cases C-141/11 *Hörnfeldt*, C341/08 *Petersen*, and joined cases C-250/09 and C-268/09 *Georgiev* (all 65, 67 or 68 years).
8. Cf. Nicola Gundt's contribution in this issue *infra*.
9. Julén Votinius (2016), *supra* n. 2.
10. S McKay, S. Jefferys, A. Paraskevopoulou, J. Keles, *Study on Precarious work and social rights*. Carried out for the European Commission (VT/2010/084), Working Lives Research Institute, London Metropolitan University 2012.
11. AGE, *Contribution to the European Commission's assessment of the transposition and application of Employment Equality Directive (2000/78/EC)*, 2013. There is growing recognition of the insight that age and gender synergize in ways that tend to discriminate against women, S. Spedale, C. Coupland & S. Tempest, *Gendered Ageism and Organizational Routines at Work: The Case of Day-Parting in Television Broadcasting*, 35 Organization Studies (11) 1585 (2014); W. Loretto, C. Duncan & P. J. White, *Ageism and employment. Controversies, ambiguities and younger people's perceptions*, (20) Ageing and Society 279, 285 and 296 (2000); and J. McMullin, *Theorizing Age and Gender Relations* in S. Arber & J. Ginn (eds), *Connecting gender and ageing: a sociological approach* (Open University Press 1995).

In many EU countries, the level of insecurity on the labour market has increased during the years following the Great Recession.[12] From an immediate labour market participation perspective, the negative effects of economic crisis can be observed primarily in relation to young employees, among whom unemployment has risen sharply during the crisis years. The group of older employees belonging to the well protected insiders has at all not been affected by the crisis, as regards their position on the labour market. On the other hand, the precarious group of older employees has been hit very hard – this group displays a level of long term unemployment that is in fact equal to a complete push-out from the labour market.

A division between insiders and outsiders in the labour market can be seen in all age groups. But for older employees, the contrast is unusually clear. This is to a large extent because the position that an older person has reached in the labour market at the entry of the early end of his or her working life is a result of the working life that this person has had so far. Successful careers tend to result in a position as a well-protected insider, while the opposite applies for a person whose path in working life has been less straightforward. Although young employees have been hit the hardest by unemployment and following labour law reforms after the crisis, effects relating to the dismantling of employment security are a concern for every employee, and especially those who belong to a group that typically is perceived as less attractive in the labour market – such as older employees.[13] Within EU law, the longstanding tradition of legislation to safeguard the fundamental principles of equal treatment and non-discrimination in working life can provide a barrier against unfair management decisions. The following section introduces the relevant provisions of EU discrimination law, with particular focus on older workes.

§15.03 THE EU BAN ON AGE DISCRIMINATION IN WORKING LIFE

The area of non-discrimination has largely evolved in the context of gender equality in working life, which has had a place on the social policy agenda within the EU since the 1970s (although progress has been slow). A comprehensive body of secondary legislation and case law on sex discrimination began to develop in the 1970s, mainly on the basis of the provision in the Treaty of Rome regarding equal pay for men and women.[14] The promotion of gender equality also appears in various policy documents, such as the European Employment Strategy, the Community Action Programmes on

---

12. S. Laulom, E. Mazuyer & C. Escande Varniol (eds), *Quel droit social dans une Europe en crise?* (Bruxelles: Larcier 2012); S. Laulom, *Dismissal Law Under Challenge: New Risks for Workers*, 5 European Labour Law Journal (3-4) 231 (2014); C. Degryse, M. Jepsen & P. Pochet, *The Euro Crisis and its Impact on National and European Social Policies*, (ETUI 2013); C. Barnard, *The Financial Crisis and the Euro Plus Pact: A Labour Lawyer's Perspective*, 41 Industrial Law Journal 98 (2012).
13. J. Prassl, *Contingent Crises, Permanent Reforms: Rationalising Labour Market Reforms in the European Union*, 5 European Labour Law Journal (3-4) 211 (2014); Eurofound, *Employment trends and policies for older workers in the recession* (2012).
14. E. Ellis & P. Watson, *EU anti-discrimination law*, (2nd ed. Oxford University Press 2013).

equal opportunities for men and women, and several recommendations and resolutions from the Council.[15] Many times, these soft-law documents have expressed a more progressive approach than the binding law.[16]

In 2000, following the Treaty of Amsterdam, the existing directives on sex discrimination were accompanied by directives prohibiting discrimination on the grounds of racial or ethnic origin, religion or belief, disability, sexual orientation – or age. Through ratification of the Lisbon Treaty, and its coming into force in 2009, promotion of equal treatment and the combating of discrimination were acknowledged as a key aim of the European Union, and the fundamental right to equality became protected under the CFREU and the ECHR.[17] Today, the prohibition against age in working life is found in the Employment Equality Directive 2000/78.[18]

The Employment Equality Directive 2000/78 distinguish between *direct* discrimination and *indirect* discrimination. The former is at hand when a person is being subjected to less favourable treatment which is associated with a protected ground, such as age.[19] The latter regards the case where the employer applies a condition or criterion that appears neutral, but in fact puts persons belonging to a protected group at a particular disadvantage, and where the criterion cannot be justified with reference to an objectively acceptable aim. A possibility for justification is built into the very construction of indirect discrimination, whereas normally direct discrimination is allowed in only the few cases that are specifically enumerated in the directive. However, in relation to direct discrimination on the grounds of age, the possibilities for exemptions are particularly comprehensive; in fact, the possibilities for justification are similar to what otherwise applies in cases of indirect discrimination.[20] In relation to age, premise 25 of the Equal Treatment Framework Directive 2000/78 emphasizes the importance of distinguishing between 'differences in treatment which are justified, in particular by legitimate employment policy, labour market and vocational training objectives, and discrimination which must be prohibited'. Accordingly, Article 6 justifies differential treatment on the grounds of age for various employment policy

---

15. Some recent examples are *Europe 2020, A Strategy for Smart, Sustainable and Inclusive Growth*, COM(2010)2020 final; *Strategy for Equality between Women and Men 2010–2015*, COM(2010)0491 final; *Reconciliation of Work and Family Life in the Context of Demographic Change* 11841/11 SOC 584 (EPSCO).
16. P. Foubert, *The Legal Protection of the Pregnant Worker in the European Community: Sex Equality, Thoughts of Social and Economic Policy and Comparative Leaps to the United States of America*, 214 (Kluwer Law International, 2002). C. McGlynn, *Reclaiming a Feminist Vision: the Reconciliation of Paid Work and Family Life in European Union Law and Policy*, 7 Columbia Journal of European Law 242 (2001).
17. Treaty of the European Union, Article 3, Charter of Fundamental Rights of the European Union, Chapter III, particularly Articles 21 (non-discrimination), 23 (equality between men and women) and 25 (the rights of the elderly), and European Convention on Human Rights, Art. 14 and Protocol No. 12.
18. Council Directive 2000/78/EC establishing a general framework for equal treatment in employment and occupation.
19. Article 2, Directive 2000/78/EC and Article 2.1, Directive 2006/54/EC.
20. Cf A. Numhauser-Henning, *The EU Ban on Age-Discrimination and Older Workers: Potentials and Pitfalls*, 29 International Journal of Comparative Labour Law and Industrial Relations (4) 391–414 (2013).

objectives.[21] To be permitted, differential treatment must be deemed appropriate and necessary, but in its case law, the CJEU imposes very undemanding requirements on Member States to prove that measures that disadvantage older workers actually provide the labour market benefits that are claimed as their justification.[22] It is clear that many times, collective and public interests that stem from the function of the labour market and societal considerations may be given priority over the interest of non-discrimination on the grounds of age.

§15.04 THE ACTIVE AGEING AGENDA IN EU EMPLOYMENT POLICIES

Before the introduction of the prohibition on age discrimination in 2000, through Directive 2000/78, old age was a fairly invisible matter in the EU labour law context.[23] The recognition of age as grounds for discrimination coincided with a general shift within the EU, towards policies that more actively addressed the looming demographic change in Europe.[24] In a short time, ageing and the situation of older persons became a central component of EU agendas regarding policies for employment and economic growth, embodied in the key concept of *active ageing*.[25] Active ageing refers to a range of areas, but in effect it has been most developed in policies regarding active ageing in employment.[26] In 2001 and 2002, two general EU targets were adopted to increase labour market participation of older workers and promote sustainable pensions: the Stockholm target, to ensure that half of those aged 55-64 were in employment by 2010, and the Barcelona target, to increase actual retirement age by five years by 2010.

---

21. Article 6.1, Directive 2000/78/EC, interpreted by the CJEU in numerous cases.
22. J. Fudge & A. Zbyszewska, *An Intersectional Approach to Age Discrimination in the European Union: Bridging Dignity and Distribution?* In A. Numhauser Henning & M. Rönnmar (eds) *Age Discrimination and Labour Law. Comparative and Conceptual Perspectives in the EU and Beyond* (Kluwer Law International 2015).
23. Council Directive 2000/78/EC establishing a general framework for equal treatment in employment and occupation. Earlier measures on older workers in the EU are few, and all have the form of non-legally binding acts. A very early example is the Council Recommendation 82/857/EEC on the principles of a Community policy with regard to retirement age, 27. Cf Ellis & Watson (2013), *supra* n. 14; M. Bell, *Anti-discrimination law and the European Union* (Oxford University Press 2002), N. ten Bokum & P. Bartelings (eds), *Age discrimination law in Europe* (Kluwer Law International, 2009).
24. *Towards a Europe for All Ages* COM (1999) 221; *Europe's response to World Ageing* COM (2002) 143; *Confronting demographic change: a new solidarity between the generations* COM (2005) 94; *The demographic future of Europe – From challenge to opportunity*, COM (2006) 571; Council Resolution 6226/07 Opportunities and challenges of demographic change in Europe; *Dealing with the impact of an ageing population in the EU (2009 Ageing Report)* COM (2009) 180.
25. Council and Parliament Decision 940/2011/EU on the European Year for Active Ageing and Solidarity between Generations (2012). A. Walker & T. Maltby, *Active ageing: A strategic policy solution to demographic ageing in the European Union*, 21 International Journal of Social Welfare, 117 (2012); A. Walker, *Commentary: The Emergence and Application of Active Aging in Europe*, 21 Journal of Aging & Social Policy 75 (2008).
26. Walker & Maltby (2012), *supra* n. 25, c.f. European Commission, Commission Staff Working Document ex-ante evaluation accompanying document to the decision of the European parliament and the Council on the European Year for Active Ageing (2012), SEC (2010) 1002 final.

The active ageing policy of raising employment rates for older workers is part of the European Union's growth and job strategy Europe 2020, where it is addressed in the flagship initiative towards full employment – the 'Agenda for new skills and jobs'. In a recent, comprehensive survey of the development of the active ageing concept both within and beyond the EU policy sphere, along with an overview of the scholarly debate on the topic, EU policy discourses on active ageing are described as comprising two contrasting models.[27] The first, and predominant, model focuses more or less completely on extending working life; this model is based on considerations about productivity and economic growth.[28] The other model is less influential on the EU level, but is a leading one for WHO and the UN. It is much more comprehensive, in that it has equal focus on including quality of life, mental and physical well-being, and social participation.[29] In some EU policy actions and documents, there is a trend towards a certain convergence between these two models, such as in the launching of the European Year of Active Ageing and Solidarity between the Generations in 2012.[30] So far, this approximation towards a more comprehensive approach to active ageing on the EU side seems to have happened more on the rhetorical level.[31] In practice, the overall emphasis is still very much on promoting labour market opportunities and enhancing employment conditions and employability of older employees.

As an integrated part of the European employment strategy, the understanding of active ageing within the EU is closely connected to the discourse on employability and its emphasis on the responsibility of the individual employee to achieve and maintain his or her own power of attraction in the labour market.[32] The concept of employability also encompasses a requirement to adjust to an increasingly changing and insecure labour market, in relation to which policies for deregulation in order to allow for more flexibility for employers are seen as key.[33]

---

27. L. Foster & A. Walker, *Active and Successful Aging: A European Policy Perspective*, 55 The Gerontologist (1) 83 (2015); E. Carmel, K. Hamblin & T. Papadopoulos, *Governing the activation of older workers in the European Union*, 27 International Journal of Sociology and Social Policy (9/10) 387 (2007).
28. K. Hamblin, *Changes to policies for work and retirement in EU15 nations (1995–2005): An exploration of policy packages for the 50-plus cohort*, International Journal of Ageing and Later Life (5) 513 (2010).
29. L. Foster & A. Walker, *Gender and active ageing in Europe*, 10 European Journal of Ageing (3) (2013).
30. European Commission, *Commission Staff Working Document* SEC (2010) 1002 final.
31. K. Hamblin, *Active Ageing in the European Union Policy Convergence and Divergence*, (Palgrave Macmillan 2013).
32. A. Fejes, *Discourses on Employability: Constituting the Responsible Citizen*, 32 Studies in Continuing Education, 89 (2010); P. Moore, *The International Political Economy of Work and Employability* (Palgrave Macmillan 2010); B. Casey, *The implications of the economic crisis for pensions and pension policy in Europe*, Global Social Policy (12) 246 (2012).
33. J. Julén Votinius, *Having the Right Attitude. Cooperation Skills and Labour Law*, 28 The International Journal of Comparative Labour Law and Industrial Relations (2) 223 (2012).

§15.05 EXTENDED WORKING LIVES AND COLLECTIVE BARGAINING ON A NATIONAL LEVEL

[A] Regulatory Approaches and Strategies to Promote Extended Working Lives

Policies for active ageing, including the fostering of extended working lives, are to some extent pursued on a national level in all of the countries in Europe.[34] While the situation of older employees is high on the agenda in countries like Sweden, Finland, the UK, Germany and the Netherlands, the matter has drawn much less attention in Poland, Slovakia, Greece and Hungary.[35] The following section presents some examples of how collective bargaining activities have added to the development of national labour market approaches to active ageing. As always, it is important to emphasize that the Member States differ in terms of their regulation of working life, not least as regards the role of the social partners, as well as the interaction between labour law and industrial relations. Many Member States have introduced at least some form of statutory regulation to promote extended working lives.[36] Normally, statutory law provides the general framework, and in many cases also financial incentives, while the social partners to varying degrees contribute to the detailed design and implementation. In a number of countries, comprehensive tripartite agreements have been concluded to introduce longer working life strategies. This is the case in, for instance, Finland, Denmark, Belgium, Ireland, Germany and France.[37] In some countries, such as France, Germany and Denmark, the social partners have also concluded sectoral-level agreements in the matter, beyond the statutory framework.

Research as well as policy documents on active ageing point to a number of key factors in the promotion of longer working lives.[38] The following section is structured around three policy areas addressing a number of these key factors (although the exact

---

34. For a detailed overview of national approaches to active ageing, see A. Zaidi & D. Stanton, *Active Ageing Index 2014. Analytical Report*, United Nations Economic Commission for Europe, Geneva, and European Commission, Directorate General for Employment, Social Affairs and Inclusion (Brussels 2015).
35. A. Walker & A. Zaidi, *New Evidence on Active Ageing in Europe*, 51 Intereconomics (3) 139-144 (2016); European Agency for Safety and Health at Work, *Analysis report on EU and Member State policies, strategies and programmes on population and workforce ageing* (Luxembourg Publications Office of the European Union 2016).
36. Eurofound, *Role of governments and social partners in keeping older workers in the labour market*, Dublin 2013.
37. *Ibidem.* Cf C. Claisse, C. Daniel and A. Naboulet, *Les accords collectifs d'entreprises et plans d'action en faveur de l'emploi des salariés âgés*, (157) Document d'études. Direction de l'animation de la recherche, des études et des statistiques, (DARES 2011).
38. The conceptualization of these key factors varies in different descriptions, and there is a lack of coherent terminology. C.E. Edge, A.M. Cooper & M. Coffey, *Barriers and facilitators to extended working lives in Europe. A gender focus*, 38 Public Health Reviews (2) (2017); A. Blackham, *Extending Working Life for Older Workers Age Discrimination Law, Policy and Practice* (Hart Publishing 2016); Eurofound (2013), *supra* n. 36; European Commission, *European Employment Observatory Review, Employment Policies to Promote Active Ageing 2012* (Publications Office of the European Union, Luxemboug 2012); R. Gould, J. Ilmarinen, J. Järvisalo & S. Koskinen, *Dimensions of work ability. Results of the Health 2000 Survey* (ETK, Kela, KTL, FIOH 2008).

phrasing may vary): working conditions, work environment and work organization; workforce and career development; and age-awareness and attitudes in the workplace. Arrangements specifically intended to promote the general health of older persons are not discussed here. Such arrangements primarily relate to policies on health and medical care, and thus primarily belong outside the area of labour law and collective bargaining.

[B] Working Conditions, Work Organization and Part-Time Pension Schemes

Measures related to work organization that may have a positive impact to prolong working lives include policies to promote flexible work and working time, adjusting workplaces and tasks to match the capacities of the employees, and special arrangements to lighten the workload of older workers.[39]

In certain cases, the requirement for reasonable accommodation of employees with disabilities in Article 5 of Equal Treatment Framework Directive 2000/78 may impose a statutory obligation on the employer to adjust the working conditions to the needs of an older employee. As stated by the CJEU in the cases *HK Denmark* and *Chacón Navas*, the only decisive factor for the definition of disability is that it refers to a physical, mental or psychological impairment that hinders the participation of the person concerned in professional life for a long time.[40] The cause of the impairment is thus not relevant. The requirement for reasonable accommodation may include an obligation for the employer to provide for special aids, especially if the impairment relates to functional capacity, but also for adjustments of work tasks, or their redistribution between employees in a workplace. Even if the impairment only means an inability to work full-time, it constitutes a disability within the meaning of the Directive. In an individual case, a national court may find that an obligation to reduce working hours for the disabled employee would impose a disproportionate burden on the employer. As a matter of principle, however, the Directive does not exclude the possibility that a reduction in working hours can be a suitable measure to meet the requirement of reasonable accommodation.[41]

The statutory requirement for reasonable accommodation of disabled employees very clearly shows how adjusted working conditions and work organization can contribute to prolonging someone's working life. However, the requirement is limited to employees with a disability, and only covers measures to allow the employee to carry out the work despite the impairment caused by that disability. By contrast, extended working-life policies cover all employees above a certain age, and when addressing working conditions and work organization, these policies typically seek to create incentives to remain in working life by facilitating the working situation of these employees in various ways.

---

39. Eurofound (2013), *supra* n. 36, 13.
40. Joined Cases C-335/11 and C-337/11 *HK Denmark*, case *Chacón Navas* C-13/05. Cf Numhauser-Henning (2013).
41. Joined Cases C-335/11 and C-337/11 *HK Denmark*.

To make a real difference in prolonging working lives, it must to some extent be possible to tailor adjustments of working conditions to the individual employee. Thus, whereas the framework for these policies can be set at the national or sectoral level, the details of the adjustment measures are normally set at the workplace level. One way in which the social partners have opened up for individual modifications of working conditions in some cases is to introduce the possibility for older employees to trade other privileges for time off. For instance, the collective agreement between the Federation of the Finnish Technology Industries and the Finnish Metal Workers' Union contains a clause on the seniority bonus – an extra top-up of the wage after a certain number of years in service. For employees who have reached 58 years, the collective agreement allows for individual agreements between the employer and employees whereby the latter can exchange their seniority bonus or a part thereof for corresponding time off.[42] Similar practices can be found in the Netherlands, where the construction industry agreement allows workers of 55 years and older to request a four-day working week (thirty-two hours) instead of claiming other rights to leave, such as extra paid vacation due to age. In the Netherlands generally, provisions on the adjustment of working conditions to spare older workers are found in collective agreements in the male-dominated sectors of industry. The collective agreement for Shell contains provisions regarding the exemption of older workers from all-round shifts, while the AKZO collective agreement contains exemptions from on-call-duties and shifts.[43]

In marked contrast to protection against strenuous shifts, or the option to trade other benefits for a reduction in working time, a number of Member States also provide the right to a part-time pension at a certain age. Part-time pension schemes can contribute to prolonging working lives, as the possibility to partly step down can serve as an alternative to full retirement, thus enabling those who want to stay in working life a bit longer to do so. There is a wide variety of solutions for partial retirement within the EU.[44] Schemes set by national legislation sometimes cover all employees, such as the Austrian schemes for partial retirement and partial pension. In other cases, such as the German Altersteilzeitgesetz, statutory law provides a voluntary framework to which companies may or may not accede. It is common to develop statutory schemes in consultation with the social partners, and for most partial retirement schemes, the details can be modified in collective agreements.[45]

---

42. Clause 14.5.3 of the Collective agreement between the Federation of Finnish Technology Industries and the Finnish Metalworker's Union 1 November 2013 – 31 October 2016, reformed through Collective agreement in the technology industries 1 November 2016 – 31 October 2017.
43. Article 34 of Collective arbeidsovereenkomst 1 Maart 2015 t/m 29 Februari 2016 Shell Nederland Raffinaderij B.V. Shell Nederland Chemie B.V. en Federatie Nederlandse Vakbeweging. Articles 3.2, 3.2, 3.4 and 6.4.2. of Deel A – I: Normatieve bepalingen (II: Obligatoire bepalingen) van de Collectieve Arbeidsovereenkomsten afgesloten voor AkzoNobel bedrijven in Nederland juli 2015–30 juni 2017.
44. Eurofound, *Extending working lives through flexible retirement schemes. Partial retirement*, Publication office of the European Union 2016.
45. For example, the Austrian scheme for partial retirement (Altersteilzeit) stipulated in section 27 of the Unemployment Insurance Act (AVIG), has been modified for employees of the Austrian Tabak AG through *(PS/015/2001) Kollektivvertrag über Altersteilzeit*, Fachverband der Nahrungs- und Genussmittelindustrie und Österrechischen Gewerkschaftsbund, Gewerkschaft der Privatangestellten. Likewise, the scheme for a partial pension (Teilpension), stipulated in

There are also examples of partial retirement schemes established by collective agreements only, for instance in the Netherlands and Denmark.[46] In 2013, the social partners in Sweden concluded collective agreements on extensive rights to apply for partial retirement for large sectors of industry, construction and transport, from the age of 60 or 62 depending on the sector. The agreements require the employer to consider in good faith the granting of partial retirement unless it would cause considerable disruption to the business.[47] An application for partial retirement can be denied only for disruptions that cannot be easily reduced or eliminated by the employer, who must consider the possibility of relocating the worker to enable their partial retirement, even if the relocation requires certain vocational training.[48] The explicit purpose of these agreements is to create conditions for generational renewal.[49]

Several studies have been undertaken to investigate the effect of part-time pension schemes on the length of working lives.[50] The results do not offer any distinct support for a positive correlation between part-time pension schemes and prolonged working lives. There are methodological difficulties in measuring the impact of part-time pension schemes, as ideally, their output should be compared with a hypothetical situation where the scheme did not exist.[51] More importantly, the effects of part-time retirement schemes can be measured from different perspectives. Thus, while such schemes might have a positive impact on the share of older employees in the workforce, their impact on the average total number of years in employment might be insignificant. Studies have questioned the benefit of introducing part-time pension schemes, due to the risk that that part-time work might crowd out full-time work without increasing the overall working-time output.

---

    section 27a of the same act, has been adjusted for employees in the Food Products Industry through *Zusatzkollektivvertrag betreffend Altersteilzeit*, Fachverband der Nahrungs- und Genussmittelindustrie, und dem Österreichischen Gewerkschaftsbund, Gewerkschaft der Privatangestellten.

46. OECD, *Ageing and Employment Policies Ageing and Employment Policies. Denmark 2015. Working better with age* (2015).
47. Swedish National Mediation Office, *Annual report 2013*, Stockholm 2014, 32.
48. Information nr 4/2013 1(7) Appendix 7 and 8, Gemensam kommentar Deltidspension 1 Teknikarbetsgivarna och IF Metall, Gemensam kommentar Deltidspension Teknikarbetsgivarna och Unionen/ Sveriges Ingenjörer.
49. This right applies after 60 or 62 years of age, depending on the area of the collective agreement; Swedish National Mediation Office, *supra* n. 47. The employer must consider in good faith the granting of partial retirement unless it would cause considerable disruption to the business; the application can be denied only for disruptions that cannot be easily reduced or eliminated by the employer, who must consider the possibility of relocating the worker to enable the partial retirement, even if the relocation requires certain vocational training. Information nr 4/2013 1(7) Appendix 7 and 8, Gemensam kommentar Deltidspension 1 Teknikarbetsgivarna och IF Metall, Gemensam kommentar Deltidspension Teknikarbetsgivarna och Unionen/ Sveriges Ingenjörer.
50. For different ways to approach the matter, *see* Eurofound (2016). *See also* P. Berg, M.K. Hamman, M. Piszczek & C.J. Ruhm, *Can Policy Facilitate Partial Retirement? Evidence from Germany*, Discussion Paper No. 9266, IZA (2015).
51. M. Takala & N. Väänänen, *Does part-time pension extend working lives? A Finnish case study*, Reports 05, Finnish Centre for Pensions 27 (2016).

[C] Lifelong Learning and Mobility on the Labour Market

The policy area of lifelong learning and mobility on the labour market is a matter for all ages, and does not concern older employees specifically. In the discourse on extended working lives, however, lifelong learning has been identified as a key area. It is therefore important to note that older employees have significantly more limited opportunities for training and development than younger employees in, for example, the UK, Germany and France.[52] In fact, Denmark is the only EU Member State in which the number of people in training (in-house as well as off-the-job) does not decrease with age.[53] Lack of willingness on the employers' side to invest in older employees, along with the reluctance of older employees to adapt to the changing requirements for workplace performance, have been identified as factors that hamper strategies for training and skills improvement opportunities for the ageing workforce.[54]

In May 2009, a strategic framework for European co-operation in education and training was adopted. The framework sets as a benchmark that by 2020 at least 15% of adults aged 25 to 64 years old should participate in lifelong learning.[55] It has proved difficult to meet, or even progress towards, this benchmark. In 2014, the EU average of adults in lifelong learning schemes was just below 11%, and in 2015 this average did not increase. In fact, in some EU countries, the 2015 average was lower than the year before, and in comparison with 2012, adult learning participation rates fell in 14 Member States.[56] As for 2016, Denmark, Sweden, Finland, the Netherlands, France, Luxembourg and Estonia display high participation rates, whereas those in Romania, Bulgaria, Slovakia, Croatia, Poland and Greece are very low.

Within the EU as a whole, employers provide around one third of non-formal education and training. In all but five Member States, employers are the most common providers of these activities.[57] In the 2016 Skills Agenda, the European Commission concludes that more can be done to support learning environments at work. The Commission furthermore stresses that the social partners will have a central role to play in the successful development of the agenda, building on initiatives at European

---

52. S. Vickerstaff, C. Phillipson & W. Loretto, *Training and Development: 'The Missing Part of the Extending Working Life Agenda?*, 25 Public Policy Aging Report (4) 139-142 (2015); U. Leber, J. Stegmaier & A. Tisch, *Altersspezifische Personalpolitik: Wie Betriebe auf die Alterung ihrer Belegschaften reagieren*, IAB-Kurzbericht, Nürnberg, 8 (13/2013); Chartered Institute of Personnel and Development CIPD, *Creating longer, more fulfilling working lives. Employer Practice in Five European Countries*, Policy Report, 32 (2016).
53. J. Schmitz, *Companies and Old Workers. Obstacles and Drivers of Labour Market Participation in Recruitment and in the Workplace*, in S. Scherger (ed.), *Paid Work Beyond Pension Age. Comparative Perspectives* (Palgrave Macmillan 2015).
54. G. Martin, D. Dymock, S. Billett & G. Johnson, *In the name of meritocracy. Managers' perceptions of policies and practices for training older workers*, Ageing & Society (34) 992-1018 (2014).
55. Council conclusions of 12 May 2009 on a strategic framework for European cooperation in education and training ('ET 2020'), Annex I, Reference levels of European average performance ('European benchmarks').
56. Eurostat, *Adult learning statistics*, June 2017.
57. Eurostat, 2017. In Estonia, Lithuania, Poland and Slovenia, formal educational institutions are the most common providers, and in Spain informal education providers, i.e., libraries, are the most common providers.

and national level, drawing on specific sectoral expertise and working within sectors and across industry.[58]

In most EU Member States, lifelong learning strategies focusing on vocational training are drawn up in consultation with the social partners, or in tripartite arrangements. The social partners can then choose to conclude sectoral or local collective agreements to set the framework for company level.[59] One example is the sectoral agreement for the Finnish Facilities Services Sector. In order to secure and increase the supply of competent workforce in the branch associations, the agreement recommends that employees should have opportunities to participate in education that supports and develops their professional skills, and that the education should be provided at the expense of the employer.[60] Another recent example specifically targeting older employees is the agreement between the German metalworkers' trade union and the employers in the information technology sector, concluded as part of an initiative to improve employment and employability for persons aged above 50 years, i.e., by offering individually designed comprehensive training opportunities.[61]

In addition to lifelong learning, labour market mobility is a central factor in the prolongation of working lives. For older employees, unemployment implies a serious risk of never re-entering the labour market. Arrangements to support labour market mobility can significantly contribute to decreasing the risk of unemployment. In Sweden, sectoral collective agreements to support employees in cases of redundancy were concluded in the early 1970s, and they are renegotiated on a regular basis.[62] These so-called transition agreements are administered by job security councils (trygghetsråd) established by the social partners. On the basis of these agreements, the councils provide redundant employees with financial support, career planning and counselling to help them find a new job. The transition agreements and job security councils play a very important role in supporting employees in the event of restructuring.[63] Although the transition agreements do not target older workers specifically, in practice they are especially important to this group. This can be illustrated by statistics from the job security council for white-collar staff in the private sector, Trygghetsrådet

---

58. Communication from the Commission, *A New Skills Agenda for Europe. Working together to strengthen human capital, employability and competitiveness*, COM(2016) 381 final.
59. The frequency and coverage of such agreements vary greatly between the Member States. Eurofound, *Contribution of Collective Bargaining to Continuing Vocational Training*, Dublin 2009.
60. Collective Labour Agreement for the Facilities Services Sector, 1 February 2017 – 31 January 2018, Real Estate Employers Services United PAM.
61. IT 50 Plus, a joint initiative between IG Metall and BITKOM. Cf 'e-Skills in Europe, Germany, Country report' (2014), within the project for the European Commission *e-Skills for Jobs in Europe. Measuring Progress and Moving Ahead*.
62. Government Report SOU 2002:59, 37. K. Ahlberg and N. Bruun, *Sweden: transition through collective bargaining*, in T. Blanke and E. Rose (eds), *Collective Bargaining and Wages in Comparative Perspective: Germany, France, the Netherlands, Sweden and the United Kingdom* (Alphen aan den Rijn: Kluwer Law International, 2005).
63. M. Rönnmar, *Intergenerational Bargaining: Sweden – Country Report*. Report to the EU-project *Intergenerational Bargaining: towards integrated bargaining for younger and older workers in EU countries (iNGenBar)* (2014).

TRR. Of those who received a new job after turning to TRR during the first three months of 2017, 80% were over 40 years of age.[64]

[D] Age-Awareness and Attitudes Towards Older Employees

In addition to measures to alleviate working conditions, introduce incentivizing benefits and create opportunities for professional development, key strategies to promote longer working lives include workplace arrangements to make the situation of older employees more visible. By increasing employer knowledge regarding the needs that may occur in later working life, and allowing older employees themselves to articulate and contribute to resolving the challenges that come with age, such arrangements may also help to counteract ageism and prevent age discrimination. The adoption of a statutory, tripartite or collectively bargained framework for such awareness-raising policies serves to create a readiness to adjust the working situation for employees in their late working life. This expectation, in turn, fosters a general anticipation that employees actually should stay longer in work.

Age management strategies primarily target persons who are already in employment. However, measures to increase the recruitment of older employees can also be a part of a comprehensive age management strategy. Some EU Member States have introduced schemes to encourage employers to hire employees above a certain age. This is, for example, the case in Spain, where employers who hire unemployed workers over 45 enjoy a year-long social security bonus and a quota discount of EUR 1,300 a year for three years.[65] In addition, the new *Programa Extraordinario de Activación para el Empleo* includes benefits for long-term unemployed workers and labour intermediation policies. The initiative has been recognized in the national framework collective agreement signed by the main employers' organizations and the two main trade unions, with the aim of providing guidelines for both branch and company agreements.[66] The framework agreement encourages the social partners at the sectoral level to promote the recruitment of e.g., workers over 45, taking into account the public system of hiring bonuses. A different approach is that of the French *contrat de génération*, a scheme introduced in 2013 requiring the social partners to conclude a collective agreement under which companies may recruit a younger worker on a permanent employment contract and at the same time keep on (or hire) an older worker. The scheme also contains supervision and education, and is financially subsidized by the state. To date, the scheme has resulted in a relatively low number of

---

64. Trygghetsrådet TRR Statistics 2017-04-18. More specifically, 38% were between 40 and 50 years of age, 35% were between 50 and 60 years of age, and 7% were over 60 years of age.
65. C.f. the Netherlands employers may apply for a subsidy when training or hiring an unemployed person over 50, Regeling van de Minister van Sociale Zaken en Werkgelegenheid van 26 september 2013, 20130000129478, tot verstrekken van subsidie voor scholing en plaatsing van oudere werklozen (Regeling scholing en plaatsing oudere werklozen), Stcrt. 2013, 27343, applicable until 1 January 2018. See M. Kullmann, *Extended Working Life. The Dutch Government Response*, 7 European Labour Law Journal (1) 31-51 (2016).
66. Chapter I, Point h) of *III Acuerdo para el Empleo y la Negociación Colectiva*, 8 June 2015, between CEOE & CEPYME and CCOO &UGT.

employment contracts. In the long run, however, account must be taken of the outcome in terms both of the numbers of employees hired and of how the scheme has contributed to changes in attitudes and the removal of prejudice.[67]

Strategies to address approaches towards older members of the workforce are the core of age management.[68] This includes recruitment policies towards older jobseekers, but equally important are measures such as consultations, planning and individually targeted measures for employees of a certain age. Some examples of such targeted measures have already been discussed above, in §15.5[B] on working conditions and §15.5[C] on workforce development. But there are also examples of how collective bargaining can introduce comprehensive structures for planning and consultation with older employees in the workplace. In Denmark, the importance of age management practices is long established among the social partners. Since 2009, the collective agreement in the public sector has provided for *senior conversations*, a voluntary dialogue with the employer on how the job demands of older workers can be met to satisfy both parties. To accommodate the needs of the employer and the individual employee, the agreement includes particular senior employment contracts with reduced working time or modified job content, and schemes that allow for financial incentives or extraordinary pension contributions to employees who choose to stay on longer in employment for a certain number of years.[69] Similarly, under the title Prolonging Working Careers, the collective agreement between the Federation of Finnish Technology Industries and the Finnish Metal Workers' Union (also mentioned above, in § 15.5[B] (footnote 42)) states that the employer shall discuss with employees attaining the age of 58 the available measures for helping an older employee to cope at work. In addition, the agreement refers to the technology industries' career-span scheme publication for examples of measures that can be taken.[70]

§15.06 DISCUSSION AND FINAL REMARKS

The topic of extended working lives is high on the EU employment policy agenda. In many Member States, the need to meet the challenges of an ageing workforce has an

---

67. S. Robin-Olivier, *Age Discrimination and Labour Law in France*, in A. Numhauser-Henning and M. Rönnmar (eds), *Age Discrimination and Labour Law. Comparative and Conceptual Perspectives in the EU and Beyond* (Alphen aan den Rijn: Kluwer Law International, 2015).
68. On attitudes towards older employees *see*, for instance C. Ulander-Wänman, *Swedish Collective Agreements and Employer's Willingness to Hire and Retain Older Workers in Employment*, 6 Journal of Working Life Studies 2:61-79 (2016); C.T. Kulik, S. Perera & C. Cregan, *Engage Me. The Mature-Age Worker and Stereotype Threat*, 59 Academy of management Journal (6) 2132-2156 (2016); M. Carlsson & S. Eriksson, *The Effect of Age and Gender on Labour Demand. Evidence from a Field Experiment*, Working Paper 2017:8, IFAU.
69. Rammeaftale om Seniorpolitik, 2015. Cf. M. Barslund, *Extending Working Lives. The case of Denmark*, CEPS Working Document No. 404, 2015. Other studies indicate is a discrepancy among the Danish companies in terms of the recognition of the problem and practical action. *See*, for instance, H. Jensen & R. Juul Møberg, *Age Management in Danish Companies: What, How, and How Much?*, 2 Nordic Journal of Working Life Studies (3) 49-66 (2012).
70. Clause 31.1.10 of the Collective agreement between the Federation of Finnish Technology Industries and the Finnish Metalworker's Union 1 November 2013 – 31 October 2016, reformed through Collective agreement in the technology industries 1 November 2016 – 31 October 2017.

important impact on policy-making and regulatory development. The crucial role of the social partners in this development has repeatedly been stressed. Indeed, many of the strategies for accommodating the challenges that come with an ageing workforce can translate into collective agreements. This article shows many examples of how collective bargaining in a constructive and applicable way can lead to the implementation of policy measures to promote extended working lives, and transform them into everyday practice in the workplace.

Against the background of legislation and policies at EU and national level, this article argues that collective bargaining may considerably contribute to the prolongation of working lives. As others have highlighted, when facing the upcoming ageing of the workforce, employers tend primarily to consider measures that are financially and practically low in cost.[71] Thus, adjustments in the working conditions, such as ergonomic measures or reduction in working time, are more likely to take place than employability-increasing practices such as vocational training. At first sight, this approach from the employer is only logical. As explained by Schmitz, from the perspective of human resource capital theory, the expected outcome for employers (and also employees) of an investment in training decreases with the age of the employee.[72] What might be more difficult to see is that investments in training and other employability-increasing measures have a significant potential to pay off, as the employer can avoid the costs of early retirement and the hiring and training of new employees. In this context, it is worth noting that research has also shown that, in addition to less costly measures, employers also tend to consider measures that are formulated in collective agreements.[73]

The impact of collective bargaining in the context of promoting extended working lives is highly significant; it has a clear potential to make a difference, and a unique ability to provide tailor-made solutions. In addition, also from a strategic perspective, it would be rational for both employers and trade unions to increase their engagement in collective bargaining for older employees. Collective bargaining enables the social partners to direct the measures towards areas that matter to them, which is not always the same as those that matter to the public policy-maker. To illustrate this, the Swedish collective agreements on part-time retirement provide an example. There seems to be scientific evidence that part-time pensions can extend working careers for certain groups in the sense that people within these groups actually stay longer in working life than they would otherwise have done. Nevertheless, there is little support for the positive impact on public finances. On a macro-economic level, it is probably more efficient if people continue to work full time for a somewhat shorter period instead of working a number of additional years on a part-time basis.[74] To counteract the effects

---

71. M. Fleischmann, F. Koster & J. Schippers, *Nothing ventured, nothing gained! How and under which conditions employers provide employability-enhancing practices to their older workers*, 26 The International Journal of Human Resource Management (22): 2908-2925 (2015).
72. Schmitz (2015), *supra* n. 53.
73. Fleischmann, Koster & Schippers (2015), *supra* n. 71.
74. Takala & Väänänen (2016), *supra* 51, n. 27. Cf A.L. Gustman & T.L. Steinmeier, *Projecting Behavioral Responses to the next Generation of retirement Policies* 28 Research in Labor Economics, 237-253 (2008).

of the ongoing demographic shift, working-life reforms should increase the overall working-time output by imposing a positive effect on income levels and tax revenues. From the perspective of public finances, this renders part-time pension schemes less interesting. Looking at the matter from the perspective of the social partners, however, the situation comes out differently. The explicit aim of the collective agreement was not primarily to contribute to the public finances, but to provide for generational renewal.[75] In the promotion of knowledge transfer or the retaining of skills and experience within business, part-time pension schemes have the potential to play a key role. Collective bargaining has an important potential to contribute to the strategies of extended working lives in way that lets the social partners impact significantly on the future shaping of this area.

---

75. Rönnmar (2014), *supra* n. 63.

CHAPTER 16
Collective Bargaining with Regard to Young Employees: Importance and Challenges

Judith Brockmann

Young employees can be considered a vulnerable group that has been particularly hit by the financial and economic crisis and its effects on the labour market. This paper focuses on collective bargaining with regard to young employees and gives examples of provisions in collective agreements targeting young employees. The role of the social partners and of collective bargaining is clearly emphasised by European policies when it comes to combating youth unemployment and promoting the labour market participation of young employees. By contrast, available data and information on collective bargaining with regard to young employees lead to the conclusion that collective agreements are of rather little importance. The paper explores possible legal and factual reasons. *Inter alia*, these are not only the functioning of the European legal framework, but also the labour market situation, and the structure and functioning of trade unions.

§16.01 INTRODUCTION

Youth unemployment and the raising of young employees' labour market participation are major concerns in European Union (EU) policy and for the Member States.

Young or future employees are a vulnerable group when it comes to labour market participation and precarious working conditions. Youth can be conceived as a specific risk factor in the labour market.[1] Youth unemployment rates doubled in several Member States and even rose to over 50% in 2014 in certain members states

---

1. Jenny Julén Votinius, *Young Employees: Securities, Risk Distribution and Fundamental Social Rights*, (3-4) 5 European Labour Law Journal 366, 367 (2014); European Commission, *Joint Employment Report 2017 as adopted by the EPSCO Council on 3rd March 2017*, 28, http://ec.europa.eu/social/main.jsp?catId=101&langId=en (accessed 21 July 2017).

such as Greece and Spain.[2] They have significantly decreased since then, but remain notably higher than the overall unemployment rates in nearly all Member States.[3] Of course, labour market situations vary in the different Member States,[4] but independently of the general labour market situation, low-skilled young people have particular problems entering the labour market.[5] This is all the more true for Member States with difficult labour market situations.[6] Vulnerability is not limited to unemployment but also concerns precarious employment relationships and working conditions.[7] Young employees are significantly more often employed in non-standard forms of employment, such as on part-time, temporary or temporary agency contracts.[8] They often earn less than the average employee.[9] Youth unemployment and precarious working conditions are a concern in different respects, especially because of long-term scarring

---

2. Eurostat http://ec.europa.eu/eurostat/tgm/table.do?tab = table&plugin = 1&language = en&pcode = tipslm80 (accessed 21 July 2017).
3. Eurostat, *Unemployment News Release 107/2017* – 3 July 2017; http://ec.europa.eu/eurostat/documents/2995521/8094245/3-03072017-AP-EN.pdf/aced038e-2af1-4a7a-a726-7e8d20d840c0 (accessed 21 July 2017).
4. *Draft Joint Employment Report from the Commission and the Council accompanying the Communication from the Commission on the Annual Growth, Survey 2015, Brussels 20 November 2014*, COM (214) 9 final, 5.
5. *See* in-depth Hans Dietrich, *Youth unemployment in the period 2001–2010 and the European crisis – looking at the empirical evidence*, 19(3) Transfer 305–324 (2013).
6. For example Council Recommendation of 12 July 2016 on the 2016 National Reform Programme of Portugal and delivering a Council opinion on the 2016 Stability Programme of Portugal, (2016/C 299/26), No. 10, 111. For a general overview *see* European Commission, DG Employment, Social Affairs and Inclusion, *Mutual Learning Programme, Thematic Paper: What works for the labour market integration of youth at risk*, 4 et seq. (2016).
7. Julén Votinius, *supra* n. 1, at 366.
8. *See* Janine Leschke, *Has the economic crisis contributed to more segmentation in labour market and welfare outcomes?*, ETUI Working Paper 2012.02; Frank Tros & Maarten Keune, *Intergenerational bargaining in the EU: Comparative report, 2016*, 6 with further references, http://intergenerationalbargaining.eu/pages/reports (accessed 21 July 2017); ILO, *Non-standard employment around the world: Understanding challenges, shaping prospects*, 135 et seq. and 140 (2016).
9. This might be due to special youth minimum wages foreseen by collective agreements (*see infra* §16.03[A]) or national legislation. Statutory minimum wages are adjusted for young employees in Belgium, Greece, France, Ireland, Luxembourg, Malta, the Netherlands and the UK, *see* Eurofound, *Statutory minimum wages in the EU 2017*, Dublin, 19 (2017). For example, Dutch law provides a youth minimum wage applicable up to the age of 23, *see* Tros, *Inter-generational Bargaining: towards integrated bargaining for younger and older workers in EU countries: The Netherlands – Country Report*, 14, http://intergenerationalbargaining.eu/pages/reports (accessed 22 July 2017). For the actual rate visit https://www.government.nl/topics/minimum-wage/amount-of-the-minimum-wage; the National Minimum Wages Act of 2000 of the Republic of Ireland provides lower minimum wages for young employees up to the age of 20 years and special trainee rates; the UK National Minimum Wage Act 1998 provides youth minimum wages up to the age of 25 and special rates for apprentices; *see also* Jeremias Prassl, *Contingent Crises, Permanent Reforms*, (3-4) 8 European Labour Law Journal, 211, 223 (2013). For an overview, *see* OECD, *FOCUS on Minimum wages after the crisis: Making them pay May 2015*, 11, http://www.oecd.org/social/Focus-on-Minimum-Wages-after-the-crisis-2015.pdf (accessed 21 July 2017); the German Minimum Wages Act of 2014 (MiLoG) does not apply to persons aged under 18 without having accomplished any vocational or professional education according to §22 (2) MiLoG.

effects. They raise the risk of on-going precarious working arrangements,[10] long-term unemployment,[11] and lead to higher poverty risks,[12] including negative effects on old-age provisions and pension shortfalls. In addition, they may have more or less severe consequences for the social structure.[13]

Policies and measures to promote youth employment are manifold. They are developed at a European as well as a national level by the Member States. European activities in favour of youth employment are included in the framework of different European policies, especially in the Europe 2020 Strategy, comprising the procedures of the European Semester and the European Youth Guarantee (EYG), to name only the most important. European policies address not only Member States but also the social partners. Social partners' action is of course institutionally embedded in the regulatory legal framework of collective bargaining in the relevant Member State and in the current economic situation,[14] but also depends on – diverse – industrial relations traditions and on the current situation and power of the social partners.[15]

After some definitions concerning the target group 'young employees' (§16.02), the paper offers examples of collective bargaining issues with regard to young employees from different Member States (§16.03). As far as data and information are available, collective bargaining seems to be of little importance when it comes to young employees as a target group. This may be explained by different legal and current conditions at the EU level and in the Member States (§16.04). But the legal framework is only one possible explanation. In reality, the reasons for the marginal role of collective bargaining with regard to young employees are manifold (§16.05). Important factors may also be found in the current labour market situation and in the structure and functioning of trade unions.

§16.02 WHO ARE 'YOUNG EMPLOYEES'?

Talking about young employees as a group of stakeholders in collective bargaining, the paper concentrates on collective bargaining agreements that include special provisions for young employees. These provisions might act in favour of young employees, e.g., involving special training or mentorship, rules or quotas for the intake of young employees. But they might also lead to a downgrading of labour conditions for young

---

10. ILO, *supra* n. 8, at 137 et seq; Maarten Keune, *YOUnion Final Report: Trade Unions and Young Workers in Seven EU Countries*, 6 et seq, https://moodle.adaptland.it/course/view.php?id=327 (accessed 21 July 2017).
11. Cf. Achim Schmillen & Matthias Umkehrer, *The scars of youth: Effects of early-career unemployment on future unemployment experience*, IAB Discussion Paper 6/2013.
12. Matthias Umkehrer, *The impact of changing youth employment patterns on future wages*, IAB Discussion Paper 31/2015.
13. ILO, *supra* n. 8, at 138, 143.
14. Kurt Vandaele, *Trade unions' 'deliberative vitality' towards young workers: Survey evidence across Europe*, in Andy Hodder, Lefteris Kretsos (eds.), *Young Workers and Trade Unions: A Global View*, 16, 35 (Palgrave Macmillan 2015).
15. See Orestis Papadopoulos, *Economic crisis and youth unemployment: Comparing Greece and Ireland*, 22(4) European Journal of Industrial Relations 409, 419 (2016) for a general appreciation. *See also* Tros & Keune, *supra* n. 8, at 26.

employees, with e.g., lower minimum wages in order to make employing them more attractive for employers thanks to reduced labour costs.

It must be taken into account that 'young employees' are far from being a legally defined group. This is true for the age structure and their limits as well as for the social structure. When speaking of young employees, one should be aware that there is no clear or legal concept defining a certain age group. Its extent depends on the policy context. European statistics usually understand by 'young workers' or 'young employees' persons aged 15 to 24.[16] In European policies, definitions might be more restrictive,[17] but also wider. The European Youth Guarantee, for example, applies to young persons aged under 25 years.[18] However, this is binding neither for the Member States and national legislation nor for the social partners.[19] Various examples show that the notion of young employees may be enormously extended. Depending on the objective pursued, national legislation sometimes defines the group of young employees reaching up to the age of 29,[20] 30[21] or even 35[22] years. For the purposes of this paper, we will just take into account the definition employed by the ruling bodies, i.e., the legislature and/or the social partners, considering their competences.

Finally, young employees are far from being a homogeneous group. They are diverse in terms of e.g., their level of education (from school dropouts to tertiary education),[23] professional situation[24] and experience (individuals with or without a degree looking for internships or their first jobs, others having their first professional experiences), and migration background. The paper will concentrate on those engaged in the labour market, i.e., young employees currently employed or unemployed and

---

16. Eurostat, *Youth unemployment rate – % of active population aged 15-24*, http://ec.europa.eu/eurostat/tgm/refreshTableAction.do?tab=table&plugin=1&pcode=tipslm80&language=en (accessed 21 July 2017). See also Dominique Anxo, *Entry and Exit Patterns from the Labour Force: A European and Live-Course Perspective*, in Ann Numhauser-Henning & Mia Rönnmar (eds.), Age Discrimination and Labour Law. Comparative and Conceptual Perspectives in the EU and Beyond, (Kluwer Law International 2015), 17, 18 et seq. In this paper, the term will be used in this sense, unless it is defined differently.
17. The Council Directive 94/33/EC of 22 June 1994 on the protection of young people at work, for example, targets young workers aged under 18 years.
18. Council of the European Union, Council Recommendation of 22 April 2013 on establishing a Youth Guarantee, OJ C 120/1, 26 April 2013.
19. See supra n. 9 for statutory youth minimum wages and *infra* §16.03[A]. for collectively bargained youth wages.
20. For example Cyprus, *National Reform Programme 2013, Europe 2020 Strategy for: Smart, Sustainable and Inclusive Growth*, p. 8, http://ec.europa.eu/europe2020/pdf/nd/nrp2013_cyprus_en.pdf (accessed 21 July 2017).
21. For example Denmark, Danish Government, *The National Reform Programme Denmark 2013*, 50, http://ec.europa.eu/europe2020/pdf/nd/nrp2013_denmark_en.pdf (accessed 21 July 2017); *see also* on the example of Portugal Margherita Bussi & Leonard Geyer, *Youth Guarantees and recent developments on measures against youth unemployment: A mapping exercise*, 37 (ETUI 2013).
22. For example Italy: Republica Italiana, *Economic and Financial Document 2013, Section III National Reform Programme*, 41, http://ec.europa.eu/europe2020/pdf/nd/nrp2013_italy_en.pdf (accessed 21 July 2017); for the example of Greece, *see* Bussi & Geyer, *supra* n. 21 at 31.
23. Educational qualifications cannot prevent especially structural unemployment, but still seem to be the best insurance against unemployment, *see* ILO, *supra* n. 7, at 143 as well as Keune, *supra* n. 10, at 7.
24. Tros & Keune, *supra* n. 8, at 12.

looking for a job. For this reason, it will specifically not consider the group known as 'NEETs' (neither in employment nor education and training).[25]

§16.03 EXAMPLES OF COLLECTIVE BARGAINING WITH REGARD TO YOUNG EMPLOYEES

Collective bargaining on young employees' matters is not monitored systematically, so for most Member States, reliable data is not available and more empirical research in this field would be desirable. That said, examples of collective agreements with special provisions concerning young employees can be found[26] and some key issues can be identified. Some of them are well known, such as youth wages (A), targets for the intake of young employees or job guarantees for apprentices (B), and vocational education and training (VET) matters (C). But with regard to demographic changes, young employees are also an important group to be considered when it comes to intergenerational bargaining that focuses on both young and older employees (D).

[A] Youth Wages

In some Member States, particularly where no statutory minimum wage is provided by national legislation, special youth wages are foreseen by collective agreements. This is the case where stipulations provide lower wages for young employees (as a defined age group) compared with 'adult professional' workers. The logic underlying youth wages is to render youth employment more attractive for employers by reducing labour costs.[27]

Youth wages exist for example in Belgium, where mandatory national minimum wages have been fixed by national collective agreements within the National Labour Council (CNT/NAR) since 1975. Until 2013 the agreements provided special youth wages. Since then, the minimum wage has basically applied from the age of 18 years onwards, but there are still increments combining age and seniority criteria up to the age of 21. Furthermore, the conventional minimum wages do not apply for young employees under the age of 18 and those employed on special student contracts or apprenticeship programmes even beyond the age of 18.[28]

Similar examples are reported from Sweden, where minimum wages are not fixed by statutory rules but by the social partners and subject to collective agreements at

---

25. For an in-depth analysis, see Bussi & Geyer, supra n. 21, at 18 et seq.
26. Also thanks to the research on intergenerational bargaining within the iNGenBar project: *Intergenerational bargaining: towards integrated bargaining for younger and older workers in EU countries*, financed by the European Commission; DG Employment, Social Affairs and Inclusion; Social Dialogue, Industrial Relations (VS/2013/0353), www.intergenerationalbargaining.eu (accessed 21 July 2017). For more examples, see also ETUC et al., *Framework of Actions on Youth Employment, Second follow-up report*, September 2015, 12 et seq., https://www.etuc.org/sites/www.etuc.org/files/circular/files/2nd_follow_up_report_foa_youth_sept_2015_-_final.pdf (accessed 24 July 2017).
27. See for example Julén Votinius, supra n. 1, at 381 et seq; Keune, supra n. 10, at 7.
28. See Conseil National du Travail/Nationale Arbeidsraad 2017, *Remuneration/Loon*, http://www.cnt-nar.be/Cct-theme.htm (accessed 21 July 2017) with further references.

different levels.[29] (Lower) youth minimum wages are common for young employees aged 16 to 19 years. In addition, periods of professional experience acquired before the age of 18 or 19 may not be taken into account for the purposes of wage calculation.[30]

When it comes to the allowances for apprentices foreseen by collective agreements in the field of vocational education and training (VET) (*see infra*), they are usually lower than statutory or conventional minimum wages. That said, it has to be taken into account that the object of apprenticeship contracts is not work but professional training. In this respect, they are not comparable to youth wages.

[B] Intake of Young Employees

Collective agreements may contain provisions to directly facilitate the integration of young employees in the labour market in the form of job guarantees. However, their extent may vary considerably. For example, sector-level collective agreements may provide numbered targets for the intake of young employees or former apprentices. They can thus be understood as declarations of intent, as they are usually not legally binding or at least not enforceable. This may be different when it comes to job guarantees for apprentices who have completed their VET (*see infra*). Job guarantees for young employees may also be linked to the employment or early retirement of older employees; examples will be given in the context of intergenerational bargaining (*see infra*).

For example, Swedish law provides special collective agreements to promote the employment of young people, the so-called introduction agreements. The state regulation results from a tripartite negotiation process and provides financial subsidies when young employees are hired in application of an introduction agreement.[31] These collective agreements deal with the hiring of young employees and combine it with education, training and supervision.[32]

[C] Qualification of Young Employees and VET

The qualification of young employees is another important subject, especially when employers need to find qualified workforce. Collective agreements may provide a wide range of skills enhancement, training on the job, mentorship and/or supervision of

---

29. Mia Rönnmar, *Intergenerational Bargaining: towards integrated bargaining for younger and older workers in EU countries, Sweden – Country Report* (2014), 5 et seq, http://intergenerationalbargaining.eu/pages/reports (accessed 24 July 2017).
30. Jenny Julén Votinius, *Age Discrimination and Labour Law in Sweden*, in Ann Numhauser-Henning & Mia Rönnmar (eds.), *Age Discrimination and Labour Law. Comparative and Conceptual Perspectives in the EU and Beyond*, (Kluwer Law International 2015), 292 with further references.
31. *See in detail* Rönnmar, *supra* n. 29, at 19 et seq.
32. *See infra* §16.04.

young employees. The importance of collective bargaining depends mainly on the VET systems of the Member States.[33]

In countries with an established (dual) VET system, status, working and learning conditions in companies are traditionally subject to collective bargaining. This is especially true for Germany and Austria.[34] The collective agreements traditionally fix allowances for apprentices, but may include guarantees to hire young workers after they have completed their VET or at least agree quotas for the intake of former apprentices. The employer's side invokes principally the need to find and bind qualified workforce and to make a return on investments in VET as motives for this kind of guarantee.[35] But in Italy too, for example, occupational standards for VET and other forms of apprenticeships are subject to collective agreements.[36]

[D] Intergenerational Bargaining

With regard to demographic changes in the active labour force, intergenerational bargaining seems to be an interesting approach for the social partners. Rather than bargaining separately for the young and the old, intergenerational bargaining is characterised by a more holistic and work-life-cycle-orientated approach.[37] Even if collective bargaining and the provisions seem to particularly focus on the concerns of older employees,[38] life-cycle-orientated rules are appropriate to meet young employees' interests at least in a medium- or long-term perspective.[39] Occasionally, collective agreements may also link the employment or intake of a young employee to either the maintenance or the (early) retirement of an elder employee. The idea of intergenerational bargaining is not new. For example, Italian law has provided instruments to promote collectively bargained 'generational relay schemes' since 1984, though they have scarcely been used in practice.[40] This also seems to be true for recently assessed forms of intergenerational bargaining.

In Germany, a new type of collective agreement is emerging, the so-called demography-related collective agreements (Demografie-Tarifverträge), at a sectoral as

---

33. Jason Heyes, *Vocational education and training and the Great Recession: supporting young people in a time of crisis*, ETUI Report 131 (2014), 56.
34. Moreover, the social partners are usually represented in the bodies that are in charge of administration and control of VET; cf. for Germany: Arts 77, 82 and 92 Berufsbildungsgesetz (BBiG) (Germany); for Austria: Arts §§19, 31-31d Berufsausbildungsgesetz (BAG).
35. Antonio Brettschneider, *Intergenerational Bargaining – National Report Germany*, http://intergenerationalbargaining.eu/pages/reports (accessed 21 July 2017) (2014).
36. Lisa Rustico & Roberto Pedersini, *iNGenBar – Inter-generational Bargaining towards integrated bargaining for younger and older workers in EU countries, Italy Country Report*, 9, http://intergenerationalbargaining.eu/pages/reports (accessed 21 July 2017).
37. See also Julén Votinius, in this issue, Part II, Chapter 15, *Older Employees, Extended Working Lives, and Collective Bargaining* (supra).
38. Bundesanstalt für Arbeitsschutz und Arbeitsmedizin (ed.), Altersdifferenzierte und alternsgerechte Betriebs- und Tarifpolitik: Eine Bestandsaufnahme betriebspolitischer und tarifvertraglicher Maßnahmen zur Sicherung der Beschäftigungsfähigkeit, inqa-Report 42, 2011, 167 et seq.
39. This is true for flexible part-time solutions or long-term working-time accounts, see Brettschneider *supra* n. 35, at 30.
40. Rustico & Pedersini, *supra* n. 35, at 6.

well as a company level. These are the product of autonomous collective bargaining and not incentivised by statutory rules. One important aim of demography-related collective agreements is to guarantee a performant workforce in times of age-related fluctuation. In this sense, they may provide a guarantee of the employment of a certain number of apprentices, former apprentices or other young employees, sometimes directly linked to the retirement of an older employee.[41] Moreover, sectoral-level agreements provide for a set of possible measures to be activated either by company-level agreements or at the plant level by the employer and works councils. Despite their growing number, the impact of demography-related collective agreements seems to be limited, as their application at company level is not very popular for various reasons.[42]

In France, there is a certain tradition in the actions of the social partners and labour market policies to facilitate the employment of young employees by linking them to the leave of older employees.[43] In 2013, a statutory law[44] – preceded by a national collective agreement[45] – introduced the legal framework of a 'generation contract' (contrat de génération).[46] The law aims to facilitate the access of young employees to open-ended contracts, to hire and maintain the contracts of older employees and to secure the transmission of knowledge and competences between both groups.[47] It provides financial subsidies for SMEs hiring a young employee on the basis of an open-ended contract linked to the maintenance or conclusion of a contract with an older employee. The law aims to promote collective bargaining and obliges the employer to establish an action plan on the employment of young and older employees and the modes of knowledge transmission in the company if no collective agreement is concluded at sector or company level.[48] Two reports recently assessed the instrument and its application and showed that the government's expectations were far from being met.[49] Even if a growing number of sectoral-level agreements have been concluded, and the scope of their application extended by decree,[50] they tend to repeat the legal provisions set by the law. Indeed, agreements may often include numbered targets for

---

41. The same mechanism can be found in the 'contrat de génération' in France. The important difference is that the instrument is not provided by German law and unlike in France, public financial subsidies are not available.
42. Brettschneider, *supra* n. 35, at 48 et seq.
43. Dominique Méda, Michèle Tallard & Jean-Louis Renoux, *Intergenerational Bargaining, Country Report: France*, 5 et seq., 48, http://intergenerationalbargaining.eu/pages/reports (accessed 21 July 2017).
44. Cf. Art. L 5121-9 et seq. Code du travail.
45. Accord National Interprofessionnel du 19 octobre 2012, *relatif au contrat de génération*, http://www.unml.info/les-missions-locales/espace-documentaire-des-missions-locales/orientation-emploi-formation/les-contrats-aides/contrat-de-generation/accord-national-interprofessionnel-du-19-octobre-2012-relatif-au-contrat-de-generation.html (accessed 21 July 2017).
46. Méda, Tallard & Renoux, *supra* n. 43, at 22.
47. Article L5121-6 Code du travail.
48. It depends on the company's size whether one or both provisions apply, DARES, *L'aide à l'embauche en contrat de génération: Une incitation à pérenniser l'emploi des jeunes*, DARES Etudes No. 025, Mars 2015.
49. *Id.*
50. For a full list, visit http://travail-emploi.gouv.fr/emploi/insertion-dans-l-emploi/mesures-seniors/contrat-de-generation/negociez-un-accord-ou-un-plan-d-action/liste-des-accords-de-branche-etendus/ (accessed 21 July 2017).

the intake of young or the maintenance of older employees, but they are usually not legally binding and have to be understood as a declaration of intent. Company-level agreements tend to copy the content of sector-level agreements, so the social partners do not seem to be making active use of their regulating power for rule setting.[51]

[E] Interim Conclusions

Examples of collective bargaining concerning young employees' matters can be found in any structural collective bargaining setting, i.e., autonomous as well as incentive-induced[52] and mandatory collective bargaining structures. Collective bargaining concerning young employees takes places on all levels, i.e., national, sectoral and company,[53] and can also be found in European group-level agreements.[54] However, following the different national or comparative reports, collective bargaining does not play an important role when it comes to young employees' matters.[55]

VET can be considered an important field for collective bargaining. But this seems to be true only if the social partner's involvement in the VET system is well established and if collective bargaining agreements are part of it. This seems to be the case in Austria and Germany, but it must be doubted if this is a model for other Member States and their collective bargaining systems, considering the wide variety of educational systems. Austria and Germany have a long tradition of highly advanced dual VET systems, combining school and on-site training.

The intake of young employees also seems to be rather important considering the demographic structure of the workforce. This is particularly true when employers are seeking generational transfer.

Finally, collective bargaining also seems to play a role when it comes to lowering labour conditions for young employees. This is often based on the conviction that alleviated charges for employers and less employment protection will improve employment opportunities for young workers. Thus, the latter end up depending on the general labour market situation. In other respects, lowering the labour conditions by collective agreements will contribute to precarious employment arrangements and may finally turn against trade unions (see infra).

---

51. Cour de Comptes, *Rapport public annuel 2016, Tome I: les observations, version intégrale*, 66 et seq., www.ccomptes.fr (accessed 21 July 2017).
52. *See* in this issue Pierre-Emmanuel Berthier & Oliver Leclerc, Part I, Chapter 3, *How to get collective bargaining decentralized: legal incentives v. Compulsory measures (supra)*.
53. For an in-depth analysis of different bargaining levels, *see* Sylvaine Laulom, in this issue, Part I, Chapter 1, *What does decentralization of collective bargaining means ?, (supra)*.
54. *See* the example of the European Framework Agreement of the Groupe Safran (Accord cadre européen en faveur de l'insertion professionnelle des jeunes) concluded on 28 March 2013, http://safran-cfdt.fr/wp-content/uploads/2014/03/Accord-Cadre-Europeen-Developpement-25-03-2015.pdf or http://fo-safran.com/wp-content/uploads/2016/03/Accordcadreeuropéen-VF.pdf (accessed 20 July 2017).
55. This appraisal is unanimously shared by all the experts engaged in the INLACRIS network as well as the social partners' representatives from different Member States that have been involved in the present research.

§16.04 THE INSTITUTIONAL FRAMEWORK: CHALLENGES FOR COLLECTIVE BARGAINING WITH REGARD TO YOUNG EMPLOYEES' MATTERS

Collective bargaining depends on many factors, and the legal framework is only one of them. Both the European and national legal conditions have to be considered. The national traditions and structures of social dialogue and industrial relations play an important role.[56] Furthermore, the labour market situation and the functioning and structures of trade unions have to be taken into account.

[A] European Policies

The involvement of the social partners seems to be one of the key concerns of the European Union when it comes to labour market policies. This is to be expected, as the promotion of the social partners is foreseen by the treaties in the context of employment regulation, especially in Articles 151, 154 and 155 TFEU. It is continually stressed in all policy documents concerning employment strategies, labour market reforms and the combating of youth unemployment/increasing of young employees' labour market participation.[57] Thus, in policy fields dealing with young employees or jobseekers, social partners are not explicitly or necessarily involved with the furthering of the policies on a European or national level. Instead, they are named as stakeholders in these fields, along with other institutions, the Member States, business and civil society. Social partners have occasionally been consulted at the European level, for example with the development of the *Quality Framework for Traineeship*.[58]

Concerning Europe 2020 and the European Employment strategy, the EU has adopted soft law strategies on the one hand[59] and combined them with financial policies and instruments on the other.[60] This can be illustrated with regard to the

---

56. *See* e.g., Papadopoulos, *supra* n. 15, at 410 et seq.
57. *See only* European Commission, Communication from the Commission, *Europe 2020: A strategy for smart, sustainable and inclusive growth* Brussels, 3.3.2010 COM (2010) 2020 final; Council of the European Union, *Council Recommendation of 22 April 2013 on establishing a Youth Guarantee*, OJ C 120/1, 26 April 2013; European Commission, *Draft Joint Employment Report from the Commission and the Council accompanying the Communication from the Commission on the Annual Growth Survey 2016*, Brussels, 26.11.2015 COM (2015) 700 final; European Commission, *Draft Joint Employment Report from the Commission and the Council accompanying the Communication from the Commission on the Annual Growth Survey 2017*, Brussels, 16.11.2016, COM (2016) 729 final; European Commission, n. 6, at 28.
58. Beryl ter Haar & Mia Rönnmar, *Intergenerational Bargaining, EU Age Discrimination Law and EU Policies – an Integrated Analysis*, p. 13, http://intergenerationalbargaining.eu/pages/reports (accessed 21 July 2017).
59. Cf. Paul Copeland & Beryl ter Haar, *A toothless bite? The effectiveness of the European Employment Strategy as a governance tool*, 23(1) Journal of European Social Policy, 21, 27 (2013).
60. *See* Manfred Weiss, *European employment policies: A critical analysis of the legal framework*, 8 (2) European Labour Law Journal, 111, 113 (2017) with further references.

European Youth Guarantee and its implementation mechanism.[61] The implementation is based on typical measures of the open method of co-ordination (OMC),[62] i.e., choices are left to the Member States as to the establishment of good practices and financial incentives.[63] At the same time, financial policies such as austerity measures or the goals and assessments in the European Semester framework focus on measures taken by the Member States. Member States, or rather their governments, are held liable towards the EU and its institutions. This leads to Member State-driven measures (i.e., by legislators or governments) to fulfil the goals,[64] which may leave little space for collective bargaining.[65] In this sense, measures taken by the Member States seem to be far more important.[66]

When it comes to the procedures provided within the European Semester, it is remarkable that youth unemployment became an important issue in the last Country Specific Recommendations (CSR) (2015/16), despite having been barely mentioned in earlier CSRs. However, the European recommendations are very general and do not systematically assess the implementation of the EYG or the social partners' involvement in this regard.[67]

Eurofound analysed the social partners' involvement in the procedures of the European Semester by the European Commission and by the Member States, i.e., especially the elaboration of the National Reform Programmes (NRP) and the CSR in

---

61. See Ales, *The European Employment Strategy as Enhanced Coordination: A holistic approach to the EU social commitment*, 8 (2) European Labour Law Journal, 122, 123 (2017) with further references.
62. Arne Pilniok, *Governance im europäischen Forschungsförderverbund*, 208 et seq (Mohr Siebeck 2011); Arthur Benz, *Accountable Multilevel Governance by the Open Method of Coordination?*, 13 European Law Journal, 505-522 (2007).
63. Cf. Copeland & ter Haar, *supra* n. 59, passim.
64. As Leclerc stated: 'Labour law reform seems to be one of the few policy instruments available to governments in the eurozone [sic!] with which to reassure the financial markets and to avoid the downgrading of their sovereign debt by the credit rating agencies. In that sense, labour market reform seems to work as a signal to the financial markets of the willingness of individual States to act positively for the sake of their economies.' – Olivier Leclerc, *Which Securities for Workers in Times of Crisis? Challenges and Perspectives*, 5(3-4) European Labour Law Journal, 410, 414 (2013).
65. Cf. Copeland & ter Haar, *supra*, n. 59, passim.
66. In this sense also Kurt Vandaele, *Union responses to young workers since the Great Recession in Ireland, the Netherlands and Sweden: are youth structures reorienting the union agenda?*, 19 (3) Transfer, 381, 395 (2013), Tros, *supra* n. 9, at 40 et seq., and Vanessa Beck & Glynne Williams, *iNGenBar – Inter-generational Bargaining: Towards integrated bargaining for younger and older workers in EU countries: UK Country Report*, http://intergenerationalbargaining.eu/pages/reports (accessed 21 July 2017), 14 et seq.
67. See e.g., the following CSR: Empfehlung für eine Empfehlung des Rates zum nationalen Reformprogramm Rumäniens 2015 mit einer Stellungnahme des Rates zum Konvergenzprogramm Rumäniens 2015 as of 13.5.2015, COM(2015) 272 final, no. 13, 5 (only available in German). Only the Report of Luxemburg mentions the challenge to actively involve the social partners in the implementation process of the EYG, *see* Commission Staff Working Document Country Report Luxembourg 2015 {COM (2015) 85 final} as of 18.3.2015, SWD (2015) 35 final/2, 26; Memorandum of Understanding between the European Commission acting on behalf of the European Stability Mechanism and the Hellenic Republic and the Bank of Greece, 16, https://ec.europa.eu/info/files/memorandum-understanding-greece-august-2015_en (accessed 21 July 2017).

the Member States. It shows that the level of involvement differs a lot in the Member States,[68] but that recently there has been a slight general improvement.[69]

On the other hand, CSR used as instruments of the European Semester and financial policy seem to rather discourage the participation of social partners, unless collective bargaining is used with the aim of promoting wage moderation or introducing more flexible working conditions. When it comes to collective bargaining or collective bargaining systems as aspects mentioned in the NRP or CSR, they usually seem to be considered a source of inflexibility and an obstacle to employment. There is a tendency to advise Member States to introduce more flexibility in collective bargaining systems, supposing that this may be reached by decentralising collective bargaining and by allowing deviation from legal rules or higher-level (i.e., on the national or sectoral level) agreements by lower-level agreements (i.e., respectively on the sectoral or company level).[70] This can be observed in the memorandums of understanding (e.g., for Greece and Spain) as well as in the CSR.[71]

---

68. See Christian Wetz, *Towards a new start for social dialogue? Collective employment relations – Q1 2015*, https://www.eurofound.europa.eu/observatories/eurwork/articles/industrial-relations/towards-a-new-start-for-social-dialogue-collective-employment-relations-q1-2015 (accessed 21 July 2017); e.g., the DGB as most important German trade union confederation complained that the consultation procedures concerning the NRP 2015 were insufficient due to a lack of communication of the Federal Government and a very tight schedule set out by the framework of the European Semester that did not allow a proper involvement of the social partners, see DGB, *Stellungnahme des Deutschen Gewerkschaftsbundes zum Entwurf des Nationalen Reformprogramms Deutschland 2015*, 1 et seq, http://www.dgb.de/themen/++co++5888c824-c26b-11e4-bfa4-52540023ef1a (accessed 21 July 2017). At the same time, the DGB stressed a good practice example from France, where the government published the social partners' observations.
69. Eurofound, *Involvement of the social partners in the European Semester: 2016 update* (Publications Office of the European Union 2017).
70. Bernadette Allinger, Jörg Flecker & Christoph Hermann, *Das Ende der Pfadabhängigkeit? – Umwälzungen in den industriellen Beziehungen seit der Krise*, (1/2) Sozialer Fortschritt, 5-13 (2014); Thorsten Schulten & Torsten Müller, *A new European interventionism? The impact of the new European economic governance on wages and collective bargaining*, in David Natali & Bart Vanhercke (eds.), *Social developments in the European Union 2012* (OSE/ETUI 2013), 181-213; for an in-depth analysis, Aristea Koukiadaki, Isabel Távora & Miguel Martínez Lucio (eds), *Joint regulation and labour market policy in Europe during the crisis: a seven-country comparison*, 8-134 (ETUI 2016).
71. See Council Recommendation of 14 July 2015 on the 2015 National Reform Programme of Italy and delivering a Council opinion on the 2015 Stability Programme of Italy (2015/C 272/16), no. 19, OJ C 272, 64 and Recommendation for a Council Recommendation on the 2016 national reform programme of Italy and delivering a Council opinion on the 2016 stability programme of Italy as of 18.5.2016, COM (2016) 332 final, no. 16, 6; Recommendation for a Council Recommendation on the 2016 national reform programme of Spain and delivering a Council opinion on the 2016 stability programme of Spain as of 18.5.2016, no. 10, COM (2016) 329 final, 5; Council Recommendation of 14 July 2015 on the 2015 National Reform Programme of Portugal and delivering a Council opinion on the 2015 Stability Programme of Portugal (2015/C 272/25), OJ C 272, no. 10, 95 et seq. and Recommendation for a Council Recommendation on the 2016 national reform programme of Portugal and delivering a Council opinion on the 2016 stability programme of Portugal as of 18.5.2016, COM (2016) 342 final, no. 9, 5.

[B] Ban on Age Discrimination

When concluding collective agreements, the social partners are bound by the legal rules prohibiting age discrimination, particularly those implementing the Employment Equality Directive (2000/78/EC).[72] This does not mean that any age-specific rules in collective agreements are prohibited. Rules that apply for a certain age group are directly discriminating. Rules applying for apprentices or first-jobbers are likely to be considered indirect discrimination, because the clear majority of apprentices or employees entering the labour market consists of younger employees and in reality the rules will mainly apply to younger employees. But following Article 6(1) of the Directive, age discrimination may be justified as long as the measures follow the principle of proportionality.[73] In this regard, the CJEU seems to leave a wide range of discretion to the social partners, relying on the collective bargaining process and the social partners' ability to reconcile interests.[74] It may be questioned for good reason, if this is always the case when it comes to young people's interests.[75] More generally speaking, the grounds for justification of age discrimination by levelling down the employment conditions of younger employees are rather weak.[76] However, one would not suppose that the current legal situation actually forms an obstacle to collective bargaining with regard to young employees' matters.

[C] Trade Unions and Young Employees

When it comes to collective bargaining on young employees' matters, it also seems appropriate to give attention to the actors and especially to the trade unions. Among other factors,[77] trade union structures and functioning may also have an impact on the relatively low importance of collective bargaining with regard to young employees. First of all, it must be stressed that the fight against youth unemployment and for decent labour conditions for young employees is expressed as a major concern of trade unions. This is not only true for the European Confederation level, but can also be

---

72. ter Haar & Rönnmar, *supra* n. 58, at 16 with further references.
73. For a critical analysis on age discrimination *see also* Julén Votinius, *supra* n. 31 at 292 and 295 and Julén Votinius,*supra* n. 38 and Christa Tobler, *EU Age discrimination law and Older and Younger Workers:Cour of Justice of the European Union Case Law Development*, in Ann Numhauser-Henning & Mia Rönnmar (eds.), Age Discrimination and Labour Law. Comparative and Conceptual Perspectives in the EU and Beyond, (Kluwer Law International 2015), 93 et seq. as well as Dagmar Schiek, *Proportionality on age discrimination cases: Towards a Model Suitable for Socially Embedded Rights*, ibid. 71, 79 et seq.
74. *See* examples given by ter Haar & Rönnmar, *supra* n. 58, at 19: *Palacios de la Villa v. Cortefiel Servicios SA*, Case C-411/05, para. 68 (2007); *Rosenbladt v. Oellerking Gebäudereinigungsges. mbH*, Case C-45/09, para. 67 (2010); *Hörnfeldt v. Posten Meddelande AB*, Case C-141/11, para. 32 (2012); *Johann Odar v. Baxter Deutschland GmbH*, Case C-152/11, para. 47 (2013).
75. In this sense *see also* Bram Foubert et al., *An EU Perspective on Age as a Distinguishing Criterion for Collective Dismissal: The Case of Belgium and The Netherlands*, 29(4) International Journal of Comparative Labour Law and Industrial Relations, 416, 430 et seq. (2013); ter Haar & Rönnmar, *supra* n. 58, at 19.
76. Julén Votinius, *supra* n. 1, at 387; Malcom Sargeant, *Young Workers and Age Discrimination*, 26(4) The International Journal of Labour Law and Industrial Relations, 467, 474 (2010).
77. Vandaele, *supra* n. 14, at 16, 34.

observed in the Member States, particularly at confederation level.[78] Confederations often seem to play a more political role and to be more involved in campaigning than the single trade unions.[79] But this may vary, of course, depending on the different collective bargaining systems of the Member States.

However, the importance of young employees and their interests are not reflected in the membership structure of trade unions. Even if systematic data is still not available,[80] there is no doubt that unionisation amongst young employees is particularly weak. Unemployed people and employees on non-standard contracts are far less unionised than employees on standard contracts.[81] That said, young people in general are less unionised than older ones. The former are highly under-represented by trade unions all over Europe, regardless of the overall rate of unionisation.[82] This may be for various reasons, which can be more or less influenced by the trade unions.[83] It has been considered that 'young workers seem to be almost invariably the most problematic group of workers to unionise'.[84] Low unionisation amongst young people may depend on (little) knowledge about[85] and (negative) attitudes towards trade unions. It has been reported that young employees often do not see the personal benefits of trade union membership.[86] But it may also be a problem based on trade unions' structures, policies and communication.[87] Hence, trade unions at the European Confederation Level and in the Member States aim to attract young employees. As Vandaele put it: 'deliberative vitality – defined here as the integration and participation of young members in union life and the internal union structure – is crucial to unions.'[88] But, as young members form a minority group inside trade unions, the organisational structures to attract and represent young people still seem to be rather weak.[89] Thus, trade unions try to build new internal structures to improve young employees' representation within trade

---

78. For the example of Sweden see Rönnmar, *supra* n. 29, at 14.
79. Torsten Geelan, *Responses of trade union confederations to the youth employment crisis*, 19(3) Transfer 399, 400 (2013); Kurt Vandaele, *Youth Representatives' opinions on recruiting and representing young workers: a twofold unsatisfied demand?*, 18(3) European Journal of Industrial Relations, 203–218 (2012).
80. Dietrich, *Youth Unemployment in Europe*, FES 2012, 34 already underlined the need of systematic data in this regard.
81. Keune, *supra* n. 10, at 2.
82. See e.g., Beck & Williams, *supra* n. 65, at 9; Rönnmar, *supra* n. 29, at 3 et seq. and 15 with further references; as well as Roberto Pedersini, *Trade union strategies to recruit new groups of workers*, European Foundation for the Improvement of Living and Working Conditions, 13, www.eurofound.europa.eu/docs/eiro/tn0901028s/tn0901028s.pdf (accessed 21 July 2017) for an in-depth analysis, who stresses the exemption of Belgium, *ibid.* at 14.
83. Vandaele, *supra* n. 66, at 395 stresses the influence of the specific national-economic context.
84. Roberto Pedersini, Trade union strategies to recruit new groups of workers, European Foundation for the Improvement of Living and Working Conditions, Dublin, May, 13,
    https://www.eurofound.europa.eu/observatories/eurwork/comparative-information/trade-union-strategies-to-recruit-new-groups-of-workers (2010) (accessed 24 July 2017).
85. Vandaele, *supra* n. 66.
86. Dietrich, *supra* n. 80, at 34.
87. Vandaele, *supra* n. 66, at 384; Keune, *supra* n. 9, at 3.
88. Vandaele, *supra* n. 13, at 16.
89. Rustico & Pedersini, *supra* n. 36, at 5; Tros, *supra* n. 9, at 11 et seq.

unions and their politics and actions.⁹⁰ Various examples show that trade unions tend to attract younger employees in different ways. On the EU level, the European Trade Union Confederation (ETUC) nowadays has an established and well-set structure with its Youth Committee,⁹¹ whereas the six Trade Union Federations on the European level have far less developed and more informal youth structures.⁹²

Trade unions use different strategies to attract new members.⁹³ They may try to canvass them by special campaigns addressed to young employees' needs, and also by using new ways of communication such as social media.⁹⁴ They may approach young employees by organising exchanges about their needs and interests in structures other than the 'classical' trade union organisations.⁹⁵

But for the time being, it must be assumed that young employees do not form an important subgroup within trade unions and that trade unions' internal structures do not facilitate the promotion of their interests.⁹⁶ Naturally, trade unions tend to represent the interests of their members.⁹⁷ The target group of collective bargaining is usually labour market insiders.⁹⁸ Thus, when it comes to collective bargaining, the influence of young members is weak.⁹⁹ Most of the members and those with influence are labour market insiders,¹⁰⁰ whereas young unemployed people are outsiders.¹⁰¹ And even if the young people are already on the job, trade unions seem to rather protect the

---

90. Vandaele, *supra* n. 14, at 16-36.
91. Despite important efforts to establish and institutionalise stable structures to represent youth and the interests of young employees, this is not the case for other trade union federations on the EU level, see Kurt Vandaele, *Youth structures in six European trade union federations: a short overview*, 21 (4) Transfer, 471–476 (2015) for an in-depth analysis. Note that industriAll European Trade Union set up a youth working group in June 2016, visit https://news.industriall-europe.euhttps://news.industriall-europe.eu/p/youth1/p/youth1 for further information.
92. Vandaele, *ibid.*
93. Vandaele, *Youth representatives' opinions on recruiting and representing young workers: a twofold unsatisfied demand?*, 18(3), European Journal of Industrial Relations, 203, 210 (2012).
94. *See* Vandaele, *supra* n. 93, at 203-218. Vandaele, *supra* n. 91, at 471.
95. Recently, the European Trade Union Federations published a collection of best practices on involving young people in trade: European Federation of Building and Woodworkers (EFBWW), Just Go For It! A Compendium of Best Practices from all over Europe on Involving Young People in Trade Unions, Chiara Lorenzini (ed.), http://www.efbww.org/default.asp?Issue = 2016%20-%20Youth%20project&Language = EN (accessed 21 July 2017).
96. *See* Vandaele, *supra* n. 91, at 203, 2011; Marcus Kahmann, *Confederal youth structures and policies: The case of CGT*, December 2015 (unpublished paper, by courtesy of the author), slides 'Representing and organizing young workers: The case of the French trade union confederation CGT, September 2016' available on http://www.ires.fr/component/k2/item/5197-representing-and-organizing-young-workers-the-case-of-the-french-trade-union-confederation-cgt (accessed 21 July 2017).
97. Bernhard Ebbinghaus, Claudia Göbel & Sebastian Koos, *Mitgliedschaft in Gewerkschaften und Wirtschaftsverbänden: Inklusions- und Exklusionstendenzen in der Organisation von Arbeitnehmerinteressen in Europa*, Mannheimer Zentrum für Europäische Sozialforschung – Working Papers Nr. 111/2008, http://www.mzes.uni-mannheim.de/publications/wp/wp-111.pdf (accessed 21 July 2017) (2008).
98. Brettschneider, *supra* n. 36, at 47.
99. Vandaele, *supra* n. 66, at 396, 211.
100. Vandaele, *supra* n. 93, at 209.
101. That said, intra-generational inequalities have to be taken into account, *see* Tros & Keune, *supra* n. 8, at 12.

established position of the members with tenure/higher seniority than to facilitate the intake or redistribution in favour of younger employees. Special contract types and internships may isolate young workers[102] and even exclude them from the application of collective agreements. Hence, trade unions cannot be conceived as guarantors of achieving distributive justice between insiders and outsiders.[103] In this sense it has even been stated that trade unions' actions for insiders have negative effects when it comes to combating youth unemployment.[104] Furthermore, there have been incentives for the social partners introduced by statutory legal provisions in some Member States to bargain collectively in order to level down the working conditions for young employees, for example to lower the legal minimum wages in order to make their intake more attractive for employers.[105] But downgrading labour conditions for young employees also 'threatens' the insiders. And even if this mechanism worked and trade unions agreed on the levelling down of labour conditions, they would lose some of their appeal for young (potential) members, who might see their proper interests concerning decent working conditions being either not represented or even betrayed.

[D] Labour Market Situation

In addition, the labour market situation has been taken into account. With regard to young employees or jobseekers, employability and qualifications are often described as problems and possible reasons for unemployment. Early school dropout, low levels of education, problems with school-to-work transition and also skills mismatch are major concerns in this regard.[106] A lack of qualifications aggravates individual risks to young employees and negatively influences their chances on the labour market. However, the problem cannot solely be described from an individual perspective.[107] But it must be stressed – as the numerous initiatives at EU and Member State level do – that the problem also has structural aspects. Thus, reforms in the educational systems, particularly secondary education and initial VET, seem crucial. It cannot be doubted that the involvement of the social partners in approaching these tasks is a necessary but not sufficient condition. Parts of the problems may be addressed by collective bargaining and collective agreements; others need state-driven remedies, i.e., the structures, functioning and funding of public employment services.[108]

---

102. Daniele Di Nunzio, *Working conditions and changes in production processes*, in: Daniele Di Nunzio (ed.), *Young people at risk: how changes in work are affecting young Italians' health and safety*, ETUI Report 129, (2013), 10,
103. Andreas Sachs & Werner Smolny, *Youth Unemployment in the OECD: The Role of Institutions*; 235(4 + 5) Jahrbücher f. Nationalökonomie u. Statistik, 403, 405 (Lucius & Lucius, Stuttgart 2015).
104. *Id.* at 412, 415.
105. Schulten & Müller, *supra* n. 71, passim.
106. *See also* Dietrich, *supra* n. 5, at 312 with further references.
107. Julén Votinius, *supra* n. 1, at 373 et seq.
108. Joachim Möller & Hans Dietrich, *Youth unemployment in Europe – business cycle and institutional effects*, (1)13 International Economics and Economic Policy, 5, 22 (2016).

Moreover, only considering the supply side of the labour market, i.e., the young employees as part of the labour force, would draw an incomplete picture.[109] The employers' side has little motivation to bargain collectively with regard to young employees as long as there is no profit or need.[110] In times of high labour supply with high youth and overall unemployment rates, the possible profits of collective bargaining on young employees' matters for the employers' side seem limited. It may become attractive if it helps to get the qualifications that are needed or if it makes employment more cost-effective and flexible, i.e., by downgrading labour conditions, especially wages.[111] The latter only works when the legal frame allows it to do so.

§16.05 OTHER OPTIONS FOR SOCIAL PARTNERS' INVOLVEMENT

With regard to European policies, it seems that collective bargaining is not as relevant as other forms of social partner activities, at least concerning young employees' matters. Other ways of involving social partners may have become more important. This means, especially, consultation processes and the participation in tripartite commissions or committees. An example can be taken from Portugal, where the social partners are members of the tripartite Economic and Social Council (ESC) and the Social Concertation Standing Committee (SPSC).[112] Other institutionalised forms of tripartite co-operation can also be found in the Netherlands, such as the Social and Economic Council (SER) that has advised the government since its establishment in 1950.[113] Rather than governing themselves in the framework of collective bargaining and 'traditional' collective agreements, social partners are involved in the policy-making process and the application of state law, also with regard to young employees' matters,[114] e.g., the implementation of the EYG.[115]

But this brings new challenges for the social partners: they are placed outside the conventional framework of labour law, as there are weak or non-existent legal foundations to these activities. Traditional modes of actions developed for traditional collective bargaining may not be appropriate. And furthermore, the outcomes of consultation processes are usually not legally binding, unless explicitly foreseen by

---

109. Bussi & Geyer, *supra* n. 21, at 42.
110. *See also* Ales, *supra* n. 61, 122, 125 analysing the changing perception of the employers' role in European Employment policies.
111. *See* for the example of Greece, Papadopoulos, *supra* n. 15, at 415.
112. Isabel Távora & Pilar González, *The reform of joint regulation and labour market policy during the current crisis: national report on Portugal*, in Aristea Koukiadaki, Isabel Távora & Miguel Martínez Lucio (eds.), *Joint regulation and labour market policy in Europe during the crisis*, 321, 324 (ETUI 2016).
113. https://www.ser.nl/en/~/media/files/internet/talen/engels/jaarverslagen/annual-report-20 14.ashx (accessed 21 July 2017).
114. Kurt Vandaele, *supra* n. 65, at 395.
115. ETUC, The Youth Guarantee in Europe, https://www.etuc.org/sites/www.etuc.org/files/ circular/files/etuc_-_the_youth_guarantee_in_europe_en_0.pdf (accessed 21 July 2017) (2014); Verónica Escudero & Elva López Mourelo, *The Youth Guarantee programme in Europe: Features, implementation and challenges*, ILO Research Department Working Paper No. 4 (2015), http://www.ilo.org/wcmsp5/groups/public/---dgreports/---inst/documents/publica tion/wcms_393024.pdf (accessed 21 July 2017), 11.

national legislation. As a consequence, it is much more challenging to promote these activities to union members.[116]

§16.06 CONCLUSIONS

Collective bargaining with regard to young employees' matters can be considered circumstantial. It seems to be complex and difficult to produce win-win situations in reconciling employers' and trade unions' interests. As long as employers do not experience any need in terms of qualifications or attractive labour conditions for young employees, and see their needs fulfilled by the supply side of the labour market, there is little motivation for them to collectively bargain on these matters. On the other hand, it might be attractive for employers to collectively bargain to downgrade labour conditions for young workers, which is particularly unattractive and might be counterproductive for trade unions. The social partners' scope for action might be limited in terms of the current European political and legal framework. However, facing the risks of young employees in the labour market by contributing to qualification and good quality employment opportunities for young employees can be considered crucial for the future of social partnership.

---

116. *See* also John Geary, *Economic crisis, austerity and trade union responses: The Irish case in comparative perspective*, 22(2) European Journal of Industrial Relations 131,142 (2016) with further references.

PART III   Expanding Spaces and New
            Boundaries of Collective
                  Agreements

CHAPTER 17
Collective Autonomy for On-Demand Workers? Normative Arguments, Current Practices and Legal Ways Forward

Auriane Lamine & Jeremias Prassl

§17.01 INTRODUCTION

The development of the digital economy has brought about advantages for workers and consumers alike – as well as new forms of employment vulnerabilities, from job insecurity to low wages and precarious working conditions. A quickly growing body of scholarship has begun to explore the practical implications of digitally mediated on-demand work, as well as potential legal responses – often with a focus on fundamental questions such as the scope of employment. Other questions are slower off the mark: on-demand workers' interests are hardly represented in the traditional industrial relations systems and institutions. This is the central focus of our contribution: *Should on-demand workers enjoy broader collective autonomy? And if so, how could this objective be achieved?* In this paper, we question the opportunity of developing institutional and/or legal arrangements to allow on-demand workers to join forces and participate more directly in the definition of their work experience and conditions, and reflect upon the features that such arrangements should entail.

This paper is interested in the legal situation of 'on-demand' or 'gig' workers: individuals who carry out their activities via a web platform or mobile app which is connecting them to their clients. Their employment status is either 'non-standard' as defined by the ILO[1] (temporary, part-time, involving multiple parties) or 'unclear' or

---

1. ILO, *Non-standard employment around the world: Understanding challenges, shaping prospects*, Geneva: ILO. November 2016, http://www.ilo.org/wcmsp5/groups/public/---dgreports/---dcomm/---publ/documents/publication/wcms_534326.pdf (accessed 7 August 2017).

'indeterminate', not least because they are often operating under contractual self-employed status, while actually exerting their activities in very constrained conditions (bogus, economically dependent or vulnerable self-employed workers).[2] In our analysis, we opt for a broad definition of collective autonomy, including worker organisation in all of its forms, collective bargaining, collective action, as well as various forms of participation in the governance of economic activities. Collective autonomy can thus be supported by many mechanisms and devices, some inspired by past arrangements or by some currently in force, others to be imagined afresh. The current legal and institutional environment might at first glance appear to be largely detrimental to the development of the collective autonomy of on-demand workers. The nature of their activities often isolates them from other workers, which hampers possible organisation, and legal obstacles stand in the way of collective action by (genuinely) independent contractors. This makes an analysis of potential opportunities to design new categories and measures conducive to collective autonomy all the more relevant and timely.

But it is not just the emergence of potentially new forms of work organisation which present a challenge: received labour and employment law structures from around the world are not necessarily favourable to this increased participation, either. They were built around a traditional figure of the worker which tends to become less and less dominant, the 'standard worker', employed full time and for an indefinite duration by one (and often only one) employer exerting exclusive authority. Representative organisations of workers are not used to, and sometimes reluctant to, represent atypical workers, not least because they might not want to support what could be perceived as an undesirable casualisation of work. Moreover, some public authorities are favourable to the development of so-called disruptive businesses which claim that the innovative nature of their products and services justifies the circumvention of existing rules. As a consequence, on-demand economy operators are frequently opposed to any measure that would stand in the way of their further growth. The collective organisation of gig economy workers, including for example attempts to bargain and impose minimum levels of remuneration by clients, might furthermore be considered to be contrary to competition or antitrust law.[3]

How, if at all, can we make the case for collective autonomy in a platform-based labour market? Given the manifold difficulties – practical, legal, philosophical – which face any attempts at replying to this question, two strands of analysis run intertwined through our piece: a theoretical exposition of different normative arguments in favour of on-demand economy workers' collective organisation, and a practical discussion of

---

2. Note that these last forms are also considered as 'non-standard' by the ILO (*id.*).
3. *FNV Kunsten*, Case C-413/13, ECJ 4 December 2014; V. De Stefano, *Non-standard workers and freedom of association: a critical analysis of restrictions to collective rights from a human rights perspective*, WP CSDLE 'Massimo D'Antona', no. 123/2015, on how legal frameworks are detrimental to the exercise, by non-standard workers, of their collective rights. They should be, according to the author, considered as human rights and thus recognized to every category of worker, whether standard or non-standard (http://csdle.lex.unict.it/Archive/WP/WP%20CSDLE%20M%20DANTONA/WP%20CSDLE%20M%20DANTONA-INT/20151111-040547_destefano_n123-2015intpdf.pdf (accessed 7 August 2017)).

how each approach under scrutiny may be translated into practice. In the former strand, we focus on the question of how different avenues to build new legal arrangements in support of on-demand workers' collective autonomy could be justified in principle. This is done by taking inspiration from several dominant schools of political theory and ethics. We consider a number of such approaches in turn, using the normative principles they develop to formulate arguments for or against the design of these arrangements, before exploring existing and potential avenues for collective representation.

To this end, discussion in the remaining sections is structured as follows: a first part briefly explores the practical challenges currently faced by those seeking to organise on-demand workers, from physical obstacles to legal pitfalls, and explains the aims and methods of our underlying normative approach. A second part then explores a number of theoretical approaches – from utilitarian and libertarian thinking to Marx and Rawls, through to more recent discourses about justice and democracy – and highlights practices developed by on-demand workers, public authorities, and even on-demand platform operators themselves which could be seen to chime with each theoretical approach.

Given present space limitations, it is important to note that neither strand, let alone our overall conclusions, claim to be anywhere near comprehensive: our goal is merely to adopt a more experimental perspective, grounding emerging practices in theoretical frameworks, and trying to project how future arrangements could take shape given the specific situation and constraints faced by on-demand workers.

§17.02 COLLECTIVE AUTONOMY FOR THE ON-DEMAND WORKER? EXPLORING THE PRACTICAL CHALLENGES

The on-demand economy is amongst the least-organised sectors in modern labour markets. The potential reasons behind this are numerous, but may loosely be grouped into two categories: practical challenges in organising workers whose shifts are intermittent and often geographically dispersed, and legal difficulties arising in competition or antitrust law given most individuals' (alleged) self-employment status.

[A] Practical Challenges

The reality of work for those labouring for a wide range of on-demand economy platforms has quickly become the subject of multiple academic and journalistic enquiries.[4] Experiences vary – unsurprisingly, perhaps, given the vast heterogeneity of self-employment and individuals' motivations to engage in gig work – but many constants of direct relevance to collective organisation emerge.

First, and foremost, there is the nature of the work: gig work is by definition intermittent, and often geographically dispersed. With online platforms connecting workers and consumers as and when jobs are required, there are no clear shift patterns:

---

4. See, for example, J. Prassl, *Humans as a Service* (OUP forthcoming 2017).

with them are gone the historically significant moments before and after work when organisers might have put their case to prospective members. The same is true for the workplace itself: in the case of platforms where work is completed and delivered online, workforces can be truly global – indeed, as a recent report by the Oxford Internet Institute finds, platform work 'is becoming increasingly important to workers living in low- and middle-income countries.'[5] Even where service provision is localised, such as in the case of transportation or delivery apps, workers will usually wait for their next task dispersed around the city.

The vast heterogeneity in gig workers adds further difficulty for organisers, who might be interacting with individuals motivated by very different reasons: compare the difference between part- and full-time workers, for example; or the reasons motivating those engaging in occasional work to earn top up income and those trying to make a living from the on-demand economy.[6] The cost of union membership, particularly early on when few if any tangible benefits are available, can be prohibitive or at least act as a strong deterrent for those struggling at the very bottom of the wage distribution. Many operators, finally, are unsurprisingly hostile to any efforts at organising genuinely independent worker representation, trying to dissuade workers from signing up to collective representation efforts: when unionisation was on the cards in Seattle, Uber's call centre representatives were instructed to call drivers to 'share some thoughts' about how 'collective bargaining and unionization do not fit the characteristics of how most partners use the Uber platform'.[7]

[B] Legal Challenges

Even if some or all of these practical obstacles were overcome, however, legal difficulties lurk in the form of antitrust or competition law. The specific details vary across jurisdictions, but the essence of the problem can nonetheless be summarised: nearly all platform operators insist in their contractual terms and conditions that they are not service providers with employees, but rather mere intermediaries connecting independent businesses with customers. On that analysis, attempts to organise on-demand economy workers with a view to collectively bargaining over wages and other terms and conditions could be seen as anticompetitive behaviour: genuinely independent business are not generally allowed to collude with each other when it comes to negotiations with suppliers and other business partners.

The challenges thus appear manifold. Indeed, as NYT correspondent Steven Greenhouse notes, 'In many ways, digital on-demand workers face far more obstacles

---

5. M. Graham, V. Lehdonvirta, A. Wood, H. Barnard, I., Hjorth, I., D.P. Simon, *The Risks and Rewards of Online Gig Work at the Global Margins* (Oxford: Oxford Internet Institute, 2017). (Electronic version available at: https://www.oii.ox.ac.uk/publications/gigwork.pdf (accessed 7 August 2017) 1-2.
6. S. Greenhouse, *On demand, and demanding their rights*, American Prospect (28 June 2016), http://prospect.org/article/demand-and-demanding-their-rights (accessed 7 August 2017).
7. A. Griswold, *This is the script Uber is using to make anti-union phone calls to drivers in Seattle*, Quartz (22 February 2016), http://qz.com/621977/this-is-the-script-uber-is-using-to-make-anti-union-phone-calls-to-drivers-in-seattle/ (accessed 7 August 2017).

to organising and being heard than workers in the traditional economy.'[8] At the same time as highlighting these problems, however, it is crucial not to see them as overwhelmingly determinative of the collective autonomy question: subsequent sections will focus extensively on innovative solutions designed to overcome many of the practical problems involved. From a legal perspective, even competition or antitrust law may pose less of a challenge than appears at first. The prohibitions on coordination and price setting only apply to *genuinely* independent business. As the Court of Justice of the European recently highlighted, competition law will not stand in the way of:

> dialogue between management and labour if the service providers, in the name and on behalf of whom the trade union negotiated, are in fact 'false self-employed', that is to say, service providers in a situation comparable to that of employees.[9]

The question of (false) self-employment in the on-demand economy is beyond the scope of the present discussion. Suffice it to say, however, that courts around the world are increasingly beginning to disregard platforms' contractual fine print which stipulates that workers are self-employment, given the realities of close control in many arrangements. As a UK employment tribunal concluded in 2016, for example, the 'notion that Uber in London is a mosaic of 30,000 small businesses linked by a common "platform" is to our minds faintly ridiculous'.[10]

§17.03 COLLECTIVE AUTONOMY FOR THE ON-DEMAND WORKER? BUILDING NORMATIVE ARGUMENTS

[A] Aim and Method

Having considered the range of potential obstacles to the collective organisation of on-demand economy workers, we now turn to exploring potential solutions. Writing in 2016, Samuel Engblom of Sweden's Trade Union Confederation TCO noted that the 'Empowerment of gig economy workers can be both collective and individual.'[11] Given the overall focus of this volume, we are particularly interested in exploring the latter of these dimensions (even though some elements of collective empowerment will of course translate into the individual sphere of employment law). Before turning to specific examples, however, we should briefly explain our theoretical approach: rather than merely focusing on *how* different models of organising gig workers might operate, we also hope to dwell on the question *why* it is that support for their collective autonomy might be desirable.

To this end, in the first paragraphs of each following section, we hope to tackle our core question from a normative standpoint: *is it desirable to develop institutional*

---

8. S. Greenhouse, *supra* n. 6.
9. *FNV Kunsten, supra* n. 3, at paragraph 31.
10. *Aslam et al. v. Uber* [2016], https://www.judiciary.gov.uk/wp-content/uploads/2016/10/aslam-and-farrar-v-uber-reasons-20161028.pdf (accessed 7 August 2017), paragraph 90.
11. S. Engblom, *Atypical Work in the Digital Age – Trade Union Strategies for the Gig Economy*, in M. Rönnmar, and J. Julén Voitinius (eds), *Festskrift till Ann Numhauser-Henning*, (Lund: Juristförlaget i Lund, 2017).

and/or legal frameworks to foster on-demand workers' collective autonomy, their ability to participate more actively in the definition of their tasks and working context? Following the method developed by P. Van Parijs and C. Ansperger,[12] we hope to build arguments to answer this question, based on the principles of justice developed in four classical traditions of political theory. To complement our lines of argumentation, we offer references to ongoing research work and examples of emerging practices of organisation among on-demand workers. Some of these illustrations are primarily intended to support our normative claims, others to show the diversified and sometimes disruptive shapes our theoretical ideas could take when put in practice.

None of the arguments developed below are exhaustive (the complexity and heterogeneity of digital economy practices could not be reflected in such a short paper) nor can they lead to a definitive conclusion. Further economic and sociological analysis is required to test the validity of the ideas put forward. Our goal is simply to start a conversation in which legal scholars and others might take an active part in the coming years.

[B] A Utilitarian Argument

> 'Nature has placed mankind under the governance of two sovereign masters, *pain* and *pleasure*. It is for them alone to point out what we ought to do, as well as to determine what we shall do.'[13]
>
> 'An action then may be said to be conformable to the principle of utility, or, for shortness sake, to utility (meaning with respect to the community at large) when the tendency it had to augment the happiness of the community is greater than any it has to diminish it.'[14]
>
> 'The best state for human nature is that in which, while no one is poor, no one desires to be richer, nor has any reason to fear being thrust back by the efforts of others to push themselves forward'.[15]

What matters most for utilitarian authors is the greatest happiness of a society, or its 'utility'. They would thus favour any solution that maximised people's pleasure and reduced their pain. The more just solution to a given issue would thus be one which increases the happiness of a majority of the population, even if this implies that some, a minority, will be in a worse off situation. Under this model, to evaluate the quality of a given decision or choice requires looking at its material consequences. The choice

---

12. This method is introduced in a book: C. Arnsperger & P. Van Parijs, *Ethique économique et sociale* (Paris: La Découverte, 2003). It is implemented in the different classes composing the Certificate in applied ethics offered by the Hoover Chair of economic and social ethics of the Université of Louvain. (https://uclouvain.be/fr/facultes/espo/hoover/certificat-en-ethique.html accessed 7 August 2017).
13. J. Bentham, *An introduction to the principles of morals and legislation*, J. H. Burns and H. L. Hart (ed), *The collected works of Jeremy Bentham*, (London: University of London Athlone Press, 1970): 11, no. 1. (first pub. 1789).
14. J. Bentham, *id.*, 12, no. 6.
15. J.S. Mill, *Principles of Political Economy* (1848), Book IV, Chapter VI, §2 *in fine*, http://www.econlib.org/library/Mill/mlP61.html (accessed 7 August 2017).

that produces the most profitable effects will be preferred to any other one. Institutionalising the collective autonomy of on-demand workers, allowing them to have a broader influence on the definition of their working conditions would likely place them in a more favourable situation. The increase in well-being would be manifold: possibility to obtain a better remuneration for their services and extra protections (insurances, limits to working hours, guarantees of payment, …); feeling of empowerment as they are able exert stronger control on their own jobs and to participate in the definition of the purposes of this activity.

Take, for example, the recent efforts by Austrian cycle couriers working for food delivery platform Foodora in Vienna. When the platform first arrived in the autumn of 2015, most couriers were directly employed, felt closely involved in the operations of the company, and enjoyed perks such as access to a local garage which served as a place to look after each others' bikes and meet before and after work. Some time later, however, things began to changes: permanent staff were dismissed, others reclassified as independent contractors; the garage was shut and communications began to break down.[16] It was as a result of these changes that the couriers elected a works council ('Betriebsrat') to (re-) engage with their employer – who was surprisingly supportive: after some initial doubts, local Foodora management was happy to engage with the works council, recognising the potential benefits of social dialogue to both sides.[17] The election of a works council was merely the first step in this direction: in cooperation with the employer, next planned steps include a works agreement, potentially leading to sectoral collective negotiations.[18] This gain realised through the exercise of collective autonomy, however, has to be balanced with the losses that such measures would create for the other members of the community. At least two groups would disapprove. First, the shareholders of the intermediaries (in particular, online platforms or app businesses) might lose a part of their benefits, at least in the short term: if gig workers are in a situation to obtain more from clients and from platforms through the use of their collective autonomy, it is likely that platform owners will get a lesser share of the intermediaries' earnings. Second, the numerous users of these services would probably have to pay more money to afford the same services. Consequently, some might decide to stop using them, to the detriment of both intermediaries and on-demand workers. At first sight, a utilitarian perspective might lead us to favour an institutional solution which does not foster the collective freedoms of demand workers, even if this leads to a further deterioration of their personal situation.

But the reasoning might lead us elsewhere, even on exclusively utilitarian terms, if we decide to evaluate not only the short-term but also the medium term and

---

16. J. Redl, *Warum bekommt foodora jetzt einen betriebsrat frau siegl*, Falter (19 April 2017), https://www.falter.at/archiv/FALTER_2017041930FD6DCA17/warum-bekommt-foodora-jetzt-einen-betriebsrat-frau-siegl (accessed 7 August 2017).
17. A.P.A. *Foodora Zusteller in Oesterreich gruenden Betriebsrat*, Die Presse (12 April 2017), http://diepresse.com/home/wirtschaft/unternehmen/5199850/FoodoraZusteller-in-Oesterreich-gruenden-Betriebsrat (accessed 7 August 2017).
18. X., *Betriebsrat fuer fahrradzustelldienst foodora*, Vida (12 April 2017) http://www.vida.at/cms/S03/S03_20.a/1342577497037/wien/betriebsrat-fuer-fahrradzustelldienst-foodora (accessed 7 August 2017).

long-term consequences that such a choice would entail. This is true for at least four reasons. First, despite their high financial valuations, some platforms and intermediaries are not profitable.[19] Their business model appears unsustainable even though most of intermediaries own almost no assets, that they have freed themselves from a lot of legal constraints, and they are gradually lowering their labour costs.[20] If the platform economy is contributing to the development of financial market bubbles,[21] then it might be that the real threat for shareholders does not come from an empowerment of its workers. Transportation economist Hubert Horan has been amongst the most prominent critics of the gig economy's underlying financial model. Using transportation platform Uber as an example, he notes how 'the staggering $13 billion in cash its investors provided is consistent with the magnitude of funding required to subsidise the many years of predatory competition required to drive out more efficient incumbents.'[22] Second, the number of on-demand workers, as well as other 'non-standard' workers, is increasing.[23] In the long run, they might no longer represent a minority of the workforce anymore, thus significantly tilting the cost versus benefit calculus.

---

19. The example of Uber is particularly significant. In April 2017, Uber disclosed its financials to Bloomberg for the first time: E. Newcomer, *Uber, Lifting Financial Veil, Says Sales Growth Outpaces Losses*, Bloomberg (14 April 2017), https://www.bloomberg.com/news/articles/2017-04-14/embattled-uber-reports-strong-sales-growth-as-losses-continue (accessed 7 August 2017). The numbers reveal that the company is still not profitable after eight years, despite its valuation at some $70 billion on private markets. Net losses for 2016 amounted to $2.8 billion. It is impossible to predict if Uber's business will end up being a success or a failure. However, despite its current impressive growth in revenue and capacity to attract investors, its financial situation and business strategy cast some doubts about its capacity to reach the level of profitability and be in a situation to pay back its investors. Its strategy consists in expanding its market share by eliminating competitors at high costs – by offering temporarily unbeatable prices to consumers – while owning almost no private assets and conducting limited R&D. The announced arrival on the market of autonomous cars along with the numerous scandals and suits in which Uber is involved, might constitute additional threats for their model. Uber's financial strategy has recently been compared to a 'Ponzi scheme': J. Sier, *Magellan's Hamish Douglass says Uber is a 'Ponzi scheme'*, Sydney Morning Herald (24 May 2017) http://www.smh.com.au/business/markets/magellans-hamish-douglass-says-uber-is-a-ponzi-scheme-20170523-gwb701.html (accessed 7 August 2017).
20. For example the opinion of S. Fabode, *Why companies like lyft, uber, postmates, instacart etc will never be profitable*, Hackernoon.com (2 March 2017) https://hackernoon.com/why-companies-like-lyft-uber-postmates-instacart-etc-will-never-be-profitable-ecdfde647175 (accessed 7 August 2017).
21. For example the opinion of S. Rajaraman, *The on-demand economy is a bubble and it is about to burst*, Quartz (28 April 2017), https://qz.com/967474/the-on-demand-economy-is-a-bubble-and-its-about-to-burst/ (accessed 7 August 2017).
22. Y. Smith, *Can Uber Ever Deliver – part 4*, Naked Capitalism (2016), http://www.nakedcapitalism.com/2016/12/can-uber-ever-deliver-part-four-understanding-that-unregulated-monopoly-was-always-ubers-central-objective.html. (accessed 7 August 2017). Monopoly concerns have been raised by a number of commentators, see e.g., also F. Pasquale, Two Narratives of Platform Capitalism, 35 Yale Law & Policy Review, 309 (2016): 316 for concerns that first-mover advantages and luck might thus be entrenched (and sources quoted there); though not everyone agrees, e.g., J. Meyer, *Uber is not (and will never be) a monopoly*, Forbes (15 February 2016) https://www.forbes.com/sites/jaredmeyer/2016/02/15/uber-guardian-not-monopoly-ridesharing/#2f4e6c377932 (accessed 7 August 2017).
23. ILO, *ILO: Non-standard forms of employment, a feature of the contemporary world of work*, ILO Newsroom (14 November 2016) http://www.ilo.org/global/about-the-ilo/newsroom/news/WCMS_534122/lang--en/index.htm (accessed 7 August 2017).

Third, some intermediaries of the gig economy are connecting peers to other peers. In these models, workers are also users, therefore solutions that would empower them as workers would also have a clear, positive impact on consumers. Finally, and most importantly, one positive impact of the association of on-demand workers is that they will be able to demand access to the benefits of private or public risk pooling mechanisms, or even to develop similar mechanisms of their own.[24] The benefit of a private health insurance might reduce public expenditure that would have otherwise been incurred to ensure workers' well-being. More importantly, a rise in pay would likely result in a correlative increase in tax income (as well as social security contributions where applicable), which will serve the interests not only of the on-demand workers but of all employees, or of whole national communities.

Viewed from a utilitarian perspective, there are thus a number of indicators in clear support of collective autonomy: any improvement of on-demand workers' situation, through the development of representation or participation devices, might increase everyone's utility. This leaves open an empirical question as to the quantification of the various costs and benefits indicated: but that is not necessarily discouraging. As Paul Davies has highlighted, 'the efficiency of employee governance is highly sensitive to both the overall configuration of the mechanisms for employee voice in the company and, probably, to society co-ordination mechanisms existing outside the company.'[25] The specifics of local arrangements matter, in other words – but the overall utilitarian case could well be proven empirically.

[C]   **A Libertarian Argument**

> 'A society that does not recognize that each individual has values of his own which he is entitled to follow can have no respect for the dignity of the individual and cannot really know freedom.'[26]
>
> 'Equality of the general rules of law and conduct (...) is the only kind of equality conducive to liberty and the only equality which we can secure without destroying liberty. Not only has liberty nothing to do with any other sort of equality, but it is even bound to produce inequality in many respects. This is the necessary result and part of the justification of individual liberty: If the result of individual liberty did not demonstrate that some manners of living are more successful than others, much of the case for it would vanish.'[27]
>
> '1. A person who acquires a holding in accordance with the principle of justice in acquisition is entitled to that holding.
>
> 2. A person who acquires a holding in accordance with the principle of justice in transfer, from someone else entitled to the holding, is entitled to the holding.

---

24. D. Hemel, *Pooling and Unpooling in the Uber Economy*, University of Chicago Legal Form (forthcoming 2017).
25. P.L. Davies, *Efficiency Arguments for Collective Representation of Workers: A Sketch*, in A. Bogg, C. Costello, A. Davies and J. Prassl (eds), *The Autonomy of Labour Law*, 395 (Oxford: Hart Publishing, 2015).
26. F. Hayek, *The Constitution of Liberty* (London & New York: Routledge, 2006): Chapter 5, p. 70. (First pub. in 1960).
27. F. Hayek, *id.*, Chapter 6, p. 75.

3. No one is entitled to a holding except by (repeated) applications of 1 and 2.'[28]

'Our main conclusions about the state are that a minimal state, limited, to the narrow functions of protection against force, theft, fraud, enforcement of contracts, and so on, is justified, but any more extensive state will violate persons' rights not to be forced to do certain things, and is unjustified; and that the minimal state is inspiring as well as right.'[29]

Though different schools can be identified in the libertarian tradition, all its proponents would agree on this principle: a just regulatory approach to the on-demand economy would be one that is compatible with each person's autonomy and more particularly, her ability of self-determination. Libertarians will thus generally favour a system of rights and institutions which ensure that the exercise of this individual freedom is not unduly restricted by State action or by other individuals. This requires the recognition of basic liberties such as freedom of expression, religion, association and the protection of rightfully acquired property and against physical harm.

Based on these premises, it could be argued that on-demand workers are simply exerting their fundamental freedoms (whether or not already recognised in the law in force) if they were to come together and bargain in the defence of their interests. A legal system allowing these freedoms to be exerted without constraints and on a more equal footing with their economic counterparts, would thus be welcomed on libertarian grounds.

However, one would then have to determine whether the promotion of on-demand workers's freedoms does not result in an undesirable attack on other actors' rights. First, one could say that the current situation (i.e., a situation where the autonomy of on-demand workers is absent or at best, very limited) is the only one compatible with the platforms' and their shareholders' rightly acquired property rights which risk being deteriorated in case this autonomy is freed from constraints. The same goes for the freedom of clients to use a large range of services, including especially cheaper ones.

However the platform does not, more than 'typical employers', own its workforce. Most of the time, as noted earlier, it does not even own the means of production or service. Contrary to capital or land owners who should be allowed to, according to most libertarians, use their goods without limitation, platforms do not own a right to treat their workforce as they please. Second, it does not seem that the right to property of the shareholders of intermediary businesses are threatened: they are still free to make use of their capital as they see fit, even if the investment context is slightly changed. Clients are similarly still free to spend their money as they wish, even if services are more expensive on average. Indeed, even from a libertarian perspective one could also argue that the financial benefits (of gig economy managers, shareholders or consumers) have not been fairly acquired if the underlying business model is

---

28. R. Nozick, *Anarchy State and Utopia*, (Philadelphia: Basic Books, 1974): Chapter 7, section 1, p. 151.
29. R. Nozick, *Anarchy, State, and Utopia, id.*, Preface, p. ix.

designed in violation of workers' autonomy.[30] Some liberals would add that the collective setting of a shared minimum floor of protections for on-demand workers, is favourable to a smooth functioning of the market and to fair competition which does not impair participants' most basic rights.[31] In all three cases mentioned above, fundamental freedoms of all other actors do not seem to be challenged by the fact that broader autonomy is recognised to on-demand workers.

Libertarian authors have not only advocated for the promotion of individual freedoms. Most of the time, they have defended in parallel a particular, minimalist, conception of the state. They would thus favour solutions to market failures with as little state intervention as possible. This does not mean that there is no space for collective autonomy. On the contrary, in some cases, collective autonomy might benefit from the inertia of public authorities (especially as opposed to interventions banning the exercise of such autonomy – *see supra*, remarks on legal constraints), at least initially, and workers are incentivised to act in common when national law is silent. UK lawyers may well recognise a variant of this approach, for example, given the country's historical experience with little state intervention during years of *Collective Laissez Faire*.[32] Much more recently, we can find a number of examples where platforms themselves have engaged with workers (or 'partners') to set up collective structures of sorts – beyond the boundaries of traditional trade unionism.

In the early summer of 2016, for example, Uber announced the creation of the 'Independent Drivers Guild', a new organisation dedicated to the collective representation of drivers' interests vis-à-vis the platform. The setup included several elements instantly familiar to students of collective labour law: driver representatives were offered monthly meetings with management to raise and discuss members' issues, and individuals in dispute with the company over 'deactivation' (firing) can request that a guild member join them during hearings.[33] The Guild is also working actively towards using the combined purchasing power of its members to negotiate better deals for key services including insurance and legal protection, and actively engages in lobbying local law-makers to create a basic floor of rights for drivers.[34]

---

30. 'Some people steal from others, or defraud them, or enslave them, seizing their product and preventing them from living as they choose, or forcibly exclude others from competing in exchanges. None of these are permissible modes of transition from one situation to another. (R. Nozick, *supra* n. 28, p. 152) or 'Seizing the results of someone's labor is equivalent to seizing hours from him and directing him to carry on various activities' (R. Nozick, *supra* n. 28, p. 160 (Chapter 7, distributive justice), though he was here referring to the process of taxation... Actually, Nozick is known to have taken stances in favour of non-coercive agreed upon slave-like contracts (*Idem*, p. 33). For a critique of this position based on its rejection of the fundamental idea of inalienable rights, which cannot be waived by a simple consent: D. Ellerman, *Translatio versus Concessio: Retrieving the Debate about Contracts of Alienation with an Application to Today's Employment Contract*, Politics and Society, 453-454 (September 2005).
31. F.H. Knight, *The Sickness of Liberal Society*, 2 Ethics, 91-93 (1946).
32. O Kahn-Freund, *Legal Framework*, in A Flanders and H Clegg (eds), *The System of Industrial Relations in Great Britain* (Oxford: Blackwell, 1954).
33. N. Scheiber and M. Isaac, *Uber Recognizes New York Drivers' Group, Short of a Union*, NY Times (10 May 2016), https://www.nytimes.com/2016/05/11/technology/uber-agrees-to-union-deal-in-new-york.html (accessed 7 August 2017).
34. Website of the Independent Drivers Guild: https://drivingguild.org/idg-benefits/ (accessed 7 August 2017).

That said, a purely market-driven system will also have a number of drawbacks: not least, because the precise nature of the arrangement will depend on parties' relative bargaining power, which will usually be slanted in favour of the on-demand platform. The Independent Drivers Guild, for example, explicitly lacks any power to engage in collective bargaining over wages or other working conditions, let alone the ability to threaten or organise industrial action to shore up any demands. As the New York Times reported less than a year after the guild's foundation, 'the group's relationship with Uber has also inspired considerable suspicion among labor leaders, activists and experts.'[35]

Another way in which libertarian arguments could be linked to collective action in the gig economy (albeit from a consumer, rather than a worker, perspective) is through certification schemes: moves towards deregulation often suggest that legal regulation (state-mandated choices) be replaced with consumer choice. In the context on on-demand work, this could be achieved through a certification regime not unlike the 'FairTrade' movement for goods. Trade Unions or other independent operators could develop a set of standards to evaluate and certify platform operators who comply with their legal obligations (or, in a tiered system, voluntarily go beyond them). This information could then be advertised prominently on the platform itself, alerting consumers to the fact that its services comply with the relevant standards. In a world of increasing cross-platform competition, where multiple operators compete to offer very similar services, consumer choice could quickly drive a re-thinking amongst platforms. In the short run, certification processes could even be combined with other assistance to on-demand economy workers, along the lines of the Independent Drivers' Guild services just seen. Germany's IG Metall, for example, has been closely involved in the creation of *FairCrowdWork Watch*, a site which allows workers to rate different platforms' working conditions, compare payment rates, and access basic legal advice.[36]

[D]   A Marxist Argument

> 'All these consequences are implied in the statement that the worker is related to the *product of his labour* as to an alien object. (...) The worker puts his life into the object, but now his life then belongs no longer to him but to the object. Hence, the greater his activity, the more the worker lacks objects. Whatever the product of his labor is, he is not. Therefore, the greater this product, the less is he himself. The alienation of the worker in his product means not only that his labor becomes an object, an external existence, but that it exists outside him, independently, as something alien to him, and that it becomes a power on its own confronting him.

---

35. N. Scheiber, *Uber Has a Union of Sorts, but Faces Doubts on Its Autonomy*, NY Times (12 May 2017), https://www.nytimes.com/2017/05/12/business/economy/uber-drivers-union.html (accessed 7 August 2017).
36. http://www.faircrowdwork.org/en/watch (accessed 7 August 2017).

It means that the life which he has conferred on the object confronts him as something hostile and alien.'[37]

'A class of labourers, who live only so long as they find work, and who find work only so long as their labour increase capital. These labourers, who must sell themselves piecemeal, are a commodity, like every other article of commerce, and are consequently exposed to all the vicissitudes of competition, to all the fluctuations of the market. (...) He becomes an appendage of the machine, and it is only the most simple, most monotonous, and most easily acquired knack, that is required of him. Hence, the cost of production of a workman is restricted, almost entirely, to the means of subsistence that he requires for his maintenance, and for the propagation of his race.'[38]

'If this labourer were in possession of his own means of production, and were satisfied to live as a labourer, he need not work beyond the time necessary for the reproduction of his means of subsistence, say 8 hours a day.'[39] 'The directing motive, the end and aim of capitalist production, is to extract the greatest possible amount of surplus value, and consequently to exploit labour-power to the greatest possible extent.'[40]

Arnsperger and Van Parijs identify the Marxist theory of justice as encompassing the fulfilment of two principles.[41] First, a just decision or measure should contribute to reduce or suppress 'alienation': it should push for a type of human activity which is not *alien* to the person exerting it, which implies that it should necessarily be driven by other aims than the only necessity of subsistence. Second, a just measure should combat situations of 'exploitation', that is, of appropriation by one person (e.g., an employer) of the surplus value created by someone else's labour.

For many individuals, work in the on-demand economy presents real risks of both alienation and exploitation in this sense. It is not uncommon to hear positive accounts about the underlying activity – which may then be reduced to no more than a means of subsistence through the business structures inherent in many platforms' models. Take cycle couriers as an example: at first glance, the notion of navigating the streets of a major city such as London or Paris on a bicycle at all times of day and night, exposed to perilous traffic and the wet and cold in inclement weather, all whilst under the tight time pressure and control of a remote controller communicating through a radio handset or phone-based app, sounds like the archetypical continuation (or resurrection) of the worst of Victorian labour practices. Yet many seem to relish the daily physical exertion. As one courier explained in an interview with *The Guardian* newspaper:

---

37. K. Marx, *Economic and Philosophic Manuscripts of 1844*, section XXII, §10, https://www.marxists.org/archive/marx/works/download/pdf/Economic-Philosophic-Manuscripts-1844.pdf.
38. K. Marx and F. Engel, *The Manifesto of the Communist Party*, 1848, section 1, §§30-31, https://www.marxists.org/archive/marx/works/download/pdf/Manifesto.pdf,
39. K. Marx, *Capital. A Critique of Political Economy*, Vol. 1, Chapter 11, §13, https://www.marxists.org/archive/marx/works/download/pdf/Capital-Volume-I.pdf.
40. K. Marx, *Capital*, Vol. I, *id.*, Chapter 13, §19.
41. They acknowledge however that Marx was not himself involved in the elaboration of a political or ethical theory (C. Arnsperger & P. Van Parijs, *supra* n. 12, 44).

'Most of us just love riding around London,' [cycle courier Andrew Boxer] says of his job with courier firm Excel, which can involve 60 to 70 miles a day in the saddle. 'Even in appalling weather, riding along the river is an exciting experience. Most low-paid jobs aren't this much fun.'[42]

Fun, that is, until alienation and exploitation kick in, and working conditions start grinding workers down. One interesting feature is that alienation and exploitation might or might not coincide in the work experience of on-demand workers. Some observers praise the gig economy because it empowers workers, helping them to become less alienated. Indeed, some of these operators can choose when and for how long they will work; sometimes they are free to define the whole organisation of their work. As we note below, however, this newly acquired autonomy does not necessarily protects them from being exploited in their work.

The systematic use of information technology is an important factor of alienation, which makes on-demand work genuinely different from other forms of precarious employment. It fosters a renewed, specific, commodification of labour.[43] Apps, platforms and the algorithms through which they operate encourage the fragmentation of work in numerous disconnected tasks. Electronic interfaces are connecting offer and demand at a high pace, whilst at the same time making workers more distant and more alien from the activities they carry out. The rating systems most platforms put in place allow for a purely quantitative (though taking the 'deliberative' form of a vote), 'dehumanising' or 'objectifying', evaluation of workers' performance. Consumers rate each 'gig' or 'task' (intermittent work relationship), with the composite score displayed to future customers. This is often sold as a key attraction of platform-based work: ratings are said to signal the quality of individual workers' services and differentiate them from the crowd – thus providing access to better jobs, at higher pay.

As Tom Slee has shown, however, on-demand economy ratings have very little value in this regard. Drawing on a range of empirical studies, he concludes that 'reputation systems fail in their basic task' of providing quality information. Reputation algorithms, he argues, should instead be seen as 'a substitute for a company management structure, and a bad one at that. A reputation system is the boss from hell: an erratic, bad-tempered and unaccountable manager that may fire you at any time, on a whim, with no appeal'.[44] Instead of merely aggregating consumer feedback, platform operators rely on constant algorithmic monitoring to ensure tight control over every

---

42. A. Boxer, *Love the Job, Hate the Way We're Treated: Life on the Frontline of UK's Delivery Army*, The Guardian (31 July 2016) https://www.theguardian.com/money/2016/jul/30/job-pay-workers-gig-economy (accessed 7 August 2017).
43. See, on this topic, the pioneering work of J. Ellul, *Les possibilités techniques et le travail*, in *Pour qui, pour quoi travaillons-nous ?*, 85-112 (Paris: La table ronde, 2013).
44. T. Slee, *What's Yours Is Mine: Against the Sharing Economy*, 100-101 (New York and London: OR Books, 2015). This is confirmed by internal Uber documents, which suggest that in 2014, fewer than 3% of drivers where 'at risk of being deactivated' due to a rating below 4.6 stars (out of 5): J. Cook, *Uber's internal charts show how its driver-rating system actually works*, Businessinsider.com (11 February 2015) http://uk.businessinsider.com/leaked-charts-show-how-ubers-driver-rating-system-works-2015-2 (accessed 7 August 2017). It might be argued that this is due to the pressure of the rating system keeping the worker pool at a high standard, with lower performing bands excluded from the market. As Slee explains, however, this is not the

aspect of work and service delivery. Additional elements – from compliance with platform policies to how quickly and often a worker accepts new tasks – are factored into the equation, with any deviation sanctioned in real time through lower ratings: TaskRabbit's 'Performance Metrics', for example, include Task Acceptance Rate, Task Completion Rate, Original Time Percentage (work at or before the requested time) and Response Rates, whilst sanctions range from denying access to better-paid work to instant termination.[45]

The direct result of this tight control is that even joyful activities can quickly become alienating in the Marxist sense, with supposedly independent contractors punished near instantly for refusing to accept assigned work.[46] As a London Employment Tribunal Judge noted when discussing courier's 'choice to work when on circuit' in a recent cycling courier case, 'this is inequality of bargaining power at work' ([49]). And it is not just alienation for which examples can readily be found: exploitation as defined earlier is similarly a frequent problem. Staying with delivery couriers as an example, London delivery firm Citysprint found itself in the crosshairs of the Independent Workers Union of Great Britain (IWGB) over particularly flagrant pay practices, beyond frequently observed issues such as duties on workers to provide their own vehicles and rent communication equipment from the employer. One of the Union's key areas of criticism was a fifteen year courier industry pay freeze, which translated into a 30% wage cut in real terms over that period.[47] This appropriation by the company (and, in turn, its customers who profited from ever-falling delivery rates) of the surplus value created by the courier's labour was thrown into particularly stark relief when a recent documentary featuring the IWGB's recruitment efforts juxtaposed courier's falling pay with the Citysprint CEO's earnings, which according to financial filings had gone up by 55% in 2013 alone.[48]

The Marxist argument for institutional support of the collective autonomy of on-demand workers is the most classic and obvious one. Alienation can first decrease if collective action allows workers to obtain a remuneration whose level is not only based on an abstract evaluation of their production or on the meeting of supply and demand – a recurring trait of the digital economy – but also on an acknowledgment of their needs. A broadened participation of these workers to the organisation of their work and to the definition of their tasks could contribute to make their relation this

---

case: 'J-curve rating distributions [where nearly all data points are at the high end of the scale], like those of the Sharing Economy reputation systems, show up whenever people rate each other.' T. Slee, *id*., p. 101.
45. https://support.taskrabbit.com/hc/en-us/articles/204409610-TaskRabbit-Performance-Metrics (accessed 7 August 2017). Amazon's rating mechanism is so complex that many requesters appear to struggle to understand it: http://www.mturkgrind.com/threads/lifetime-approval-rate-misunderstood-by-requesters.27458/ (accessed 7 August 2017).
46. S. Butler, *London Cycle Courier 'Was Punished for Refusing Work after Eight Hours in Cold'*, The Guardian (21 March 2017), https://www.theguardian.com/business/2017/mar/21/london-cycle-courier-was-punished-for-refusing-work-after-eight-hours-in-cold (accessed 7 August 2017).
47. X., *Pressure grows on tax dodging CitySprint to stop exploitation of couriers*, ReelNews YouTube channel (12 November 2015), https://www.youtube.com/watch?v=_pnwWwxfNX0 at 1:10 (accessed 7 August 2017).
48. *Ib.*, 2:26.

work less alienating. It will offer them an opportunity to voice some new claims (especially if the state of the labour market does not leave space for exit strategies), for example to allow subjective dimensions of their working experience to be more taken into account by their different contractual partners. It might also allow these workers to recreate some coherence or continuity in their work experience, which is currently often fragmented into a series of unrelated tasks. It could also offer an opportunity to develop and exercise different kinds of checks and balances on the people exerting authority and control over them.

The IWBG's organising strategy in London reflects many of these elements: in seeking payment of at least the equivalent of the London living wage plus costs,[49] the Union organised large-scaled protests, bringing couriers together not just at their employer's headquarter, but also outside a number of significant customers, including well-known companies such as television station ITV, the Guardian Newspaper, financial services firm HSBC, consultants PWC, and law firm Linklaters.[50] Slogans such as 'we dodge death to meet your deadlines' and "your profits are made at our loss" expressed drivers' frustration with their high-pressure, low-wage working conditions, and sought an acknowledgment of their working realities not just from the operator, but also their consumers directly.

Exploitation could be reduced, in turn, if on-demand workers could unite to defend their interests and are consequently put in a situation to impose the payment of a decent wage. Collective action could rebalance the distribution of the value created by the activity, for the benefit of the workers. This would thus not be far from one of the most advocated rationales of labour law: to rebalance an unequal contractual relationship. This distribution would likely involve, in this case, at least three actors: the worker, the platform/intermediary and the client, the two latter ones currently being in the position to unilaterally capture an undue part of the value created by the on-demand worker. Through association and the use of this potential surplus of income, there is also a chance that the workers will be able to make the intermediary superfluous, by developing their own connecting and contracting devices. This will be even easier when workers already own their main means of production.[51] By doing so, they would put an end to their exploitation by the platform, in Marxist terminology.

The IWGB's campaigns have already begun to bear fruit in this regard. In London, for example, Citysprint dropped some of its lowest payment rates, and other companies agreed to substantial pay rises.[52] In addition to engaging in wage bargaining with courier firms and other gig economy employers in the transportation sector, the Union has also begun to fund a series of high-profile lawsuits against other platforms, with hitherto impressively consistent success.[53] Examples of successful collective pushes against alienation and exploitation, finally, are by no means limited to the UK.

---

49. *Id.*, 4:46.
50. *Id.*, 7:30ff.
51. Shifts in governance and property here happens in parallel. This is central to the current 'platform cooperativism movement'. See https://platform.coop/ (accessed 7 August 2017).
52. *Pressure grows on tax dodging CitySprint to stop exploitation of couriers, supra* n. 47, at 9:30.
53. Website of the Independent Workers Union of Great Britain: https://iwgb.org.uk (accessed 7 August 2017).

In Australia, for example, a concerted campaign by Unions NSW led to a detailed agreement with gig economy platform Airtasker, including above-minimum wage pay rates and recourse to independent dispute resolution mechanisms.[54]

[E] A Rawlsian Argument

> 'As a first step, suppose that the basic structure of society distributes certain primary goods, that is, things that every rational man is presumed to want. These goods normally have a use whatever a person's rational plan of life. For simplicity, assume that the chief primary goods at the disposition of society are rights and liberties, powers and opportunities, income and wealth. (...) These are the social primary goods. Other primary goods such as health and vigor, intelligence and imagination, are natural goods; although their possession is influenced by the basic structure, they are not so directly under its control. Imagine, then, a hypothetical initial arrangement in which all the social primary goods are equally distributed: everyone has similar rights and duties, and income and wealth are evenly shared. This state of affairs provides a benchmark for judging improvements.'[55]
>
> 'First principle. Each person is to have an equal right to the most extensive total system of equal basic liberties compatible with a similar system of liberty for all.'[56] (Principle 1)
>
> 'Social and economic inequalities are to be arranged so that they are both (a) to the greatest benefit of the least advantaged, consistent with the just savings principle and (b) attached to offices and positions open to all under conditions of fair equality of opportunity'[57] (Principle 2)

According to Rawls' first principle, a just decision is one which ensures that each person will benefit equally from the enjoyment of her basic liberties of association, expression, religion, ... As we began to outline above (§17.03), the collective organisation of on-demand workers can be considered as the realisation one of these basic freedoms. Institutions or laws that would support such a development can thus be considered desirable. We also argued above that, even though such recognition would necessarily restrict the freedom of other actors, these limitations would not seem to be important enough to question the proportionality of measures intended to promote on-demand workers' most basic freedoms. In Rawlsian terms, any such measure would actually contribute to a more equal enjoyment of freedoms whose exercise was restricted to some. Given the fact that Rawls gives priority to this first principle,[58] we

---

54. A. Patty, *Airtasker and Unions Make Landmark Agreement to Improve Pay Rates and Conditions*, Sydney Morning Herald (1 May 2017) http://www.smh.com.au/business/workplace-relations/airtasker-and-unions-make-landmark-agreement-to-improve-pay-rates-and-conditions-20170427-gvtvpo.html (accessed 7 August 2017).
55. J. Rawls, *A Theory of Justice*. Revised Edition, 54 (Cambridge: Harvard University Press, 1999).
56. J. Rawls, *A Theory of Justice, id.*, 266.
57. *Id.*, p. 266. Note that when asked on which principle should be granted the priority, Rawls responded principle (1); then Principle 2 (b) and Principle 2 (a) to end up with (*Idem*, 266 and C. Arnsperger & P. Van Parijs, *supra* n. 12, p. 58 ('clause de priorité lexicographique').
58. J. Rawls, *supra* n. 55, p. 266.

could argue that the demonstration of an imbalance in the enjoyment of basic freedoms already gives solid grounds for the measures we advocate for.

In the gig economy, one key ingredient for the realisation of this very basic freedom is information, ranging from the quality of particular tasks to the reliability and trustworthiness of repeat customers. In the absence of platform cooperation, this information can only be acquired, compiled and disseminated through collective action: a form of electronic self-empowerment to realise basic liberty, without harming others. When Lilly Irani and Six Silberman, then graduate students at the University of California, Irvine, realised that workers on Amazon's digital microtask platform MTurk had no easy way of providing feedback about dishonest and abusive customers, they developed feedback software to be installed in workers' browsers. TurkOpticon, as the plugin is called, allows Turkers to rate requesters for factors from accuracy of task description to promptness of payment, thus warning future users off unreliable clients.[59]

However, Rawls completes this first principle with a second one and its application to the issue at stake makes the argumentation even stronger. Inequalities, when they do not concern the most basic freedoms, are acceptable if two criteria are met. First, people with same abilities and endowments should be ensured to have access to the same social opportunities and goods. Second, the famous 'difference principle' requires that a particular situation of inequality must benefit the least-advantaged members of society. The question thus becomes: in the situation of economic vulnerability of on-demand workers and in the absence of a framework allowing them to voice their interests collectively, are these two conditions met? Most likely not.

Though on-demand work can sometimes result from a personal choice to organise one's life with more latitude, it is very often driven by the need to bring a living wage to one's household.[60] The latter group of individuals have thus not been granted the same access to a job and a living wage as the workers who are employed in a typical, more lasting and stable working relationship (b).[61] Some of these on-demand workers are University graduates – in their case, the inequality of opportunity concerns foremost the access to the labour market. For lots of other on-demand who might also come from an (ethnic, religious, social) minority background,[62] this inequality goes back much further in time. Such an observation clearly pleads in favour

---

59. L. Irani and M. Silberman, *Turkopticon: Interrupting Worker Invisibility in Amazon Mechanical Turk* (CHI 2013: Changing Perspectives, Paris, France Session: Smart Tools, Smart Work), available at https://hci.cs.uwaterloo.ca/faculty/elaw/cs889/reading/turkopticon.pdf (accessed 7 August 2017).
60. See recent work by American sociologist J. Schorr (J. Schorr, *From Moral Aspiration to Cynical Predation: Diversity in the Platform Economy*, SASE Conference featured speech, University of Lyon (1 July 2017)). She develops two categories of on-demand workers – people doing it for a living, who are more likely to have to suffer very bad working conditions and people who choose to do it to get supplemental earnings, who tend to enjoy a broader autonomy and satisfaction in their work experience.
61. Research is currently conducted on how the on-demand economy impacts particular categories of workers – young people, women, migrant workers ... The results might likely shed a useful light on these particular normative questions.
62. See for example, the demographics of Uber drivers in the US: J. Hall & A. Krueger, *An Analysis of the Labor Market for Uber's Driver-Partners in the United States*, study commissioned by Uber

of the adoption of any institutional mechanism that would foster a better equality of opportunities among workers and citizens. The organisation of on-demand workers would not only allow them to make their relationship with their contractors more economically balanced. It could also lead them to voice their interests in the political sphere. As political agents, they could advocate for broader reforms intended at opening access to education and the labour market to people with equal talents and abilities ('natural goods').

On the second point (a), the answer is more debated nowadays. If on-demand workers are considered as the most-disadvantaged members of society then the status quo clearly does not benefit them. This pleads for putting them in a more favourable bargaining position and supporting them in their attempts to organise and to voice their interests. If we consider that the most-disadvantaged people are the ones who don't have access to any paid activity, our appreciation might differ. Would the possibility to obtain the respect of minimal protection standards, including a minimum wage, harm the unemployed by making their hire in the on-demand context more expensive for businesses and thus less probable? Debates are being held on the potential damages that social protection can have on the labour market, some arguing that less rigid social standards and less collective action would help the fight against unemployment. This mantra is however highly questioned by both classical and non-classical economists.[63] It might indeed be that on-demand workers and the unemployed, as well as standard-workers, have a lot in common and that they would better imagine mechanisms that would allow them to collaborate in making their interests heard. As we stated above (*see* §17.01), depending on the nature of social security systems, collective action could also benefit the least-favoured people. Collective action might result in a larger participation of enterprises and workers to public insurance schemes, following potential wage raises. As a consequence, other workers could be granted benefits for periods of unemployment (or a basic income?); the sick and the old, who lack access to the labour market, will benefit from wider redistribution mechanisms.

Let us add that Rawls was primarily concerned, in the definition of his justice principles, with the access of citizens to primary goods, both 'natural' (intelligence, imagination, health, speed) and 'social' (rights, liberties, income and wealth), desirable for all. The most important primary good was for him 'self-respect' or 'self-esteem'

(22 January 2015), https://s3.amazonaws.com/uber-static/comms/PDF/Uber_Driver-Partners_Hall_Kreuger_2015.pdf (accessed 7 August 2017).

63. For an account of these debates about the potential consequences of introducing a minimum wage on the employment rate: R.A., *Minimum Human Wages. The Economics of Minimum-Wage Laws Is Very Tricky*, The Economist (15 February 2013) https://www.economist.com/blogs/freeexchange/2013/02/labour-markets (accessed 7 August 2017); *see* also A. Eydoux, *La dérégulation de l'emploi permet-elle de réduire les inégalités*, Alternatives Economiques (7 July 2017) https://www.alternatives-economiques.fr/anne-eydoux/deregulation-de-lemploi-permet-de-reduire-inegalites/00079739 (accessed 7 August 2017). The author explains how we have shifted in dominant political discourses, from the liberal claim that the removal of labour protections of employees (including severance pay) would encourage hiring new workers and thus lower unemployment rates, to another one, more nuanced, that this removal would at least reduce the distance between 'standard' (aka well protected) and 'non-standard' (aka not protected enough) workers. She argues that none of these claims can be sustained. The debate thus becomes one of 'insiders' against 'outsiders'. The age-old policy of divide and rule?

that is, 'a person's sense of his own value, his secure conviction that his conception of his good, his plan of life, is worth carrying out. (...). It also 'implies a confidence in one's ability, so far as it is in one's power, to fulfil one's intention.'[64] For Rawls, the benefit of self-respect is inherently social, dependent on a recognition of one's worth and dignity by people he shares interest with, who are part of a common association.[65] This requirement is close from the normative criterion developed later by A. Honneth in *The Struggle for recognition*.[66] The potential gain in self-respect that the on-demand worker might obtain by associating with peers sharing the same fate, or by being able to voice her concerns in the public arena, might be the strongest argument formulated, in Rawlsian terms, in favour of the adoption of legal mechanisms enabling the organisation and participation of on-demand workers in the government of their own working activities and projects.

Ultimately, state support for the organisation of on-demand economy workers and their eventual engagement in collective bargaining with platform employers is thus a crucial step in ensuring a fair – and sustainable – operation of the gig economy. It is not difficult to find examples of targeted and promising legislative intervention, both at the local and national level. In December 2015, for example, the Seattle City Council unanimously enacted an ordinance granting the city's drivers 'a voice on the job and the opportunity to negotiate for improved working conditions at their companies'. This was presented as a measure of last resort, other avenues having failed. As Council Member Mike O'Brien explained:

> We've heard from Seattle drivers making sub-minimum wage, and companies like Uber have turned a deaf ear to their concerns. This bill was only introduced out of necessity after witnessing how little power drivers themselves had in working for a living wage.[67]

In 2016, the French Labour Code was similarly modified to ensure the protection of basic collective labour rights vis-à-vis gig economy platforms. Several articles were introduced in the 7th section of the Code by the highly contested 'Loi travail'.[68]

---

64. J. Rawls, *Theory of Justice*, supra n. 55, p. 386.
65. *Id.*, 386.
66. A. Honneth, *The Struggle for Recognition. The Moral Grammar of Social Conflicts* (Cambridge: MIT Press, 1995): 'Just as, in the case of love, children acquire, via the continuous experience of "maternal" care, the basic self-confidence to assert their needs in an unforced manner, adult subjects acquire, via the experience of legal recognition, the possibility of seeing their actions as the universally respected expression of their own autonomy. [...] What is required are conditions in which individual rights are no longer granted disparately to members of social status groups but are granted equally to all people as free beings; only then will the individual legal person be able to see in them an objectivated point of reference for the idea that he or she is recognized for having the capacity for autonomously forming judgments.'
67. City of Seattle, *Giving Drivers a Voice. Council Unanimously Adopts First-of-Its-Kind Legislation to Give Drivers a Voice on the Job*, Press Release (14 December 2015), http://www.seattle.gov/council/issues/giving-drivers-a-voice (accessed 7 August 2017).
68. Articles L7341-1 to L7342-6 of the Code du travail ('Travailleurs utilisant une plateforme de mise en relation par voie électronique'), introduced by the Loi no. 2016-1088 du 8 août 2016 relative au travail, à la modernisation du dialogue social et à la sécurisation des parcours professionnels, JORF no. 0184, 9 August 2016, available at https://www.legifrance.gouv.fr/affichCode.do;jsessionid=477C7170C222AE05ECF8817BB26DFA0E.tpdila17v_2?idSectionTA=LEGISCTA

On-demand workers are granted several important prerogatives if the revenue they make trough the platform reaches a certain level:[69] the platform has the duty to pay contributions to an insurance scheme against accidents at work benefitting each worker, who also enjoys a right to vocational training. More relevant for our analysis, on-demand workers are afforded the right not to be retaliated if they 'refuse to provide their services in a concerted way' in order to 'defend their professional demands' (Artice L7342-5), as well as a right to 'constitute a trade union, to become its affiliates, and to use it to defend their collective interests' (Article L7342-6). These prerogatives are applicable to self-employed on-demand workers only.[70]

The success of individual initiatives notwithstanding, the overall problems for organised labour remain acute. As we noted at the outset, employee classification might very likely be an essential stepping stone to most large-scale collective efforts. If work in the on-demand economy was properly classified as employment, workers would be able to organise themselves and form trade unions to bargain directly with platforms over their terms and conditions – backed up if necessary by the power to mandate negotiations and threaten industrial action.

§17.04 CONCLUSION: FROM JUSTICE TO DEMOCRACY – FINDING INSPIRATION IN HABERMAS AND DEWEY

> 'The task of universal pragmatics is to identify and reconstruct universal conditions of possible mutual understanding.'[71] 'I shall develop the thesis that anyone acting communicatively must, in performing any speech act, raise universal validity claims and suppose that they can be vindicated.'[72] 'Reaching and understanding is the process of bringing about an agreement on the presupposed basis of validity claims that are mutually recognized.'[73]
>
> 'Every experience is a moving force. Its value can be judged only on the ground of what it moves toward and into.'[74] 'The method of democracy is to bring

---

000033013020&cidTexte = LEGITEXT000006072050&dateTexte = 20170531. Interestingly, we find in the section 7 of the French labour code, a list of professionals that are recognized the status of employee (or some of its correlated advantage) despite not performing their activities under the authority of an employer.

69. This level was fixed in a recent Décret: Décret no. 2017-774 du 4 mai 2017 relatif à la responsabilité sociale des plateformes de mise en relation par voie électronique, JORF no. 0107, 6 May 2017.
70. This choice of wording could be questioned because it gives the impression that on-demand workers are necessarily self-employed. In this regard, an important case is pending in French courts: the URSSAF (Union de recouvrement des cotisations de sécurité sociale et d'allocations familiale, the administration in charge of the perception of social contributions) asked for the a 'requalification' of Uber drivers' service contracts into employment contracts. Uber objected to this order, bringing the case to court. In its last decision, the Tribunal des affaires de sécurité sociale dismissed this claim. But the URSSAF already appealed. (C. Alix, *Devant la justice, l'Urssaf perd face à Uber*, Libération (17 March 2017) http://www.liberation.fr/futurs/2017/03/17/devant-la-justice-l-urssaf-perd-face-a-uber_1556255 (accessed 7 August 2017).
71. J. Habermas, *What Is Universal Pragmatics?*, in M. Cooke (ed.), *On the Pragmatics of Communication*, 21 (Cambridge: MIT Press, 1998).
72. *Id.*, 22.
73. *Id.*, 23.
74. J. Dewey, *Experience and Education*, 38 (New York: Simon & Schuster, 1997).

conflicts out into the open where their special claims can be seen and appraised, where they can be discussed and judged in the light of the more inclusive interests than are represented by either of them separately.'[75] 'As believers in democracy we have not only the right but the duty to question existing mechanisms of, say, suffrage and to inquire whether some functional organization would not serve to formulate and manifest public opinion better than the existing methods. It is not irrelevant to the point that a score of passages could be cited in which Jefferson refers to the American Government as an experiment.'[76]

In this article, we have examined the question of the desirability of introducing institutional or legal measures to support on-demand workers in their capacity to organise, to associate in order be better placed to voice their interests, and to have a broader say on the circumstances in which their activities are taking place. The theories we have used have provided us with substantive principles of justice. On their basis, we have defended the notion that on-demand workers should benefit from broader collective autonomy. We will conclude by referring to two authors who have pushed for a pragmatic or pragmatist-inspired account of institutional and legal design. Their focus has switched from the content of justice principles to the context and the procedures which allow bringing common norms or principles about.[77] As a consequence, the idea of democracy, as a process allowing for different conceptions of what is good or just to be expressed and confronted, occupies a central role in their work. Not only do they offer additional arguments in favour of supporting legally the exercise by workers of the gig economy, of their collective autonomy; they also inform our own effort by giving us some hints about the nature of the potential contribution of legal scholars in the analysis of this sensitive issue.

Habermas has largely pleaded for the development of democratic institutions, in which everyone would be granted with an equal right to defend the norms he or she considers as indispensable for the members of a community to live successfully together. Using shared language and codes, each person is formulating claims that are founded in reason, trying to persuade his/her peers of their relevance and universality. Through this ongoing process of discussion, the community is able to adopt norms that can be agreed upon by all. A strong argument could thus be built in favour or

---

75. J. Dewey, *Liberalism and Social Action*, 81 (New York: Prometheus Books, 1999) (First pub. 1935).
76. J. Dewey, *Freedom and Culture*, in J. A. Boydston (ed.), *John Dewey. Later Works 1925-1953*, vol. 13, 175 (Southern Illinois University Press, 2008).
77. 'In contrast to sociological skepticism about law, philosophical theories of justice resolutely work out the moral content of modern legal orders. These rational constructions of law serve to justify principles according to which a well-ordered society should be set up. In the process, however, they lose touch with the reality of contemporary societies and thus have difficulties in identifying the conditions necessary for the realization of these principles.' (J. Habermas, *Between facts and norms: Contributions to a Discourse Theory of Law and Democracy*, (Cambridge: MIT Press, 1992): Chapter 2); 'A man is intelligent not in virtue of having reason which grasps first and indemonstrable truths about fixed principles, in order to reason deductively from them to the particulars which they govern, but in virtue of his capacity to estimate the possibilities of a situation and to act in accordance with his estimate.' (J. Dewey, *The Quest for Certainty: A Study of the Relation of Knowledge and Action* (The Gifford Lectures 1929) in J. A. Boydston (ed.), *John Dewey. Later Works 1925-1953*, vol. 4, 170 (Southern Illinois University Press, 2008) (First pub. in 1929).

arrangements that would allow on-demand workers to express their normative priorities in the public realm, and in this way, participate in the adoption of more just legal norms. They could do so by making use of all arguments developed above. It is no coincidence if workers participation in the governance of firms and collective bargaining have been described as forms of 'industrial democracy'.[78] One could argue that as much as an industrial economy had created a need for an industrial democracy, a digital democracy must ensue from the rise of the digital economy, making use of its intrinsic immaterial qualities.

For Dewey, democracy is the most desirable institutional arrangement, not because it would allow the members of a community to agree on shared norms following a process of deliberation, but because it allows for a constant experience of learning. The author encourages scholars in social sciences to give particular attention to people's claims and actions: only from this observation can an informed knowledge of what matters for a given society develop. Each person values specific aims and acts to fulfil them. By a process of trial and error, she adapts her ends and means according to the lessons of experience. The science Dewey is advocating for is one which helps societies define their collective purposes, identify obstacles, and formulate solutions to overcome them. Education is the indispensable basis of this learning process. Democracy is in turn, 'more than a form of government; it is primarily a mode of associated living, of conjoint communicated experience'.[79] Democracy is fundamentally defined by the social context in which it emerges. There is thus another argument to build on the basis of Dewey's thought. We should favour institutional solutions which are directly inspired from on-demand workers' expressed aspirations and from their various creative attempts to realise them. This requires first to look closely at these initiatives. Then, we should as legal scholars, perpetuate and extend their experiment, proposing solutions aimed at being tried and tested in reality.

In this article, we intended to lay some foundations for this ambitious task. To do so, we offered normative arguments, complemented with numerous examples of how the collective autonomy of on-demand workers actually develops and of how it could be supported by adequate legal arrangements. We hope to be able to elaborate more on emerging practices and possible legal reforms in the future, and that these first ideas might inspire more scholars to take part in this crucial debate. Together we could frame reform proposals and apply them to data collected in the field. The specificities of work in the gig economy and the solutions developed to respond to the challenges it poses might subsequently help us to question traditional legal categories and frameworks. Seen thus, the desirability of on-demand workers' autonomy is but another small part of a larger inquiry into the adequacy and future of our democratic institutions and models in the context of a changing economy.

---

78. B. & S. Webb, *Industrial Democracy*, (London, New York & Bombay: Longmans, Green & Co, 1897).
79. J. Dewey, *Democracy and Education: An introduction to the philosophy of education*, 87 (New York: The Free Press, 1966) (First pub. 191).

CHAPTER 18
Are Agency Workers Protected by Trade Unions?: A Case Study from the Netherlands

Nicola Gundt

§18.01 INTRODUCTION

This contribution analyses the position of employees in triangular employment relations in the collective bargaining process at the example of the Netherlands. The contribution aims to show that regulating the employment conditions of these employees is difficult for several reasons. In the first place, the category of persons employed in triangular employment relationships covers a wide range of – sometimes very different – situations. Therefore the question is whether the same legal rules should apply to the whole group. Here, questions concerning the reasonableness of derogations from protective labour law will be raised. In the second place, due to their short stay in an enterprise or sector combined with the usually fragmented employment history and frequent spells of unemployment, most persons working in triangular employment relations, specifically the classic agency workers, are hard to organise. Many will not remain in the enterprise or sector long enough to gain anything from (lengthy) collective bargaining processes, and therefore lack the motivation to join a trade union which could speak in their name. This means that trade unions as classic employee representation bodies may be legitimised to a lesser extent than usually. In addition and consequence, they may simply lack bargaining power to ensure a balanced mix of rights and duties, flexibility and protection. This in turn leads to questions concerning the desirability of collective labour agreements applicable to triangular employment relations which derogate *in peius* from statutory law provisions.

The contribution starts with a discussion of the Dutch statutory regulation of triangular employment relations. It aims to show the different possibilities of derogation *in peius* the law offers, resulting in diluted employment protection for all groups of employees falling under the legal definition of agency worker. The second paragraph analyses the personal scope of application of the statutory provisions. Here, the Supreme Court's decision of 4 November 2016 on the definition of triangular employment relations, its reception in doctrine and its possible consequences will be discussed in depth, in order to show just how broad the meaning of 'agency work' in Dutch law has become. In a third part, the generally binding collective labour agreement applicable to triangular employment relations is discussed. The discussion will focus on equality, flexibility and protection, at the example of several employment conditions such as protection against dismissal, wage level and other rights and duties. It will become clear that the freedom offered by the statutes is generally used to its full extent. The question then, of course, is: Why is the collective labour agreement as it is? Are there reasons to be given for (some of the) particular agreements? Finally, the question will be raised whether, concerning the specific characteristics, such as low union density and trade union agendas, collective bargaining is the proper way of ensuring employee protection for this specific group, which dangers exist and how these dangers can be contained.

§18.02 THE DEFINITION OF THE TRIANGULAR EMPLOYMENT RELATION

In Dutch law, Article 7:690 Civil code (Burgerlijk Wetboek, BW) defines the agency contract as an employment contract between an employee and an employer. The employer's business must be to assign employees to a user undertaking in order to work temporarily under that undertaking's supervision and direction.[1] This assigning of people to different factual users is the so-called allocative function. This feature does not figure in the text of any legal provision and has therefore been the subject of much debate, in substance as well as in definition. During the Parliamentary discussion, the term has been frequently used, but was not included in the legal definition of agency work. It describes the fact that there is some go-between between the user undertaking and the employee and the fact that there is no direct legal link between the user and the worker.

According to the legislator, this allocative function, in which the employer acts as intermediary between labour demand and labour supply, implies a necessity for greater freedom concerning contractual arrangements for employers as well as for employees.[2] It therefore seems to be the core argument for more flexibility and (therefore) less employment protection. However, its precise meaning and ambit are hotly debated. This is due to the fact that the legal provision following the definition of

---

1. The aspect of temporariness of the hiring out, so prominently existent in the EU directive, is absent in the Dutch definition. Under Dutch law, it is perfectly possible (though unlikely) that an agency worker is employed by the agency on a permanent contract.
2. *Kamerstukken II*, 25263, Nr. 3, p. 9.

agency work in Article 7:690 BW, Artice 7:691 BW, allows for substantial derogations from protective statutory law for agency work. As both, Articles 7:690 and 7:691 BW are placed in the same section of the Civil code headed 'specific rules regarding agency work contracts', this suggests that both provisions use identical terms and concepts on agency work and agency worker. The impact of the discussion on the ambit of Article 7:690 BW becomes obvious, as soon as the possibilities to derogate from protective statutory provisions are envisaged.

The impact of some of the derogations made possible by Article 7:691 BW, is quite stark. For example, Article 7:691 subsection 1 BW states that the rules concerning chains of consecutive fixed-term contracts which, after a certain time or number of contracts, will be converted by law into a permanent contract only apply after twenty-six weeks of work for the agency. This means that during the first twenty-six weeks in which the agency worker has actually worked, the number of contracts between the agency and the agency worker is irrelevant.[3] As such, this is already a differential treatment of agency workers. What is more, the period of twenty-six weeks can be extended by collective agreement to a maximum of seventy-eight weeks in which work has been done,[4] meaning (at least) one and a half year during which protection against consecutive fixed-term contracts is suspended.[5] However, the biggest hole in the agency workers' protection is the so-called agency clause from subsection 2. This clause effects the termination by law of the employment contract, in case the user firm notifies the agency that they do not wish to make use of the agency worker any more. This clause effectively means that the rules on dismissal do not apply.[6] The clause applies during the first twenty-six weeks of actual employment, but its applicability can be extended by collective agreement to seventy-eight weeks in which work has been done.[7] Furthermore, as the employment contract terminates as soon as the hiring company terminates the assignment, the employee bears the risk of there not being sufficient work, while generally speaking, this is a risk that should be borne by the employer.[8]

§18.03 WHICH TRIANGULAR RELATIONS ARE COVERED BY ARTICLE 7:690 AND/OR ARTICLE 7:691 BW?

As already mentioned briefly, one of the most heatedly debated questions in Dutch labour law was and still is which triangular employment relations come within the

---

3. At least as long as the agency is the employer. For a successive employer not being an agency, things are different, which might affect the user company's decision to offer a contract.
4. Article 7:691 subs. 8 (a) BW.
5. E.M. Hoogeveen, *Payrolling: uitholling werknemersbescherming of gat in de markt?* 6 ArbeidsRecht (2012).
6. As will become clear in the analysis of the collective labour agreement, neither do rules concerning protection in case of sickness. Usually, being medically unfit for work means that the employee enjoys protection from dismissal during the first 104 weeks of incapacity (Article 7:670 BW). In agency contracts, instead, calling in sick triggers the termination by law of the contract (see *infra*).
7. Article 7:691 subs. 8 (a) BW.
8. Article 7:628 BW.

material scope of Article 7:690 BW.[9] The question of the necessity of an allocative function of the employer and the possible meaning of this notion in particular has led to much discussion. Another question is whether the definitions in Article 7:690 BW and Article 7:691 BW should be identical. The discussion may seem academic, but the outcome decides which employers can rely on the derogations from protective provisions in Article 7:691 BW and whether the generally binding collective labour agreement applies.[10]

[A] Parliamentary Debates

Applicability of the 'diluted' labour law from Article 7:691 BW seems justified in case of real agency workers, persons who really do not have a single employer and use the agency to find a temporary job. This was the group of persons, everyone had in mind when debating on Articles 7:690 and 7:691 BW. At least, this is how the Council of State, a state organ that offers guidance and counsel concerning legislation to Parliament, primarily understands the concept. In that case, flexibility on the employer side is needed, as the agency itself does not have jobs, but merely allocates persons to job offers from outside. On the other hand, the classical agency employee differs from core employees of the user firm to such an extent, that less 'involvement' of the user enterprise in the form of reasonable care for an employment perspective may be justified.

However, the parliamentary discussion, particularly the answer to the Council of State, shows that the concept of 'agency work' is understood much broader by the government. The answer states explicitly that not only typical agency work should be covered by Article 7:690 BW, but that it covers other forms of triangular employment situations as well, as long as the employer makes it his business to deploy employees to user firms to work there under the direction of that user firm.[11] In these cases, whatever the government thought in 1999, application of these, rather more lenient rules may become problematic as the developments on payrolling, posting and similar constructions show. Payrolling is a term that describes a range of employment relations in which employees are selected by the user and then stalled at another company acting as agency.[12] The employees, which have been selected by the user, will then be seconded permanently and exclusively to the user who selected them. The user therefore, in the most extreme cases, just outsources his responsibilities as employer – partly with the help of Article 7:691 BW. These constructions are not forbidden, even

---

9. *See* for example the PhD thesis by J.P.H. Zwemmer, *Pluraliteit van werkgeverschap*. (Deventer: Kluwer 2012) on the subject, in particular pp. 84-91; E.M. Hogeveen, *De inlener en het werkgeverschap*, ArA 4-35 (2007/3).
10. E.M. Hoogeveen, *Payrolling: uitholling werknemersbescherming of gat in de markt?* 6 ArbeidsRecht (2012); M. Tanja, J. den Hoedt, *De uitzendovereenkomst, een beperkende uitleg met verruimende gevolgen*, TRA paragraph 3 (2017/15).
11. *Kamerstukken II*, 1996-1997, 25263, B, p. 9.
12. *See* e.g., the definition used by Hoogeveen: E.M. Hoogeveen, *Payrolling: uitholling werknemersbescherming of gat in de markt?* 6 ArbeidsRecht (2012).

though, according to some (lower) courts[13] and part of the doctrine,[14] they reek of abuse. However, whether they should be treated the same as the much more instable classical agency relations, is a different question. The same goes for another form of triangular employment, the so-called posting (*detachering*). The Dutch term *detachering* – usually rendered in English as posting – is used to describe situations in which highly specialised staff is hired out in order to work in a user company. Typical fields of application are ICT and accounting, but also the medical world. Consultancy, however, remains outside the ambit of the 'agency' contract in Articles 7:690 and 7:691 BW.[15]

[B]   Doctrine

As it became clearer that the derogations made possible by Article 7:691 BW were also used in situations that did not differ much from a normal employment relation, discussions in literature and case-law on the meaning and ambit of that provision intensified. Many scholars and judges tried to find a system that differentiates between classical agency work and other employment relations, because (seemingly) they thought the application of the more lenient rules of Article 7:691 BW inappropriate in some cases. One of the core concepts in that debate was and still is the allocative function of the employer. As has already been stated above, the parliamentary discussion offers neither a clear reference to nor a definition of the concept.[16] It therefore remains hotly debated. Several opinions can be distinguished. A first opinion is that an allocative function is necessary for an employment relation to come within the ambit of Article 7:690 BW.[17] Once an employment relation is covered by Article 7:690 BW, this then opens the possibility to apply Article 7:691 BW. The difficulty with this approach is that it depends on the definition of 'allocative function' in order to delineate the scope of application of Articles 7:690 and 7:691 BW. If the scholars stick with the Parliamentary debates and follow the broad view, this leads to a broad applicability of Article 7:691 BW as well, something they generally seem to be keen to prevent.[18] Others contend that within the ambit of Article 7:690 BW no allocative function is needed, but that Article 7:691 BW can only be invoked if the allocative

---

13. Rb Noord-Nederland (ktr Assen), 1 mei 2015, ECLI:NL:BRNNE:2015:2205; Rb Oost-Nederland (ktr Enschede), 21 maart 2013, ECLI:NL:RBONE:2013:BZ5108; Rb Overijssel (ktr Almelo), 11 maart 2014, ECLI:NL:RBOVE:2014:1214.
14. E.M. Hoogeveen, *Payrolling: uitholling werknemersbescherming of gat in de markt?* 6 ArbeidsRecht (2012).
15. M. Tanja, J. den Hoedt, *De uitzendovereenkomst, een beperkende uitleg met verruimende gevolgen*, TRA paragraph 4.4 (2017/15).
16. *Kamerstukken II*, 1996/97, 25 264, nr. 5.
17. The greatest advocate of the allocative function is Zwemmer in all his publications, see e.g.: J.P.H. Zwemmer, *Pluraliteit van werkgeverschap* (Deventer: Kluwer, 2012); *Waarom de payrollonderneming geen (uitzend)werkgever is*, TRA (2009/12); *De payrollonderneming, de inlener en het werkgeverschap*, TAP 19-23 (2010/1), 19-23; E. Knipschild, *Annotation of Gerechtshof Arnhem-Leeuwarden (zp Arnhem)*, 3 februari 2015, ECLI:NL:GHARL:2015:679, in *JAR* 2015/69.
18. It seems that e.g., Hoogeveen does not like her own conclusion in E.M. Hoogeveen, *Payrolling: uitholling werknemersbescherming of gat in de markt?* 6 ArbeidsRecht (2012).

function is present.[19] In this case, the differentiation would allow to align the definition in Article 7:690 BW with the political debate in Parliament, but leads to the delicate outcome that the same term 'agency contract' is interpreted in different ways in two statutory provisions, that entered into force at the same moment, were debated together and are placed under the same heading 'agency contracts' in the civil code.

[C] Supreme Court

On 4 November 2016, the Dutch Supreme Court (Hoge Raad, HR) rendered a long-awaited judgment in the matter.[20] The case concerns an employer, Care 4 Care, who specialises in hiring out highly qualified medical staff to user enterprises on the one side and a foundation that runs pension funds for agency workers on the other side. Participation in the pension funds is compulsory for all employers in the agency sector. Care 4 Care started proceedings in order to obtain a declaration that it is not an agency and therefore is under no obligation to pay fees to the funds. Proceedings quickly boiled down to the question of how to interpret Articles 7:690 and 7:691 BW.

The Advocate-General offers a thorough overview of the Parliamentary debate, case law and doctrine, which mainly shows just how widely positions differ on the matter. He then tries to offer some guidance by distinguishing a traditional (narrow) interpretation of the 'allocative function' from a broader reading thereof. According to the A-G, the traditional meaning encompasses just the classical agency work which provides employees in case of short-time need, e.g., in case a replacement is needed or the workload suddenly grows.[21] The broader meaning, according to the A-G, includes all kinds of intermediary functions and all kinds of employers who engage in any kind of intermediary function with the exception of pure consultancy.[22] In the eyes of the A-G, this allows for at least partial reconciliation of different statements in the Parliamentary debate. The outcome is that according to the A-G, an allocative function in the widest sense was deemed necessary in Article 7:690.[23] He then follows the line in the doctrine that opts for a different interpretation of the allocative function in Article 7:691 BW: '... a classical or traditional interpretation of allocative function as would be the case in art. 7:691 BW...'.[24]

The judgment itself is surprisingly short. The Supreme Court simply states that the Parliamentary debates on the matter show that no other requirements are relevant than those expressly mentioned in the provision itself. In particular, there is no requirement concerning the temporary nature of the work, nor does a restrictively understood allocative function apply. On the contrary: according to the Supreme Court,

---

19. F.B.J. Grapperhaus, *Tekst & Commentaar Arbeidsrecht*, inleideinde opmerkingen bij Afdeling 11, aant. 5, (Deventer: Kluwer 2015).
20. ECLI:NL:HR:2016:2356.
21. The so-called 'ziek en piek', literally sickness and peak workload (see Conclusie A-G G.R.B. van Peursem, ECLI:NL:PHR:2016:238, nr. 3.28).
22. M. Tanja, J. den Hoedt, *De uitzendovereenkomst, een beperkende uitleg met verruimende gevolgen*, TRA paragraph 4.4 (2017/15).
23. ECLI:NL:PHR:2016:238, paragraph 3.25.
24. ECLI:NL:PHR:2016:238, paragraph 3.29.

the Parliamentary debates show that next to the classical agency relations other triangular employment relations were also meant to come within the ambit of Article 7:690 BW.[25] The court therefore accepts an allocative function in the widest possible meaning, being that the employer's business must be to act as go-between between labour supply and labour demand. Second, according to the Supreme Court, Parliamentary debate and the fact that both provisions follow each other within the same subsection of the Civil code show that the concept of work through intermediaries as understood in Article 7:690 BW is the same as in Article 7:691 BW. This means that the possibilities to derogate from protective provisions apply to more triangular employment relations than the classical agency relations.[26] The Supreme Court, however, is not blind to the danger of abuse of these freedoms in situations which resemble agency work only in name. Still, the Court quite clearly states that if the concept of agency work in the two provisions is to be interpreted in different ways, it is first and foremost a task for the legislator to provide for this. However, judges retain the possibility to interpret Article 7:691 BW in a way that ensures compatibility with the provision's ratio and even the possibility to refuse its use in case its application must be deemed unacceptable.[27]

[D] Assessment

Concerning the debate on the applicability of the derogations contained in Article 7:691 BW, this means that the ambit of Articles 7:690 and 7:691 BW is the same. The line of argumentation that a distinction between the two should be made, as put forward by e.g., Grapperhaus has explicitly been ruled out by the Supreme Court. On the other hand, the line of argumentation that a classical form of allocation must be present, has also been ruled out. Limitations concerning the definition of agency work therefore are not to be found in the definition of an allocative function or in a distinction between Article 7:690 BW on the one hand and Article 7:691 BW on the other hand. Still, the Supreme Court itself seems to feel the need to offer an emergency exit for extreme cases in which the applicability of the derogations in Article 7:691 BW will have to be considered abusive.

This is the part of the judgment that some parts of legal doctrine, in spite of the Supreme Court's clear language, use as a basis when they (still) argue in favour of a differentiation in scope between Article 7:690 and Article 7:691 BW.[28] In their view, if for certain types of triangular employment relations the diluted labour law of Article 7:691 BW is inapplicable from the start, this leads to greater clarity than judges trying to delineate the borders with the help of an unreasonableness-test. They particularly think of payrolling, as a construction which can be stretched so far that a user selects a candidate himself and puts him to work under his own direction and guidance and does everything a 'normal' employer does, except for being the contractual party to the

---

25. ECLI:NL:HR:2016:2356, paragraph 3.4.2.
26. ECLI:NL:HR:2016:2356, paragraph 3.4.3.
27. Ibidem.
28. P.Th. Sick, A.M. Wevers, *De allocatiefunctie 'alloceren'?*, TRA (2017/16).

employment contract. The scholars' justification for this delineation can is that in payrolling relations, because they differ from the typical agency contracts due to their exclusive and long-term allocation to one single user who chose the candidate himself, the standard rules on dismissal apply instead of the rules applicable to triangular relations.[29] In this view, little would change if compared to the situation before the ruling. Others, however, though recognising that applicability of the less stringent rules of Article 7:691 BW can lead to abuse, particularly (again) in payroll constructions, find little possibility for judges to disapply the law on the basis of an unreasonableness test.[30] In Dutch legal doctrine, it is generally accepted that the unreasonableness-test merely allows for a marginal test on whether a certain decision is manifestly unreasonable.[31] As long as this is not the case, a judge cannot 'interfere'. On the one hand, this leads to security about the applicable law, particularly concerning the overwhelming majority of persons with good intentions. On the other hand, this extremely high threshold, could incite malevolent employers and / or users to try and find the limits of the system, leaving employees without protection.

To conclude: at the moment, the prevailing opinion seems that any triangular employment relation in which an element of bringing together labour demand and labour supply exists, comes within the ambit of Article 7:690 and thus also within the scope of application of Article 7:691 BW, regardless of further characteristics of that work, like its temporary or low-skilled nature. This means that the derogations form protective law are available in many more situations than employers – including the employer before the Supreme Court, Care 4 Care – realise. It encompasses not only the classical agency relation, but also posting (e.g., of highly specialised and trained staff) or payroll-constructions.

§18.04 THE COLLECTIVE LABOUR AGREEMENT

Another consequence of the broad personal and material scope the Supreme Court has given to Articles 7:690 and 7:691 BW is that the collective labour agreement which has been declared generally binding applies to more situations than many thought before. The question then is, whether the provisions laid down in these two instruments, and particularly in the collective labour agreement, suit all the situations that the Supreme Court has declared do come within its ambit. On first sight, it seems that the collective labour agreement is tailored to the needs of the classical agency relations. This can be seen most clearly in the phased system explained below, which makes full use of the possible derogations in Article 7:691 BW. These provisions are useful in agency situations, but less so in posting, particularly in posting of highly specialised and highly trained staff for whom there is much demand.

---

29. *Ibidem*, paragraph 6.
30. M. Tanja, J. den Hoedt, *De uitzendovereenkomst, een beperkende uitleg met verruimende gevolgen*, TRA paragraph 3.2 (2017/15).
31. A. M. Luttmer-Kat, *Tekst & Commentaar Arbeidsrecht*, Article 7:681 (oud) BW, aant. 2 (Deventer: Kluwer 2010).

However, the generally binding collective labour agreement will – in principle – apply and supersede the individual employment contract.[32] In case these rules do not really fit the employment relation, this can be a problem. Though the collective labour agreement offers quite some possibilities to derogate from provisions by expressly providing otherwise in individual contracts,[33] this still means that an employer, who was maybe not even aware that the collective labour agreement applies, must re-negotiate or modify employment contracts. This may be much more burdensome than a one-time exemption of certain types of employment relations form the scope of application of the agreement.

[A]   Scope of Application

In the agency sector (the collective agreement itself uses this term), two collective labour agreements exist, of which one is declared generally binding.[34] Parties to the other agreement are exempted from the generally binding collective labour agreement.[35] This means that not only employers who are either signatories or represented by signatory organisations are bound by the agreement, but that its rules apply throughout the whole sector as described in the collective labour agreement itself.

The Supreme Court's ruling of November last year showed just how broad the meaning of agency work is. In the literature, criticism and concern has been voiced on the possible applicability of the Agency work collective labour agreement to other forms of triangular employment relations because of the different character of e.g., posting of highly qualified staff.[36]

Article 2(1) of the agreement encompasses the classical agencies. After the Supreme Court's ruling, it is clear that all employers, regardless of the name of the business, whose wage payroll consists for more than 50% of wages paid to workers that are hired out to a third party to work under its direction and command, fall within the ambit of the agreement. For those employers who until now did not consider themselves to be agencies in the sense of the agreements, applicability of the collective agreement can be a bit of a shock, as the agreement contains many provisions that cater for the specific needs of classical work agencies and their workers (*infra*). Therefore, the 'non-classical' agencies, like firms that post specially trained medical or technical staff to user firms, would be interested in finding a way out.

The easiest way would be to clarify the personal scope of application of the Collective Labour Agreement during the next bargaining round. Another possibility would be an ad hoc exemption from the agreement by the Minister or the social partners. If neither exemption has been requested or granted, the question is whether

---

32. Article 3(1) Wet algemeen verbindend en onverbindend verklaring cao.
33. See e.g., Article 13(1)(c) of the Collective Labour Agreement (CLA).
34. Available in English at: https://www.abu.nl/yourpassage/collective_labour_agreement_temporary_agency_workers/index.html#10 (accessed 20 July 2017).
35. Article 2(2) CLA.
36. P.Th. Sick, A.M. Wevers, *De allocatiefunctie 'alloceren'?*, TRA (2017/16); M. Tanja, J. den Hoedt, *De uitzendovereenkomst, een beperkende uitleg met verruimende gevolgen*, TRA (2017/15).

the employer company falls within another sectoral collective labour agreement. If that is the case, Article 2(4) of the collective labour agreement may still ensure the applicability of the agency collective agreement. Article 2(4) describes employers who are not considered agencies, but which, if the cumulative criteria stated in the provision are fulfilled, fall within the scope of application of the collective labour agreement. In the first place, the business's activities must consist entirely of placing workers, as defined in Article 7:690 BW. As discussed above, this is a very broad concept and does not help in limiting or defining the scope of application. Second, the employees must be involved in work regulated by a different collective labour agreement as their employers' for at least 25% of the wage sum. In the third place, the employer must deploy workers for at least 15% of the total annual wage and salary bill on the basis of contracts that include an agency clause as defined in Article 7:691(2) BW.[37] In my view, when hiring out highly qualified staff, which is not readily at hand, two things may happen that prevent the applicability of the collective labour agreement. In the first place, it is quite possible that the legal employer uses the collective labour agreement that also applies to the user to which the employees are seconded, in other words, he uses a different agreement than the one he himself is bound by. Second, and this seems the much more valuable argument, I cannot imagine an agency clause being applicable in these employment relations. After all, these postings concern highly trained, specialised and therefore sought after staff. In spite of the very broad range of employment relations coming within the ambit of Articles 7:690 and 7:691 BW, the collective labour agreement may not be applicable to all these relations due to Article 2(4). If the collective labour agreement is applicable while not really fitting the situation, it remains to be seen whether all the unfitting provisions can be contracted away.

[B] Flexibility

One of the core provisions of the Collective labour agreement is Article 13, containing the phase system, that regulates the accumulation of rights and the strengthening position of the agency worker. The so-called phase-system describes the three phases of the agency contract. Phase A is the least secure: the agency clause from Article 7:691(2) BW will apply and the chain of contracts-provision (Article 7:668a BW combined with Article 7:691(1) BW) will be inapplicable, unless explicitly provided differently. This means that the employee will enjoy no security concerning employment and that dismissal law provisions do not apply. Instead, every contract terminates as of law as soon as the user tells the agency that they no longer wish to employ the worker. Phase A lasts for seventy-eight worked weeks which is the maximum period allowed by law.[38] If an employee does not work every week, this – already long – period of one and a half years is extended. Interruptions of more than six months lead to a new start in phase A at zero. During the applicability of the agency clause in phase

---

37. There are two more criteria, but these are the most important ones. See for more information Article 2(4) d and e of the CLA.
38. Cf. Article 7:691(8) BW.

A, another provision from the collective labour agreement applies which adds to the insecurity. This clause is Article 14 of the collective agreement. It states that the employee must notify both, the employer and the user in case of sickness, which is a normal requirement in triangular employment relations as both, the employer and the user feel the consequences of the employee's sickness. The interesting aspect of this clause is hidden in section 4, which defines the consequence of the notification of sickness. It states that as long as the employee works in phase A and the agency clause applies, the notification of incapacity to work is deemed to be the user company's request to terminate the contract for services. Combined with the existence of the agency clause, this provision means the immediate termination of the employment contract as of law. The collective labour agreement, with the trade unions' consent, stipulates that the obligatory notification of being unfit to work triggers a resolutive condition. The resolutive condition leads to a termination by law of the contract, so the usual prohibition of dismissal concerning sick employees does not apply.[39] Compared to the near absolute prohibition of dismissal in case of sickness during 104 weeks applicable to permanent employment contracts, this looks rather bleak. It is also interesting to note that the provision remains unchanged, even though since 1 July 2015, the possibility to derogate from the prohibition of termination on grounds of sickness has been deleted from the law. To be fair, technically, the agency clause as such does not bring about a dismissal but a termination as of law. However, construing a resolutive condition from a prohibited ground for dismissal shows a very different idea of employee protection.

As said before, all these rules apply during the first seventy-eight weeks in which the agency worker has actually worked. In the (unlikely) case an employee successfully completes phase A, phase B starts. This phase offers much more security. It consists of a maximum of six fixed-term secondments in four years' time. In fact, these contracts are fixed-term contracts and a minimum of employment security is provided. However, in contrast to the usually applicable rules on termination, Article 15 CLA stipulates that different, much shorter, periods of notice apply. Thus, here also, flexibility reigns.

Finally, in phase C, after a minimum of seventy-eight weeks in phase A and a maximum of four more years in phase B, the agency worker enters into a permanent employment contract with the agency, provided his employment history shows no gaps of more than six months.

[C] Wages

Concerning payment, to which a whole chapter is devoted, the principal rule is payment at the user's rate (Article 19). The entitlement to payment at the user's rates starts on the first day of employment for the user firm. Article 20 specifies how the agency worker's tasks are to be classified and which elements of the user remuneration

---

39. Cf Article 7:670(1) BW.

apply. These elements are then specified in great detail.[40] The exceptions to the rule that the user's wages apply can be found in section 3 of the chapter on wages. For employees described here, the agency work wage scales apply. According to Article 27 CLA, the agency wages apply to a whole range of persons who have in common that they are (seemingly) hard to integrate in the first employment market. The enumeration includes long term (= more than twelve months) unemployed, reintegration target groups, e.g., under the Work and Income (Capacity for Work) Act, job-seekers who are unable to earn the statutory minimum wage, drop-outs from school, people who are re-entering the labour market after an absence of at least three years and holiday workers. Specific rules apply to a so-called transition group, where employees are guided towards new employment, to non-gradable workers with respect to the user's job list and to employees in phase C enjoying a permanent employment contract.

During phase A and in secondment contracts which explicitly exclude continued payment of wages, wages are only due for those periods in which the employee really shows up at the user firm and actually works, unless explicitly agreed otherwise.[41] However, if the employee shows up at the user enterprise at the agreed time and is not put to work, he has a right to wages over three hours of work.[42] In case the secondment contract contains a right to continued payment of wages, the agency must pay the employee the reversion wages (*terugvalloon*). If the employee loses part of his working hours, he is entitled to the reversion wages over the lost hours. However, in this case, the agency must look for suitable job offers and if possible, place the employee in a suitable job.[43]

[D] Other Provisions

The collective agreement contains several more chapters, dealing with health and safety, holidays and days off (and wage payment over these days), pensions and vocational training. It also contains a complete chapter with rules applicable in international and cross-border situations. They mainly relate to an alternative payment of holiday wages, housing and travel costs and to social insurance. These rules are adapted to the (usually short) spells of employment across the border.

§18.05 ASSESSMENT OF THE COLLECTIVE LABOUR AGREEMENT ON AGENCY WORK

It is interesting to note that the collective labour agreement in the agency sector offers a different range of protection according to the subject in question. Concerning wages, employee protection has improved a lot. Under the previous collective agreement, agency workers could be paid the (lower) agency wages during the first twenty-six weeks of employment in a user enterprise. This led to substantial unrest amongst

---

40. Articles 21-26 CLA.
41. Article 40 CLA.
42. This is actually a statutory right, see Article 7:628a BW.
43. Article 44 CLA.

workers, after all, employees of the user firm saw others do their job for less money. Fears of being outpriced rose, particularly in cases of cross-border agency work, in which, in accordance with Directive 96/71/EC, the home law remains applicable, save for the issues mentioned explicitly and exclusively in Article 3(1)(g). Under the new agreement, the general principle of equal value for equal work is taken into account from the beginning onwards, even though, strictly speaking, triangular relations fall out of the ambit of equal treatment law due to the fact that the unequal treatment cannot be traced back to a single (responsible) source.[44] Still, it should be borne in mind that concerning wages, the collective agreement ensures a reasonable standard. The categories exempted from the right to pay according to a user are those with immense difficulties entering the labour market, whose labour value simply may be less and who need this lower wages in order to re-enter the labour market at all.

The provisions on health and safety, holidays, holiday pay, pension and vocational training also show a balanced approach in which the employee is offered a reasonable range of rights which, e.g., in the case of holiday pay are modelled according the employee's needs. One reason for the equal treatment on these issues is that it seems rather impractical to imagine e.g., a work floor where different safety rules apply to different categories of employees. Other aspects, like vocational training, holidays and pensions correspond to higher employment costs and therefore limit the competitive advantage of agency workers. This, like wage costs as such, helps to prevent unequal treatment on the work floor and competition on employment conditions, which has always been a traditional concern of trade unions. Therefore, protection with regard to wages and cost-related employment conditions as well as security should not come as a surprise.

However, with regard to protection of employment, the picture is a very different one. Here, the statutory possibilities to derogate in peius from protective provisions have been used to their fullest extent. The best illustration is the phase system with the very extensive phase A of complete insecurity which lasts for a minimum of one and a half years and is followed by a period of slightly more security for four more years and only then, after a minimum of 5.5 years, a permanent contract is reached. Even if there is agreement on agency work to be flexible in nature, this is a lot of flexibility combined with very little security.

Still, the most striking clause in the whole agreement is the clause that construes a termination as of right in case of a notification of being unfit for work. This is so out of tune with the rules that apply to standard employment contracts, where being medically unfit for work amounts to a prohibition of dismissal and strict wage and re-integration duties that one really wonders why this provision was made, or rather, why trade unions accepted it. However, it has been there from the very start, and after some discussion in the very beginning[45] it has never been challenged.[46]

---

44. C. Barnard, *EU Employment Law*, 309 (4th ed. Oxford University Press 2012).
45. E. Verhulp *De uitzendkracht in het flex(s)t(r)ijdperk*, Sociaal Recht 322-328 (1998).
46. Another question is, whether this possibility to terminate the employment contract immediately really leads to saving money as the agencies have specific social security obligations (they carry their own unemployment risk). Discussion on that would, however, lead too far away from the core question of this contribution.

§18.06 WHY IS THE COLLECTIVE LABOUR AGREEMENT AS IT STANDS?

This very mixed picture with regard to protecting employee rights certainly triggers the question why the collective agreement was agreed in this form. Even if one agrees on the idea that agency work is flexible by nature, one could definitely ask why the collective agreement offers this much flexibility, particularly with regard to the termination of the employment contract and the extensive derogations from protective provisions.

In my view, several explanations are possible. All of them relate to the specific industrial relations in triangular employment relations, particularly the classical agency work.

In the first place, trade unions do not bargain from a position of strength in the agency sector. Union density is low, even lower than the already low overall union density. One possible explanation for this is that agency workers often are young persons. In the Netherlands, young persons are more likely not to be members of a trade union than older workers.[47] Another explanation is that temporary agency workers may be much harder to organise than employees enjoying a permanent contract. It may be that agency workers will not easily join trade unions, because for them the possible benefits of a collective agreement are too unsure. Agency contracts usually are concluded for relatively short periods. Collective agreements, in contrast, are usually concluded only after (lengthy) negotiations. A long process of negotiations does not appeal to agency workers, because they do not see how, if at all, they can benefit from it.

In the second place, trade unions, being weak in the agency sector due to low union density, and therefore not having an incentive to bargain hard or simply lacking bargaining power, may prefer to protect their core members. Generally speaking these are the relatively old, white males in permanent employment.[48] As these employees make up most of the trade union members, there may be a strong preference in the unions to keep available a flexible crust of employees that enjoy (almost) no employment protection, but as such serve as employment protection for the core workers. During economic upheavals, they are the first to be dismissed[49] and thus cushion the core workers in case of economically hard times. This preference could explain the extreme flexibility and near total lack of employment protection in the Agency collective labour agreement.

Both aspects combined may explain why the collective labour agreement in the agency sector offers relatively little employment protection, but aims at making agency work no less costly for an employer in terms of wages and other employment conditions than regular work.

---

47. See for figures: http://statline.cbs.nl/Statweb/publication/?VW = T&DM = SLNL&PA = 80598 NED&D1 = 0&D2 = 0&D3 = a&D4 = 0-1,3-5&D5 = a&HD = 160804-1645&HDR = T,G2,G1,G3&STB = G4 (accessed 23 July 2017).
48. *Ibid.*
49. Article 7:671b(5)(c) BW.

§18.07 IS THE TRADE UNION THE MOST APPROPRIATE PROTECTOR OF AGENCY WORKERS?

The final question to be discussed in this contribution is, whether the legislator should offer as much leeway to derogate in peius from protective employment law provisions in a sector where union density is low, the unions' bargaining position is correspondingly weak and the unions may be more interested in the fate of other employees.

Generally speaking, particularly after an analysis of the collective labour agreement in the Agency sector, one could doubt the legislator's faith in trade unions to ensure equitable protection for all employees. That the legislator shares some of these doubts, can also be inferred form the fact that during the latest round of amendments to Dutch labour law in 2015, the possibilities to derogate from the law by collective agreement have been limited. One of the reasons was to counter the 'excessive flexibility'[50] on the Dutch labour market. In that light, it is interesting to note, just how much flexibility has been retained. After all, the Dutch legislator set the limits to derogatory provisions at the maximum period agreed upon by former collective labour agreements. Still, there now is an absolute limit set by the legislator.

Considering the extremely wide margins allowed – the period of near-total job insecurity being tripled from twenty-six to seventy-eight weeks – and the fact that the collective labour agreement has consistently used this legislative leeway to the fullest extent, one could ask whether trade unions, in view of their unenviable position due to lack of bargaining power and maybe also bargaining will due to conflicting interests within the federation are best placed to achieve equitable employment protection for agency workers.

---

50. Kamerstukken II, 2013/14, 33818, nr. 3, p. 3.

CHAPTER 19
Multi-Employer Situations and Collective Bargaining: The Hungarian Cases

Gábor Kártyás

§19.01 INTRODUCTION

There is a long-standing discussion in labour law literature concerning the notion of 'employer'. Numerous studies have challenged the unitary concept of the employer and pointed out situations where multiple entities exercise employer functions.[1] Yet the collective aspects of such scenarios have not gained as much attention as their effects on the individual employment relationship. This chapter aims to discover the obstacles trade unions face in collective bargaining caused by the proliferation of employer positions. After an analysis of the most common cases of multiple employers, there are some concluding remarks and questions for the future.

The scope of the study is limited by two factors. First, in the settings assessed, employee status – the legal form of employment – is not questioned. Although employment rights beyond the employment relationship (including questions of collective labour rights[2]) are a major problem in contemporary labour law,[3] this chapter focuses only situations based on the typical employment relationship. Nonetheless, it will be seen that even in this 'traditional' setting, multi-employer cases can

---

1. See for example: Paul Davis, Mark Freedland, *The Complexities of the Employing Enterprise*, in Guy Davidov & Brian Langille (eds), *Boundaries and Frontiers of Labour Law. Goals and Means in the Regulation of Work* (Hart Publishing 2006); Jeremias Prassl, *The Concept of the Employer* (Oxford University Press 2015).
2. In the *FNV Kunsten* case the European Court of Justice ruled that a collectively bargained minimum wage applicable for self-employed musicians may be contrary to the prohibitions of competition law (*FNV Kunsten Informatie en Media kontra Staat der Nederlanden*, C-413/13., ECLI:EU:C:2014:2411).
3. See for instance the Comparative Labour Law and Policy Journal's special issue on the network economy (Volume 37, Issue 3 – Spring 2016).

challenge the very structure of collective labour law. Second, collective bargaining in temporary agency work is not tackled here. Agency work significantly differs from the cases analysed below, as the employer-like responsibility of the user company/non-contractual employer is recognised by law.[4] Needless to say, the division of the employer's position between the agency and user company still raises several questions on collective bargaining in the agency work sector.[5]

§19.02 A CASE STUDY: LOST BETWEEN FOUR 'EMPLOYERS'

The nature and complexity of multi-employer situations is well illustrated by the following case study. At the end of 2015, a leading Hungarian online media company was sold. The firm operated as a subsidiary of the biggest telecommunication service provider in Hungary, while the whole group was controlled by a huge international company. The mother company had a long-standing history of developed social dialogue with two unions active within the organisation. Both the mother company and the subsidiary had collective agreements. When the first rumours of the acquisition leaked out, the union represented in the subsidiary immediately started negotiations on the future of working conditions – and especially of the collective agreement. But no matter how desperately the union tried to find a partner to negotiate with, it met with closed doors.

First, the union officials approached the subsidiary, the legal employer with whom the collective agreement had been concluded. They were rejected, as the management felt no longer competent on future working conditions and said the mother company was responsible for conducting the vending process. When the union knocked on the mother company's door, the answer was negative again: the Hungarian management pointed to the group's international headquarters, as all questions relevant to the transition were determined there. On reaching the international managers, the union learned that the vending contract strictly stipulated that the vendor should not alter any working conditions prior to the acquisition taking place. Thus the union was politely referred to the buyer. As the final step, the new owner of the company expressed a warm welcome to the union and requested patience: the new management confessed that they needed at least a year to become familiar with the organisation and did not wish to enter into negotiations on the working conditions until then. After nearly eight months of chasing a competent bargaining partner, the union's

---

4. *See* especially the user's right to supervise and direct agency workers and its obligation to offer equal working conditions as prescribed in directive 2008/104/EC of the European Parliament and of the Council of 19 November 2008 on temporary agency work, Articles 3 and 5.
5. James Arrowsmith, *Temporary Agency Work and Collective Bargaining in the EU* (European Foundation for the Improvement of Living and Working Conditions, 2008); Eurociett, UNI-Europa: *The Role of Temporary Agency Work and Labour Market Transitions in Europe: Institutional Frameworks, Empirical Evidence, Good Practice and the Impact of Social Dialogue* 54-63 (2013); Tamás Gyulavári, Gábor Kártyás, *The Hungarian Flexicurity Pathway? New Labour Code after Twenty Years in the Market Economy* 148-150 (Pázmány Press 2015).

overtures remained unanswered. In the event, the union was involved in the acquisition process only as far as was required by law, which meant merely formal consultations and no real influence. At the time writing this chapter, the employer's side of the bargaining table remains unoccupied.

§19.03 GENERAL REMARKS: IS THIS JUST A QUESTION OF POWER?

Before turning to the specific cases involving more employers, some common features may be pointed out. Such situations are always initiated or designed by the employer. It is never the employees' interests that drive these organisational changes, but rather it is the within the employer's autonomy to shape the employing organisation. This principle appeared in the European Court of Justice's (ECJ) practice concerning the mass dismissals directive. In the *Fujitsu Siemens* case, the ECJ stated that the way the management of a group of undertakings is organised is an internal matter and that it is not the purpose of the directive to restrict the freedom of such a group to organise their activities as they think best suits their needs.[6] In most cases, the shaping of the employer's organisation is not considered a labour law issue, but rather handled as a transaction governed by civil law. Nonetheless, such civil law contracts have grave labour law implications, which are often seen as unintended side effects. The above-mentioned characteristics also explain the huge diversity of the cases.

Multi-employer situations mean at least a twofold challenge for unions. First, it is definitely more difficult to organise workers in complex organisations. Most employers are not structured as a sole legal person operating out of unitary physical premises and led by one manager exercising and fulfilling the full range of employers' rights and obligations. Even a matter as simple as informing employees about the union's position on the current wage policy becomes a challenge if such workers are separated into small employing entities all acting as legally independent employers – or alternatively, controlled by a central body. Second, as the above case study suggests, the real decision-maker might easily disappear in the maze of complex organisational structures, leaving the union without a partner to bargain with. As a contrast to the above-mentioned *Fujitsu Siemens* case, the European Court of Human Rights pointed out how employers might abuse their freedom to organise their business to escape some legal obligations in a case concerning the right to strike and a UK ban on secondary actions. Delocalising work centres, outsourcing work to other companies and adopting complex corporate structures in order to transfer work to separate legal entities or to hive off companies could make trade unions 'find themselves severely hampered in the performance of their legitimate, normal activities in protecting their members' interests'.[7]

Before proceeding any further, a possible solution can be highlighted which would make the present long story very short. That is the power of the union. If the

---

6. *Akavan Erityisalojen Keskusliitto AEK ry and Others v. Fujitsu Siemens Computers Oy.*, C-44/08., ECLI:EU:C:2009:533, paragraph 59. *See also Rockfon A/S v. Specialarbejderforbundet i Danmark*, C-449/93., ECLI:EU:C:1995:420, paragraph 21.
7. *RMT v. UK* (no. 31045/10) paragraph 98.

relevant union is strong enough and has sufficient members to ensure that its threat of a strike is thus taken with due seriousness, the employer will surely appoint a bargaining partner, no matter how complex the organisational structure. We can still agree with Otto Kahn-Freund that when employees negotiate with the employer, it is 'a negotiation between collective entities, both of which are, or may at least be, bearers of power'.[8] While choosing this quick ending for the story is rather tempting, we might wonder whether today's unions are powerful enough to overcome the challenges of multi-employer structures. We might be rather doubtful. In my view, the least labour law can do is to eliminate the legal barriers blocking the route to the bargaining table. In the following sections, some of the most common multi-employer scenarios are presented, mostly from the Hungarian experience, with a focus on the (legal) obstacles they imply for unions and some possible solutions.

§19.04 PUBLIC FUNDING ENTITIES

Probably the most common cases where other entities appear behind (or next to) the legal employer are those where employers do not enjoy financial independence. This occurs in public funding entities, where the legally independent employer has no or very limited competence over financial issues and such decisions are made by a sustainer that funds the employer. For example, a local government runs different institutions, such as a kindergarten, concert hall or museum. While these may have their own legal personality and act as employers of their staff, all decisions with financial implications require the consent of the town hall. In this setting, collective bargaining without the mayor's representative at the table is meaningless.[9] The issue is the same when the employer has a complex ownership background.[10]

It is obvious that there are always owners or shareholders behind an employer who in one way or another will have their say during collective bargaining. The issue becomes complex if the employer is not the owner's or sustainer's only business, meaning its decision does not reflect solely the interests of the relevant employer. The more complex the interests at stake become, the harder it is for the union to achieve its goals. For example, even if the museum supports the union's claim for a pay raise, the local government might reject it to allocate more budget for its other institutions. It is not rare in such cases for the employer and union to stand on common ground and bargain with joint forces against the sustainer. Here the factual bargaining situation (union + employer against the sustainer) is totally different from that mapped by labour law (union against the employer).

---

8. Otto Kahn-Freund, *Kahn-Freund's Labour and the Law* 17-18 (Stevens&Sons, 1983).
9. This is exactly the case with Hungarian public employees. Public institutions act as the legal employer of their public employees; however, the financial background for their activity is guaranteed by the sustainer. As unions cannot negotiate directly with the sustainer, collective bargaining with the legal employer becomes rather formal, especially in the most important questions, such as wages. Csilla Lehoczkyné Kollonay, *A magyar munkajog I–II.* 82 (Vincze Kiadó 2001).
10. See for example Prassl's thorough analysis of the employer's functions in Private Equity Investments. Prassl, *supra* n. 1, at 73-80.

While it seems unrealistic to legally oblige the owner/sustainer to negotiate directly with the union if requested, such a concept appears partly in EU labour law. Directives on mass dismissals and transfer of undertakings prescribe that the employer has to fulfil its obligation to inform and consult the workers' representatives irrespective of whether the relevant decision regarding the collective redundancy or the transfer is being taken by the employer or by an undertaking controlling the employer.[11] Nonetheless, the ECJ pointed out that even if these decisions are made by a separate entity, it does not have the status of employer and the obligation to inform, consult and notify is imposed solely on the employer and not the controlling entity.[12] Thus, from a legal point of view, the two organisations are to be approached as different employers; however, union law recognises that certain decisions are made outside the unitary employer.

§19.05 COMPANY GROUPS

If different companies are connected by ownership, the identity of the union's bargaining partner might become blurred. 'Once the majority, or at least a significant proportion of voting rights, are vested in a single shareholder, it will be able to exert considerable power over management.'[13]

In the *Albron* case,[14] the ECJ recognised that the employers' functions and responsibilities might rest beyond the party who signed the employment contract as employer. The case concerned a group of companies where all the staff were employed by one employer, which acted centrally and detached the staff to the group's various operating companies. One member provided catering services in various locations for the group's employees. These activities were outsourced to a third party. The ECJ had to decide whether such an arrangement constituted transfer of an undertaking within the meaning of directive 2001/23/EC,[15] considering that there was no actual employment contract between the employees affected and the economic entity transferred.

Article 3(1) of directive 2001/23 requires an employment contract, or alternatively and thus as an equivalent, an employment relationship at the date of the transfer. From such wording the Court concluded that a contractual link with the transferor is not required in all circumstances for employees to be able to benefit from the protection conferred by the directive. In its reasoning, the ECJ differentiated the 'contractual' from the 'factual' employer, where the former was not responsible for the economic activity of the economic entity transferred. The Court ruled that if there is a plurality of

---

11. Council Directive 98/59/EC of 20 July 1998 on the approximation of the laws of the Member States relating to collective redundancies Article 2(4) and Council Directive 2001/23/EC of 12 March 2001 on the approximation of the laws of the Member States relating to the safeguarding of employees' rights in the event of transfers of undertakings, businesses or parts of undertakings or businesses Article 7(4).
12. C-44/08, paragraphs 57–58.
13. Prassl, *supra* n. 1, at 54.
14. *Albron Catering BV kontra FNV Bondgenoten and John Roest*, C-242/09., ECLI:EU:C:2010:625.
15. Council Directive 2001/23/EC of 12 March 2001 on the approximation of the laws of the Member States relating to the safeguarding of employees' rights in the event of transfers of undertakings, businesses or parts of undertakings or businesses.

employers, the contractual employer must not systematically be given greater weight and take precedence, for the purposes of determining the identity of the transferor, over the position of a non-contractual employer who is responsible for that activity. The ECJ also referred to the aim of the directive – that is the protection of employees in the event of a change of the employer – and found that the above interpretation is in line with such an aim.[16]

One might wonder what message this ruling has for unions. The separation of the factual and contractual employer would be useful for unions to identify who to bargain with in multi-employer cases and there is little in the judgment to suggest that this purposive interpretation is limited to the transferor concept.[17] Nevertheless, such a functional approach can only be relied on if it is incorporated into national law; otherwise, it is less likely that courts will apply it to oblige employers to bargain with the union.

§19.06 LARGE EMPLOYING ENTITIES

The union's bargaining goals can be seriously hampered if a huge and diverse employing organisation is centralised. Even numerous physically separated premises with diverse activities can come under the umbrella of one organisation (one legal person) which acts as a sole legal employer. Only a very detailed collective agreement could cover all the various needs of the different divisions of such an organisation, not to mention that these needs might contradict each other. The more diverse interests appear in the activities and workplaces to be covered, the more challenging it becomes to find the common ground to represent against the employer.

The collective agreement concluded in the public education sector in Hungary is a good example. From 2013 an umbrella organisation called the Klebelsberg Centre for Public Education Institution Management (KLIK) was set up to centralise the operation of all public (primary and secondary) schools in the country. This meant an enormous reorganisation, putting one government agency in the place of over 5,000 independent education institutions with their own legal personality.[18] In November 2013, KLIK concluded a collective agreement with the teachers' union.[19] While the union welcomed reaching such an agreement, a closer look at its content reveals that it is rather an empty shell. Most of the nearly ten-page document merely repeats the statutory regulation and contains but a handful of substantive provisions (e.g., on substitution fees, disciplinary actions or breaks). Nonetheless, one should not forget that the agreement is applicable to all schools maintained by KLIK. Both tiny village schools with only one teacher and prestigious urban secondary schools with laboratories and sports centres are covered, although they have little in common as workplaces.

---

16. C-242/09, paragraphs 25–29.
17. Prassl, *supra* n. 1, at 104.
18. 202/2012. (VII. 27.) Governmental Decree Article 6.
19. Available in Hungarian at: http://klik.gov.hu/download/7/fe/80000/KLIK_PSZ%20kollekt%C3%ADv_1122.pdf (accessed 20 July 2017).

Considering such heterogeneity, it is not surprising that the bargaining partners could not touch upon more relevant issues.

Although Hungarian labour law traditionally builds on the system of multi-level collective agreements[20] – that is to say, it recognises that agreements can be concluded at sector level, mezzo level (covering more employers) and employer level –, it must be emphasised that KLIK is one unitary employer. Thus legally all public schools have to be covered by one collective agreement. Nonetheless, court practice recognised the possibility of a collective agreement containing annexes applying only to specific workplaces of the employer and which might prescribe special (even less favourable) rules to certain groups of employees.[21] This could be a way to enrich the content of KLIK's collective agreement. However, it is quite apparent that the government's intent was the fullest possible centralisation of public education. Thus most probably only the union would call for such annexes.

§19.07 MICRO-EMPLOYING ENTITIES

The way a business is organised may be diametrically opposite to that described above; moreover, the disintegration of the employing organisation is much more common. In this case, the separate divisions of the organisation have legal personality and act as the employer of their own staff. Although these 'cells' are independent (and could also appear as separate companies), they cooperate under the auspices of an umbrella organisation. This is how a franchise system is usually structured. Numerous franchisees, acting on their own account as legal persons, contribute to the operation of the franchisor's business, retailing the latter's product or providing its service. Nonetheless, the franchise contract generally contains detailed provisions on how the franchisee can carry out its activities, which means strict control for the franchisor.[22] The franchisee's bounds can be as tight as between a division and the headquarters within one organisation.[23]

In labour law systems based on the unitary concept of the employer, it can be difficult if not impossible for employees in small franchise outlets to organise and bargain effectively.[24] Separate legal persons mean separate bargaining partners for the union if it intends to conclude an agreement covering all workers. For example, if a restaurant chain operates on the franchise model, each restaurant will be approached to cover all staff in the chain. While it seems much more convenient to bargain with the franchisor directly, it can easily refuse the union's approach with the excuse of not being the legal employer of the workers affected. Moreover, the franchisor might

---

20. Gyula Berke, *A kollektív szerződés a magyar munkajogban*, 142 (Utilitates Bt. 2014).
21. See Supreme Court decision no. Mfv. II. 11.082/2001/3.
22. This is well reflected in the Hungarian Civil Code, prescribing that the franchisor shall have the right to give orders and to control; however, the franchisee acts on its own account during its retailing activity [Act 5 of 2013 on the Civil Code Articles 6:376(2) and 6:380(1)].
23. Joellen Riley, *A Blurred Boundary between Entrepreneurship and Servitude: Regulating Business Format Franchising in Australia*, in: Judy Fudge, Shae McCrystal & Kamala Sankaran, *Challenging the Legal Boundaries of Work Regulation* 103-104 (Hart Publishing 2012).
24. Riley, *supra* n. 23, at 107.

organise its business precisely in this way to outsource employment risks and obligations to its partners.[25] While the franchisor may have little or no intent to bargain, it is also burdensome to negotiate with the franchisees. Approaching the separate employers requires a lot of time and resources the union might not have, and besides the franchisees can be small organisations where the union cannot attract members or meet the statutory criteria to be eligible for collective bargaining.

§19.08 EMPLOYEE SHARING

Employee sharing (or labour pooling) is built on the clear multiplication of the employer's position. In this new form of employment, a group of employers hires workers jointly and is jointly responsible for them. Each participating employer's position is identical in that all enjoy and bear the same employers' rights and obligations. Unlike with agency work, variations in employer status are not qualitative but quantitative. For example, each employer may give orders to the shared employee, but has to respect the other employers' same right. Thus the employers have to agree among themselves how to split the employee's working time and define the time limits the employee is available for each of them. Joint employment also means that the employers bear the costs of employment together without a 'central' employer who would charge the others for the assigned workforce (as a temporary work agency would do with the user company). Employee sharing is a rather rare but spreading phenomenon, which has not yet been regulated in most European countries. It can be legally construed in various ways. One possible model is that all employers sign a common employment contract with the employee, or there can be an umbrella organisation (embracing the employers) that enters into the employment relationship. Shared employment is mostly used to cope with seasonal or unbalanced workforce needs (e.g., in ports or agriculture). It may also be favourable for SMEs to hire highly trained specialists (e.g., a tax lawyer or a marketing expert) jointly and split the costs or risks. From the employee's side, permanent joint employment is more advantageous than a set of consecutive short-term contracts with the members of the group would be.[26]

An employment relationship involving more employers leads to confronting collective agreements if more participating employers have agreements in force. At this point, legal regulation should step in and guide the parties as to which agreement to apply to the shared employee.[27] As an illustration, the Hungarian Labour Code

---

25. The employment contract, understood as a bilateral relationship, 'allows (and, perhaps, invites) firms to shift the risks associated with employing labour' to various forms of intermediaries (Judy Fudge, *The Legal Boundaries of the Employer, Precarious Workers, and Labour Protection*, in Guy Davidov, Brian Langille, *Boundaries and Frontiers of Labour Law. Goals and Means in the Regulation of Work* (Hart Publishing 2006). Now, we can add, the burdens of collective bargaining may also be outsourced.
26. Eurofound: *New forms of employment* 11-13, 17 (Publications Office of the European Union 2015).
27. Certain authors argue that Hungarian labour law will enable employers to conclude more collective agreements, for instance if more trade unions are represented within the organisation

prescribes that the collective agreement concluded by the employer liable for wages shall apply to the shared employee, in the absence of an agreement to the contrary.[28] It is up to the employers to decide which one of them is responsible for wages. Thus great discretion is offered to the parties. As collective agreements usually set out detailed rules on remuneration, it is a logical choice to follow the Labour Code rule and apply the collective agreement of the employer responsible for wages. However, the employers might specifically want to exclude the employee from its scope. For instance, where another employer's agreement offers less generous benefits, the parties might choose it for cost-cutting reasons. Nonetheless, it would clearly be an abusive exercise of rights[29] to select an employer where there is no collective agreement in force, and such an agreement is therefore void. Note that deviation from the statutory rule needs the agreement of all employers and the employee, and not just of the employers alone.[30]

§19.09 CONCLUSIONS AND QUESTIONS

'Will the real employer please stand up?' Unions could quote this smart title two British scholars used in their paper on the employer's rights and obligations in agency work.[31] In the cases presented, the difficulties unions face do not lie in the legal construction of employment, in the sense that they are all involve employees in the traditional, typical employment relationship. In these scenarios, it is rather the employer who is atypical. While it is undoubtedly within the employer's autonomy to design its organisation to best fit its activities, such freedom is not without boundaries. The chase after cost-effective business models cannot outsource the responsibilities an employer has towards workers' representatives to no man's land. 'No public or private entity should be permitted to profit from violations of the four core labour rights in the ILO's 1998 Declaration of Fundamental Principles and Rights at Work', among them the denial of freedom of association.[32] The cases analysed show some of the first examples of labour law stepping in to defend such basic principles. The number of similar multi-employer situations will surely grow in the near future. It remains to be seen whether the body of applicable labour law will follow.

---

and each agreement would be applicable to the members of the signatory union. However, this is not possible under the Labour Code in force. Tamás Prugberger, *Az új Munkatörvénykönyv az uniós normák és a tagállami szabályozások tükrében*. In: Attila Kun, *Az új Munka Törvénykönyve dilemmái* (Acta Caroliensia Conventorum Scientiarum Iuridico-Politicarum V 2013).
28. Act 1 of 2012 on the Labour Code Article 279(4).
29. Labour Code Article 7.
30. This solution is similar to a previous but still relevant court practice, which recognised that parties may stipulate in the employment contract the application of a certain collective agreement, even if the employer falls under no collective agreement (Supreme Court, Mfv. II. 10.137/2001/5).
31. Michael Wynn, Patricia Leighton, *Will the Real Employer Please Stand Up? Client Companies and the Employment Status of the Temporary Agency Worker*. Vol. 35. Industrial Law Journal (2006).
32. Alan Hyde, *Legal Responsibility for Labour Conditions Down the Production Chain*. In: Judy Fudge, Shae McCrystal & Kamala Sankaran, *Challenging the Legal Boundaries of Work Regulation* 98 (Hart Publishing 2012).

CHAPTER 20
A Study in Red and Blue: A Comparison of Collective Bargaining in Carrefour in Some EU Countries

José María Miranda Boto, Teresa Coelho Moreira, Florence Debord, Sonia Fernández Sánchez, Yolanda Maneiro Vázquez & Łukasz Pisarczyk

§20.01 GOALS AND FOUNDATIONS OF THIS CHAPTER

[A] Into the Heart of Collective Bargaining

Previous INLACRIS research and meetings have arrived at several useful conclusions on collective bargaining, decentralisation, the mutation of the roles of the bargaining agents, and other interesting issues. These findings, however, have been mainly focused on the abstract, theoretical level. They were based on the study of national legislations and found some hints of legal harmonisation, spontaneous or otherwise. The EU documents encouraging the growth of collective bargaining as a tool are well known.[1] If we drew up a well-organised table, we could probably fill its gaps with many common answers throughout the Member States.

---

1. Recently, in the Communication from the Commission, *Launching a consultation on a European Pillar of Social Rights*, (COM (2016) 127 final). The 10th item in Chapter II reads as follows: 'Well-functioning social dialogue requires autonomous and representative social partners with the capacities to reach collective agreements. Given the decreases in terms of organisational density and representativeness, social partners need to further build their capacities to engage in a better functioning and effective social dialogue. The engagement of social partners at EU and national level is crucial for the success of design and implementation of economic and social policies, including in efforts to safeguard employment in periods of economic downturns. Moreover, new forms of work organisation such as in the services sector and in the digital economy make the involvement of workers uneven, and their information and consultation more complex. a. Social partners shall be consulted in the design and implementation of employment and social policies. They shall be encouraged to develop collective agreements in matters relevant

But the reality of collective bargaining can only be grasped through the reading and studying of actual collective agreements.[2] They will show whether the legislator's will has been implemented or if, on the other hand, social partners have their own points of view about the management of industrial relations. That is the main justification for a case study: a trip into the heart of collective bargaining, taking on the role of a collective Marlow, trying to identify if the legal harmonisation has also meant an actual harmonisation of the structures, actors and contents of collective bargaining.

In a certain way, a case study could also mean a synthesis of very important parts of current INLACRIS research, incorporating a transversal approach. The most specific parts, concerning, e.g., work-life balance, older and younger workers, the role of agency work, or the impact of crisis on collective bargaining, could easily be incorporated into it.

A first, obvious approach is the quantitative one. We could easily describe this possibility as 'the *Eurostat* temptation'. The irresistible attraction of figures showing differences is, at first glance, a major asset. But, after a little thought, the main defects of this approach are quickly seen: we lack the context to fully evaluate these quantities. It is all very well to find a salary gap of EUR 300 between two countries, but it would be better to have a general idea about the meaning of that money, linked to the minimum and average salaries in those countries, the cost of living, the price of a coffee or a glass of wine...for isolated numbers do not usually say very much, though they are useful for citing easy examples and showing contrasts.

This should lead us to the necessity of the qualitative approach. And that is, hopefully, the real value of this chapter, a reality-based exercise in theoretical comprehension of the differences and resemblances between collective bargaining in Member States. The comparative vision is very helpful in building mental schemes and also in demolishing *a priori* national opinions about the role of collective bargaining, effectively reminding us 'that we cannot take for granted that rules or institutions are transplantable'.[3] Many things that are considered essential in one country can be of negligible relevance in another. Thus, in a sense, this chapter is of great value for teaching Collective Labour Law, as it can help to give a clear idea of the meaning of collective bargaining.

The winning argument for embarking on this project was the human factor. The INLACRIS network comprises a team of labour lawyers who know their own systems inside out. This is not the classic situation of misuse of comparative law, with someone

---

to them, respecting national traditions, their autonomy and right to collective action. b. Information and consultation shall be ensured for all workers, including those working digitally and/or operating across borders, or their representatives in good time, in particular in the case of collective redundancies, transfer, restructuring and merger of undertakings.'

2. Always bearing in mind the reality pointed out by F. Schmidt and A.C. Neal, in *Collective Agreements and Collective Bargaining*, Chapter 12 of volume XV of the *International Encyclopedia of Comparative Law* (J.C.B. Mohr – Martinus Nijhoff Publishers, 1984), p. 3: 'A definition of a collective agreement depends upon the use to be made of it (...). Our definition thus refers to social relationships, and not to the legal structure, which may, and indeed does, differ radically from one country to another.'
3. O. Kahn-Freund, *On Uses and Misuses of Comparative Law*, 37 (1) Modern Law Review, 27 (1974).

reading foreign law through their own, national eyes. The foundation of the case study would be peer evaluation, not a foreign take on a given agreement. The inside knowledge of the team members would thus offer the greatest added value.

As for the time frame, there are two obvious approaches to choose. First of all, there is the simplest one, the static dimension: evaluating the status of collective bargaining in the first semester of 2016. The second one is dynamic: monitoring how collective bargaining developed within a single scope during the crisis years.[4] As this case study is, in itself, a hypothesis about a work method, the first position was preferred, because it is the simplest. Nonetheless, the second point of view has great advantages and should be taken into consideration for future research papers.

Theoretically, we could even contemplate the possibility of 'a case within the case', the individualisation of the comparison. The creation of a 'topical worker' could be the basis for a *narrative* approach, drawing a prototype and the comparison of their rights and position in each country. It would also provide an effective and current comparison of comparable workers and working conditions. Not just 'salaries are established in collective agreements', but 'for this kind of employee, the salary is X in country X and Y in country Y, he/she would be entitled to this type of allowance, etc.'. This is a promising possibility that could be tested in further research, but we were unable to implement it on this occasion.

[B] On the Methodology of the Study

After all these considerations, we have to decide on the scope of the case study. One of the main findings of the INLACRIS research is the radical differences between Member States in the role of sectoral agreements. The contrast between Hungary (four sectoral agreements in the whole country)[5] or Poland (six, with two of them in the private sector) and Spain (several hundred)[6] illustrates this perfectly. Thus, a comparison

---

4. Generally speaking, V. Glassner, M. Keune & P. Margison, *Collective Bargaining in a Time of Crisis: Developments in the Private Sector in Europe*, 17 (3) Transfer 318 (2011): 'Looking to the implications for the medium term, the crisis has indeed reinforced the predominant substantive and procedural trajectories of the past 20 years. Substantively, restoring competitiveness and maintaining employment are not only central to the agenda of crisis-response agreements, but have been the principal issues subject to trade-off. The wider effect is further to entrench the role of employment as a new "general equivalent" (Léonard, 2001) against which competitiveness-enhancing, or -restoring, measures to reduce costs and/or increase flexibility are negotiated. On the one hand, this evidences the prevalence of a certain type of integrative agreement. On the other hand, such agreements resemble concession bargaining in which workers make concessions in exchange for some form of employment guarantee.'
5. T. Gyulavári, G. Kártyás, *The Hungarian Flexicurity Pathway? New Labour Code after Twenty Years in the Market Economy* (Pázmány Press, Budapest, 2015), p. 25: 'This deficiency may be partly explained by the fact that employers' organizations represented in the above mentioned committees employ only a small proportion of employees, therefore, it would be pointless to conclude a sector level collective agreement in order to establish uniform working conditions in the entire sector.'
6. H. Ysás Molinero, *Recent Collective Bargaining Articulation Reforms in France and Spain*, 3 Spanish Labour Law and Employment Relations Journal (2014), p. 8: 'These rules led to a certain degree of fossilization of bargaining units, as the chronological preference made it extremely difficult to create new units. In addition, bargaining units were frequently derived from labour

between sectoral agreements is not, apparently, the easiest way to find a common path. It is not just a question of numbers, but also of the definition of what a branch or industry or sector is, according to national labour systems.

Accordingly, the simplest solution, guided as ever by Ockham's methodology, is to choose a company and observe its practice. The choice of company is the MacGuffin in this story. In Alfred Hitchcock's well-known words, a MacGuffin is 'an apparatus for trapping lions in the Scottish Highlands', but it is, in fact, a cinematographic technique, a plot device that acts as the driving force, with little or no narrative explanation. In our case study, this means that there is no special interest in taking one or other company as the object of the study.

Carrefour was chosen for various different reasons. First of all, it is a multinational company, one of the biggest in the European retail sector, established in several Member States with representation in the INLACRIS network (at least in France, Italy, Poland, Turkey, Romania, Greece and Spain). The retail sector is wider, for example, than the automobile sector, which is limited to fewer Member States.

Second, real collective bargaining actors in Carrefour could be found within the reach of the team, so their opinions could easily be incorporated in the academic results and we would be able to check the actors' perceptions of reality with the academic analysis in the final conference of the INLACRIS project. Unfortunately, this actual possibility turned out to be unachievable, as it would have meant finishing our study at an earlier time to circulate it among stakeholders.

The starting point for this ensemble research was a questionnaire, tackling the main points of interest. Each national author prepared a short report on these, and then all of the materials were melded in this common text. The comparison followed, trying to draw common trends or to show notable differences. Here, the debate among the authors led to the finding of national explanations, 'Montesquieu's environmental criteria which determine *l'esprit des lois*':[7] the role of the sectoral agreement, the main bargaining actors, the presence of old institutions, the relative position of foreign capital, the existence of different management philosophies within the same company, etc.

The participation of Portugal in this chapter has an added interest. Counter to the general trend of concentration in the retail sector, Carrefour left the Portuguese market and sold its assets to Continente.[8] Thus, the comparison with this country is a double

---

regulations dating back to the Franco era, as those units covered a territorial and sectoral regulatory field that were previously covered by Francoist labour regulations (identification of sectors and subsectors on a provincial basis). Moreover, jurisprudence has always tended to protect previously-created units.'

7. O. Kahn-Freund, *On Uses and Misuses of Comparative Law*, 37(1) Modern Law Review, 7 (1974).
8. https://run.unl.pt/bitstream/10362/9640/1/Goncalves_2009.pdf. (accessed 20 July 2017). The Italian case could have been very similar, as Carrefour sold several of its assets to another company, Coop, due to leadership and marketing issues. This decision led to a restructuring and rationalisation process, which implied collective redundancies for nearly half of its staff (http://www.lecceprima.it/economia/carrefour-saluta-il-salento-e-puglia-tocca-alla-coop.html) (accessed 20 July 2017). A court in Rome ruled some of the redundancies unfair and ordered the readmission of 115 employees and the payment of due wages. Up to now, this ruling has not been implemented, without any consequence.

one, as we can discover in it the possible effects of splitting the group. But we also have to take into account the situation of the Portuguese labour market after the intervention of the *Troika*, as reforming collective bargaining was seen as part of the solution in addressing external imbalances and achieving a recovery by the *Troika*; and Portugal made several reforms regarding sectoral collective bargaining, wage-setting institutions and rules governing industrial conflict, which led to a fall in collective bargaining coverage and also, to a certain extent, to a decentralisation of collective bargaining down to firm level.[9]

Finally, the Polish case is very special. The specific features of social dialogue in Poland are the weakness of trade unions and the lack of stable elected representation. The result is a breakdown of collective bargaining and very limited coverage by collective agreements. Sectoral agreements are almost non-existent. Social dialogue is concentrated at the plant level. The number of agreements is still very limited. The gap is partially filled by internal regulations issued by employers (the regulations concern not only work rules but also remuneration).

As a conclusion on our methodology, we must say that this chapter is a first step on a road that goes ever on and on. Bertrand, 3rd Earl Russell, wrote in the second chapter of his well-known book, 'The Scientific Outlook': 'In arriving at a scientific law there are three main stages: The first consists in observing the significant facts; the second in arriving at a hypothesis, which, if it is true, would account for these facts; the third is deducing from this hypothesis consequences which can be tested by observation. If the consequences are verified, the hypothesis is provisionally accepted as true, although it will usually require modification later on as a result of the discovery of further facts.' The itinerary of this chapter has followed all those steps, and further modifications are still needed in order to build a proper case study. But many lessons have been learned and we think that this methodology could have very positive results both in researching and teaching Labour Law.

§20.02 THE INTERNATIONAL AGREEMENT

Another key factor in the choice of the subject of the study was the global dimension. On 30 September 2015, Carrefour signed an international agreement on social dialogue and diversity with UNI-Global Union.[10] Their first agreement had been signed in 2001, leading to a close cooperation that has finally brought about this new text. Its second chapter deals with the promotion of social dialogue, described as part of Carrefour's corporate culture. In this text, social dialogue has a broader meaning than classic

---

9. *See* in this issue, T. Coelho Moreira, *The Revival of Sectoral Collective Bargaining: The Portuguese Experience* (Part I, Chapter 7 *infra*). However, Portugal is also interesting because, after the end of bailout programme, collective bargaining is slowly picking up with an increase in the collective agreements at sectoral level reaching sixty-five in 2015 when compared with twenty-seven in 2013 or forty-nine in 2014. On the other hand, there were only fifty-three company agreements, while in 2014 there were eighty.
10. http://www.carrefour.com/sites/default/files/CP_Carrefour_UNI_fren.pdf for the press release.

collective bargaining. It includes alternative dispute resolution mechanisms, information and consultation, and the creation of regular meetings between the firm and the union in order to smooth their relationships, which are to be based on trust and mutual respect.

The third chapter of the agreement deals with fundamental rights. In our second piece of INLACRIS research, one main conclusion had been that their role is 'essentially twofold. First, in their capacity as superior legal standards, [they] can be used to evaluate and question previous labour law reforms and existing legal solutions to promote flexibility in employment. Second, fundamental social rights have considerable potential to influence the drafting of forthcoming changes to labour market regulation, as an increased awareness of fundamental rights will inevitably have implications both for legislative activity and collective bargaining.'[11]

This agreement uses several international documents on social fundamental rights in the second dimension. First of all, there is the proclamation of collective bargaining in itself as a key issue. Second, collective bargaining should be the tool to develop other rights, such as those proclaimed in the texts referred to by the agreement. The eight ILO fundamental conventions,[12] the ten principles of the UN Global Compact,[13] and the OECD Guidelines for multinational companies[14] all deal with this dual perspective.

Chapter 3.1 of the agreement develops more specific commitments on collective bargaining. First of all, it will be implemented according to local legislations and following the OECD Guidelines. Furthermore, it grants its exercise without reprisals, repression or any other action, opposition or discrimination. This is a typical example of corporate responsibility, acknowledging the rule of law and putting in writing what is obvious: that multinational companies are subject to national legislations.[15]

Finally, Chapter 5 of the agreement establishes an autonomous procedure for dispute resolution, with competence to conduct an investigation on the facts and take the appropriate measures. It creates two different pathways, one for each of the parties to the agreement. They are clearly parallel, as they establish a 'growing' mechanism of

---

11. S. Laulom & C. Teissier, *Which Securities for Workers in Times of Crisis? An Introduction*, 5 (3-4), European Labour Law Journal, 209 (2014).
12. Conventions No 87 and No 98, especially.
13. Principle 3: 'Businesses should uphold the freedom of association and the effective recognition of the right to collective bargaining?'.
14. Guideline V.1.b: 'Respect the right of workers employed by the multinational enterprise to have trade unions and representative organisations of their own choosing recognised for the purpose of collective bargaining, and engage in constructive negotiations, either individually or through employers' associations, with such representatives with a view to reaching agreements on terms and conditions of employment.'
15. Y. Maneiro Vázquez, *Derechos fundamentales de los trabajadores y responsabilidad social corporativa*, in VV.AA., *Gobierno corporativo y responsabilidad social de las empresas* (Madrid: Marcial Pons 2009), pp. 314-315: 'En los países que cuentan con un ordenamiento jurídico desarrollado y completo, tanto en el reconocimiento como en las garantías a las que se sujetan los referidos derechos fundamentales, las medidas de responsabilidad social no parecen presentar mayor utilidad que cualquier orden o indicación amparada por el poder de dirección empresarial. Si se trata de una medida concertada, es, en todo caso, más deseable, su inclusión en un convenio colectivo, vinculante para ambas partes firmantes y, por tal motivo, jurídicamente exigible en caso de incumplimiento por alguna de ellas'.

denouncements to the other party. The procedure is thus based on mutual collaboration. On the other hand, such clauses can usually be found in transnational collective agreements.[16]

Concerning the formal aspects of the agreement, it must be mentioned that it was signed by Carrefour central management and the trade union federation Uni-Global. Even if the European Works Council is an active element in firms of this size,[17] the supra-European scale of Carrefour made it advisable to look for a global counterpart. According to the European Commission,[18] 143 of all identified transnational collective agreements in its database are signed by global federations, making them the most usual signing party.

In spite of all of this, we have not been able to find any mention of the international agreement in any of the texts studied. Most of them pre-date it, but there were other international agreements beforehand, which probably means that these kinds of text are focused on the multinational, worldwide management of the company, and are still in a developing phase at the national level.

§20.03 FORMALITIES OF THE AGREEMENTS: SCOPE, SUBJECTS, DURATION

[A] Scope of the Agreement

One of the main issues in collective bargaining nowadays is the tension between centralisation and flexibility. In fact, one of the main hypotheses of the INLACRIS research is that collective bargaining in Europe is following a path that leads to a competitive decentralisation. If that proved correct, we should find many countries in this situation.

France is the perfect example of this theory, as the Carrefour group is split into several minor bargaining units. Following a reform and regrouping of all the different Carrefour establishments, a holding *Carrefour France* was created under a single direction, but including 200 different legal structures. They are indeed different companies, with their own works councils. Within this framework, the one structure that is taken into account is the *Carrefour Hypers*, the firm's hypermarkets, which are subject to the *Convention Collective d'Entreprise Carrefour*, dating from 1999 and modernised in 2015. Other parts of the group, such as Carrefour Market or Carrefour

---

16. According to the European Commission (http://ec.europa.eu/social/main.jsp?catId = 978& langId = en), (accessed 20 July 2017) 98 of 265 identified transnational agreements included this kind of provision.
17. http://www.presencegroup.eu/ewc/2015/10/19/ewcs-as-a-strategic-tool-in-developing-best-practices/ (accessed 20 July 2017). On the role of the EWC, the report by Eurofound, generally speaking, has pointed out: 'The overall conclusion that can be drawn from this is that the efforts made by management and employee representatives to further develop their EWCs can benefit both the company as well as its employees. Clearly, the practices presented in the EWC case studies in this report are examples of innovative industrial relations practices based on win-win situations.' (http://www.eurofound.europa.eu/sites/default/files/ef_publication/field_ef_doc ument/ef1511en.pdf accessed 20 July 2017).
18. http://ec.europa.eu/social/main.jsp?catId = 978&langId = en (accessed 20 July 2017).

Montagne (smaller dimensions or a more specialised scope of sales), have their own collective agreements. Finally, there are several framework agreements that affect the whole organisation, linked to specific issues such as crisis, restructuring, disability and diversity, but they do not have the legal rank of a collective agreement.[19]

Along the same lines, we can point out the *Contratto integrativo aziendale* for the Carrefour Group in Italy, signed in 2016 and affecting all the group's different types of establishment, in contrast to the French situation. It is called 'integrative' because it integrates the content of a nationwide collective agreement to which all issues not covered by the Carrefour agreement are referred.[20]

The Polish case is the exception in the list, as collective bargaining takes place within the company, but beyond the rules of the Labour Code, which regulates the conclusion of the typical collective agreement (*układ zbiorowy pracy*), formally treated as a source of Labour Law. The main reasons for this decision are allegedly the complicated negotiation and registration procedure, the denial of a role for social partners in its implementation and the lack of flexibility that it implies (difficulties with amendments or termination). As a result, employers are afraid to conclude typical collective agreements (there are none in the entire sector). The result is the atypical collective agreement (*porozumienie zbiorowe*) for the whole of Carrefour Poland, which is in theory binding *inter partes* and which is endowed with such great stability that it could even be defined as a 'cooperation agreement'. In practice, such agreements are respected by social partners as an important source for the rights and duties of the parties to individual employment contracts as well as for the proper functioning of social dialogue in the company. There are currently two agreements in force. The first, concluded a few years ago, regulates, *inter alia*, some conditions of work as well as the relationship between the company and trade unions. The second, which concerns remuneration, has been concluded recently (at the beginning of April 2017). A new non-wage agreement is now being negotiated and should be concluded this year.[21] These atypical collective agreements may afterwards be implemented by means of internal regulations issued by employers, even at the establishment level.[22] Nonetheless, the agreement has played a positive role in developing working standards. The current situation is much better than in other supermarkets/hypermarkets in Poland. Carrefour Poland is considered a company that maintains good relationships with trade

---

19. One example is the *Accord cadre relatif aux mesures d'accompagnement en cas de mise en oeuvre d'un plan de sauvegarde de l'emploi et/ou d'un plan de départs volontaires* (30 June 2015) – http://www.cfdt-carrefour.com/images/catalogue/id_1/images/877_ACCORD_CADRE_2015_derni_re_version.pdf (accessed 7 August 2017).
20. They were being called 'integrative' in the 1960s, as they were understood as *nearer* agreements.
21. Trade unions expect e.g., an increase in the number of the days of annual leave to achieve the standards existing in western Europe or a guarantee that all the workers will enjoy two days off within each week (at the moment, the number of days off is calculated in a reference period of three months).
22. According to Polish Law, they must be issued by employers with at least twenty employees not covered by collective agreements: remuneration, work rules (including working time). The social allowances in them are financed from special funds created by some employers with at least twenty employees in FTE. The conditions for granting social allowances are ascertained in internal regulations agreed with trade unions. Internal regulations (formally issued unilaterally by the employer) are agreed with trade unions.

unions. Perhaps in the future this will result in the conclusion of a typical collective agreement.

By contrast, the sector agreement is present in Spain. There, the collective agreement governing Carrefour activity is the *Convenio colectivo estatal de grandes almacenes*,[23] a sector agreement for all big department stores with a long tradition.[24] The inclusion in this category is very wide, as several criteria are used: membership of the employers' organisation, franchises, firms with a total shop surface of more than 30,000 m^2, both department stores and hypermarkets, and also specialist department stores like Ikea or Leroy Merlin. Only supermarkets are specifically excluded, as they have their own sector agreement. This means that competition through collective bargaining is excluded in this sector,[25] as none of the great companies is outside the scope of the agreement.

In parallel with Spain, Continente in Portugal finds itself within a sector agreement, a *contrato coletivo de trabalho*,[26] the highest level of collective bargaining in that country,[27] dating from 2008. Following an extension ordinance (*portaria de extenção*) of 2010, it covers 101 companies and 85,003 workers (data from 2010), being the only agreement containing such a quantification. In this case, the surface of the establishment is a requisite for membership of the employers' organisation that bargained the agreement, so every shop of over 200 m^2 is included in its scope. This means that all the great retail groups such as Continente or Pingo Doce come within the same agreement, in a repetition of the cartelisation already observed in Spain.

As indicated, there was in 2010 an extension ordinance of this agreement that established: 'The signatory associations requested the extension of the collective bargaining agreement to all companies not affiliated to the employers' association in the area of its application, belonging to the same economic sector and workers in its

---

23. https://www.boe.es/boe/dias/2013/04/22/pdfs/BOE-A-2013-4278.pdf (accessed 7 August 2017).
24. Broadly speaking, the retail activity sector in Spain is very widely regulated. According to data from the trade union CC.OO. (http://www.1mayo.ccoo.es/nova/files/1018/DAlonso.pdf accessed 7 August 2017)), 'Hay excesivos convenios tanto sectoriales como de empresa. (Aproximadamente existen más de 250 convenios sectoriales y más de 100 convenios de empresa. Entre todos afectan aproximadamente a dos millones de trabajadores y trabajadoras). De los convenios sectoriales, solamente siete son convenios sectoriales de ámbito estatal, el resto son convenios sectoriales de ámbito provincial o de Comunidad Autónoma'.
25. About competitition Law and collective agreements, J. M. Goerlich Peset, *Negociación colectiva y Derecho de la competencia: un complejo panorama*, in *Cláusulas de vanguardia y problemas prácticos de la negociación colectiva actual* (Thomson Reuters – Lex Nova, Cizur Menor, 2015), p. 121: 'No implica vulneración de la normativa *antitrust* (...) por más que las similitudes en el comportamiento de las empresas pueden resultar llamativas (...). No cabe descartar (...) un impacto indirecto, pero colectivo, de la regulación de las condiciones de trabajo por el convenio colectivo en las decisiones que las empresas toman en el mercado.'
26. http://bte.gep.msess.gov.pt/completos/2008/bte22_2008.pdf; http://bte.gep.msess.gov.pt/completos/2010/bte18_2010.pdf (accessed 7 August 2017).
27. In Portugal, the collective agreements can be sectoral collective agreements – *contrato coletivo de trabalho* – signed between a trade union association and an employers' association; or they can be an ACT, a multi-employer agreement signed between a trade union and several employers; or they can be a company agreement signed between a trade union and an employer (a firm-level agreement under Article 3 of the Portuguese Labour Code).

service category professional therein, represented by employees' unions.' This collective agreement applies to large areas equivalent to Carrefour – which in Portugal are, among others, Continente and Pingo Doce. The latter belongs to the Jerónimo Martins Group and is also represented in Poland.

Nonetheless, it must be pointed out that this agreement is one of the most obvious exceptions to the rule, as the trend after the *Troika* intervention shows a change in the predominant type of collective agreement. The traditionally preponderant sectoral top-level branch and professional agreements (CCT and ACT), such as this one, have given way to firm-level agreements, which has also led to a decrease in the number of workers covered. The number of employees covered by collective agreements fell from almost 1.9 million in 2008 to some 225,000 in 2014.[28]

However, more recent data shows an increase in the workers' coverage and in 2015 it is recovering slightly, to around 568,900 workers. Nevertheless, in 2015, the number of sectoral agreements signed was still only 37% of the number signed in 2008, and the level of worker coverage was still only 26% of the 2008 figure.

[B] The Bargaining Agents

According to the national questionnaires, the answer is unanimous concerning the subjects present in collective bargaining, and points to the absolute importance of trade unions. Elected representatives did not have any role in the different procedures. However, this lack of presence is in contrast to some trends detected by the doctrine.[29]

The *convention collective nationale Carrefour* was bargained, on the company's side, by the General Direction of Carrefour Hyper. On the workers' side, national delegates from representative trade unions were present, in accordance with the law. Those trade unions were the CFDT (Confédération française démocratique du travail), CGT (Confédération générale du travail), FO (Force Ouvrière) and CGC (Confédération générale des cadres, a trade union for managers).[30]

In Italy, the main trade unions signed the agreement: FILCAMS CGIL (Confederazione Generale Italiana del Lavoro), FISACAT CISL (Confederazione Italiana Sindacati Lavoratori) and UILTUS UIL (Unione Italiana del Lavoro). They are the retail branch of the three main Italian trade unions.[31] The most interesting aspect is to be found on the employer's side, as there were six different companies, represented by five senior Carrefour Group managers.

---

28. T. Coelho Moreira, *supra* n. 9.
29. The best comparative study in Spanish on this issue is J. J. Fernández Domínguez, 'Legitimación y protagonistas de la negociación colectiva', in *Perspectivas de evolución de la negociación colectiva en el marco comparado europeo*, Cinca, Madrid, 2015, pp. 15 ss.
30. C. Nicod, P-E. Berthier, F. Debord, S. Laulom, 'France', INLACRIS working papers, p. 3: 'Since the 1 January 2009, a company agreement is valid only if it is signed by representative unions, which totalize 30% of the votes at the last elections, and if the main part of unions (which has obtained more than 50%) don't oppose it. The opposition has to be sent to the signatory unions within eight days, it must be written and motivated.'
31. In Italy there is no *erga omnes* efficacy and collective agreements are only binding for their signers. Hence the importance of the presence of these three subjects, which are also present in the trade sectoral agreement.

The Polish scenario, within this first, decentralised ensemble of countries, is defined by its own organisational conditions. There is no employers' organisation that would assume a certain measure of the representation of megastores and/or supermarkets. Working conditions quite often constitute an element of competition between the companies.[32] Thus, a sector-wide agreement is impossible to achieve, resulting in a constellation of agreements (if any at all) in the retail trade sector.[33] When it comes to worker representation in Carrefour, we find it is a monopoly of Solidarność, the only trade union acting on behalf of employees. There are certainly works councils in some shops, but they lack the right to negotiate collective agreements, as they only have information and consultation privileges (quite often they are under the informal influence of trade unions). Thus, we have the simplest couple: Carrefour Poland and Solidarność. Moreover, supermarkets and shops are treated as separate employers that can regulate working conditions autonomously, e.g., by means of internal regulations. However, they must fall within the framework created by agreements concluded with trade unions.

The Spanish situation presents a very different picture. The bargaining party on the employers' side is a specific organisation, ANGED (Asociación Nacional de Grandes Empresas de Distribución), within the framework of the CEOE, the main, general employers' organisation in Spain. The originality comes from the workers' side, as the trade unions that bargained this agreement are not the 'typical' most representative trade unions in Spain, CCOO and UGT, nor the regionally most representative trade unions, ELA-LAB and CIG. On the contrary, they were the much smaller FASGA (Federación de Asociaciones Sindicales de Grandes Almacenes) and FETICO (Federación de Trabajadores Independientes de Comercio).[34] This is a very special situation in the Spanish labour market, as they are constantly reported as 'yellow unions' by the other trade unions,[35] but they have close to a very solid monopoly of representation in the *grandes almacenes*.

In Portugal, we find a similar scenario to the first one. The APED (Associação Portuguesa de Empresas de Distribuição) is the bargaining organisation on the employers' side. The trade union responsible is FEPCES (Federação Portuguesa dos

---

32. There are rigid statutory provisions, mainly the employee privilege principle that implies that modifications *in peius* must be expressly indicated by the law.
33. This is a trend in Poland: 'In principle, the social dialogue takes place on the enterprise level. However, the bargaining power of trade unions on this level was weakened in times of crisis. Multienterprise collective bargaining is rare and the procedure of extension of multienterprise collective agreements is not used.' (D. Skupień, M. Łaga & Ł. Pisarczyk, *Polish Labour and Social Security Law: The Impact of the Economic Crisis and Demographic Problems*, XI European Congress of Labour and Social Security Law, Dublin 2014).
34. Article 87.2.c Estatuto de los Trabajadores: 'Los sindicatos que cuenten con un mínimo del 10 por ciento de los miembros de los comités de empresa o delegados de personal en el ámbito geográfico y funcional al que se refiera el convenio' and Article 88.2 Estatuto de los Trabajadores: 'La comisión negociadora quedará válidamente constituida cuando los sindicatos, federaciones o confederaciones y las asociaciones empresariales a que se refiere el artículo anterior representen como mínimo, respectivamente, a la mayoría absoluta de los miembros de los comités de empresa y delegados de personal.'
35. One example: http://navarra.ugt.org/noticias/noticias/denuncia-complicidad-fasga-fetico-patronal-6825.html.

Sindicatos do Comércio, Escritório e Serviços, e Outros).[36] It is integrated in one of the main Portuguese confederations, the CGTP (Confederação Geral dos Trabalhadores Portugueses). The most remarkable aspect concerning the Portuguese case is the concentration on the workers' representatives' side. As a rule, there are no legal criteria to assess the representativeness of trade unions. As collective agreements may be extended to employers and employees that are not represented and affiliated respectively by employers' organisations or trade unions through administrative procedures, the government has a discretionary power to extend the personal scope of collective agreements even when the signatories of that collective agreement may be insignificant, having only a very small number of members. These extensions of collective agreements to third parties may be particularly dangerous if the employers' organisations represent a minority of big or very big enterprises who then attempt to extend their agreement to small or medium size competitors.[37]

[C] Duration of the Agreement

This is the first quantitative issue that will be dealt with in this chapter. In some of our debates in the successive INLACRIS seminars, it was suggested that perhaps the conjunctural crisis implied shorter timespans for collective agreements. This would be a consequence of flexibility, opening and reopening scenarios for a new establishment of working conditions. This hypothesis has been proved wrong, at least in our 'laboratory'.

The longest agreement by far is the French one, as it is open-ended. Nonetheless, it is of course subject to later revisions.[38] The previous agreement in Carrefour dated back to 1999 (the earliest one from 1969), so the main conclusion is great stability in this field, even by the standards of French Law.[39]

The Polish agreements are also open-ended. This is indeed understood as a token of stability. Not being a single text and with flexibility derived from its informal nature, its capacity for adaptation is far bigger than that of other agreements. The 'time' factor here must therefore be taken into account from a different perspective.

All other agreements are, on the other hand, temporary, but not necessarily short-lived. The Spanish agreement establishes a duration of four years; the Portuguese, at least two years; and the Italian is the shortest, at just fifteen months (the

---

36. The Portuguese Constitution gives competence to conclude collective agreements only to the trade unions. However, there is the possibility – Article 491, No 3 – for the workers' council to negotiate collective agreements at firm level, within legally defined and rather restrictive terms. Such terms included a delegation-like empowerment by trade unions granted in the context, and stated in the text, of a collective agreement of broader scope and a firm-size threshold of 150 or more workers.
37. T. Coelho Moreira, *supra* n. 9.
38. Loi du 17 août 2015: Articles L.2242-5 à L.2242-20.
39. It is habitual in the French system to have agreements that date from long ago. These agreements are re-bargained regularly, even by different subjects from the original ones. This situation is more usual in sectoral bargaining.

sectoral agreement has a two-year duration).[40] In any case, the relativity of these figures must be taken into account. According to Spanish law, an agreement keeps its validity until denounced, through tacit prorogations of one year, the same as in Italy.

Beyond these general considerations, there are also special duration clauses for certain specific issues in some of these agreements, especially those establishing wages. This can be considered normal in the national systems of industrial relations, so no connection with the crisis can be clearly established.

§20.04 MATERIAL CONTENT OF THE AGREEMENTS

[A] Working Time

Two issues are of primary interest in this field: obviously, the duration of the working time; but also the regulation of flexibility tools. Thus both sides of the legal regime of working time – the classical limitation and the *modern* adjustment – will be considered.

On the first issue, there is clearly a strong link with the maximum legal working time in France and Portugal. Of course, this does not mean that the time is the same, as it is thirty-five and forty hours respectively. The Italian agreement also uses the hours-per-week system, establishing a normal thirty-eight-hour week.[41] The Spanish agreement, on the other hand, uses the more flexible hours-per-year system, with 1,798 yearly hours, between 39 and 40 per week.[42]

Breaks and rest periods are also organised in many of these texts. In the French agreement, a better regime than the legal one is established. Thus, four hours of work imply a break of fifteen minutes; six hours, twenty minutes; and more than seven hours, half an hour. In the Italian agreement, the time threshold is five and a half hours: more than that, and a fifteen-minute break is required; less than that, ten minutes; for workers on a split shift, ten plus ten. The Portuguese agreement is by far the most generous, as there should be a rest period of no less than one hour and no more than two after five hours of work. However, the break can be restricted to thirty minutes by agreement in some circumstances.

Concerning holidays, the Spanish agreement is more generous than the legal standard, as it establishes thirty-one natural days instead of the legal thirty. In the Italian case, it is the sectoral agreement and not the Carrefour agreement that deals with this issue: twenty-six working days. The Portuguese agreement, on the other hand, includes a list of compulsory holidays. Its main utility is the connection with the remuneration provisions about working on these days. The most original provision on working time in this agreement is the leave to perform voluntary firefighter or Red Cross functions when necessary, and also once every three months to donate blood.

---

40. In this agreement there is an open statement about the reasons for this duration: 'the particular conditions of the socio-economic and contracting context'.
41. On the other hand, the parties to the agreement also talk about the goal of a daily/weekly scheduled-flexible system.
42. Forty hours per week means, in Spanish Law, 1,826 hours and 27 minutes per year.

The Italian agreement, on the other hand, leaves this issue to the sectoral agreement.

The flexibility, meanwhile, comes from several mechanisms and is present in all of the agreements studied. This confirms a trend that we have already detected in previous INLACRIS seminars.

In the French agreement, there are clauses on the modulation of working time in every employee category. The managers are the group with the most flexibility. In the Italian text, we can find a general clause talking about pursuing a 'flexible scheduled daily/weekly timetable' (*flessibilità programmata*), nearly an oxymoron. We have to remark that this flexibility has led in some shops to twenty-four-hour opening.

As for the Polish case, working time amounts to forty hours per week (on average). Collective agreements and internal regulations issued by employers define a general framework of the process of work while specific working hours are usually set up in individual schedules of working time determined by shop or department managers. It is necessary to stress that Polish law allows work on Sundays, which may constitute a normal element of work.[43] Agreements and internal regulations may flexibilise the organisation of work by introducing e.g., shift work (also on Sundays) and flexible working time (working hours can be extended from eight to twelve hours per day, with shorter working hours on other days and additional days off). Finally, as we have seen in other documents, there are special provisions for managers concerning task-based working time (in practice, they have relatively stable working hours). In the Polish case, the reference period for calculating working hours is three months.

The Spanish agreement dedicates its Article 27 to the distribution of working time.[44] It includes many clauses about the redistribution of working time, in spite of the annual planning. The agreement on this issue plays a very important role in Spanish law, as there is a legal provision that allows collective bargaining to implement measures on irregular distribution of working time, directly giving enhanced power to the company.[45] Even then, there are exceptions to this flexibility, establishing the possibility of urgent modifications in cases of absence of other workers, no matter the day of the week. This last clause was a great novelty in the agreement, as there were no comparable provisions affecting work on Sundays in the previous collective bargaining.[46] There is also a remarkable provision forbidding 'habitual overtime hours' that should be substituted by part-time or fixed-term contracts.

In the Portuguese case, there are several clear mentions of flexibility, as ordinary working time can be raised by two hours daily, up to a limit of ten hours/day and fifty

---

43. A draft of a law amending the Labour Code provides for more rigid rules concerning Sunday work. At the moment the law requires at least one free Sunday within a period of four weeks. In Carrefour shops with a larger number of workers, employees may enjoy more free Sundays (quite often it is regulated by individual schedules of working time).
44. For company level, P. Gimeno Díaz de Atauri, *La flexibilidad en el tiempo de trabajo en los más recientes convenios de empresa*, in *Cláusulas de vanguardia y problemas prácticos de la negociación colectiva actual*, 305 et seq. (Thomson Reuters – Lex Nova, Cizur Menor, 2015).
45. About this mechanism, N. Martínez Yáñez, *El Régimen Jurídico de la Disponibilidad Horaria*, 39 et seq. (Thomson Reuters – Aranzadi, Cizur Menor, 2011).
46. It currently includes one strange, specific provision, declaring derogated and without force any provision opposing this one. That is unnecessary, as the rule in Spanish law is that new agreements derogate old agreements, unless there are specific exceptions.

hours/week. This measure is not considered overtime and must be compensated with free time within eight weeks at most. This is a legal possibility according to Article 204 of the *Código de Trabalho*.[47] Furthermore, employees with direction, supervision or coordination tasks may be exempted from all the rules about working time, always on the employer's initiative. This exemption is linked to a salary raise.

[B] Professional Classification

The Spanish agreement clearly shows the effects of the latest reforms. The 'categoría profesional', the detailed description of a specific occupation deriving from the Francoist system, was substituted in 2012 by the broader idea of 'grupos profesionales', professional groups that organise several occupations in one homogeneous ensemble.[48] This agreement is one of the first to have incorporated this technique, as bargaining agents are apparently reluctant to adopt this change.[49] We can thus find five different groups: core staff (*personal base*), professionals (*profesionales*), professional coordinators (*profesionales coordinadores*), technicians (*técnicos*) and managers (*mandos*).[50] This structure is the base of the remuneration system. It is completed by a large chapter on promotions, where several procedures are included, ranging from

---

47. T. Coelho Moreira, 'Portugal', INLACRIS working papers, p. 16: 'Working time accounts can be introduced by collective agreement. Working time may be increased by four hours per day, 60 hours per week and 200 hours per year. Individual work contracts or collective agreements may establish that normal working time is concentrated in four days. By collective agreement it is furthermore possible to establish that schedules are concentrated in periods of three days, followed by rest periods of at least two days. In this type of regime, average normal working time shall be reached in periods of 45 days. This provision is designed to help companies adapt to breaks or large variations in the intensity of their activity. The total working time per year must not drop below six months of full-time work. During periods of inactivity, the employee receives 20% of their basic pay (or more, if the corresponding collective agreement sets higher standards).'
48. M. L. Martín Hernández, *La regulación convencional de la clasificación profesional y de la movilidad funcional tras las últimas reformas laborales*, in *Observatorio de la negociación colectiva: los espacios de las negociación colectiva tras las reformas laborales de 2010, 2011 y 2012*, 15-46 (Madrid Cinca, 2013).
49. See D. Pérez del Prado, *Modernas tendencias en materia de clasificación profesional*, in *Cláusulas de vanguardia y problemas prácticos de la negociación colectiva actual*, (Thomson Reuters – Lex Nova, Cizur Menor, 2015), p. 287-288: 'La categoría profesional (...) seguía siendo el elemento central de vertebración en materia de encuadramiento, a pesar de su progresiva relativización legal (...). Existen una serie de indicios que nos llevan a pensar que la influencia de la categoría profesional no ha desaparecido completamente (...). No son pocos los convenios colectivos que tras realizar una completa definición de las variables sobre las que se articulan los grupos y los grupos en sí (...) a continuación insertan sin más (...) las antiguas categorías (...). Algunos convenios aluden expresamente a la reforma, pareciendo dejar a las claras que es la ley y no el propio deseo lo que les lleva a adoptar esta nueva forma de clasificación profesional (...). También se observa una cierta tendencia a definir el grupo a los meros efectos formales, aplicándose *de facto* la categoría como elemento vertebrador de la clasificación professional.'
50. This group asks for theoretical or practical training equivalent to a University degree or a PhD. It is a real challenge to imagine the translation to real life of a 'practical training' equivalent to a PhD in the retail sector.

free designation (managers and technicians), to internal exams (coordinators) or performance evaluation (base level to professionals).

The French structure is numerically different, as it shows nine different levels, according to the responsibility and capacities of the employees. They are organised in three 'courses' (*filières*): employees and workers (*employés et ouvriers*), technicians and supervisors (*techniciens et agents de maîtrise*), and managers (*cadres*). In any case, it follows the same logical, organisational pattern.

The Portuguese system is the most prolix, as it includes fifty-three descriptions of occupations, classified into thirteen groups (some of them including just one occupation, such as Group I, 'Director'). This was the old pattern in Spain, before the above-mentioned reform. It also has a provision on promotions, mainly based on seniority for the lowest levels.

In the Polish case, a lot depends on shop size. In smaller shops, the job descriptions are very general. Employees are just 'shop employees/cashiers'. Their tasks are internally diversified. In supermarkets/hypermarkets, due to the existence of specialised departments, such a situation is impossible. Consequently, job descriptions are more detailed. Workers are also assigned to specific departments. In the Italian case, the structure of the company is established in the sectoral agreement, with a similar technique to those mentioned, including seven different levels.

It is easy to conclude from above that, as a rule, collective bargaining is a useful tool in the organisation of the working of the enterprise.

[C]   Remuneration

According to Benjamin Franklin, 'money has never made man happy, nor will it, there is nothing in its nature to produce happiness. The more of it one has the more one wants'. This can easily be understood as an accurate take on collective bargaining. The monetary issues are, of course, present in these agreements.

The French agreement contains a very detailed system of remuneration, especially for levels I to V. However, this system was considered unlawful by the *Cour de Cassation*, as it included an erroneous schedule of breaks and rest periods, according to which wages were inferior to the SMIC and thus ruled out by the court. Beyond this, there are general dispositions on bonuses, such as special holiday payments or a special end-of-year benefit. There are also special rules for salesmen, linked to productivity, in a mixed system of wages. As for wages in kind, there are also provisions on restaurant tickets and discounts when shopping in Carrefour.

The Italian agreement is the most distinct, as it does not follow this common trend. There is no general design for remuneration, but many detailed clauses on individual aspects, ranging from productivity bonuses, compensation for working on

Sundays, or flexible benefits.[51] But the main tool for fixing salaries is the national sectoral agreement.[52]

In the Polish case, the new wage collective agreement provides for basic remuneration and some additional elements. The basic remuneration has been recently increased and is higher than the national minimum wage.[53] It depends on position and responsibility, and is thus linked to the professional classification in the company, by means of wage bands. The remuneration increases with seniority (experienced workers have some additional duties, e.g., training new staff). Typically, remuneration differs according to geographical area (Warsaw has the highest rates, followed by other big cities, then small towns). This is justified by, *inter alia*, the variation in the costs of living. Sometimes there are also additional elements of remuneration. Without being exhaustive, we can point to seniority allowances (after five, ten or fifteen years of work in the company) or specific bonuses connected with performance and/or the results of work. However, the company has recently cancelled its 'secret client' programme (there were some problems with the identification of workers). Performance bonuses are used in special departments such as household goods (e.g., depending on turnover). Employees are incentivised to increase sales. Although the general wage policy is shaped by the company, there is some leeway for lower-level managers, who may e.g., grant special bonuses and allowances within their budgets.

The Spanish agreement includes the traditional salary structure, linking professional classification with base salary, and later developing a catalogue of bonuses. The first one is calculated on a yearly basis (excluding managers) that is afterwards shown as an hourly rate. This part of the salary ranges from EUR 13,951.11 to EUR 17,072.58, frozen in 2013 for the duration of the agreement,[54] with an exceptional annual revision

---

51. In the sectoral agreement, we can find that the remuneration is composed of a basic payment and several bonuses, including seniority, fourteen times per year (July and Christmas). On the other hand, we have to take into account that this retributive system may not be implemented in establishments 'in crisis'.
52. Vid., M. Rusciano, *I diversi livelli attuali di cotnrattazione collettiva riguardo alla determinazione dei trattamenti retributivi*, in *Relazione in Atti del Convegno 'Il trattamento retributive dei lavoratori, la contrattazioen colelttiva e la legge'*, Roma, 22.23/04/2010; M. D'Antona, *Appunti sulle fonti di determinazione della retribuzione*, in I, RGL, (1986); G. Ferraro, *Retribuzione e assetto della contrattazione collettiva*, in I, RIDL, (2010).
    According to the Italian Constitution (Article 36), there are to two main principles for the calculation of salaries: proportionality (to the quantity and quality of work) and sufficiency (enough remuneration to guarantee the worker a free and worthy for him and his family). In case of controversy, the judge will establish it according to the rules of equity, not necessarily according to the collective agreement (Article 2099 *codice civile*). Vid., S. Bellomo, *Retribuzione sufficente e autonomia collettiva*, (Torino: Giappichelli, 2002); M.C. Cataudella, *Determinazione giudiziale della retribuzione sufficente e ruolo della contrattazione collettiva*, in GI, (2010); L. Del Vecchio, *Retribuzione sufficiente e condizioni territoriali: gli orientamenti della giurisprudenza*, I, ADL, (2003); M. Dell'Olio, *Retribuzione, quantità e qualità del lavoro, qualità di vita*, ADL, (1995); P. Ichino, *La nozione di 'giusta retribuzione' nell'articolo 36 della Costituzione*, I, RIDL, (2010); M. Madera, *Contratto collettivo aziendale e giusta retribuzione*, GI, (1996); M. Magnani, *Il salario minimo legale*, I, RIDL, (2010).
53. Due to the problems with engaging workers, almost all companies operating supermarkets/hypermarkets have slightly increased the level of wages.
54. This situation was an exception to the trend even during the harshest years of the crisis. See S. Olarte Encabo, *Cláusulas de revisión salarial en la negociación colectiva durante la crisis económica*, I, Actualidad Laboral, 32 et seq. (2012). For an economist's global point of view, J.

clause based on the 'trade index'. It must be paid on sixteen occasions, two more than the ordinary legal provision.

The most important of the bonuses is the seniority bonus, calculated for every four years and ranging from EUR 255.79 to EUR 192.32. It is important to point out that the majority of bonuses, i.e., those that are personal or linked to specific jobs or quality performance, can be regulated by the different firms within the scope of the agreement. The sectoral agreement merely offers a minimum floor that must be respected by them.

There are also some provisions on travel expenses, social allowances such as compulsory life insurance for the employees, clothing (including a 35% discount on work clothes in some sectors) and general discounts for employees.

The first version of the Portuguese agreement contained, like the Spanish and the French ones, a meticulous system for the setting of salaries. It was modified in 2010 and these remain in force (they were modified in order to adjust them to the national minimum salary). It is important to underline this *freezing* of remuneration, for nearly six years, in parallel with the mandate of the *Troika*. On the technical side, it follows the habitual link between professional classification and remuneration, the lowest salary being EUR 475 and the highest fixed salary EUR 1,146. The top three levels establish a bonus of 20% at least over this quantity. The most remarkable thing in the Portuguese case is the geographical differences established between the shops in Lisbon, Setúbal and Porto (higher salaries) and those located in the rest of the country. The first version of the agreement, from 2008, contains further special provisions on bonuses: Sunday work, holiday work, thirteenth pay for Christmas and, finally, a food subsidy (*subsídio de alimentação*) of EUR 4.55 per day. The renewal of these provisions is currently being bargained, through a difficult process of conciliation with the Ministry of Employment.

[D] Work Contracts and Employment

The Spanish agreement includes several provisions on the modalities of work contracts. This is a usual situation, as Spanish legislation delegates to collective agreements the role of establishing several details, such as duration, number of repetitions, etc.[55] Thus, the agreement contains provisions on part-time work (e.g., giving employees on such contracts preference for new full-time posts) and fixed-term contracts (establishing the maximum flexibility allowed by the legislation).

The Polish system of agreements also deals with this subject, establishing a maximum duration of thirty-three months for fixed-term contracts, unless a longer one is objectively justified. In Carrefour there are more rigid limitations on fixed-term employment, encouraging the company to apply open-ended contracts. Nonetheless,

---

I. Pérez Infante, *Las reformas de la negociación colectiva y la devaluación salarial*, http://aeet-jel.es/sites/default/files/comunicaciones/perezinfante_2015.pdf (accessed March 2017).

55. A general panorama in A.B. Muñoz Ruiz, *Líneas de tendencia en materia de empleo, contratación y formación en los convenios colectivos de empresa*, in *Cláusulas de vanguardia y problemas prácticos de la negociación colectiva actual*, 217 et seq. (Thomson Reuters – Lex Nova, Cizur Menor, 2015).

the most difficult problem concerns one main trait of central and eastern European countries, well studied within the INLACRIS network:[56] civil law contracts and the role of economically dependent workers. The trade unions insist on limitations for civil law contracts as well. Although this is not regulated by collective agreements, the company endeavours to decrease the number of civil law agreements.

Finally, the Portuguese agreement reflects a strange situation, as it reproduces the legal contents, without establishing a better regime. Furthermore, it establishes a lower threshold for some specific fixed-term contracts, being thus *contra legem*. According to Article 139 of the Labour Code, the whole legal framework for fixed term contracts can be regulated by collective agreement. The only exceptions are Articles 140, No. 4, b) and Article 148, Nos 1, 4 and 5.

Once again, this issue is dealt with in Italy in the sectoral agreement, with a remarkable extension.

[E] Health and Safety

French Carrefour deals with these issues in specific agreements of a temporary nature. One recent example is the 2012-2015 agreement (not signed by the CGT), about a policy of occupational risk prevention, including psychosocial risks and the prevention of arduousness at work (*penibilité du travail*). On the other hand, the improvement of life quality at work is one of the subjects that must be forcefully bargained every year. This kind of agreement includes provisions on employees' clothing,[57] working in special sectors or some budget for maintenance and renewal of working tools.

There is a commitment on the part of the Italian Carrefour Group to apply the legislation to health and safety. This includes the organisation of meetings with workers' representatives to improve working conditions. All of this is the translation of legal obligations, so the agreement does not play a real role here.[58]

In the case of Poland, we can find two main items related to this subject: first, lists of jobs prohibited for women and young workers; and second, the provision to employees of tools and materials as well as working clothes, footwear and items of individual protection and personal hygiene.

The Spanish agreement has very little on this subject, as it only deals with the powers of the *comité intercentros* (a central works council established only through collective bargaining) and support in case of illness. In summary, the company must pay the difference between the state benefit and the employee's base salary (bonus excluded).

In the Portuguese agreement there is also a full chapter dedicated to these issues, following the principles of the Act on Work Accidents. The main creations are the

---

56. Complementing each other, T. Gyulavári, *Trap of the Past: Why Economically Dependent Work Is Not Regulated in the Member States of Eastern Europe*, 5, 3-4, European Labour Law Journal, 267 et seq. (2014), and F. Rosioru, *Legal Acknowledgement of the Category of Economically Dependent Workers*, 5, 3-4, European Labour Law Journal, 279 et seq. (2014).
57. Paying special attention, by the way, to managers' clothing.
58. M. Lai, *Il diritto della sicurezza sul lavoro tra conferme e sviluppi* (Torino: Giappichelli, 2016).

establishment of a similar benefit, according to which the employer must pay the difference between the state benefit and the employee's salary, with a limit of ninety days per year. The Italian agreements also include this kind of benefit, in the same amount, but with a six-month limit.

[F] Trade Union Rights & Representation

The French agreement contains a huge chapter (eighteen pages) on these issues, aimed at the organisation of the workers' representatives and their powers and functions. Thus, there are dispositions on national delegates, mixed commissions, travel expenses, material resources and a very *French* indication on the funding of social and cultural activities organised by the works councils. This agreement is not the only text to deal with the subject, as there is another specific text on the creation of a Central Committee. It was not signed by CGT and establishes a central body of representation, composed of twenty people (with their deputies), chosen according to rules written in the same agreement.

The Italian text mainly deals with paid leave for representation tasks. On the other hand, it contains a lot of literature about information and consultation.[59] This is due to the more programmatic nature of this text and the main role played by the national sectoral agreement, with one specific title on these issues.

In the Polish case, there are auxiliary rules on the development of the activity of the trade union. According to these, the company provides rooms and technical equipment, with Solidarność given one office in the headquarters and granted use of the rooms reserved for employees in the shops. The bulletin boards are also dealt with in the agreements (a bulletin board in each shop). Moreover, there are special bodies supervised by trade unions (social labour inspectors) that control the enforcement of the labour law, mainly health and safety standards. They may control employer premises at any time. The company organises special training sessions for workers engaged in this activity.

The Spanish agreement is certainly the most extensive on this issue, as nearly twenty articles are dedicated to such different matters as the role of trade unions in the companies, the powers of the *comité intercentros*, payment of union dues and reinforced guarantees for workers' representatives. There is also a remarkable development of elections within companies, absolutely atypical of Spanish practice.

A very interesting part of the agreement deals with alternative dispute resolution procedures. As a trend, these are established in Spain through inter-professional agreements, but this agreement takes advantage of the legislation and creates its own conciliation/arbitration mechanism, in order to develop the procedure for opting out of its conditions, according to the legislation.[60]

---

59. M. Corti, *I diritti di informazione e consultazione in Italia dopo il d.lgs.n.25 del 2007 tra continuità e innovazione*, 10 RUTC (2009).
60. J. Calvo Gallego, *Algunas notas sobre el papel de los sistemas extrajudiciales en los procesos de inaplicación de los convenios colectivos*, in *Reformas estructurales y negociación colectiva*, 343 et seq. (Junta de Andalucía, Sevilla, 2012).

Along the same lines, the Portuguese agreement gives more favourable rights to workers' representatives, as it provides them with eight hours per month of 'representation time' (*crédito*), instead of the legal five hours. There are also provisions on meetings, material resources, payment of union dues and other organisational rights.

[G] Discrimination and Diversity

As previously stated, within the framework of the French Carrefour, we have to point out several agreements on this issue. First of all, there is the text on disability. Its two main contents are a goal of 6% occupation at every employment level for disabled people; and a general ergonomics aim, involving the adaptation of workplaces and the funding of equipment. On the other hand, there is a text on diversity and social cohesion that includes, among others, provisions on the anonymity of CVs or the sensitisation of employees towards their colleagues. Finally, in the above-mentioned agreement about the *contrat de génération*, there are specific provisions about hiring young people from disadvantaged areas (*quartiers sensibles*), linked to the employability of populations coming from recent, post-colonial immigration.

The Spanish agreement deals also with discrimination, creating a commission on equal opportunities and non-discrimination and making mandatory the existence of a protocol on mobbing and sexual harassment[61] in every company within the scope of the agreement.[62] Collective bargaining is playing a very important role in the implementation of the equality principle.[63]

In Carrefour Poland, there is also an anti-harassment procedure, based on anonymous information and a special committee dealing with harassment claims. The procedure is established for the headquarters. The trade unions expect the adoption of a procedure covering the whole company.

[H] Other Provisions

The Polish agreement includes remarkable provision of staff benefits, ranging from support for employees and other persons (family members) in need in the form of price reductions in shops (5% with a family card) or the organisation and funding of sports activities (including sports equipment). The company supports the functioning of small

---

61. On this type of protocol in Spain, Y. Maneiro Vázquez & J.M. Miranda Boto, *Las obligaciones de la empresa en materia de acoso moral, acoso sexual y acoso por razón de sexo: los protocolos antiacoso*, in *Mobbing, acoso laboral y acoso por razón de sexo. Guía para la empresa y las personas trabajadoras*, 65 et seq. (2nd edition, Madrid: Tecnos, 2011). As recent news shows, there is still a lot to do on this issue in Spain: http://politica.elpais.com/politica/2016/09/06/actualidad/1473165018_143499.html (accessed 7 August 2017).
62. This clause is included in the Best Practices Guide (p. 14) of the trade union UGT, even in spite of the fact that it did not sign the agreement: http://www.ugt.es/Publicaciones/GuiaBuenasPracticas_brechaSalarial_UGT_Mujer.pdf (accessed 7 August 2017).
63. See C. Martínez Moreno, *Últimas tendencias en los contenidos de la negociación colectiva en materia de igualdad entre mujeres y hombres*, in *Cláusulas de vanguardia y problemas prácticos de la negociación colectiva actual*, 403 et seq. (Thomson Reuters – Lex Nova, Cizur Menor, 2015).

libraries where workers may exchange books as well as organises courses for employees (e.g., cookery courses run by French chefs). Another interesting initiative is competitions for employees (e.g., 'Our talents').

In the Spanish agreement, there is a very important clause about the probation period. This is one of the very few situations where a collective agreement can derogate *in peius* the legal provisions, establishing longer periods. The sectoral agreement takes advantage of this possibility, extending the period by up to four months for coordinators and by up to three months for professionals and core staff. The legal ceiling is two months for any of these groups.

One of the most distinctive features of the Spanish agreement is the regulation of the disciplinary power of the company. The whole of Chapter II of this agreement is dedicated to this subject, which can be never dealt with unilaterally and covers the full range of misdemeanours and sanctions or procedures, according to the tradition established since the advent of democracy.

Turning to the Italian case, there is a highly original provision on the preservation of the jobs of terminally ill employees.[64] Under Italian law, a sick employee can be fired after the *periodo di comporto*, so the agreement creates an exception that is mainly focused on social security benefits, as this extended period of employment can imply higher widow and orphan benefits.

Another remarkable clause, this time in the sectoral agreement, deals with non-EU workers. According to the parties, the presence of foreign workers is growing in importance in the retail sector. Therefore, measures concerning their integration are needed, such as paid leave for participation in educational courses. There is also a clause, probably against EU law, that allows them to accumulate holidays over two years in order to enjoy longer periods.

§20.05 SPECIFIC ISSUES DERIVED FROM OTHER PARTS OF THE RESEARCH

[A] Work-Life Balance and Gender Equality

There is remarkable attention to this matter in the French agreement in its Chapter 8. Some of the more innovative measures include are a 'disposition for joint mobility', in order to help couples to be transferred to the same shop, or at least to the same city. Similarly, we have to point out the *Chèque Emploi Service Universel*, a monetary bonus to finance family-linked costs, such as babysitters and kindergartens. These provisions are developed through the annual mandatory bargaining. Within this type of agreement, we can find more innovative provisions, such as the use of videoconferencing for meetings, the promotion of training for female workers or the neutralisation of

---

64. R. Voza, *Licenziamento e malattia: le parole e i silenzi del legislatore*, in 248 WP CSDLE Massimo D'Antona.it, (2015). Schiavone, *L'impossibilità sopravvenuta della prestazione lavorativa*, I, RIDL, (2010); Santini, *Licenziamento per giusta causa: immediatezza del recesso ed efficacia durante il periodo di comporto*, II RIDL, (2003).

maternity and parental leave. In this frame, there are also several agreements on equality that go further than gender equality and will be commented on later.

The Spanish agreement also deals with this issue, greatly encouraged by the *Ley Orgánica* 3/2007 on effective equality between women and men.[65] It is one of the most relevant parts of the agreement, as it actually improves working conditions. For example, concerning the suspension of the contract due to risk during pregnancy, the company will pay a bonus on top of the social security benefit. There is also a pioneering provision on leave, which in some situations can be paid, for taking a child under fifteen to medical examinations.

In contrast, the Portuguese agreement is very short in such content and its provisions are even not in line with the legal dispositions, as a result of later reforms. Along very similar lines, the Polish documents do not establish a clear policy. Only part-time work can be identified in the range of tools for this issue. Likewise, the Italian agreement only deals with part-time jobs, in spite of the great reforms brought in by the *Jobs Act*. This can be understood as a lack of interest by the bargaining parties, in spite of the inclusion in the text of a provision concerning the creation of a consultative commission on this matter.

[B] Agency Work

The French agreement simply mentions that temporary agency work can be used in the legal situations, without any further development. On the other hand, the Portuguese agreement does not deal with this issue at all.

This void shows a clear paradox with the theoretical proposals in our colleagues' work. The reality of the sector, according to the opinions received during the preparation of this chapter, is a huge presence of temporary agency work, estimated at up to even 30% or 40% in some occupations within the sector, mainly security services.

[C] Age

In the French case, the age factor is mainly present in the later segment of working life, affecting senior workers. The agreement includes better provisions on rest periods (those older than 55 can have two full days of rest every two weeks), holidays (right to three consecutive weeks, but in December), night shifts (preferential right for switching to morning shift) and, on a voluntary basis, part-time work. There are also very interesting provisions on the *contrat de génération*, giving more facilities as the legal age is reduced to 45 years.

On the other hand, younger workers only benefit from some advantages linked to training contracts (*contrats en alternance*), in order to prepare a professional career.

---

65. N. Mendoza Navas, R. Menéndez Calvo, *Igualdad entre mujeres y hombres. Aspectos laborales de la Ley 3/2007*, in R. Escudero Rodríguez (coord.) *Observatorio de la negociación colectiva: Empleo público, Igualdad, Nuevas tecnologías y Globalización* (2010), http://www.bollettinoadapt.it/old/files/document/13207observatorio_neg.pdf (accessed 7 August 2017).

This kind of clause is very similar to one in the Italian text (*apprendistato*), which does not refer to age in any other part. The only mention of age in the Portuguese agreement is linked to training contracts (*regime do trabalhador-estudante*), but is not really developed.

Once again, in the Italian case, the main role in this issue is played by the national sectoral agreement, which is mainly focused on young workers, specifying the ages that make possible several fixed-term contracts.

This coincidence in nearly every agreement, even if minor, is remarkable, as it clearly shows the same spirit of incorporation of younger workers, through specific types of contracts, linked to training. The idea of a cheaper transition from school and university to the labour market is clearly present in many systems of industrial relations.

BCLR - BULLETIN OF COMPARATIVE LABOUR RELATIONS

Vol. Author/Title/Year/ISBN

1. Roger Blanpain, *Individual Employment Contracts: Collective Agreements*, 1970.
2. Roger Blanpain, *Social Planning*, 1971 (ISBN 90-312-0018-2).
3. Roger Blanpain, *Guaranteed Income Funds*, 1972 (ISBN 90-312-0019-0).
4. Roger Blanpain, *Employee Participation at the Level of the Enterprise*, 1973 (ISBN 90-312-0020-4).
5. Roger Blanpain, *Vastheid van Betrekking: Staking en Bezetting*, 1974.
6. Roger Blanpain, *Labour Law and Industrial Relations (International Bibliography)*, 1975 (ISBN 90-312-0023-9).
7. Roger Blanpain, *Multinational Enterprises*, 1976 (ISBN 90-312-0024-7).
8. Roger Blanpain, *Worker's Participation in the European Company*, 1977 (ISBN 90-312-0044-1).
9. Roger Blanpain, *Women and Labour*, 1978 (ISBN 90-312-0077-8).
10. Roger Blanpain, *European Conference on Labour Law and Industrial Relations: Multinational Enterprises*, 1979 (ISBN 90-312-0091-3).
11. Roger Blanpain, *Job Security and Industrial Relations*, 1980 (ISBN 90-312-0147-2).
12. Roger Blanpain, Greg Bamber & Russell Lansbury, *Technological Change and Industrial Relations: An International Symposium*, 1983 (ISBN 90-312-0205-3).
13. Roger Blanpain, James Janssen van Raay & A. Moulty, *Worker's Participation in the European Community: The Fifth Directive*, 1984 (ISBN 90-654-4187-5).
14. Roger Blanpain, *Equality and Prohibition of Discrimination in Employment*, 1985 (ISBN 90-654-4215-4).
15. Roger Blanpain, *Restructuring Labour in the Enterprise: Law and Practice in France, F.R. of Germany, Italy, Sweden and the United Kingdom*, 1986 (ISBN 90-654-4283-9).
16. Roger Blanpain & E. Kassalow, *Unions and Industrial Relations: Recent Trends and Prospect: A Comparative Treatment*, 1987 (ISBN 90-654-4294-4).
17. Roger Blanpain & Marco Biagi, *Trade Union Democracy and Industrial Relations*, 1988 (ISBN 90-654-4394-0).
18. Roger Blanpain & Jelle Visser, *In Search of Inclusive Unionism*, 1990 (ISBN 90-654-4439-4).
19. Roger Blanpain, *Flexibility and Wages: A Comparative Treatment*, 1990 (ISBN 90-654-4461-0).

20. Roger Blanpain, Stephen Frenkel & Oliver Clarke, *Economic Restructuring and Industrial Relations in Industrialised Countries*, 1990 (ISBN 90-654-4488-2).
21. Roger Blanpain & Friedrich Fürstenberg, *Structure and Strategy in Industrial Relations*, 1991 (ISBN 90-654-4559-5).
22. Roger Blanpain, Amira Galin & Ozer Carmi, *Flexible Work Patterns and Their Impact on Industrial Relations*, 1991 (ISBN 90-654-4572-2).
23. Roger Blanpain, *Workers' Participation: Influence on Management Decision-Making by Labour in the Private Sector*, 1992 (ISBN 90-654-4600-1).
24. Roger Blanpain, Brian Brooks & Chris Engels, *Employed or Self-Employed*, 1992 (ISBN 90-654-4613-3).
25. Roger Blanpain & Tiziano Treu, *Industrial Relations Developments in the Telecommunications Industry*, 1993 (ISBN 90-654-4642-7).
26. Roger Blanpain & Marco Biagi, *Industrial Relations in Small and Medium Sized Enterprises*, 1993 (ISBN 90-654-4696-6).
27. Roger Blanpain & Marco Biagi, *Participative Management and Industrial Relations in a Worldwide Perspective*, 1993 (ISBN 90-654-4769-5).
28. Roger Blanpain, Jacques Rojot & Hoyt N. Wheeler, *Employee Rights and Industrial Justice*, 1994 (ISBN 90-654-4804-7).
29. Roger Blanpain & Ruth Ben-Israel, *Strikes and Lock-Outs in Industrialized Market Economies*, 1994 (ISBN 90-654-4841-1).
30. Roger Blanpain, Kazuo Sugeno & Yasuo Suwa, *The Harmonization of Working Life and Family Life*, 1995 (ISBN 90-411-0064-4).
31. Roger Blanpain & Laszio Nagy, *Labour Law and Industrial Relations in Central and Eastern Europe*, 1996 (ISBN 90-411-0298-1).
32. Roger Blanpain, *Labour Law and Industrial Relations in the European Union*, 1997 (ISBN 90-411-0527-1).
33. Taco Van Peijpe, *Employment Protection under Strain*, 1998 (ISBN 90-411-0528-8).
34. Roger Blanpain, Takashi Araki & Ryuichi Yamakawa, *The Process of Industrialization and the Role of Labour Law in Asia*, 1999 (ISBN 9-041-1104-7-X).
35. Roger Blanpain & Marco Biagi, *Non-standard Work and Industrial Relations*, 1999 (ISBN 90-411-1117-4).
36. Roger Blanpain, *Private Employment Agencies: The Impact of ILO Convention 181 (1997) and the Judgment of the European Court of Justice of 11 December 1997*, 1999 (ISBN 90-411-1118-2).
37. Roger Blanpain, *Multinational Enterprises and the Social Challenges of the XXIst Century: The ILO Declaration on Fundamental Principles at Work, Public and Private Corporate Codes of Conduct*, 2000 (ISBN 90-411-1280-4).
38. Roger Blanpain, Ryuichi Yamakawa & Takashi Araki, *Deregulation and Labour Law: In Search of a Labour Concept for the 21st Century*, 2000 (ISBN 90-411-1370-3).
39. Roger Blanpain, *The Council of Europe and the Social Challenges of the XXIst Century*, 2001 (ISBN 90-411-1543-9).

40. Roger Blanpain, *On-Line Rights for Employees in the Information Society, Use & Monitoring of E-Mail & Internet at Work*, 2002 (ISBN 90-411-1626-5).
41. Roger Blanpain, *The Evolving Employment Relationship and the New Economy: The Role of Labour Law & Industrial Relations*, 2001 (ISBN 90-411-1691-5).
42. Roger Blanpain, *Involvement of Employees in the European Union, Works Councils, Company Statute, Information and Consultation Rights*, 2002 (ISBN 90-411-1760-1).
43. Michele Colucci, *The Impact of the Internet and New Technologies on the Workplace: A Legal Analysis from a Comparative Point of View*, 2002 (ISBN 90-411-1824-1).
44. Roger Blanpain, *White Paper on the Labour Market in Italy: The Quality of European Industrial Relations and Changing Industrial Relations*, 2002 (ISBN 90-411-1841-1).
45. Roger Blanpain, Russell D. Lansbury & Young-Bum Park, *Impact of Globalisation on Employment Relations: A Comparison of the Automobile and Banking Industries in Australia and Korea*, 2002 (ISBN 90-411-1850-0).
46. Roger Blanpain & Antoine Jacobs, *Employee Rights in Bankruptcy: A Comparative-Law Assessment*, 2002 (ISBN 90-411-1942-6).
47. Roger Blanpain, Takashi Araki & Shinya Ouchi, *Corporate Restructuring and the Role of Labour Law*, 2003 (ISBN 90-411-1949-3).
48. Roger Blanpain, *Collective Bargaining, Discrimination, Social Security and European Integration*, 2003 (ISBN 90-411-2010-6).
49. Roger Blanpain & Luis Aparicio-Valdez, *Labour Relations in the Asia- Pacific Countries*, 2004 (ISBN 90-411-2239-7).
50. Roger Blanpain & Ronnie Graham, *Temporary Agency Work and the Information Society*, 2004 (ISBN 90-411-2252-4).
51. Roger Blanpain, *The Actors of Collective Bargaining: A World Report*, 2004 (ISBN 90-411-2253-2).
52. Roger Blanpain & Michele Colucci, *The Globalisation of Labour Standards: The Soft Law Track*, 2004 (ISBN 90-411-2303-2).
53. Roger Blanpain, Takashi Araki & Shinya Ouchi, *Labour Law in Motion: Diversification of the Labour Force & Terms and Conditions of Employment*, 2005 (ISBN 90-411-2315-6).
54. Roger Blanpain, *Smoking and the Workplace*, 2005 (ISBN 90-411-2325-3).
55. Roger Blanpain, *Confronting Globalization: The Quest for a Social Agenda*, 2005 (ISBN 90-411-2381-4).
56. Roger Blanpain, Thomas Blanke & Edgar Rose, *Collective Bargaining Wages in Comparative Perspective: Germany, France, the Netherlands, Sweden and the United Kingdom*, 2005 (ISBN 90-411-2388-1).
57. Roger Blanpain & Anne Numhauser-Henning, *Women in Academia & Equality Law: Aiming High - Falling Short?*, 2006 (ISBN 978-90-411-2427-6).
58. Roger Blanpain, *Freedom of Services in the European Union: Labour and Social Security Law: The Bolkestein Initiative*, 2006 (ISBN 978-90-411-2453-5).
59. Roger Blanpain, Frans Pennings & Nurhan Sural, *Flexibilisation and Modernisation of the Turkish Labour Market*, 2006 (ISBN 978-90-411-2490-X).

60. Roger Blanpain & Boel Flodgren, *Corporate and Employment Perspectives in a Global Business Environment*, 2006 (ISBN 978-90-411-2537-X).
61. Roger Blanpain, Shinya Ouchi & Takashi Araki, *Decentralizing Industrial Relations and The Role of Labor Unions and Employee Representatives*, 2007 (ISBN 978-90-411-2583-3).
62. Roger Blanpain, *European Framework Agreements and Telework: Law and Practice: A European and Comparative Study*, 2007 (ISBN 978-90-411-2560-4).
63. Roger Blanpain, Jim Kitay, Leanne Cutcher & Nick Wailes, *Globalization and Employment Relations in Retail Banking*, 2007 (ISBN 978-90-411-2620-1).
64. Roger Blanpain, Russell Lansbury, Jim Kitay, Nick Wailes & Anja Kirsch, *Globalization and Employment Relations in the Auto Assembly Industry: A Study of Seven Countries*, 2008 (ISBN 978-90-411-2698-6).
65. Roger Blanpain & Michele Tiraboschi, *The Global Labour Market: From Globalization to Flexicurity*, 2008 (ISBN 978-90-411-2722-8).
66. Roger Blanpain, Michele Colucci & Frank Hendrickx, *The Future of Sport in the European Union: Beyond the EU Reform Treaty and the White Paper*, 2008 (ISBN 978-90-411-2761-7).
67. Roger Blanpain, Linda Dickens, *Challenges in European Employment Relations: Employment Regulation, Trade Union Organization, Equality, Flexicurity, Training and New Approaches to Pay*, 2008 (ISBN 978-90-411-2771-6).
68. Roger Blanpain, Hiroya Nakakubo & Takashi Araki, *New Developments in Employment Discrimination Law*, 2008 (ISBN 978-90-411-2782-2).
69. Roger Blanpain, Andrzej Marian wiątkowski, *The Laval and Viking Cases: Freedom of Services and Establishment v. Industrial Conflict in the European Economic Area and Russia*, 2009 (ISBN 978-90-411-2850-8).
70. Roger Blanpain, William Bromwich, Olga Rymkevich, Silvia Spattini, *The Modernization of Labour Law and Industrial Relations in a Comparative Perspective*, 2009 (ISBN 978-90-411-2865-2).
71. Roger Blanpain, Juan Pablo Landa & Brian Langille, *Employment Policies and Multilevel Governance*, 2009 (ISBN 978-90-411-2866-9).
72. Roger Blanpain, European Works Councils; *The European Directive 2009/ 38/EC of 6 May 2009*, 2009 (ISBN 978-90-411-3208-6).
73. Roger Blanpain, William Bromwich, Olga Rymkevich & Silvia Spattini, *Labour Productivity, Investment in Human Capital and Youth Employment: Comparative Developments and Global Responses*, 2010 (ISBN 978-90-411-3249-9).
74. Greg J. Bamber & Philippe Pochet, *Regulating Employment Relations, Work and Labour Laws: International Comparisons between Key Countries*, 2010 (ISBN 978-90-411-3199-7). General Editor: Roger Blanpain.
75. Roger Blanpain, Desislava Nikolaeva Dimitrova, *Seafarers' Rights in the Globalized Maritime Industry*, 2010 (ISBN 978-90-411-3349-6).
76. Roger Blanpain, Hiroya Nakakubo & Takashi Araki, *Regulation of Fixed- Term Employment Contracts*, 2010 (ISBN 978-90-411-3356-4).

77. Roger Blanpain, William Bromwich, Olga Rymkevich & Iacopo Senatori, *Rethinking Corporate Governance*, 2011 (ISBN 978-90-411-3450-9).
78. Roger Blanpain & Frank Hendrickx, *Labour Law between Change and Tradition: Liber Amicorum Antoine Jacobs*, 2011 (ISBN 978-90-411-3424-0).
79. Roger Blanpain, Thomas Klebe, Marlene Schmidt & Bernd Waas, *Trade Union Rights at the Workplace*, 2012 (ISBN 978-90-411-3460-8).
80. Roger Blanpain, William Bromwich, Olga Rymkevich & Iacopo Senatori, *Labour Markets, Industrial Relations and Human Resources Management: From Recession to Recovery*, 2012 (ISBN 978-90-411-4004-3).
81. Roger Blanpain, Hiroya Nakakubo & Takashi Araki, *Systems of Employee Representation at the Enterprise: A Comparative Study*, 2012 (ISBN 978-90-411-4080-7).
82. Roger Blanpain & Frank Hendrickx, *Temporary Agency Work in the European Union and the United States*, 2013 (ISBN 978-90-411-4769-1).
83. Roger Blanpain, Toker Dereli, Y. Pınar Soykut-Sarıca & Aslı en-Tabaı, *Emerging Patterns of Work and Turkish Labour Market Challenges under Globalization: Readings on Labour and Employment Relations*, 2014
(ISBN 978-90-411-4983-1).
84. Roger Blanpain, Pablo Arellano Ortiz, Marius Olivier & Gijsbert Vonk, *Social Security and Migrant Workers: Selected Studies of Cross-border Social Security Mechanisms*, 2014 (ISBN 978-90-411-4770-7).
85. Roger Blanpain & Nikita Lyutov, *Workers' Representation in Central and Eastern Europe: Challenges and Opportunities for the Works Councils' System*, 2014 (ISBN 978-90-411-4746-2).
86. Roger Blanpain, Ulla Liukkunen & Chen Yifeng, *China and ILO Fundamental Principles and Rights at Works*, 2014 (ISBN 978-90-411-4984-8).
87. Roger Blanpain, *The Use of Languages and Employment Relations*, 2014 (ISBN 978-90-411-5606-8).
88. Roger Blanpain, Hiroya Nakakubo & Takashi Araki, *Protection of Employees' Personal Information and Privacy*, 2014 (ISBN 978-90-411-5608-2).
89. Roger Blanpain, Jan Wouters, Glenn Rayp, Laura Beke & Axel Marx, *Protecting Labour Rights in a Multi-polar Supply Chain and Mobile Global Economy*, 2015 (ISBN 978-90-411-5662-4).
90. Roger Blanpain & Stefania Marassi, *Globalization and Transnational Collective Labour Relations: International and European Framework Agreements at Company Level*, 2015 (ISBN 978-90-411-4748-6).
91. Roger Blanpain, Frank Hendrickx & Petra Herzfeld Olsson, *National Effects of the Implementation of EU Directives on Labour Migration from Third Countries*, 2016 (ISBN 978-90-411-6257-1).
92. Roger Blanpain, Frank Hendrickx & D'Arcy du Toit, *Labour Law and Social Progress: Holding the Line or Shifting the Boundaries?* 2016 (ISBN 978-90-411-6747-7).

93. Roger Blanpain & Frank Hendrickx, *Reasonable Accommodation in the Modern Workplace: Potential and Limits of the Integrative Logics of Labour Law*, 2016 (ISBN 978-90-411-6258-8).
94. Roger Blanpain, Frank Hendrickx & Bernd Waas, *New Forms of Employment in Europe*, 2016 (ISBN 978-90-411-6239-7).
95. Roger Blanpain, Frank Hendrickx, Hiroya Nakakubo & Takashi Araki, *The Notion of Employer in the Era of the Fissured Workplace: Should Labour Law Responsibilities Exceed the Boundary of the Legal Entity?*, 2017 (ISBN 978-90-411-8470-2).
96. Elena Sychenko, *Individual Labour Rights as Human Rights: The Contributions of the European Court of Human Rights to Worker's Rights Protection*, 2017 (ISBN 978-90-411-8629-4).
97. William Bromwich & Olga Rymkevich, *Improving Workplace Quality: New Perspectives and Challenges for Worker Well-Being*, 2017 (ISBN 978-90-411-8628-7).
98. Sarah De Groof, *Work-Life Balance in the Modern Workplace: Interdisciplinary Perspectives from Work-Family Research, Law and Policy*, 2017 (ISBN 978-90-411-8630-0).
99. Sylvaine Laulom, *Collective Bargaining Developments in Times of Crisis*, 2018 (ISBN 978-90-411-8999-8).